EMBODIED POLITICS IN VISUAL AUTOBIOGRAPHY

From reality television to film, performance, and video art, autobiography is everywhere in today's image-obsessed age. With contributions by both artists and scholars, *Embodied Politics in Visual Autobiography* is a unique examination of visual autobiography's involvement in the global cultural politics of health, disability, and the body. This provocative collection looks at images of selfhood and embodiment in a variety of media and with a particular focus on bodily identities and practices that challenge the norm: a pregnant man in cyberspace, a fat activist performance troupe, indigenous artists intervening in museums, transnational selves who connect disability to war, and many more.

The chapters in *Embodied Politics in Visual Autobiography* reflect several different theoretical approaches but share a common concern with the ways in which visual culture can generate resistance, critique, and creative interventions. With contributions that investigate digital media, installation art, graphic memoir, performance, film, reality television, photography, and video art, the collection offers a wide-ranging critical account of what is clearly becoming one of the most important issues in contemporary culture.

(Cultural Spaces)

SARAH BROPHY is an associate professor in the Department of English and Cultural Studies at McMaster University.

JANICE HLADKI is an associate professor of Theatre and Film Studies in the School of the Arts at McMaster University.

Embodied Politics in Visual Autobiography

Edited by SARAH BROPHY
and JANICE HLADKI

UNIVERSITY OF TORONTO PRESS
Toronto Buffalo London

Toronto Buffalo London
www.utppublishing.com

ISBN 978-1-4426-4660-5 (cloth)
ISBN 978-1-4426-1609-7 (paper)

Library and Archives Canada Cataloguing in Publication

Embodied politics in visual autobiography / edited by Sarah Brophy and Janice Hladki.

(Cultural spaces)
Includes bibliographical references.
ISBN 978-1-4426-4660-5 (bound). ISBN 978-1-4426-1609-7 (pbk.)

1. Visual communication – Political aspects. 2. Visual communication – Social aspects. 3. Autobiography – Political aspects. 4. Autobiography – Social aspects. 5. Human body in mass media. 6. Human body in popular culture. I. Brophy, Sarah, author, editor II. Hladki, Janice, 1949–, author, editor III. Series: Cultural spaces

P93.5.E43 2014 302.23 C2014-903350-8

University of Toronto Press acknowledges the financial assistance to its publishing program of the Canada Council for the Arts and the Ontario Arts Council, an agency of the government of Ontario.

Canada Council for the Arts Conseil des Arts du Canada

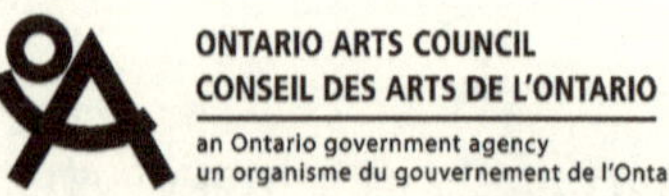

University of Toronto Press acknowledges the financial support of the Government of Canada through the Canada Book Fund for its publishing activities.

Contents

Acknowledgments

As co-editors working closely together over a number of years, we have had the pleasure of developing a rewarding collaborative practice, and we are grateful for the many other partnerships that have sustained this long-term project. Our greatest debt of gratitude is to the academic and arts-based contributors to this volume, who have been so patient and encouraging with us as we worked to weave their excellent contributions into book form. A book on works and practices of visual autobiography would be impossible if not for the creations of the artists and cultural producers, and so we thank the makers of the material that is the foundation of this project. When we first imagined this collection and sent out a call for papers, we received many remarkable proposals. We would like to acknowledge the authors who could not be included in this volume: we appreciate their interest and support.

Sarah Trimble provided stellar research assistance for this edited collection over three years. Trimble, your deep intelligence, patience, and attention to detail and to the larger vision have been invaluable. Thank you for being such a pleasure to work with and for keeping us organized and progressing with the project at its more daunting moments!

We entrusted the final preparation of the manuscript to Kathryn Allan, who, not surprisingly, carried this work out perfectly. Kathryn, we are grateful and also very proud of the inspiring example you set of bridging research and professional writing and editing work. We're appreciative, too, of Sarah O'Byrne's assistance with image permissions, and for the work of the archivists, artists, and technicians who furnished the images, especially the timely help of Simon Oakley.

Thanks to our University of Toronto Press editor, Siobhan McMenemy, for her expertise and for her work on behalf of this project over the course of time. We are especially grateful to her for securing engaged and helpful external reports and for guiding us through the stages of development. The contribution of the external reviewers was invaluable: their insightful comments on individual chapters and the overall structure and argumentation helped us to strengthen the manuscript.

Many colleagues, staff, and students at McMaster and beyond have offered feedback and cheered us along. Lorraine York generously read an early draft proposal and has consistently been a model of collaborative support: thank you so very much, Lorraine! We're grateful for lively and thoughtful conversations with colleagues, including Sara Ahmed, Phanuel Antwi, Jane Aronson, Nadine Attewell, Lisa Cartwright, Daniel Coleman, Amber Dean, Kari Dehli, Susan Fast, Margot Francis, Don Goellnicht, Marnina Gonick, Merri Lisa Johnson, Shoshana Magnet, Robert McRuer, Rick Monture, Susie O'Brien, Mary O'Connor, Kathleen Rockhill, Anne Savage, Sue Spearey, Helene Strauss, Tanya Titchkosky, Y-Dang Troeung, and Jean Wilson. Antoinette Somo has, with her characteristic warmth and grace, provided crucial administrative support for many of our activities, including this book. It's been a great experience to collaborate with Carol Podedworny, Ihor Holubisky, Nicole Knibb, and Rose-Anne Prevec at the McMaster Museum of Art; the opportunity to curate exhibitions has deepened our thinking about the field of visual culture and museology-as-pedagogy. We would like to honour colleagues who passed away during the development of this collection and whose work will continue to shape our own: Victoria Littman, Sharon Rosenberg, and Roger I. Simon.

We thank each and every one of our graduate students for involving us in their political and critical projects, and, thinking more particularly of the intellectual context for this edited collection, we are grateful to the group with whom we worked closely to plan and mount a conference on the topic of "Health, Embodiment, and Visual Culture" in 2010: Melissa Carroll, Emily Hill, Dilia Narduzzi, Jessie Travis, Sarah Trimble, and PhebeAnn Wolframe.

This project enjoyed funding from the Arts Research Board at McMaster University, and we would like to thank the Associate Vice-President (Research), Fiona McNeill, for her enthusiasm and support. Fiona, you are a rare gem.

Finally, we thank family and friends for sustaining care, conversation, and love.

Sarah Brophy:

I have learned and continue to learn so much from Janice's rich knowledge, creative thinking, and exemplary skills in the art of friendship. Working with Janice makes it newly possible to do academic work: to do it with heart. My loving thanks to the wonderful Peter Walmsley, who gives me everything, and to our boys, Patrick, Ben, and Sam, who create the best joyful mess. My parents, Lorraine and George Brophy, are outstandingly generous, shining in the role of grandparents. A shout out to the Brophy siblings, Rachel, Jane, Joe, and Ben, and their partners: I think we have mellowed together into the very finest company. The loss in the last few years of my grandparents, Rita and Tom Tobey, and of my father-in-law, Bob Walmsley, sharpens both the sense of cherishing family and friends, including my grandmother, Dorothy Kelly, and my mother-in-law, Ruth Walmsley, and the importance of savouring good times together. I am grateful for superb friends and neighbours, who provide support and laughter in equal measure, especially Tom Allen, Millie Allen, Scott Bunyan, Wayne Cass, Carolyn Finlayson, Grace Kehler, Liz Koblyk, Miranda Koblyk, Jen Lee, Mary O'Connor, Michael Ross, Sarah Trimble, and Lorraine York. My thanks also go to adored babysitter Sophie Goellnicht and to the kindly teachers at Patrick's daycare and elementary school.

Janice Hladki:

Special appreciation to Sarah, who brought her smarts, panache, and care to both the work and our friendship. Sarah, it has been a profound pleasure to work with you, and I am inspired by your insights and dedication. I would like to thank my generous friends, who provide life lessons, guide me through the rough patches, and remain patient when I am absent during demanding projects: Mary Bower, Kari Dehli, Marnina Gonick, Martino Lee, Shoshana Magnet, Carol Podedworny, Kathleen Rockhill, Andre Rosenbaum, Bunny Siegel, Kelly St John, Peter Walmsley, and Meredith Ware. I am grateful for the emotional and intellectual community these friends have offered over many years. I also extend my thanks to colleagues in my home areas of Theatre & Film Studies and the School of the Arts and in the affiliated areas of Gender Studies and Feminist Research, English and Cultural Studies, and Communication Studies and Multimedia. I would like to acknowledge the influence of numerous artists whose politically impassioned work has shaped my understanding of bodies and culture. My wonderful Mum and Dad, Josephine and Neil Watson, have always offered their loving support, and I deeply appreciate their encouragement of curiosity. For daily life sustenance, particularly through heart care and the gift of his incredible music, I am indebted to Wayne Cass.

EMBODIED POLITICS IN VISUAL AUTOBIOGRAPHY

1 Visual Autobiography in the Frame: Critical Embodiment and Cultural Pedagogy

SARAH BROPHY AND JANICE HLADKI

At the beginning of her performance video, *Worth* (2010), renowned visual artist Rebecca Belmore (Anishinaabe) sits quietly on the sidewalk in front of the Vancouver Art Gallery. Above her is a large stencilled placard that reads: "I am worth more than one million dollars to my people." Gallery visitors pass by, barely glancing her way, as they move towards the entrance of the museum. Belmore uses water to wash a rectangular section of the pavement and then arranges pieces of long dark hair- and fur-fringed red fabric that she has removed from three carefully wrapped packages.[1] A small crowd gathers. The climax of the performance involves Belmore, clad in a Jesus T-shirt and having just washed her feet, lying down on the cloth with her arms extended. At the end of the piece, Belmore, who lives in Vancouver, presents one of the blankets as a precious artefact for safekeeping to Daina Augaitis, Chief Curator at the Vancouver Art Gallery. While low-volume Aboriginal drumming provides an aural backdrop to the performance, Belmore is vocally silent throughout – until she says "I quit" to Augaitis. Available on YouTube in the form of a recording dated, not coincidentally, 11 September 2010, a date that reminds us of competing catastrophic memories and the ways that dominant national narratives of loss can screen out other losses, *Worth* has energized Belmore and her supporters in the context of a vexing legal case, in which her art dealer sued Belmore for breach of contract. A fleeting, poignant, public self-crucifixion outside the doors of a major national art institute, *Worth* also stands in its own right as a powerful work of art.[2]

We begin by invoking *Worth* (and return to this performance video in our concluding chapter) because it brilliantly exemplifies the texts and tactics that animate this book. Belmore's performing body is "a lived space marked by events, in which the consequences of violence are felt" (Bennett 2005, 60). Rather than telling a story about that violence that could be readily summarized, she uses her body as a medium for communicating the material conditions that shape both her career as an artist and the histories of Indigenous women. In this way, *Worth* intervenes in a heterogeneous cultural field – criss-crossed by power relations – that is emerging at the intersection of the everyday, the arts, and public culture. Engaging closely with such arts projects, and working in unprecedented ways across visual culture, autobiography, disability, feminist, Indigenous, and postcolonial studies, *Embodied Politics in Visual Autobiography* reflects on how visual autobiographies today envision, situate, and circulate multiple forms of critical embodiment.

Visual Autobiography as Political Cultural Practice

From reality television, to film and video, to performance art, to graphic memoirs, auto/biography is everywhere in today's visual mediascape. Coined by Arjun Appadurai (1990) to refer to the accelerated transmission of visual culture in an era of global flows, the term "mediascape" reminds us, too, of visual culture's world-making role, including its role in producing "proto-narratives of possible lives" (9). Globalization and cultural studies critics tend to cast the proliferation of autobiography in contemporary culture as a symptom – and a mechanism – of neoliberal privatization. Zygmunt Bauman (2009), for example, sees the new prominence of "individual life politics" as signalling the evacuation of the public sphere of collective, democratic potential (14). And we would add that privatization of the responsibility for health through stories and images of individuals heroically overcoming risk is an especially troubling development (Alaimo 2010; Metzl and Kirkland 2010; Rose 2006). Visual mediation has been identified as particularly problematic in this regard. In *Bodily Natures: Science, Environment, and the Material Self*, Stacy Alaimo (2010) stresses the need for new "knowledge practices" that can show how "the very substance of the self is interconnected with vast biological, economic, and industrial systems" (95), but is wary of how, because "photojournalism and documentary" continue to be read as simple "factual evidence," they may be unable to depict the full complexity of many health and environmental justice concerns (71). Even more cautiously, in *Signifying Bodies: Disability in Contemporary Life Writing*, G. Thomas Couser (2009) warns that "the danger of presenting visible impairment as a voyeuristic freak show is far greater in visual media like photography, especially in video and film" (49).

Attentive to (and critical of) visual autobiography's potential complicity with the privatization of health politics, we draw attention to the many visual autobiographers who are engaged in reinvigorating public spheres, articulating multiple embodiments, and fostering new forms of analysis and coalition. The essays that make up this book explore how visual practices of "self-narration and self-portraiture" (Miller 2007a, 545) imagine unruly bodies and, in so doing, respond to the urgent need for what Patricia Zimmermann (2000) describes as "radical media democracies that animate contentious public spheres" (xx). By elucidating visual autobiography's critical contributions to the cultural politics of embodiment, health, disability, and agency, *Embodied Politics in Visual Autobiography* offers a politically hopeful account of the surge in autobiographically oriented visual cultural production.

If the state of the visual public sphere was a pressing concern in 2000, when Zimmermann issued her call for "radical media democracies," the situation has become even more urgent in the intervening years. The environment of heightened security that has prevailed since 9/11 has intensified the conditions of "optical scrutiny," to borrow a phrase from Wendy S. Hesford (2000, 362), under which lives are lived in North America and globally. As states deploy new visualizing technologies to identify and screen bodies, definitions of the "healthy," the "normal," and the "productive" regulate citizen status in increasingly stringent ways (Casper and Moore 2009; Magnet and Gates 2009; Mirzoeff 2011). Borders are being intensively policed against bodies figured as outside, and therefore threatening, to the nation (Butler 2009; R. Hall 2009; Magnet 2011; Puar 2007), and, in a climate of fiscal crisis, even those deemed full citizens are finding it difficult to access increasingly scarce public resources. In this context, LGBTQ activists, artists, and academics critique inequities in access to health care as well as to forms of public recognition and memory (Butler 2004a, 2004b; Namaste 2000; Noble 2006; Singer 2006). Indigenous media have become a site of urgent contestation of the settler nation-state's authority (Claxton, Townsend, and Loft 2005; Emberley 2007; Ginsburg, Abu-Lughod, and Larkin 2002; Hafsteinsson and Bredin 2010; Shohat and Stam 1994; Wilson and Stewart 2008). And contemporary disability media and theory not only highlight processes of pathologization, normalization, and exclusion, but, just as important, the contestatory possibilities that multiple embodiments enact (Chivers and Markotić 2010; Couser 2009; L. Davis

1995; Garland-Thomson 2009; Hladki 2005, 2009; LeBesco 2001; McRuer 2006; Mintz 2007; Snyder and Mitchell 2006; Titchkosky 2007; Tremain 2005; Wendell 1996). Taken together, the contributors to this book respond to the urgencies of health, embodiment, and visual media in our moment, with each chapter historically and geopolitically situating the modes of visuality that allow and disallow forms of embodiment to appear in public venues.

A central argument of this book is that the cultural and political salience of visual autobiographies inheres in how they generate and critically mobilize affect for pedagogical purposes. Cultural studies and critical theory are increasingly conceptualizing emotion as materially embodied, discursively constructed, and politically motivated and mobilizing. Jill Bennett (2005) calls for "a politics of empathy" and "unsettlement" in visual art (151); Elizabeth Grosz (2008) theorizes art as an intensification of sensory responses that draw viewing and feeling subjects *towards* the unknown; and Roger I. Simon (2005) considers how the audiovisual experience produces immediacy, a sense of "'being there'" (166) that offers pedagogical potential and disruptive possibility. Visual autobiographies elicit visceral responses to multiple embodiments – and to the ways in which they are pathologized, regulated, and surveyed. In turn, visual autobiographies frequently demand and reflect on the necessity and the difficulty of "ethical spectatorship," a concept that Wendy Kozol theorizes in her contribution to this book. These works agitate heart, head, and gut, making it possible for them to incite what, we argue, are newly critical modes of learning and remembrance.

There are precedents within the dynamically changing field of auto/biography studies for considering a broad range of contemporary projects and practices as "autobiographical." While Enlightenment traditions of autobiography tended to privilege recognizable life narratives of successful, even exemplary subjects, they were always supplemented, enlivened, and imperilled by their converse: the confessional and the scandalous (Rak 2004). Interested in the critical cultural meanings and counter-memories that contemporary autobiographers, often marginalized subjects, seek to generate, and in keeping with the often elusive and/or risk-taking articulations of subjectivity in these works, our book is premised on an expanded concept of the autobiographical signature or trace (Brophy 2004; Egan 1999; Hesford 1999, 2000; Hesford and Kozol 2000; Hirsch 1997; Naficy 2001; Perreault and Kadar 2005; Rak 2005; Smith and Watson 1996, 2002a). Written with a forward slash, as we do tactically in this volume from time to time, the term auto/biography highlights the varied, complex, and relational ways that "self and life" might be articulated in cultural production (Rak 2005, 16).

More specifically, we understand autobiography's relation to visual culture in terms of embodied political cultural practice. Rather than assuming the public sphere as a universally accessible forum premised on equity, following Judith Butler (2004a), we consider bodies as "formed within the crucible of social life" (26): bodies are made to appear/materialize, or are barred from doing so, within a field whose boundaries are constituted by what is presumed to be outside its sense of material reality, aesthetic value, affective and epistemological legitimacy, and ethical concern. And yet, as Butler points out in *Frames of War* (2009), possibilities for critical responses inhere in visual culture's "*thematizing* [of] the forcible frame, the one that conducts the dehumanizing norm, that restricts what is perceivable and indeed what can be" (100, emphasis added). Not coincidentally, Wendy Hesford's (1999) foundational work on visuality, autobiography, and pedagogy stresses the conceptual salience of "framing" (x). Persistently "determined and mediated" by the assumptions about documentary authenticity that "surround" and "structure" autobiographical representations, the embodied testimonies of marginalized subjects cannot escape "the risks of self-disclosure" (130, x, 131). By putting pressure on conventional frames, visual autobiographies may create the conditions for transforming themselves into what Alaimo (2010) terms "material memoirs": that is, into autobiographical texts that convey a material and trans-corporeal sense of the self (86), a phenomenon that Margrit Shildrick (2009) suggests is fundamentally and significantly intercorporeal (18). Where Alaimo is primarily interested in ecology – that is, in visions of "the self as coextensive with the physical environment" (96) – we combine her insights with Shildrick's emphasis on bodily interconnections in order to re-broaden and deepen the definition of materiality, considering visuality itself as a form of material mediation that can generate critical perspectives on embodied histories, cultural sedimentation, intersubjectivity, and critical witnessing practices. Our book is inspired, then, by Hesford's (2000) and Butler's (2009) Foucauldian intimations that "frames" are not only constraining, inescapable, and forceful, but also productive. We build on their "framing" insights by exploring autobiographical projects that engage in various forms of frame testing and theorize the "force" – as well as the critical pedagogical potential – of intercorporealities, emotions, and frames alike.

Even as we argue that the essays in this volume are united by a shared commitment to elaborating critical embodiment perspectives and tactics, we are cognizant of incommensurabilities that make juxtaposing diverse forms of marginalization and trauma tricky – and sometimes problematic. Some of these incommensurabilities stem from the particularities of forms of violence: as Bennett (2005) points out, for instance, "images of trauma and loss do not automatically map onto bodily memories as do images of physical pain" (69). Other complications are epistemological: Indigenous emphases on land, kinship, generational knowledge, and time, for example, do not align easily with those post-structuralist and/or postcolonial critiques that take capitalist modernity and its conceptions of progress and property as a given (Byrd and Rothberg 2011). We are aware, too, of the pressures that come to bear on witnessing projects according to the particular spheres of visual cultural production and circulation – the popular or alternative or institutionally established screen cultures – that they occupy and address (Chang 2007; Cvetkovich 2003; Hafsteinsson and Bredin 2010; Zimmermann 2000). Nevertheless, we take note of Ien Ang's (1997) argument that "incommensurable realities" (62) and incompatible repertoires of meaning are productive for signalling the im/possibilities of communication and affiliation across differences. Incommensurabilities can unsettle frames, generating what we are describing as the frame-testing work of visual autobiography and underlining the contentious, contingent relationships between histories, experiences, epistemologies, and visualities. We suggest, as well, following Cvetkovich (2003), that mobilizing multiple texts and genres "enables attention to how publics are formed in and through cultural archives" (9).

In this collection, interdisciplinarity and comparativism signal more than a mixing of differences; rather, they involve the unsettling of knowledges, discourses, theories, and methods, as well as a commitment to integrating new modes of study and thought. There has been an emphasis, historically and currently across the humanities and social sciences, on interrogating disciplinary boundaries, valuing a cross-fertilization of theoretical and methodological approaches, and destabilizing disciplinary claims to authoritative knowledges and paradigms. Exploring counter-methods of knowledge production by Indigenous peoples, Linda Tuhiwai Smith (1999) generates epistemological trouble-making that disorients assumptions about Indigenous difference and demands new understandings about ways to "know" "others." Smith's emphasis on "decolonizing methodologies" (1999) resonates with Tobin

Siebers' (2010) idea of "using disability studies as a pivot point" for visual culture analysis (133).[3] We pick up a major thread in critical disability studies, namely, the interrogation of the classification of bodies and the production of normal/abnormal regulations (Cohen and Weiss 2003; McRuer 2006; Shildrick 2009; Snyder and Mitchell 2006; Titchkosky 2007; Titchkosky and Michalko 2009). We are committed to challenging how "bodies are compared, differentiated, hierarchized, diagnosed" (Sullivan 2005, 29), and we understand our book as contributing to important emerging discussions, including the following: critiques of the pathologization of Indigeneity (Francis 2012; Greensmith 2012; A. Smith 2005); interrogations of impairment (Chivers 2011; Michalko 2002; Tremain 2002, 2006); meditations on crip and queer intersections (Garland-Thomson 2009; LeBesco 2001; McRuer 2006; McRuer and Mollow 2012; Shildrick 2009); attention to subjectivity and multiple differences within feminist disability studies (Driedger and Owen 2008; Garland-Thomson 2009; K. Hall 2011; Herndl 2002; Wendell 1996); and considerations of the complexly layered forms of address that characterize late twentieth- and early twenty-first-century memory projects (Bennett 2005; Rosenberg 2000; Rothberg 2009; Simon 2005). The critical practice of bringing diverse forms of trauma and marginalization into dialogue entails responding responsibly to Bennett's (2005) observation that trauma is never "unproblematically subjective" in the first place, but, rather, "always lived and negotiated at an intersection" (12). Visual autobiography projects, we suggest, may learn from one another, finding ways to "pivot" (Siebers 2010, 133) on the forms of critical embodiment that each, in all its situatedness, unfolds.

Corporeal Dilemmas: Visuality, Autobiography, and Embodied Emotion

Conceptually, our collection tracks critical theories and research methods that attend to the materiality, discursivity, and sociality of embodiment. We build on the legacies of feminist post-structuralism, including theoretically informed autobiographical work, and emphasize the interconnectedness of embodied being, social space, biomedical discourse, and political agency.[4] In *Feminism, Foucault, and Embodied Subjectivity*, for example, Margaret A. McLaren (2002) suggests that understanding the body as simultaneously produced in relations of power and producing resistance offers an important conceptual tension for feminist thought – one that requires us to attend to the inter-implication of the material and the discursive, the personal and the political. The tensions of feminist embodied knowing and politics are lived as textures, as Erin Manning points out in *Politics of Touch* (2007): an "against the grain" conceptualization of bodies as processual and in motion "makes us more sensitive, at each juncture, to how the body is defined, composed, and compartmentalized" (xii). Similarly, in her rethinking of ontology and epistemology, Karen Barad (1996) links sensuous knowledge production to power, offering the term "agential realism" to underline how "boundaries are interested instances of power, specific constructions, with real material consequences" (182). And, in *Frames of War* (2009), which we mentioned earlier, Judith Butler not only highlights the prevalence of dehumanizing visual logics, but also notices that "When those frames that govern the relative and differential recognizability of lives come apart," "other possibilities for apprehension emerge" (12). If, when frames "come apart," viewers begin to question the logic by which some lives (Western ones, in the context of Butler's critique of the US-led invasion of Iraq) are envisioned as more human and more valuable than others, then we may edge towards "a sensate understanding of war," thereby creating "the conditions of a sensate opposition to war" (100). In the spirit of McLaren's, Manning's, Barad's, and Butler's understandings of bodies as materially and discursively implicated in power relations, the chapters in this book are committed to thinking about the critically charged relationship between visual culture and lived embodiments. Our contributing authors attend to a variety of visual projects and technologies that re-envision what it means to live an embodied life; as the analyses collected here show, in a significant number of cases, visual autobiographies invite spectators to feel and think about possibilities for social justice in the worlds we inhabit together.

Since the 1990s, questions of embodied agency have also emerged as significant within the field of autobiography studies. In *Interfaces*, their examination of women's visual autobiographical practices, Sidonie Smith and Julia Watson theorize bodies as complexly built of neurochemical, anatomical, imagined, and sociopolitical elements, taking their examples from a range of visual representational and performative practices. They emphasize that feminist art practitioners have been at the forefront of mobilizing multilayered understandings of embodiment (2002b, 10). Another founding critic, Linda Kauffman (1996), focusing on the exploration of sexuality in post-humanist performances by Bob Flanagan, ORLAN, and others, sees visceral imagery as key to political contestation because it "reinstall[s] tactility and materiality …

without, however, resorting to sentimentality or essentialism" (43).[5] What is important to us about Kauffman's formulation is the idea that defamiliarizing strategies – in which visual autobiographers "objectify *themselves*, desacralizing and desecrating the body's terrain" – work to intensify rather than to cancel out the "tangible, material" body (43, original emphasis; 34). Such strategies support what Patti Lather (1993) evocatively describes, in her discussion of feminist methodologies, as an emergent form of "voluptuous validity" (681), whereby autobiography may be understood not as truth telling but as a "'leaky' practice" characterized by "a self-conscious partiality, an embodied positionality, and a tentativeness that leaves space for others to enter" (683). For a life artist such as Rebecca Belmore, with whose video *Worth* we opened this discussion, the performative coupling of material substance (her own body, the streetscape, the fabrics she is arranging), on the one hand, with self-reflexivity and testimonial address, on the other, is what constitutes the very ground of critique.

What are the implications of these re-conceptualizations of embodiment for theorizing visual self-narration and self-portraiture? Bodies come into view as fundamentally technological, in that "the senses prosthetically alter the dimensions of the body, inciting the body to move in excess of its-self toward the world" (Manning 2007, xiii). Elaborating on the implications of an emphasis on bodies as continually extending themselves into the world, Lisa Cartwright (2008) recasts the concept of viewer identification as involving

> the aspects of the psyche that are constituted through a hodgepodge of affective forces that are intersubjective and recognized as non-isomorphic but reciprocal, in a field of empathetic resonance whose material sites may include not only the body of another but also the photograph, the cinema, and the networked computer, between subjects and through intersubjective, communicative mechanisms of fantasized object-projection and introjection. Fantasy moves us and takes objects into its path, externally and internally (35).

Thinking about bodies as processual, emotion as embodied, and forms of media in terms of "material routes of feeling" (Cartwright 2008, 35) allows us to develop, in this book, a "thick" notion of cultural pedagogy – to posit that encounters with visual media are sensuous and multilayered, and that they may generate new ways of relating to life images and stories. Influenced, like Manning's discussion of prosthetics, by a Deleuzian emphasis on feeling as circulating via complexly visual-material pathways and on bodies and relational networks as continuously recreating themselves, Cartwright's formulation offers an important qualification, though, by reminding us that intersubjectivity is a "volatile and mutable" process (35, 26).

Taking seriously the affective instability and political ambiguity that Cartwright identifies at the heart of visual identificatory processes, we maintain in this study a focus on the *visuality* of new autobiographical forms. Our reasons for doing so are at once political, theoretical, and historical. Theorizations of the multi-sensing, interfacing, and world-creating body inform and inspire our analyses, but, in an ocularcentric culture (Jay 1988), visual representations of bodies, specifically, are fundamental to the elaboration of biopolitical power. As Hesford (2000) points out, there is a tradition, dating back to nineteenth-century photographs of hysterics, of conjuring women's bodies as *"pedagogical spectacles"* (351, original emphasis). And, in the early twenty-first century, "the ideal citizen-traveler is transparent or see-through," and "the 'good' global citizen" is being asked "to translate her heterogeneous body into useful, visual information" (R. Hall 2009, 45). The essays in our collection engage with the problem of transparency/opacity, focusing on how this opposition conditions public visibility and inclusion. For instance, Dan Irving's essay on how photographs of trans embodiment resonate with the ideal, resurgent in neoliberal times, of the "self-made man" testify to the fact that photographic portraiture, in particular, remains caught up in the production of national spectacles of inclusion and exclusion. Given the history of medical and state authorities' relationship to forms of "optical scrutiny" (Hesford 2000, 352), it remains imperative to query what forms of power/knowledge are being produced and circulated through autobiographical image-making practices.

Our contributing authors explore how image-based and often collaborative, sometimes serial autobiographical practices enact vital modes of cultural pedagogy in relation to health, illness, and disability. Many of the case studies they address demonstrate that visual autobiography is both resistant to and conditioned by the imperatives associated with new and old forms of "optical scrutiny." Allyson Mitchell's discussion of collaborative strategies for re-performing fat embodiment attests to the significance of critical alternative media. Mebbie Bell's analysis of anorexics' appropriations of popular culture images and Simon Strick's exploration of cosmetic surgery as a new bodily epistemology in the reality TV series *The Swan* foreground how trajectories of escape, resistance, or improvement are mapped for and by consumers.

Nuanced analyses of visual self-fashioning – and its imbrication in processes of normalization and self-discipline – are essential, these essays show, to theorizing autobiography's role in re-constituting what it means to exercise embodied agency in contemporary visual public spheres.

Given the accelerated transmissibility of visual culture in the digital era and the related pervasiveness of bodily surveillance, critical inquiry into visual subjectivities and pedagogies has become more urgent than ever before. As Jennifer González (2009) observes, the face is "the most reproduced visual sign on the Internet," and, as it has done since the Enlightenment era, it "continues to operate as the threshold to public space" (55). Paradoxically associated with universalizing conceptions of humanness, digital photographs and scans of bodies and especially of faces have emerged as key sources of biometrical data.[6] Whether we are thinking about faces in the context of biometric technologies that are used to regulate political borders or reflecting on the self-fashioning in which many of us engage on Facebook, faces are anything but politically neutral (55). Our book explores how digital-arts practitioners are re-scripting racialized and gendered embodiments and, along with them, the possibilities and constraints of digital public spaces. This re-scripting project is evident in Sayantani DasGupta's analysis of the online installation *Pop!*, a fictionalized account of male pregnancy that engenders a critical perspective on the role of medical visualizing technologies in biological reproduction and in the reproduction of preconceived race, gender, and sexual fixities. Not only do digital artworks intervene in envisioning the future, but they also shed new light on the past: as Sheila Petty's essay on African American artist Carmin Karasic's hypertext artwork elucidates, digitalization makes it possible for historical images and family memories of the Civil Rights era to be archaeologically investigated and reassembled; such a reassembly project offers critical purchase on the present, allowing us to see it as shaped by histories of both violence and activism.

While we, together with the contributing authors, are committed to drawing out politically hopeful potentials in contemporary visual autobiographies, our collective critical work in this volume is also inspired by Sara Ahmed's (2004, 2006) caution, which corresponds with Cartwright's (2008) emphasis on volatility and with Bennett's attention to what is "irreducible and different" (2005, 10), against seeing affect as an ethical solvent that inevitably leads towards reciprocity and responsibility. Ahmed (2006) asks that we attend to how emotions can propel us away from objects or, just as problematically, towards them in aggressive, appropriative ways: "The body extends its reach by taking in that which is 'not' it, where the 'not' involves the acquisition of new capacities and directions" (115). So, while engaging with visual autobiographies may open up complex and mobilizing "material routes" of identification for viewers, we stress that it remains important to account for historical and emergent visual regimes of power/knowledge that privilege whiteness, heteronormativity, masculinity, and ableism. More specifically, it is essential to account for the work that emotions do in elaborating and securing what Ahmed (2006) describes as "straight lines" of interpretation that militate against the "delayed," "astray" (78, 79), or, we would add, "opaque" (R. Hall 2009, 64).

In the rest of this introduction, we explore a selected handful of texts drawn from across diverse media modes, engaging them closely as works of visual philosophy (Bal 2006, 2007; Van Alphen 2005). While extended close readings may not be the norm for critical introductions, we would be remiss to centre our attention on prose theory and criticism. As Mieke Bal (2006) suggests of interdisciplinary methodology in visual culture studies, it is important to counter the false alternatives of either pure aestheticism or discursive overwriting. Instead, "the question is: How do images *think*? How can they ... offer ideas for reflection and debate, ideas in which the political and ideological flavour cannot be distinguished from the domain of visuality itself?" (252, original emphasis). Our aim in what follows, then, is not to survey the contemporary field so much as to model ways of "thinking with" the embodied politics of visual autobiography.

New Sensations: Critical Self-Portraiture and Installation

Like the essays by DasGupta and Petty that focus on digital re-scriptings of embodied lives (and on the conditions that shape their public visibility), *Embodied Politics* as a whole aims to reconfigure intercorporeal, interaffective encounters by emphasizing sensing, moving, remembering bodies in ways that significantly contest the primacy of normative forms of recognition. Visual artists working offline, in portraiture and installation, are presenting significant challenges to the fetishism of the human – and of the autonomous, able-bodied subject that human faces and figures are still often presumed to represent. Exemplified by Rebecca Belmore's *Worth*, site-specific installation work ties visual-intellectual analysis to the tumult of embodied feeling and a sense of "'being there'" (Simon 2005, 166). In *Chaos, Territory, Art* (2008), Elizabeth

Grosz writes: "Sensation fills the body with the resonance of (part of) the universe itself, a vibratory wave that opens the body to these unrepresented and unknowable forces, the forces of becoming-other. The body does not contain these forces but rather is touched by them and opened up to some of the possibilities of being otherwise, which the universe contains through them" (80–1).

What we draw from Grosz's rereading of evolutionary novelty is the insight that sensation's opening up of the body to "possibilities of being otherwise" might be the enabling condition for effective social critique and transformation. Autobiographical installation and performance work plays with visual self-portraiture in ways that conjure new forms of being and, in turn, new forms of relation and critical reflexivity (see figures 1.1 and 1.2). The field that we are calling "critical embodiment" was galvanized by the feminist and queer energies of 1970s visual experimentalism. Consider, for instance, how Lisa Steele's iconic video self-portrait, *Birthday Suit – with scars and defects* (1974), counters normative "*pedagogical spectacles*" of women's bodies (Hesford 2000, 351; original emphasis), particularly those deemed unhealthy, by insisting on scrutiny of her scarred body in ways that forcefully enact embodied agency.[7] Made two years earlier, Colin Campbell's groundbreaking video, *True/False* (1972), also generates an intense gazing encounter.[8] Campbell's work has been described as "hands-on and home made" (Greyson 2008, 51), and this description, which is readily applied to the style of Steele's *Birthday Suit*, draws attention to visual simplicity as key to self-portraiture, testamentary expression, and practices of staring back. In offering their own bodies as objects of scrutiny and scientific-like investigation, Steele in *Birthday Suit* and Campbell in *True/False* interrogate how tropes of truth and authenticity are attached to autobiography, and, in turn, insist on "the lived body as, at once, both an objective *subject* and a subjective *object*" (Sobchack 2004, 2, original emphases). Visual simplicity, the home-made, and oscillating subject/object dynamics continue to characterize visual autobiography in the first decade of the twenty-first century, as exemplified in the essays presented in this book by Ann Fudge Schormans and Adrienne Chambon (on the viewing practices of people with intellectual disabilities) and by Laura McGavin (on representations of cancer in graphic memoirs) that illuminate innovative practices of self-inscription and critical agency.

Installation work stages bodily encounters that ask viewers to locate ourselves as much as to look at images, and, in the process, to become

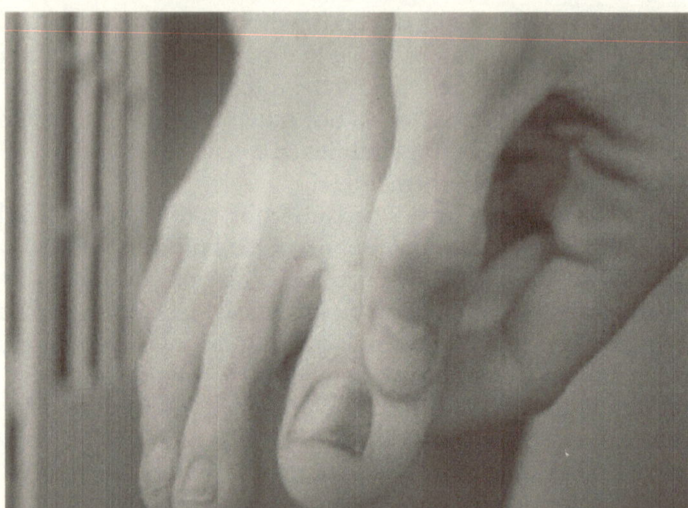

1.1. Video still from *Birthday Suit – with scars and defects* (Lisa Steele, 1974). © CARCC 2013.

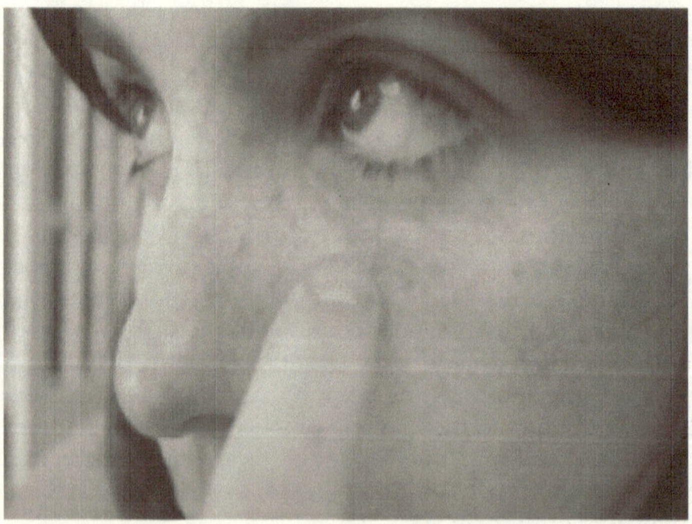

1.2. Video still from *Birthday Suit – with scars and defects* (Lisa Steele, 1974). © CARCC 2013.

differently aware of how we move through and/or around the spaces, bodies, images, objects, and ideas arranged by the artists (Bennett 2005). In this volume, Kim Sawchuk explores how multidisciplinary artist Mona Hatoum's exhibition *Corps étranger* draws viewers into what at first seem like abstract works but are, in fact, visual projections of the recesses of her own body: its orifices and entrails. We position Sawchuk's reading of Hatoum as representative of a wealth of autobiographically oriented installation work that plays dramatically with scale, distance, artifice, and juxtaposition. One particularly provocative example is filmmaker and official war artist Steve McQueen's *Queen and Country* (2007–10), which reproduces, in collaboration with families of the war dead, images of British combatants killed in Iraq since the 2003 invasion. Scaled down to the size of postage stamps, multiplied by the hundreds, and stored in sliding vertical drawers that the gallery visitor must pull out to access, these images highlight the tensions between national culture's lionizing of fallen heroes, on the one hand, and the disposability of young, often working-class and racialized enlistees, on the other.[9] By contrast, Allyson Mitchell's *Ladies Sasquatch* (2009b), an ongoing feminist installation project since 2005, is a maximalist work that takes the form of a collection of gorgeous beasts made of fun fur, taxidermy eyes, and dollar store costume fingernails. When we viewed the sasquatches at the McMaster Museum of Art in the winter of 2009, the group of five "ladies" rose in the space as a set of monumental figures, casting even taller shadows (along with our own) on the bare gallery walls and marking it, literally and figuratively, as intercorporeal space (see figure 1.3).

As Ann Cvetkovich (2009) points out, the sasquatches are autobiographical figures: by virtue of Mitchell's gathering and re-crafting; because they reference the bodies of particular dykes she has known (including two fat activist-performers); and because the small, ferocious pink familiars – the strange offspring or companions who populate the circle, frolicking in the shelter of the gathering – are named after friends and lovers (29). And as Mitchell (2009a) writes in her "Deep Lez I Statement," these "lesbian feminist monsters" are made to be seductive, to draw you in (12). While Hatoum's close-ups of her own orifices and entrails make human physiology at once familiar and strange, Mitchell embellishes the mouths and genitals of her monumental "ladies" so as to conjoin the sexually alluring and the monstrous: special details – a rose tattoo, a particularly lovely tuft of pubic fake fur – await the adventurous hand and eye. Given that sasquatches are significant

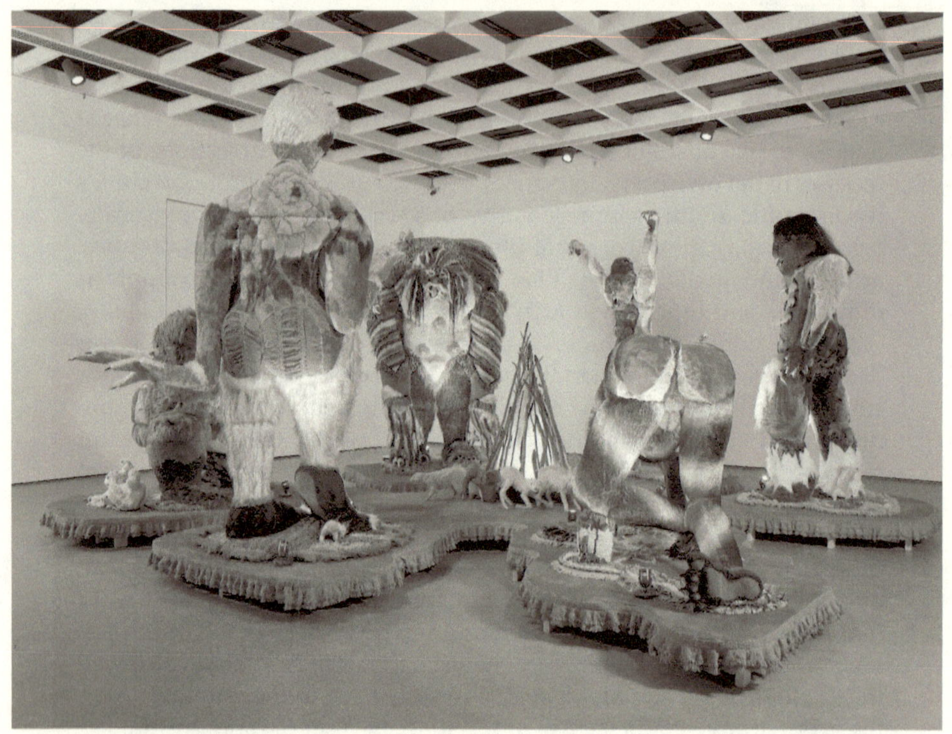

1.3. *Ladies Sasquatch.* Gallery installation view (Allyson Mitchell, 2009b) Courtesy of the artist.

entities in Indigenous histories and have been historically hunted and feared, Mitchell's project also brings race together with disability, via monstrosity. Mitchell's feminist monsters remind us that "the monstrous is not only an exteriority" and that "what is at issue is the permeability of the boundaries that guarantee the normatively embodied self" (Shildrick 2002, 1). Calling up questions about biological variation, abjection, insufficiency, human/animal dichotomies, and the "irreducible and different" (Bennett 2005, 10), Mitchell's installation materializes Shildrick's view of "the monstrous … as hopeful, the potential site of both a reconceived ontology, and a new form of ethics" (2002, 131).

While auto/biographical subjects nearly vanish into the miniaturizing format of McQueen's postage stamp images, the embodied materiality of Mitchell's sasquatches is writ large. Across these works by McQueen, Mitchell, and Hatoum, we note in particular how, in each case, the play with scale suggests a shared strategy of what disability theorist Rosemarie Garland-Thomson (2009) conceives of as the "disrupt[ion of] the placid visual relation that we expect between foreground and background" (166). For Garland-Thomson, "the sight of a radically unusual body provokes cognitive dissonance," and art does the "cultural work" of turning staring into a potentially transformative "beholding" encounter rather than a merely stigma-assigning moment of rebuff (156–7, 194). Characterized by their multisensory impact, hyperbolic visual effects of magnification/miniaturization, and no mean degree of unstable irony, contemporary auto/biographical portraiture and installation dynamically re-fabricate embodiment, perception, and, perhaps most importantly, the social spaces of display and viewership.

"I Want to Know Why": Video Art, Ethical Spectatorship, and Social Justice Imaginaries

The artists whose work we have explored in this introduction (and that our contributing authors consider) create nuanced, provocative, often discomfitting visions of embodiment – and, in turn, insist on political contestation as a key project for visual autobiography. The phenomenological and political dimensions of critical visual autobiography entail, we argue, a distinctive set of ethical and pedagogical demands. Roger I. Simon (2005) proposes the term "historiographic poetics" to refer to forms of cultural work that can generate "a community of rememberers and learners" (147) and that summon a spectatorial practice of ethical relationship to others: "Testament in this sense refers to images, text, and/or sound written and assembled to constitute ... an address that attempts to initiate a public memory" and to produce "witness as a form of collective study" (147, 149). We understand many contemporary visual autobiographies in Simon's terms, as "bringing into presence a figure whose corporeality and narrative performance might elicit a series of ethical and pedagogical considerations" (166). At stake here is a question of transformative social relations that follows from what Jill Bennett (2005) calls "empathic vision." She argues that visual language is unique: expressive and imaginative artefacts that take up difficult, troubling, complex, and critical/political rememberings have the potential to develop forms of visual philosophy and affective investment that create connective tissue with others (see also Bal 2007).

Counter to an emphasis on the representational and illustrative, Bennett underlines what art "does," that is, the understandings, theories, and affects it generates. Concerned with embodied politics and testimonial address, autobiographical film and video art illuminate remembering both as a contestation of forgetting and as a memory provocation – or an imprint – in and for the present, rather than simply as a return to a past. We maintain that visual autobiographies are producing important forms of collective learning that are profoundly tied to responsibility and accountability.

Critical and political film and video activates – and further theorizes – the pedagogical dynamics addressed by Simon and Bennett and by Wendy Kozol's essay on the complications of "ethical spectatorship" in projects of remembering genocide (this volume). Produced for non-commercial distribution, alternative film and video circulates in public spheres such as galleries, museums, film festivals, and community, activist, and educational locations. Marginalized subjects, in particular, mobilize alternative film and video practices to create critical cultural meaning (Brophy 2008; Chang 2007; Evans 2008; Gale and Steele 1996; Hladki 2010; Marchessault 1995; Shohat and Stam 1994; Waugh 2006). Practitioners use documentary, experimental, and/or narrative approaches to highlight the relationship of the maker's specific histories and embodiments to representation, calling attention to a film or video author's multiple "presences" in the text – or the way that filmmakers inhabit their films "as real empirical persons, enunciating subjects, structured absences, fictive structures, or a combination of these" (Naficy 2001, 35; see also Lee and Sakamoto 2002; Marchessault 1995; Rascaroli 2009; Russell 1999).

For example, Richard Fung's *Sea in the Blood* (2000) uses "video essay" (Biemann 2003) style to explore the history of his Chinese Trinidadian Canadian family and his lifelong attachment to his sister, Nan, who died from the inherited blood disease thalassemia (see figures 1.4 and 1.5). Fung combines this personal history with a portrait of his partner, Tim McCaskell, who is HIV-positive and engaged in HIV/AIDS activism.[10] Lyrical and slow motion sequences, which animate a gay eroticism, thread throughout the work: the men entwine in underwater swimming, often in light-fractured, red water that undulates over and around their bodies. At the same time, archival images in the video depict thalassemia patients with features marked by race and disability: as "mongoloid" and as similar to an individual with Down's Syndrome. Fung's images linking disability and race call up eugenicist discourses marked

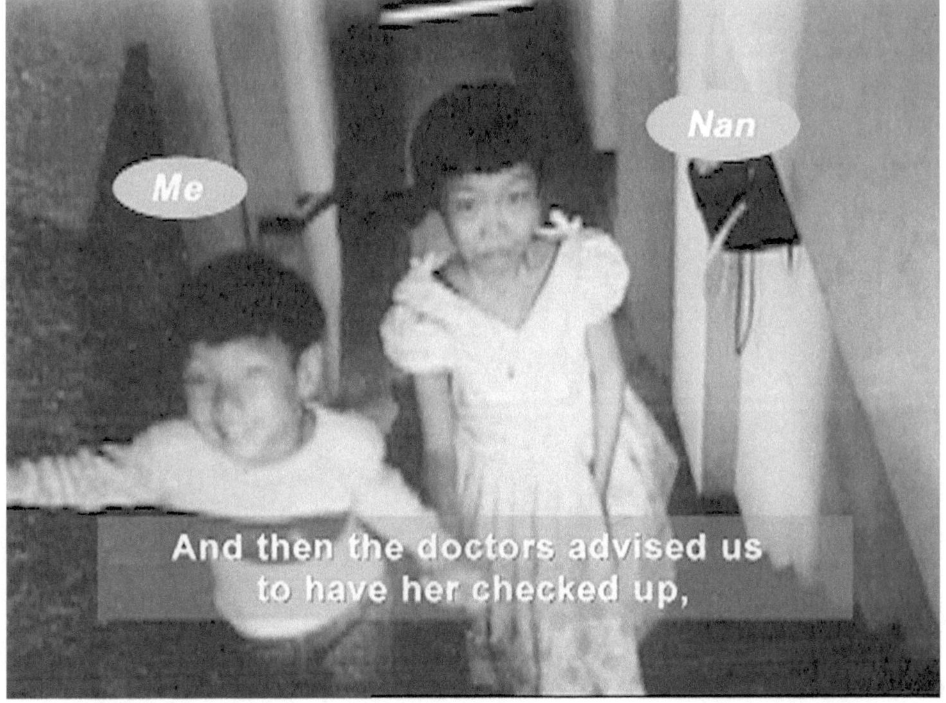

1.4. Video still from *Sea in the Blood* (Richard Fung, 2000). Courtesy of the artist.

by violent social controls, genocides, and biological atrocities, critically investigating the idea of a "Eugenic Atlantic," that is, the "fold[ing of] disability and race into a mutual project of human exclusion based upon scientific management systems successively developed within modernity" (Snyder and Mitchell 2006, 101). Fung's grainy home movies, emails, snapshots, archival medical footage, and visually obscure print text that moves across the screen all combine to disturb a sense of the veracity of photographic documentation and of medical categories (i.e., normal vs. major or minor "carriers"), instead emphasizing the relational imbrication of "desiring subjects" (Waugh 2006, 312–13). *Sea in the Blood* intervenes in commonsense assumptions about documentary and authenticity: it not only interrupts the realism and the comforting sentiments conventionally assigned to the family-album photographic record

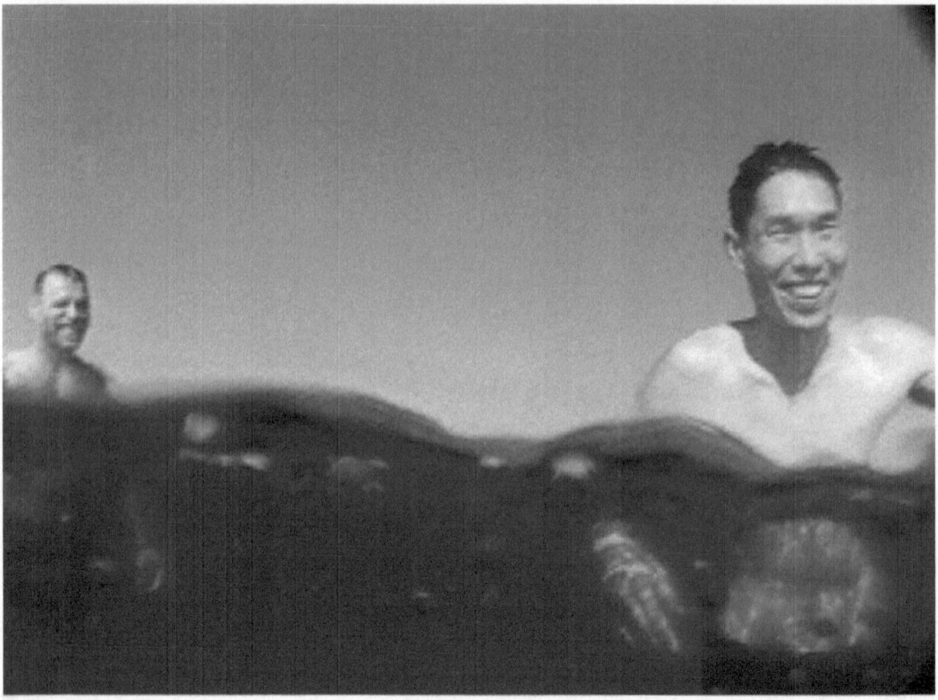

1.5. Video still from *Sea in the Blood* (Richard Fung, 2000). Courtesy of the artist.

(Hirsch 1997), but also contests how "racialized and sexualized populations continue to be ordered in the social imaginary through discourses of hygiene located in the blood" (Francis 2002). Bringing a theorist-practitioner's perspective to this collection, Fung's chapter in this book considers the transferability of such critical insights and strategies to recent autoethnographic video projects by straight men.

Fung's queer and diasporic investigation of the contested relationships among embodiment, place, medicine, and history resonates with the question posed in the title of another video autoethnography: *I Want to Know Why* (1994) by Dana Claxton (Hunkpapa Lakota Sioux). With particular attention to Claxton's artwork, we conclude this introduction by meditating on the contributions of Indigenous artists to autobiographical moving image culture (Claxton et al. 2005; Evans 2008; Masayesya 2000; Wilson and Stewart 2008). Incendiary reinvigorations of history, memory, and resistance characterize many of these works, and Claxton's relentless and gut-wrenching cry, "I want to know why," makes her video a particularly moving example of the critical and impassioned grip of unruly bodies in autobiographically oriented visual cultural production.

Kinship, family history, matrilineal heritage, and Aboriginal women's experiences are made palpable throughout Claxton's video. With throbbing sound, disturbing voice-over, and jarring imagery, this decolonizing testimonial work creates spectatorial unease and presses for responsible learning about and answerability to "why." "Tapping into the transgressive power of montage," the video "challenges viewers to think again about the history of colonialism in the cities they inhabit" (Bell 2010–11, 104). The soundtrack includes rhythmic techno music that, in its contemporaneity, underscores the re-historicizing and counter-memory work of Claxton's project. The voice-over, which includes both screaming and quiet emphases, demands accountability for the impact of colonial conditions on the women in her family and on generations of Aboriginal women who have been – and continue to be – obliterated:

> Mastachila, (Mas-tee-chel-a), my great grandmother, walked to Canada with Sitting Bull. Mastachila, (Mas-tee-chel-a), my great grandmother, walked to Canada starving. AND I WANT TO KNOW WHY. Pearl Goodtrack, my grandmother, died of alcohol poisoning. AND I WANT TO KNOW WHY. Eli Goodtrack, my mother, OD'ed at the age of 37. And I want to know why.

Claxton's demand for answers to this pattern of devastation in her genealogy points to genocidal policies in nineteenth-century America, to land expropriation, and to cross-border displacements within North America – as well as to the long-standing disavowal of these systemic oppressions. The sound text intertwines with pulsing black and white image fragments, many of which are stereotypical representations produced by mainstream white culture about Indigenous cultures (see figure 1.6).

Like artist Peter Morin (Crow clan, Tahltan Nation), who, in his contribution to this book, describes the material epistemology that animates his performance and teaching work within museum spaces, and like Rebecca Belmore in *Worth,* Claxton retrieves images from the colonial archive, producing a reversal of the normative ethnographic

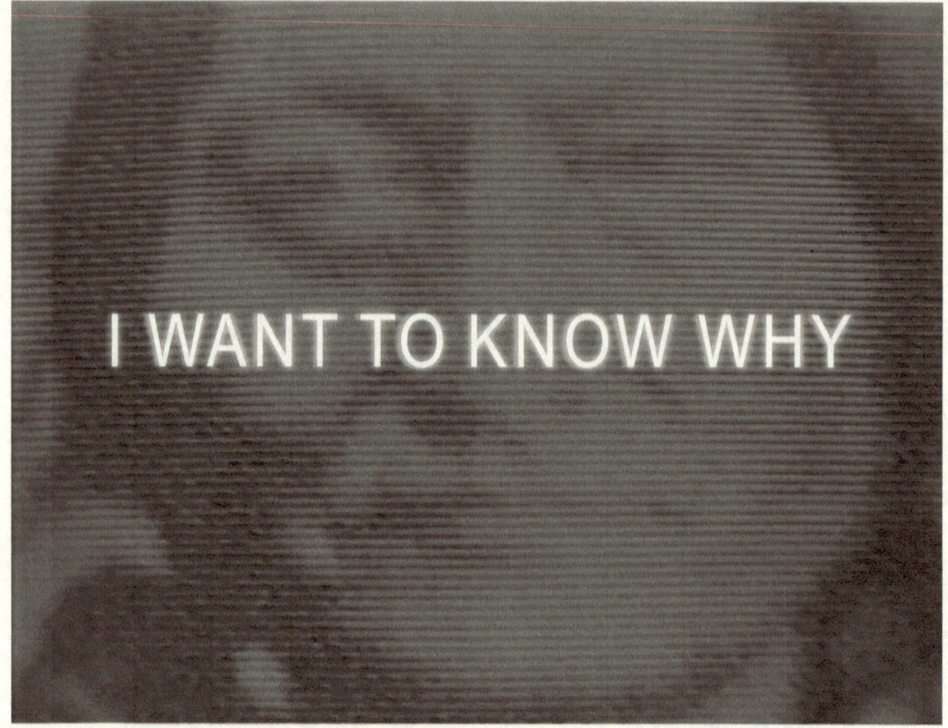

1.6. Video still from *I Want to Know Why* (Dana Claxton, 1994). Courtesy of the artist.

method such that the Indigenous subject now "examines" the "other." Juxtaposing a close-up of her great-grandmother and an image of the Statue of Liberty, Claxton "reveals the violent paradox in white Enlightenment culture, which proclaimed liberty, justice and freedom for some while justifying the displacement and dispossession of others" (Bell 2010–11, 104). The images of Sitting Bull reference the migration of the Lakota Sioux people, particularly in terms of settlement in Saskatchewan, where Claxton's reserve is located, and, consequently, they underline survival despite overwhelming violence. Monika Kin Gagnon (2000) observes that Claxton's art, including her mobilization of the archive, functions "temporally": "Underlying Claxton's version of events is an insistence that colonialism's effects continue to rupture the present" (37). This practice of constructing a past/present imbrication characterizes the photographic work of contemporary Indigenous artists who "deconstruct the representation of indigenous peoples by playing with, responding to, and turning over established tropes that are recognized as part of an ongoing colonial gaze" (Rickard 2010, 81).

I Want to Know Why disrupts the linear views of time that are central to Western understandings of history and progress. Maori theorist Linda Tuhiwai Smith (1999) argues that Western conceptions of time are fundamental to colonialist practices: linear views of time shape Western history's privileging of science, reason, and "progress" (55). Smith observes:

> What has come to count as history in contemporary society is a contentious issue for many indigenous communities because it is not only the story of domination; it is also a story which assumes that there was a "point in time" which was "prehistoric" … Traditional indigenous knowledge ceased, in this view, when it came into contact with "modern" societies, that is, the West. (55)

Claxton's work – and that of the other visual autobiographers we have discussed in this introduction – may be understood as engaging what Simon (2005) has referred to as "public time," whereby testamentary material does not simply offer evidence but also creates an interrogation of history and time along with their structures of authority (8).

Visual autobiography has been and continues to be in the forefront of generating what Linda Kauffman (1996) describes as a "new paradigm of spectatorship," in which visual and aural traces of "the human body" constitute "simultaneously the spectacle, the performance space, the subject and the object of pleasure and danger" (43–4). Premised on affective engagement *and* self-reflexivity for their efficacy, visual autobiographies call attention to the cultural assumptions that structure how embodied life histories and memories are communicated. And, because they are implicated in "public time," they create and often reinvigorate multiple public spheres, "in which learning is not simply the acquisition of new information, but … a difficult 'gift' that in its demand for a non-indifference, may open questions, interrupt conventions, and set thought to work" (Simon 2005, 7). Making visual autobiographies forceful, interruptive, engaging, and thought-provoking entails, as Kauffman and Simon each imply, a significant degree of critically embodied risk taking on the part of visual autobiographers.

It is precisely the quality of riskiness – a quality inherent in visual autobiographers' embracing of strategies that can make the frames that "govern" embodied reality "come apart" – that allows us to characterize contemporary visual auto/biographical projects as significant and potentially transformative forms of cultural pedagogy (Butler 2009, 12). Altered frames of visuality: shaky, home-made, multiple, historical, insistent. Bodies out of bounds, unruly, circulating. New life possibilities and constraints. This is the political cultural work of visual autobiography.

Contributions to the Collection

This book encompasses four parts, each of which crystallizes a pedagogical dynamic that we see as vital to the field of visual autobiographical production and theory. We begin in part 1 by investigating how visual autobiographical texts generate "multiple becomings" in the world, with an emphasis on the disruptive and critical cultural work performed by their "uncertainty" (Shildrick 2009, 176). Part II offers a cluster of essays that highlight how visual autobiographical practices, particularly those concerned with articulating embodied differences, are significantly shaped by neoliberal expectations of self-actualization and autonomy. Then, anchored by Peter Morin's Indigenous and materialist rethinking of visual knowledge practices, the essays in Part III reflect on what it might mean to instantiate a "thick" cultural pedagogy and politics of embodiment. Finally, Part IV meditates on the numerous contradictions that accompany attempts to mobilize ethical spectatorship through visual autobiography. By foregrounding projects that connect the articulation of selves to historical memory, Part IV offers a concluding reminder of a key critical premise for our study as a whole: that embodied politics are profoundly embedded in the worlds that visual autobiographers inhabit, imagine, contest, and address.

NOTES

1 *Worth* reuses material from *Wild* (2001), Belmore's installation and performance in the master bedroom of the colonial-era Grange house (1817) that comprises part of the Art Gallery of Ontario in Toronto. As Belmore (2008) writes of *Wild*, "To lie in this historic bed covered in a mass of hair is evocative of a time when the newcomers to this land viewed us as wild.

The decorative fur detail of the canopy refers to the taking and taming of this 'wilderness.' My black hair is a celebration of survival" (49).

2 See http://www.youtube.com/watch?v=Cv9DfVAzok4

3 We elaborate the concept of epistemological troublemaking in visual cultural production in our forthcoming article, "Cripping the Museum: Pedagogy, Disability, and Video Art."

4 Feminist post-structuralist works that continue to be influential for us include Braithwaite et. al. (2004); Butler and Scott (1992); Davies (2000); Rosenberg (2000); Sawicki (1991); Spivak (1999); and St. Pierre and Pillow (2000). And in the area of critically inflected autobiographical writings, we admire and are informed by, to name just a few from a wide field, Allison (1996); Anzaldúa (1987); Moraga (1983); Rockhill (1996); Spence (1995); and Walkerdine (1991). It also strikes us as crucial to note that, while critics such as Stacy Alaimo and Susan Hekman (2008) and Laura Tanner (2006) have called for feminists to get over our anti-essentialism in order to embrace anew the body's physical materiality – and nature's agentic, world-shaping powers – we find Sara Ahmed's (2008) critique of the "founding gestures" of the "new materialism" persuasive: in the drive to posit materiality as a pure theoretical object, there is a risk of ignoring earlier feminist investigations into material-semiotic interfaces (35). As the contributions to this volume by DasGupta, McGavin, Sawchuk, and others suggest, earlier feminist science studies, such as Donna Haraway's *Simians, Cyborgs, and Women* (1991) and Lisa Cartwright's *Screening the Body* (1995), continue to energize cultural analysis.

5 Key discussions of Bob Flanagan's bdsm and crip engagement with ideas of "sickness" include McRuer (2006) and Hladki (2005). Extended commentaries on ORLAN's cosmetic surgeries-as-performances can be found in Faber (2002) and Donger, with Shepherd and ORLAN (2010).

6 Corroborating González's critique of the pre-eminence of the face, Mieke Bal (2004) argues that portraiture, with its traditional focus on the humanistic emblem of the face, can be complicit with "a ferocious but disingenuous and, indeed, dangerous, individualism" (n.p.). Butler (2004a) notes that assuming the individual human face as an obvious reference point for identification (assumed at once to be universal, but usually constituted as "familiar") implicitly denies "grievability" to lives and losses deemed "other" to the nation (38–9, 131 ff.).

7 See http://www.steeleandtomczak.com/video/birthdaysuit.html

8 See http://www.colincampbellvideoartist.com/videos/true-false-clip.php

9 McQueen, who devised *Queen and Country* after he was refused the permission he needed to make a short documentary film in Iraq, maintains that his work will not be complete until the Royal Mail agrees to publish a series of stamps based on the project (McQueen 2007–10).

10 For more on autobiographical projects that bear witness to HIV/AIDS, see Brophy (2004, 2008); R. Chambers (2004); Egan (1999); Hallas (2010); and Juhasz (1995).

PART ONE

Proliferating Monstrosity

2 Quickening Paternity: Cyberspace, Surveillance, and the Performance of Male Pregnancy

SAYANTANI DASGUPTA

The New York City skyline. A taxi door opens, and a visibly pregnant man exits into Times Square. The camera tilts up to the skyscrapers all around him, phallic symbols of steel and chrome stretching to the sky.

The voice-over begins. "There's a lot of questions in my mind, because I'm going to be the first one, the first male to carry a baby to term if I survive," says the man, later identified as "Mr Lee" Mingwei.

"Oh my goodness finally! It's about time!" a passing woman exclaims. "My sister has six children. By the time she had her last one, she said, my husband is carrying the next one!" But a taxi driver has reservations. "Ethically [male pregnancy] is not allowed by Christianity, Muslim religion, I think Buddhism ... none of the religion(s) accept this ... this is a very unnatural way."

In the voice-over, Mr Lee muses, "[Male pregnancy] challenges the very nature of what it is to be a man and what is to be a woman ... The more I ask myself, the more confused I am ... the more I ask, the further away from the answer [I get]."[1]

Directed by Sophie Lepault and Capucine Lafait, *When men are pregnant* (2006) is a part of the online and real life (RL) installation, *POP! The First Male Pregnancy*. Intentionally blurring the lines between representation and reality, the website (Wong 2008h) is part of a series of interconnected sites about the fictitious RYT Hospital/Dwayne Medical Center (Wong 2008c), a cyberlocation created by artist Virgil Wong, who is the real life director of web services at a large academic hospital. While fellow artist Lee Mingwei appears as the pregnant "Mr Lee," Wong appears both online and at installation events as Dr Phineas Liu, RYT's director of genetic medicine and reproductive endocrinology. According to the site, "Dr Liu appears at speaking events, galleries, and malls to recruit patients for male pregnancy clinical trials and promote reproduction technology services at the GenoChoice Institute" (Wong 2008b).

This chapter will examine Wong and Mingwei's collaboration, *POP! The First Male Pregnancy*, a cyber- and real-world installation that simultaneously replicates and undermines the medical gaze and the biological paradigms of pregnancy through its envisioning and re-visioning of reproductive, gendered, and racial embodiment. This multigenre project – which includes the documentary film, blogs by Dr Liu and Mr Lee, reports of media coverage, and "daily" EKG and ultrasound images of the pregnant Mr Lee – can be read as a site of visual auto/biography that not only (re)produces pregnancy and medical surveillance, but also redefines the boundaries between North and South, male and female, queer and straight, science and art, and technology and the body. While Wong and Mingwei's project is firmly rooted in the soil of a postcolonial, globalized world order where technology – whether cybernetic or reproductive – threatens to turn human bodies into Heideggerean "stock," it simultaneously explores the soaring possibilities of fantasy and the fantastic in cybernetic self stories.

Autobiography as Transformation: Persona

In *Autobiography: Narrative of Transformation* (2001), Carolyn A. Barros suggests that despite the vast variations in the genre, autobiography "as a text of a life" can be considered a "narrative of transformation" (9), the plot of which is "I have changed" (10). Barros goes on to utilize three heuristic perspectives to understand autobiography: persona, figura, and dynamis. Persona – "the who" that is the "I" of the transformation (12) – is complicated in *POP!* due to the fact that there are not one but two potential "I"s: Wong and Mingwei. Both are transformed through this project from their RL personas to cybernetic ones: Virgil Wong to Dr Phineas Liu, and Lee Mingwei to the pregnant Mr Lee.

Consider Virgil Wong's description of the birth of this project: *POP!* was apparently conceived when Mingwei expressed a RL desire to experience parenthood. "Will you and your [male] partner adopt? Have a surrogate?" Wong asked, to which Mingwei answered, "No, I want to physically have a baby. I want to be pregnant." After consulting a reproductive endocrinologist and discussing the scientific and physical challenges of both ectopic wombs and abdominal ectopic pregnancy, Wong suggested that Mingwei become cybernetically, rather than materially, pregnant. From this narrative, it seems that *POP!* is a virtual realization of Mingwei's RL desires, with Wong as the artistic and cyberscientific father/facilitator (Wong 2008a).

Although Mingwei may not "really" be pregnant, the corporeal expression of *POP!* is consistent with his larger body of artistic work, which explores "the evanescent and diurnal cycles of living [and] is based on such basic human activities as cooking, letter writing, and now child-bearing." In his words:

> I see this pregnancy as being very much in keeping with Buddhist philosophical thought. There is a strong connection I feel between myself, the child within my body, and the world around us both. And I think there is a greater awareness and empathy I now share with my mother and sister as a result of my pregnancy. Most of all, there is a level of insight and understanding about being alive – of sharing your life – in ways that I've never realized before. (Wong 2008j)

For example, *100 Days with Lily* ([1995] 1998), a project based on Ch'an Buddhist philosophy and undertaken to honour his deceased grandmother, documented Mingwei's relationship with a flower that he had "planted as a bulb, nurtured to maturity, and carried everywhere, even after the flower died" (Mingwei 2008). Of course, recalling Edward Said's (1979) formulation of Orientalism as a mode of discursive colonization whereby the "exotic" East is visually, culturally, and politically produced, this visual representation of the queer Asian Pacific Islander (API) man in monk's robes is mediated by a (potentially self-inflicted) Orientalizing gaze.

In contrast, Wong's artistic voice is that of the medical cultural critic. Consider the other RYT Hospital/Dwayne Medical Center websites created by Wong: *Nanodocs* (Wong 2008g), microscopic nanotech robots that help RYT physicians monitor the health of patients by travelling through their blood and tissue; *Clyven* (Wong 2008d), a genetically engineered mouse with human intelligence who is able to communicate with website and RL installation visitors; and *Genochoice* (Wong 2008e), a program that allows you to "create your own genetically healthy child online!" Altogether, RYT hospital's websites are realistic and detailed, with well-researched medical information, links to actual websites and news reports, and an aesthetic sensibility that lends credibility to these not-yet-realized, bioethically vexed medical advances. Although this essay analyses the *POP!* site, it does so remembering its context: the fictitious medical projects to which *POP!* is linked in cyberspace, which are also displayed together as RL installations during Wong's art exhibitions (Liu and Wong 2008).

Much as the digital and RL installations partake of medical discourse, so too is the figure of Dr Phineas Liu a hyper-realistic portrayal of a medical scientist. "A number of years ago, we determined that male pregnancy was possible, based on the success of a number of ectopic pregnancies in women," he explains during the Lepault and Lafait film. Donning his white lab coat before a projected image of a moving fetus, he continues, "Here we have a 4D sonogram illustrating the fetus of Mr Lee Mingwei, the first human male to become pregnant." Then, he projects an image representing the interior of Mr Lee's body: "The same way that this child would grow inside the uterus of a female, you can see that happening within the abdominal area of Mr Lee ... The surgical procedure will be a bit more extraordinary than your average C-section [though] we're actually very confident the fetus will be perfectly fine" (Wong 2008i).

Dr Liu's focus on fetal visualization, rather than the health of the gestating parent, invokes the discourse of a biotechnically driven reproductive medicine (Martin 1992; Stabile 1998) and the "cult of the public fetus" (J.S. Taylor 2000). In the words of Paul Brodwin (2000), "laparoscopy and fetal photography ... furnish ever more invasive and naturalized depictions of the fetus, which performs the crucial ideological work (in the context of American new Right politics) of visually separating mother and fetus, asserting fetal autonomy, and reducing women to passive reproducing machines" (4). By positioning his alter ego before a giant 4D ultrasound of a fetus, Wong references the critical role of ultrasound technology in mediating the mother's relationship with her own body. The pregnant woman's reports of her biological processes, including fetal movement or "quickening" – once used as evidence of a healthy pregnancy – are now subordinated to images of her body's internal spaces on a screen, interpreted for her by a clinician (Martin 1992; Stabile 1998; J.S. Taylor 2008). Such biotechnologies have transformed the maternal body from a site of private knowledge construction to a site of public surveillance. Certainly, "a large part of ultrasound's appeal for doctors is that it allows them technologically to bypass pregnant women as a source of knowledge about pregnancy" (J.S. Taylor 2000, 149). The Lepault and Lafait film takes this cleaving of parental corporeality from fetal embodiment one step further, bringing the fetus before the gaze of both Dr Liu and the audience without the presence of Mr Lee anywhere in the room.

Although Dr Liu virtually dons the scientific mantle of Wong's RL medical centre working environment – in aspect, language, and cultural orientation – the "good doctor" can be read as part parody and part hyper-realistic portrayal of a medical practitioner. According to Sidonie Smith and Julia Watson ([2001] 2010), "Autobiographical acts involve narrators in 'identifying' themselves to the reader. That is, writers make themselves known by acts of identification, and, by implication, differentiation" (38). They suggest that such identities are discursive, dialogical, and that identity is "a 'production' which is never complete, always in process, and always constituted within, not outside, representation" (Stuart Hall quoted in Smith and Watson, 39).

In addition, *POP!* can be included in the category of what Helen Kennedy (2003) has called "technobiographies," autobiographical acts that investigate techno-social relations. As such, persona in *POP!* exemplifies the dynamic, fluid notion of the cybernetic self – the variable and interconnected "I"s that an Internet user manifests, for example, in the contexts of email, social networking portals, and avatar-using gaming sites. The transformation of Wong can be understood as a process of identification and de-identification with Liu, the fictive autobiographer. However, as Kennedy has argued, there can be no study of online lives without an understanding of their offline contexts, particularly in the case of marginalized or counter-hegemonic identities. The boundaries between Wong the artist and Liu the medical avatar are permeable rather than rigid; offline realities construct the technologically situated online self, and technological realities mediate the biologically and socially situated offline self.

In his online blog, Dr Liu refers to Virgil Wong as his "artist/filmmaker collaborator," suggesting a psychological twinning of the medical and artistic selves. What one imagines as Wong's artistic voice seeps through in Dr Liu's online writing; his blogs become self-conscious examinations of the connections between science and art, medicine and cyberspace. One entry, dated 5/21/05 and called "Ebola Dream," reads:

> I dreamt last night of a patient coming into the emergency room with myalgia, a maculopapular rash, desquamation, hepatomegaly, and pharyngitis. And she was bleeding from a strange split encircling her entire neck. While nurses and residents started showing the same signs of some acute

> febrile illness and collapsing onto the floor, I was calmly sitting in the middle of the cacophony looking for polymerase chain reaction products in the patient's vaginal secretions.
>
> My half-blind mother and I are then walking through the Hospital corridors, and she starts removing flyers she can barely see from a bulletin board. "So silly putting paper on walls, no?" she asks. "I'm going to make a web site for the Hospital." She explains how the entire site will be composed of word fragments that billow like leaves from tall trees that land into tidy little piles of color-coded information.
>
> Exasperated, I begin describing the actual mechanics of information architecture and design usability like some wayward geek only to find that she has disappeared. I shuffle quickly from the Hospital's main entrance and ride each of the major elevator banks to every floor of the building …
>
> I find my mother in a dilapidated room filled with hay and wandering sheep and goats. Dozens of nurses, interns, and attendings walk by ignoring her. She pulls me aside and points to a young African American girl in the corner. Despite being anemic and convulsing herself, my mother says, "Please help that young girl, Phinny. Her name is Lindsey. She plays the violin."
>
> I try to help my mother into the bed, but she protests, "I'm fine. Go make her better." (Wong 2008f)

While the initial paragraph of the blog is steeped in medical language – "maculopapular rash," "myalgia," "hepatomegaly" – this diary-like entry is surreal in tenor, with its "word fragments that billow like leaves" and hospital rooms "filled with hay and wandering sheep and goats." It both registers the anxiety of real clinician dreams – regarding a seriously ill patient or a frightening, contagious disease (Marcus 1999) – and critiques the technically driven micro-gaze that can overshadow physicians' abilities to holistically *see* the suffering of their patients. When faced with not only a presumably contagious, acutely bleeding patient, but also clinical staff who are "collapsing" with the same illness, Dr Liu neither reacts nor clinically attends to these sufferers, but "calmly sit[s] in the middle of the cacophony looking for polymerase chain reaction products in the patient's vaginal secretions." His dissecting gaze is mediated here by technology (presumably a microscope), and privileges reproductive body parts and body products over human interaction and an integrated vision of suffering. The loss of the "half-blind mother" may signify the entrapment of Wong's own artistic origins in the structures of medicine; in searching for her, he becomes initially even more ensconced in the architecture of the hospital, eventually becoming reborn from the womb of medicine as Dr Liu. Yet, Liu is urged by his artistic origins (even while they are "anemic and convulsing") to recognize patients as three-dimensional individuals and, in doing so, to "make [medicine] better."

As a reproductive endocrinologist might implant a fertilized ova or embryo into a woman's uterus, Wong not only implants a cybernetic pregnancy into "Mr Lee's" body, but he also implants the idea of male pregnancy into our popular cultural narratives: the Lepault and Lafait film is posted on YouTube, and Wong answers emails in the voice of "Dr Liu." Virgil Wong's transformation, then, is circular. He transforms from artist to scientist, from cultural critic to one who upholds traditional medical culture; but he also transforms back again, since his portrayal of the traditional physician becomes a critique of the very medical culture he embodies.

Male Pregnancy in Myth and Movie: Figura

Before delving further into these issues of embodiment, subjectivity, and cyberart, it is useful to understand the mythic and generic contexts that shape this visual autobiography. According to Barros (2001), figura is "the image or metaphor for the type of change described in the autobiography ... It stands as the term for the narrative of transformation, as it is particular *and* universal" (13, original emphasis). In the case of *POP!*, the central figura, of course, is male pregnancy itself, a seemingly "impossible" embodied state that is also a rich cultural site for both reinforcing and critiquing patriarchal power – and one that, through a tactic of re-doubling of the seemingly stable reference point of the individual male body, allows us to explore the politics and possibilities of fantastical embodiments in autobiography.

Medical anthropologist Janelle S. Taylor (2000) has used feminist critiques of reproduction as production – which posit doctors as managers, women as workers/consumers, and fetuses as commodities (Martin 1992) – to suggest that the pleasures of modern reproduction have been constructed in terms of the maternal consumption of commercial goods, of food, and, at a symbolic level, of fetuses themselves. Significantly, however, in Greek mythology, both male pregnancy and *paternal* consumption are common themes. The Titan Cronos, father of Zeus, is said to have consumed each of his newborn infants for fear that the children would eventually overthrow him. Hidden by his mother from his ravenous father, Zeus eventually carries out this prophecy. Later, fearing a similar prophecy foretelling that a son born of his wife, Metis, would overthrow him, Zeus swallows her while she is ostensibly pregnant, only to have the fully grown goddess Athena eventually emerge from Zeus' head (Aliki 1994).

The masculine body not only consumes, but also occasionally serves as a substitute for the unavailable female body. When Zeus' second wife, Hera, who was famously jealous of Zeus' lovers, kills Dionysus' mother with a lightning bolt, Zeus sews the unborn baby into his leg and later gives birth to him from his thigh (Aliki 1994). This narrative is consistent with the *POP!* site itself, whereby the fetus implanted into Mr Lee's abdomen is said to have been the result of a premature delivery in which the mother had died (Wong 2008a). Although these narratives could possibly be read as surrogate pregnancies, in both cases, the pregnant father does not carry the fetus for the benefit of another parent; he continues the pregnancy so that, presumably, he can parent the child himself. These are not surrogacy narratives, then, but narratives of male bodies taking over where female bodies have failed. In doing so, they manifest a different sort of incorporation, such that the maternal contribution to the fetus becomes effectively erased, and the resultant fetus (even when genetically unrelated) becomes wholly the product of paternal reproduction. Such narratives evoke seventeenth-century notions of preformation, or animaculism – the idea that fully formed babies existed in the head of sperm, and that women's bodies were simply incubators with no other biological contribution to their offspring. Here, *POP!* potentially undermines the subject-hood of the absent, pregnant female subject even as it uncouples the female body from essentialist constructions of reproduction, effectively "queering what counts as nature" (Haraway 1991, 300).

Pregnant gods and kings abound in other mythological traditions as well. When the Hindu Lord Vishnu gave birth to Lord Brahma, a lotus emerged from his navel, a sort of umbilical cord attached to an external uterus, carrying Lord Brahma within. Lord Brahma, in turn, gives birth to his "mind-born son," Narada, one of the *ayonijia* or "one-not-born-of-the-womb. Since the womb is the gateway into the cycle of rebirths, Narada is untouched by space and time … and unaffected by the fear of death" (Pattanaik 2002, 53). Here, male pregnancy is the mechanism by which individuals become purified of all things material. While female pregnancy delivers humanity unto the never-ending cycle of life and death, male pregnancy – like, it may be argued, male or female cyberpregnancy – delivers the newly born away from death itself. Indeed, on gaming sites such as Second Life, pregnancy and delivery are possible, but such virtual babies, which are bought and sold in stores on Second Life and are genetically alterable on sites such as Heavenly Bodies, are not enacted by real people. Rather, they are robotic NPCs (non-player characters), unaffected both by cycles of life and death and by the materiality – and maternality – of corporeal existence (Krotoski 2006; MMOrgy.com 2005).

As a visual autobiographical narrative that draws heavily on scientific medical technology, *POP!* can be productively read against the more common visual narratives of male pregnancy in "mad scientist" science fiction cinema. If feature films are our modern mythologies, then the techno-scientific constructions of male reproduction in this filmic genre inherit the mythological narratives of paternal gestation with which I began this section. From the various remakes of *Frankenstein* (Whale 1931; Branagh 1994) and *The Island of Dr Moreau* (Kenton 1932; Taylor 1977; Frankenheimer 1996), to *Blade Runner* (Scott 1982), *Gattaca* (Niccol 1997), and *AI: Artificial Intelligence* (Spielberg 2001), the monster/android/robot/post-human is often the result of metaphoric (or "virtual") male pregnancy on the part of the physician/scientist. For instance, Kenneth Branagh's 1994 adaptation of *Frankenstein* (1818) brings female and male reproduction into particularly sharp contrast. Distraught at witnessing his mother's bloody death during the birth of his younger brother, Victor Frankenstein – the son of a prominent obstetrician – embarks on scientific experiments to create life and cheat death while circumventing the flawed necessities of female reproduction. He constructs an enormous womb/tomb out of a metal tub, filling this ectopic uterus with buckets of amniotic fluid he has obtained from local midwives attending the deliveries of labouring women. Then Frankenstein (played by Branagh himself) places in the tub a monstrous body made from sewn-together "spare parts" of the dead, his grotesque version of a fully grown fetus. In a frenetic scene, Branagh dashes about in paroxysms of scientific delight, hooking up his metal womb to an enormous balloon-and-funnel structure resembling a penis and giant testicle. Through this externalized reproductive system, hundreds of wriggling eels – giant sperm – travel into the amniotic bath, biting and electrifying the dead body as Branagh sits astride the metal uterus and shouts, "Live! Live!"

As opposed to the reproductive myths of Greek and Hindu gods, "mad scientist" films problematize rather than glorify the narrative of male pregnancy. Scientific fathers are, by and large, killed by their progeny, who are enraged at their own "freakish," non-human identities. These films suggest that, like the maternal imagination, which is seen as vulnerable to "dangerous" thoughts and visions (Braidotti 1996), the paternal scientific imagination can (re)produce monstrosity. If these pregnant fathers are Prospero-like in both their scientific fantasies and their imperialistic hubris, then their offspring, like the postcolonial subject Caliban, threaten the white patriarchal world order with violent rebellion. Yet, *POP!* offers a different, counter-hegemonic narrative of the male scientific imagination and corporeal male reproduction. It speaks not from the centre, but from the postcolonial, queer margin, not from a singular "I," but in and through a conspicuously doubled and deliberately contradictory entity.

Producing and Reproducing the Body: Dynamis

In Barros' (2001) words, "If autobiography can be read as narrative of transformation, the 'something happened' characterized as the figura, and the 'to me' identified as the persona, then in terms of the narrative the dynamis can be understood as the motive force to which the narrative persona attributes the change" (14). If the personae of *POP!* are its twinned autobiographers – Wong/Dr Liu, Mingwei/Mr Lee – and the figura is male pregnancy with all its cultural symbolism, then the dynamis of this project is, perhaps, embodiment itself. In its phenomenological experience, as well as in the relationship of the corporeal to the medical and the cybernetic, corporeality drives this narrative. Smith and Watson (2010) note that "the body is a site of autobiographical knowledge" and, moreover, that "cultural discourses determine which aspects of bodies become meaningful – what parts of the body are there for people to see. They determine when the body becomes visible, how it becomes visible, and what that visibility means" (49, 50). It is, of course, Mingwei's body that becomes the site for the visual and discursive production of male pregnancy. His predominantly unclothed, pregnant body is displayed on the website, served up not only for the gaze of medical science, but also for viewing by installation attendees and website users (Wong 2008h). The site invites the public to "join physicians and scientists around the world in monitoring Mr Lee's pregnancy online" by viewing ultrasound images and medical diagrams of Mr Lee's abdomen, as well as graphs of daily EKG, weight, blood pressure, and fundal height readings. Indeed, scholars of visual biotechnologies have suggested that X-rays, ultrasounds, and CT scans are ways in which individuals become dis-embodied – disconnected from their own embodied experiences and reliant on the interpretation of professionals who peer behind, as it were, their corporeal curtains (Cartwright 1995; Treichler, Cartwright, and Penley 1998).

POP! not only reproduces the gestating body as a site of surveillance, but it also produces a body firmly situated according to particular gendered, sexual, ethnic, and national subject positions. Consider that, in the comedic film *Junior* (dir. Reitman 1994), in which a scientist implants a fertilized egg into his own abdomen in a procedure not unlike Mr Lee's, the pregnant man is played by the hulking white heteropatriarch, Arnold Schwarzenegger. In choosing the über-masculine Schwarzenegger to play pregnant (rather than his scientific partner, Danny DeVito), the film mitigates the viewer's discomfort with male pregnancy, creating, as Dan Irving suggests in his contribution to this book, a reassuring masculine embodiment rather than an anxiety-provoking one. In this sense, *Junior* strikes what Irving, following Anthony Chen, describes as a "hegemonic bargain" (110), since Schwarzenegger's gender, sexual, class, and racial identities are seen as normative, and therefore as invisible and inviolable.

POP! affords the viewer no such false securities. Rather than a narrative of the normative body, *POP!* enacts reproduction at the margins. Cyberviewers of the Lepault and Lafait film not only express confusion and resistance in response to Mr Lee's pregnancy, but also refuse to recognize him, repeatedly conflating him with RL pregnant transgender man Thomas Beatie (Beatie 2008), whose highly mediated production of his pregnancy – exemplified by his appearances on *Oprah* and in *People Magazine* – ultimately challenges any meaningful distinctions between RL and virtual pregnancy. As publicly constructed images of queer, pregnant, API male bodies, both *POP!* and Thomas Beatie challenge the hegemonic gaze, which responds by attempting to "undo" them through withholding its recognition. In the words of Judith Butler (2004b):

> If the schemes of recognition that are available to us are those that "undo" the person by conferring recognition, or "undo" the person by withholding recognition, then recognition becomes a site of power by which the human is differentially produced ... The question of who and what is considered real and true is apparently a question of knowledge. But it is also, as Michel Foucault makes plain, a question of power. (2, 27)

Consider the following message board comments from *When men are pregnant* (Lepault and Lafait 2006):

> A WOMAN takes some testosterone therapy to become what she thinks is a man. SHE DOES NOT HAVE male genitalia, only that of a female with which she was born. Why then is this such a big deal now that she is pregnant? SHE is NOT a man. Men simply cannot become pregnant without ovaries and a uterus. – sfinkx
>
> o my god he is gay no wonder he wants to give birth – cardcaptorsakura 99
>
> Hey I thought the first pregnant man was a Hawaiian guy that used to be a Girl. His name is Thomas Beatie. So this must be a fake, don't seem like it ... OH IM CONFUSED – MusicGirl2409
>
> ... most of you are confusing Lee Mingwei with Thomas Beatie ... 'Thomas' WAS born female and gave birth naturally since she still had her original equipment ... This is something different ... Personally, im pretty enlightened but I do believe that there should be clearly defined gender roles and this pretty much steps over the line. – grinningsphinx

Part of the homophobic, trans-intolerant dis-ease of the above comments can be traced to the fact that while *POP!* reproduces the pregnant body for surveillance, it simultaneously undermines, or "undoes," gender itself. In her now classic *Gender Trouble* ([1990] 1999), Butler asserts that identities of gender and sexuality are performative – that gender is not somehow imposed or written upon the body but is, rather, a stylized repetition of acts. As such, *POP!* can be read as a drag performance; although Mr Lee does not adopt other traditional signifiers of femininity (makeup, lipstick, a dress), he does "don" pregnancy, which has until now been considered "inherently" the sole experience of female bodies. In doing so, *POP!* brings attention to the performativity of pregnancy itself (Osborne and Segal 1993). One only has to look at the wide variety of cross-cultural and cross-historic behaviours, expectations, and even symptoms of pregnancy, or to look at the ability of some women to have "hidden" (even from themselves) socially unacceptable or inconvenient pregnancies, to suggest that pregnancy as a social identity is similarly produced and undone (Butler 2004b).

POP! operates within cultural frameworks that define white heterosexual (non-pregnant) male bodies as normative and API heterosexual and queer male bodies – pregnant or not – as feminine/freakish/other (Leong 1996). The public fascination with Beatie is symptomatic of these cultural divisions, while the tenor of this fascination clearly reveals how differently the mainstream gaze envisions an API FTM (female to male) body as compared with a white or Black FTM body. Unlike "Chase," the virile, hypermasculine African American FTM subject that Irving discusses in this volume, Thomas Beatie's API ethnicity facilitates his pregnant presence in the popular cultural imagination. His is what Wendy Kozol, in her chapter in this book, discusses as a *destabilized* Asian male masculinity (221) – both feminized and marginalized.

The *POP!* project forces viewers to ask both themselves and one another the fundamental questions, "What am I looking at?" and "How am I looking?" In asking either question, the viewer must first acknowledge engagement in the process of looking; in this acknowledgment, the viewer risks being made to articulate the position of the viewing self in relation to the viewed body. Here, we see some of the tensions that structure Wendy Kozol's conception of "ethical spectatorship" (this volume). In the words of Wendy Hui Kyong Chun (2007), the "gawker" is one who, "caught by visual forms of the commodities, becomes a spectacle just by standing and staring. The intense spectacularity of the object at which it gazes enables the gawker to forget its own status as a spectacle" (248). As viewers interact with the cyberbiotechnology of male pregnancy, "profound anxieties emerge about the conventional social hierarchies which are rooted in the body and which the body's truth silently certifies" (Brodwin 2000, 9). The message-boarders that I quoted above engage in nothing less than "high-tech Orientalism" (Chun 2007), turning a hostile and colonialist gaze on Lee and/or Beatie as the non-normative Eastern "Other."

POP! demystifies some of the "utopian" promise of cyberspace. Consider a now oft-quoted television commercial for MCI called "Anthem," which proclaims, "There is no race. There is no gender. There is no age. There are no infirmities. There are only minds. Utopia? No, Internet" (quoted in Nakamura 2007, 255). Such assertions are in keeping with formulations of cyberspace as freedom from embodiment: where "virtual gender-swapping" can occur in online gaming MUDs (multi-user dungeons) (T. Chambers 2004); where First World children can make virtual field trips to the Amazon jungle (Nakamura 2007); or where a disabled person prevented from attending a loved one's RL funeral can attend the cybernetic memorial as an able-bodied avatar (DasGupta and Hurst 2008). As Sheila Petty argues, in another chapter in this volume, such assertions of a post-ethnic, post-gender, post-disability, post-human existence are decidedly vexed (228–30). Far from being a disembodied or "out of body" space, cyberspace is extraordinarily corporeal. *POP!* not only enacts the technobiographical intertwining of on- and off-line identities (Kennedy 2003), but also extends Merleau-Ponty's formulation of the "virtual body" of reflection and subjectivity, imagination and memory (Robinson 2000). As both a subjective and an intersubjective location, moreover, cyberspace affords bodies "an invariably public dimension; constituted as a socially bound up power phenomenon in the public sphere, my body is and is not mine" (Butler 2004b, 21).

Ultimately, *POP!* not only challenges viewers to consider and articulate their views on gender, sexuality, and ethnicity, but also it locates these questions in the context of a shrinking global (cyber)space. Dr Liu's last blog entry (7/1/05) is called "Chinese Takeover – The Gay Pornography Video," and it reads:

> Eight years ago today, Hong Kong returned to Chinese rule after 156 years as part of the British colonial empire. On that very day, I was there in Hong Kong, attending a medical conference on HIV/AIDS prevention and research … I was sitting in the opulent hotel bar looking out the window as a bright red Chinese flag was slowly being cranked and hoisted into the humid air … A handsome man … sat down next to me … and introduced himself as Adam – a Hong Kong citizen whose parents came … from Great Britain many years ago. After telling him that I'm Chinese, he … winked, "Well, since I'm a Hong Kong native, I guess I belong to you now."
>
> I … rolled my eyes and then lifted my backpack to make a polite exit. Unfortunately, I didn't realize that my bag was open and out cascaded a flood of over 400 condoms, packs of lubrication, and dental dams that I was planning to distribute right after my HIV prevention seminar the next day.
>
> "My, my, it looks like you have a fun week planned," Adam quipped … "Mind if I tag along?"
>
> The whole scene smacked of a set-up for a bad gay pornography video. It turns out that Adam was an internist at a local medical practice, and we ended up sitting next to each other at a lecture on protease inhibitors. We marched in a democracy protest together the next night and sat talking until morning on a quiet pier overlooking the glittering Hong Kong skyline. (Wong 2008f)

Here is a complex text, located in a global moment of transition, as Dr Liu is literally positioned to watch the spectacle of Hong Kong's handover to China. The blog entry complicates the North to South, colonial to communist narrative of an (inter)national body by superimposing it on the bodies of two gay men. The men themselves embody the complexities of transnational migration and ethnic diasporas: the white man of British extraction is a Hong Kong native, while the API man of Chinese extraction is an American on conference in the East. Complicating all of this even further is the potential of the "rice queen"/"Madame Butterfly" dynamic (Eng 1996), with the white man sexually approaching the API man, turning the evidence of his intellectual work into the potential for sexual play. Like HIV prevention work, *POP!* risks being interpreted as "pornographic" by bringing sexuality and bodily experiences from the margins of medical and popular cultural attention to the centre. Yet, this is not a case of the mysterious Easterner "playing" femininity for the dominant West, like the Chinese spy Song Liling in David Henry Hwang's *M. Butterfly* (1988), who convinces his French diplomat lover of twenty years that he is a woman (at one point, even "bearing" him a child). Rather, *POP!* is a subaltern "takeover" of discourse around gender (and gestation) performance, embodiment in medicine, and viewership in cyberspace. This "takeover" does not occur at the expense of the exoticized API "Other." Rather, it is authored by, through, and of API bodies.

Conclusion: Cyberpregnancy and the Collaborative Potential of Fantasy

Wong and Mingwei's collaboration, *POP! The First Male Pregnancy*, performs pregnancy online and in RL art installations while complicating the viewer's own position in relation to issues of race, gender, sexuality, reproduction, and transnationalism. In doing so, it taps into what Judith Butler (2004b) calls the "critical promise of fantasy" (29):

> I think that when the unreal lays claim to reality ... something other than a simple assimilation into prevailing norms can and does take place. The norms themselves can become rattled, display their instability, and become open to a resignification ... Fantasy is part of the articulation of the possible ... The critical promise of fantasy ... is to challenge the contingent limits of what will and will not be called reality. Fantasy is what allows us to imagine ourselves and others otherwise; ... it points elsewhere, and when it is embodied, it brings the elsewhere home. (27–9)

As a collaborative project involving fictional narratives manifested in cyberspace, *POP!* effectively undermines the presumption of singular autobiographical authority. Is this Wong's narrative or Mingwei's? Is it Liu's or Lee's? *POP!* can be understood as "commingl[ing] the boundaries of separate identities into a shared subject" such that "'I' and 'you,' 'eye' and 'other' become indistinguishable" (Smith and Watson 2010, 36).

This commingling of identities continues beyond the computer screen, such that the transformational project of *POP!* engages its viewers in discourse and raises questions regarding their own embodiment and their assumptions regarding embodiment. In a sense, Wong/Liu and Mingwei/Lee carry their pregnancy *for* the viewer, much like the surrogate mother in an ethnographic study by Gillian M. Goslinga-Roy (2000); in this case, the surrogate mother happily "embraces the idea of surrendering the privacy of her womb" (125), as well as notions of her body as a collective space shared by herself and the genetic mother and father. In keeping with Butler's formulation of fantasy, the viewer's challenge is to envision an "elsewhere" beyond "the idea that the body is an organism that 'ends at the skin'" (Haraway 1991, 168) – and one that an "'I' inhabits as an owner" (Goslinga-Roy 2000, 127). In other words, *POP!* challenges the viewer to envision this cyberpregnancy as belonging to the viewer's own self as much as it belongs to the artists.

POP! The First Male Pregnancy works at the interstices of reality and fiction, biology and technology, sexuality and reproduction, power and humility, West and East, male and female, medicine and spirituality, science and art. It simultaneously signals an escape from these ultimately reductive binarisms and the possibilities of a chimerical mutuality. It points to an elsewhere that is an intersubjective space constituted socially, which, like Donna Haraway's famous assertions about the potential of the cyborg (Haraway 1991), exists at the boundaries and borderlands – an elsewhere pregnant with the potential to interrogate and reconceive the biologically and culturally real. Like the democratic space of the new Genesis myth created by Phineas Liu and his Adam, so too does the viewer have the potential to "tag along" for the ride that is *POP!*, connecting with this art installation and responding to its spectatorial demands (Wong 2008f). Ultimately, *POP!* is an intellectual, imaginative, and corporeal quickening, conceived in the "quiet pier" of the body, gestated in the intersubjective space of viewership, and born on the "glittering trans-national skyline" of cyberspace.

NOTE

1 This is my own description of the opening of Lepault and Lafait's 2006 film, *When men are pregnant*. A 7:30 minute excerpt is available online under the title "The World's First Male Pregnancy": http://www.youtube.com/watch?v=AiU-KZ_KADY

3 "Virtual" Autobiography? Anorexia, *Obsession*, and Calvin Klein

MEBBIE BELL

"Is anyone out there pro-ana?" This minute hail of graffiti calls out from the dingy walls of a women's bathroom stall, escaping from its origins in the Internet-based pro-anorexia movement. Stark in its longing for recognition, it exemplifies the tenuous realities of "pro-anas" (as participants in the movement often call themselves), as well as their subsumption within the overriding identity of "Ana." This graffiti also hails like-minded individuals into another space eerily appropriate for these bodily struggles: the virtual, disembodied forums of cyber-exchange that enable an anonymous pursuit of the thin feminized aesthetic.

With little space for such voices in mainstream discourse, the pro-anorexia movement began to cyber-circulate in the late 1990s, challenging cyberculture idealizations of the Internet as a utopian forum of free speech, malleable self-expression, and escape from the constraints of the "meat" of the body (Lupton 1995; Robins 2000). Due to its often graphic content, the movement itself and individual pro-anas faced repeated censorship from Internet service providers (Holahan 2001), as well as social censure in mainstream and virtual cultures. Anti-pro-ana material now pops up alongside pro-anorexic websites, and numerous organizations, such as the National Association of Anorexia Nervosa and Associated Disorders (2009), run electronic campaigns to educate individuals about the dangers of pro-anorexia. In response, pro-anas argue that "anorexia is a lifestyle, not a disease" (Wasted Shadow 2005); they warn critics away from entering their websites and subvert medical pathologization in their texts (Bell 2009).[1]

Pro-anorexia "trigger" material called "thinspiration" exemplifies the contradictions of women's autobiographical cultural production. Thinspiration is meant to initiate and sustain pro-anorexic practices, and includes lists of poetry, movies, books, and websites, along with "tips and tricks" for weight loss and images digitally produced and/or posted by pro-anas (ranging from celebrity photos to self-portraits to mainstream images often illegally "borrowed" from other sources). These particular textualizations also signify a series of displacements of self, body, struggle, and subversion, slippages that reveal ongoing material and discursive negotiations of feminized identities. Pro-anas enact a paradoxical doubled disappearance by entering disembodied virtual space to pursue their practices, which parallels the productive/prohibitive tensions of disciplinary normalization (cf. Foucault [1975] 1995): pro-anas first evade their unruly female bodies by entering virtual space, and the (only ever temporarily) displaced embodiment of virtual exchange is then further effaced through the overarching identity of "Ana." Behind this digital mask, however, pro-anas collectively self-interpellate through these slippages of body and self. While ethereal faeries and butterflies symbolize the pro-ana desire to escape embodied constraints – as do site names such as "Am I Invisible Yet?" (2004) – the performative production of "Ana" identity embraces the self-disciplinary imperatives of contemporary femininity.

Virtual expressions of pro-ana subjectivity raise compelling questions about the "incoherence, contradiction, and challenge" of women's autobiographical representation (Gilmore 1994, 2). Informed by "experiences of the everyday, of the body, of the sites of contact with and isolation from the read-about and lived-in worlds," pro-anorexia image-texts enact what Jeanne Perreault (1995) names "autography":

> As women write themselves, categories of difference (inner, outer, body, world, language) do not disappear, but take shape as "I" and in relation to "I." This shift in relations between persona, body-specific identity and communal, or ideological, identity (the I who says we) both maintain ongoingness and require discontinuity ... The texts that are effected anticipate and extend the problematic of subjectivity ... [the] world as the writer lives it can be imagined, felt, and recognized only from the writing. (7)

Existing in the "nowhere-somewhere" of cyberspace (Robins 2000, 135), pro-anorexic images and texts are produced by individuals eliding their own unstable identities in an attempt to eradicate fraught relationships with their embodied selves. As Judith Butler (1993) suggests, such gendered interpellations are at once violating and enabling. They emerge in "the non-space of cultural collision," and their constitutive instability necessitates their repetition (124). The near endless hyperlinks and shared content of the pro-anorexia movement enable "Ana" identity while effacing its anonymous participants. Tensions within and between these representations challenge the knowability of the autobiographical subject, suggesting, as Smith and Watson (2010) argue, that the domains of language and image must be placed "into sociohistorical context in order to 'know' how they contradict each other and destabilize forms of identification" (24–5). Though deeply engaged with contemporary discourses of femininity, pro-anorexic autobiographical representation exposes the historical objectification of women and its contemporary articulations through apparatuses of heternormativity, youth, white privilege, abilities, and affluence. However, these representations also resist the simultaneous passivity and excess encoded in the female body. If Ana "writes the body," then she does so as a "provisional self" exploring "a tentative grammar of transformations" (Perreault 1995, 7).

This chapter examines visual/textual representations of these identity negotiations, and then undertakes a discursive analysis of the pro-anorexic (mis)use of the Calvin Klein *Obsession* perfume campaign. The grainy black and white nudes of supermodel Kate Moss languishing on a couch epitomized the waiflike feminine aesthetic of 1990s "heroin chic." Pro-anorexic websites have replicated not only the original *Obsession* images, but also Adbusters' satirical reworking of the campaign, in which a woman crouches over a toilet. Thinspiration thus exposes a process of mimetic cultural sedimentation that traces dominant cultural narratives of feminine embodiment, passivity, and control. It also illustrates the ongoing negotiation of what counts as acceptable cultural critique: *Adbusters'* appropriation is read as satirical political praxis, while pro-anorexic usage is dangerous. At issue in this slippage is whether mainstream objections to pro-anorexic content are directed at pro-anorexia itself, or at the critique embedded in such counterculture (mis)appropriations of feminized iconography. In other words, (how) do they expose the constraints of disciplinary femininity and call out mainstream culture as, itself, "pro-anorexic"? Pro-anas are rejected for being "Ana," but they are also rebuked for displacing iconic symbols of contemporary femininity beyond their conventional cultural readings.

Self-Interpellation and Thinspiration

While I am particularly interested in how visual trigger material, or thinspiration, mediates pro-anorexic identity, I first want to briefly consider the constructions of "Ana" identity within the movement, as this identity provides the collective framework through which participants – mostly women – engage in their anonymous and pseudonymous exchange. Because they argue that pro-anas do not need to be cured, pro-anorexic texts are interpreted in mainstream culture as prescriptive, as teaching individuals how to become anorexic (or bulimic) and how to sustain their practices. In the *New York Times Magazine*, for instance, Mim Udovitch (2002) suggests the basic premise of "pro-ana" is "that an eating disorder is not a disorder but a lifestyle choice ... very much an ideology of the early twenty-first century, one that could not exist absent the anonymity and accessibility of the Internet, without which the only place large numbers of anorexics and bulimics would find themselves together would be at in-patient treatment" (20). This automediality of self, community, and technology (Smith and Watson 2010, 168) facilitates self-actualization that is impossible in "real" space: "this is a place where anorexia is regarded as a lifestyle and a choice, not an illness or disorder. *There are no victims here* ... We are not 'ED [eating disorder] sufferers'... The core praxis of anorexia involves control over oneself" (Ana's Underground Grotto 2005b, original emphasis). Some attest, in fact, that they are only expressing their "true" selves (House of ED 2005).

Whether pro-anorexia is defined via authenticity, self-control, or a particular lifestyle choice, such identificatory frameworks mask the complexities and regulatory pressures of bodily norms. Though pro-anorexia is entwined with the disciplinary impetus of contemporary femininity, mainstream culture nonetheless rejects it as having exceeded the boundaries of appropriate feminine behaviour; its transgressive potential requires containment. As Perreault (1995) suggests of autography, "bringing to speech parts of one's self that one has had reason to keep silent is frightening, painful, and even dangerous" (133). Pro-anas are condemned as not only "dangerous" but also "infectious," as if a viral threat to vulnerable (female) individuals (Bell 2009). Yet, pro-anas' textualizations of their bodily struggles may mediate their embodied pain. Pain, disability, or illness, Susan Wendell suggests (1996), brings the body's presence into consciousness, thereby disrupting its absence and alienation from the self: "the body itself takes us into and then beyond its sufferings and limitations" (178). This strategic potential not only parallels feminist arguments that disordered eating is a response to embodied traumas experienced by women (Thompson 1994), but also, paradoxically, intuits the bodily transcendence complexly produced through pro-anorexic virtual exchange. Many pro-anas, in fact, articulate a troubled connection to their assumed identity. Cerulean Butterfly (2005) states, "If you've come here to 'learn' to be anorexic or bulimic, then you really need to leave. Eating disorders are painful, life-destroying creatures that are not worth their cost. They are not cool or glamorous. They are not a quick fix. They are not a diet. They are a living, breathing hell." While revealing, such acknowledgments cannot easily be read as self-conscious feminist autography because pro-anas are neither consistently and collectively self-aware nor critically engaged. On a broader level, however, pro-anorexic discourse nonetheless (re)writes feminized bodily erasure as fraught embodied subjectivity.

"Ana" is personified both as anorexia, abstracted from the individual, and as disordered eating, distinctly embodied in the individual, facilitating "her" resignification beyond medical control and social stigma. In either case, "Ana" takes over in virtual space. A "Letter from Ana," reproduced on numerous websites, illustrates this slippage between erasure and interpellation:

> Allow me to introduce myself. My name, or as I am called by so called "doctors," is Anorexia. Anorexia Nervosa is my full name, but you may call me Ana … I am beginning to imbed myself in you. Pretty soon, I am with you always. I am there when you wake up in the morning and run to the scale … I'll force you into the bathroom, onto your knees, staring into the void of the toilet bowl. Your fingers will be inserted into your throat, and, not without a great deal of pain, your food binge will come up … No one must find out, no one can crack this shell that I have covered you with. I have created you, this thin, perfect, achieving child. You are mine and mine alone. Without me, you are nothing. (AnOreXic AdDiCt 2002)

Symbolizing the all-consuming struggles of pro-anas, "nothing" exists beyond this overriding identity, and "Ana" demands a commitment to reiterated regimes of self-erasure.

This simultaneous erasure and interpellation generates a doubled disappearance that can be read as an attempt to mediate feminized bodily dissatisfaction and the conflicting demands of normative femininity. Rendered anonymous by pseudonyms and webnames, pro-ana individuals pursue the identity of "Ana" while effacing their own, a process that is materialized through the (disappearing) bodies of these individuals and their hyperlinked thinspiration. As extensive feminist scholarship now attests, contemporary womanhood is constituted via the disciplinary regimes of diet, dress, and exercise and through the angst upon which these regimes rely (Gremillion 2003; Malson 1998), but pro-anorexic discourse underscores the instability of such disciplinary subjectivation. Its textualizations reveal the impossibilities of feminized discipline: women's identities are constituted through their disciplinary practices but can never achieve their disciplinary goals (Bartky 1990). Participants thus become "Ana" in an attempt to rid themselves of the troubled embodiment that prompts their feelings of inadequacy; they, in turn, produce the contradictory possibility of identity within these disciplinary constraints. This ongoing process signals the impossible task of eviscerating the contents of their unbearably female bodies: they take on the terms of the regimes within which they are enmeshed and embark on the unending task of finding a stable identity to replace their fraught embodiment. This pursuit aligns pro-anorexia with negative cultural constructions of female corporeality that constitute womanhood through de-signification and disassociation from material and social ontologies, an emptying out – or what Simon Strick, in this volume, refers to as a "gutting out" – of women's excessive corporeal and discursive presence (126–9). Moreover, as Strick outlines in relation to resignifications within "cosmetic femininity," such practices may produce self-change, but they do so via disempowerment and self-eradication (129). These disciplinary technologies enact the ideological instabilities of the female body in contemporary cultural, political, and economic milieux. Susan Bordo (1993) astutely observed similar tensions within the then emergent thin/fit feminine aesthetic of the 1980s and 1990s, stating that "the slender body codes the tantalizing ideal of a well-managed self in which all is kept in order despite the contradictions of consumer culture," while the irreconcilable demands of cultural consumption and moral restraint are worked out in the binge/purge cycle of bulimic practice (201). Contrary, then, to conventional readings of anorexia as narcissistic food refusal, pro-anorexia exposes these complex – even generative – negotiations of feminized embodiment. As Angela Failler (2006) suggests, if we are to understand anorexia from the diverse perspectives of individuals struggling with these practices, we must recognize the simultaneous and sometimes contradictory experiences of self-denial, alienation, control, refusal, "hunger," loss, and power within the anorexic self.

Pro-anorexic trigger material, or thinspiration, both mediates and reveals what I argue are the troubled autographic negotiations of thinspiration texts. While pro-anas sometimes create self-expressive "Ana/Mia artwork," most trigger images are reproduced and manipulated from other online sources, usually without acknowledgments or copyright data. Representing the extremes of thinspiration, many sites include "hardcore bone" triggers (images of severely emaciated women) and "reverse" triggers (often near-pornographic images of large women). Typically focused on gaunt ribs and pelvises, "bone" images tend to be uncaptioned, as if they speak for themselves. Reverse triggers, however, seem to require additional interpretation, at once mirroring and exposing mainstream treatment of "fat bodies" as "subjectless" objects of pity, shame, derision, and humour (Kent 2001, quoted in Mitchell, this volume, 68). For example, at Ana's Underground Grotto (2005c), a reverse trigger image of a large woman in underwear, lying on a sofa, is captioned "couch surfing like a beached whale." Mediating this derision slightly, the "Grotto" declares, "these images represent what we never want to become. If you want to know why ... just look around you at how these people too often end up being treated. Perhaps you yourself have been guilty of this at times. For the record, this site does not condone bashing fat people. We just choose not to be among their number, is all." On the other end of the spectrum, Victoria's Pro-Ana Journal (2005) posts images of extremely skeletal women, but cautions, "I think these pictures are disgusting but some people might find them useful. I definitely believe there is a difference between being Ana and being anorexic."

A slippage between disgust and desire emerges in such statements, revealing a complex and often contradictory relationship between pro-anorexia and mainstream culture. On the one hand, pro-anorexia reproduces the cultural desire for a particular thin feminized body: thinspiration images are not those of "ugly" women. And the grotesque of pro-anorexic discourse is represented by reverse triggers: the "fat girl" is called out as freak. This interpellation firmly delineates the boundaries of "normal" women's embodiment and demonstrates the politicization of fatness as a vehicle of abhorrence in contemporary culture (LeBesco 2001, 75). On the other hand, women who are too thin are also coded as disgusting – the same charge levelled at pro-anas themselves. To mediate this impasse, pro-anorexic discourse inverts the revulsion it elicits by situating disgust in obesity. Though all female bodies provoke anxiety, this inversion locates the monstrosity of feminized "corporeal disorganisation, lack of resemblance, [and] ontological impropriety" (Shildrick 2002, 32) in fat women alone. While pro-anorexia is not necessarily about beauty, its thinspiration reproduces the cultural message that thinness is beautiful and aligns with the pervasive cultural disdain of fat. This construction of desire folds in on itself, though, as the pro-anorexic desire for intelligibility also implies disgust: pro-anas seek the desirable bodies they feel they lack, but are rejected for having the disgusting bodies they desire.[2]

Yet, the presence of anorexic pornography on the Internet displaces the dominant disgust prompted by the anorexic body with desire. With images mimicking the "bone thinspiration" of extremely thin women, the text of anorexic porn sites mirrors that of other cyberpornography: sex for sale. Whether the desire for these particular thin bodies is constructed as passive, iconic, controllable, or enticing, its elevation of the anorexic body to sex object elicits pseudo-private desire out of public disgust. Analogous to the identificatory structure of "body genres" such as horror and melodrama (Williams 2003), this visceral reaction enacts the projection of subjectivity onto hypersexualized anorexic bodies, potentially recuperating their abject status through mutual bodily experience.[3] Laura Kipnis' (1998) analysis of the fetishized genre of "fat porn" reveals further slippages in these economies of desire. Instead of reiterating dominant narratives of hetero-eroticization, large-bodied women oppose "the conformist desire to simply take up an assigned place in the regime of normal" (211). As Kipnis notes, with large-bodied women, "pornography becomes something of an archive of the contemporary unaesthetic," and one against which the aesthetic realm and national sensibilities must be constantly vigilant (200). "The fat are seen to be violating territorial limits" (208) of feminized disgust, overconsumption, unruliness, and moral failure. The pro-anorexic reverse trigger is established in this spatial violation, consolidating pro-anorexia's valorization of an appropriately contained feminine form.

This valorization lays bare the self-interpellation and subjectivation of pro-anas via the thin feminized aesthetic. Where their bodies and identities fail to measure up, their thinspiration instead reiterates the ideals of young, white, thin femininity encoded with affluence, ability, and heteronormativity. Celebrity thinspiration is the most prevalent example of such representations. Sites such as Prothinspo (2010), for example, are devoted to celebrity gossip and photos, posting thousands of borrowed images (updated daily) as "a muse of sort[s] to keep you focused on your goals." Other sites focus on specific celebrities for motivation, such as A Walking Barbie (2005), which gives special attention to celebrity Paris Hilton. And, offering a clear commentary on pro-ana struggles, the numerous celebrity pages on Go Pro: Ana Lives (2010) each end with the statement "one thing's for certain i'm insecure." Taken from mainstream culture and used against their conventional meanings, these (mis)uses establish a kind of discursive feedback loop that disrupts dominant cultural meanings and through which pro-anas contextualize their identities. While reproducing conventional narratives through repeated hyperlinks, copies, and modifications, these images also resignify the meanings of pro-anorexia in virtual form. In so doing, pro-anorexia challenges the presumed stability of these narratives and usurps cultural authority over feminized embodied subjectivity.

Pro-Anorexia, Calvin Klein, and Mimetic Cultural Sedimentation

The intertwined representations of pro-anorexic self-interpellation and self-erasure rely on the reiteration of dominant cultural forms – their thinspiration. Where mimesis or repetition signals cultural intelligibility (Benjamin [1933] 2007), pro-anorexic reiterations of pop-cultural images interpellate "Ana" identity through, and against, culturally recognizable discourses. Whether subversive or normalizing, this provisional "self engages only in a (community of) discourse of which she is both product and producer" (Perreault 1995, 7). Each thinspiration post rearticulates the sedimentation of gender norms, which, "over time has produced a set of [reified] corporeal styles" (Butler 1999, 178). This performative iterability functions, as Shildrick (2002) notes, "not simply as the repetition that seeks to authorize and sediment meaning by repeated reference to a prior context, but as the moment of slippage inherent in repetition, that destabilises meaning even as it establishes it"; and, in turn, this "rearticulation ... introduces the interval of transformation" (83). The multiple and often contradictory reiterations of "Ana" identity effect an unstable, though constitutive, performative through their mimetic cultural sedimentation of dominant cultural forms.

The Calvin Klein *Obsession* perfume campaign represents a particularly provocative example of such slippery cultural references within the pro-anorexia movement. American fashion designer Klein's black and white images of supermodel Kate Moss came to epitomize the grunge aesthetic of "heroin chic" in the mid-1990s: a young, very thin, and nude Moss lay prone on a black couch, buttocks exposed, staring out at the camera. Timothy A. Hickman (2002) notes that heroin chic (associated with dingy settings, vacant gazes, pale skin, awkward positioning, and, most importantly, waiflike thinness) was applauded in the fashion industry as a "more authentic depiction of 'beauty' than that embodied by the typically airbrushed, polished images in glossy fashion magazines" (134). Its "dirty realism" was an homage to 1970s art/punk/pop/drug culture (131–4). But this counterculture aesthetic was also challenged in mainstream discourse as a dangerous valorization of self-abuse; President Clinton condemned its glamorization of heroin use (Arnold 1999, 279), and anti-drug groups called for the boycott of Calvin Klein merchandise (Richey 1996). Concerns over its supposed depravity connected heroin chic with social anxieties about embodiment and the unruly female body (Arnold 1999). Explicit use of such imagery has since faded, but its aesthetic force still resonates in popular culture: Moss was recently ousted from fashion royalty for her drug use, but images of waiflike thinness continue to haunt our cultural milieu.

Furthermore, images of Moss continue to cyber-circulate within the pro-anorexia movement. Though not its only visual narrative, this reiteration of heroin chic links pro-anorexia to the broader cultural ethos of bodily perfection. The Pro Ana Lifestyle (2007), for instance, devotes an entire section to Moss-based thinspiration, including the *Obsession* nudes. These triggers are accompanied by a visual montage of an unidentified woman throwing up into a toilet, then weighing herself. The following "Thin Commandments" (ibid.) run alongside:

1 If you aren't thin, you aren't attractive.
2 Being thin is more important than being healthy.
3 You must bu[y] clot[h]es, cut your hair, take laxatives, anything to make yourself look thinner.
4 Thou shall not eat without feeling guilty.
5 Thou shall not eat fattening food withou[t] punishing afterward.

Where "Ana" has no specific visual representation, Moss serves as a proxy for conflicting demands to both consume (food, clothes, laxatives) and constrain feminized needs, wants, and desires.

The *Obsession* campaign also emerges in pro-anorexic discourse in another form, as an *Adbusters* image reproduced on pro-anorexic websites (Ana's Underground Grotto 2005d). Deliberately conflating Klein's perfume campaign with bulimia, *Adbusters* (a Canadian anti-consumerist magazine) produced a "spoof ad" entitled "Obsession for Women (see figure 3.1)." The satire was one of its "culture jamming" enterprises and part of a broader campaign to upset the authority of corporate mass media advertisements for products such as Absolut Vodka and Camel cigarettes. Lester Faigley (1999) notes that the *Obsession* spoof sought to

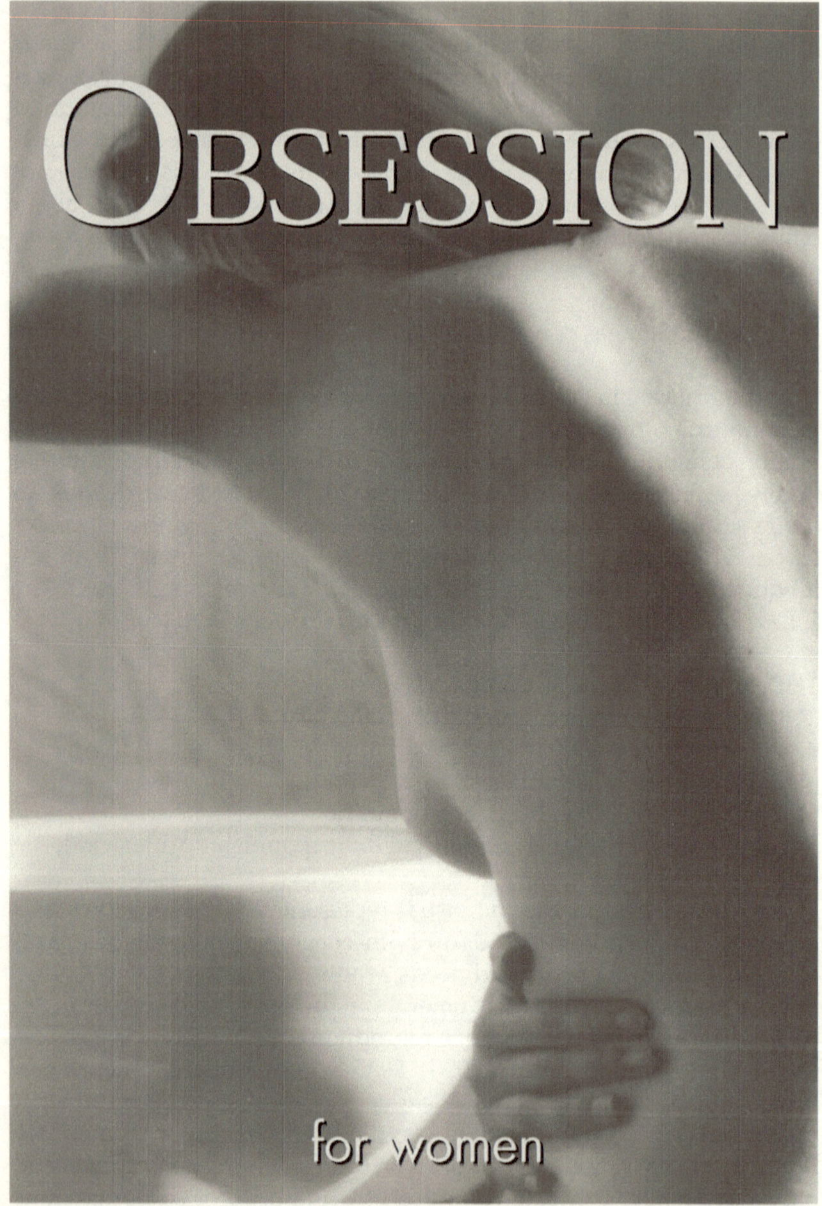

3.1. "Obsession for Women" (*Adbusters*, 2009). Used by permission of Adbusters Media Foundation.

point out "the connection between eating disorders and the worship of the adolescent body" (191), as well as to critique "the iconography of the perfect body" (193).[4] In her analysis of these "guerrilla visual tactics," Marilyn Bordwell (2002) suggests such "subvertisements" offer "*a kind of perspective by incongruity*: by co-opting familiar themes and logos, they not only caution readers about the dangers of smoking and drinking [but] they also jar us into contemplating the damage done by the advertising industry itself" (247, original emphasis). Resignifying familiar narratives, such parodies disrupt their dominant readings. Thus, in skewering both the thin feminized aesthetic and 1990s heroin chic, the *Adbusters'* image reproduces the grainy black and white photography associated with Calvin Klein while inverting its aesthetic appeal. Reminiscent of pro-anorexic "bone thinspiration," the doe-eyed model turns away from the camera, presenting the consumer instead with the naked, bony back of a woman crouched over a toilet. The relationships between subject/object and viewer/viewed thus disturbed, the paradox of conspicuous cultural consumption – mapped onto the waif aesthetic – is replaced by a voyeuristic glimpse of the bulimic purge. While the viewer now gazes on a private struggle, the woman gazes away into a porcelain bowl. This image disturbs the hetero-eroticization of the female form found in the original campaign: the shadow of a breast and the woman's hand clutched at her stomach no longer invoke conventional readings of either the hetero-male gaze or the female nude.

Adbusters' representation of bulimic practice challenges familiar narratives of cultural consumption on a number of levels. First, while disordered eating is afforded considerable attention in cultural discourse, stereotypical (and often inaccurate) representations of anorexia are the norm, such as the too-thin/very chic celebrity plastered on tabloid covers. Against this discursive presence, bulimia warrants little attention even though no clear separation between "anorexia" and "bulimia" exists in either virtual or material space. Bulimic practices are marked by their invisibilization; that is, while the specificities of disordered eating vary greatly, bulimic practices are largely hidden by individuals, masked by bodies that hover around "normal weight" (Bordo 1993, 203). Moreover, while the anorexic is often pitied, the bulimic figure is frequently derided for her seeming failure to control her unruly female body (Bray 1996, 413); the bulimic's "lack" of extreme thinness signifies her inability to contain her feminine struggles. Where anorexia is valorized via the thin aesthetic, bulimia exposes the impossibility of complete feminine erasure. In rearticulating a now-iconic global marketing campaign with private struggle, the *Adbusters'* image also reveals media manipulations of the eroticized hetero-female form. Sex sells not only a product but also a lifestyle, thereby establishing the terms by which feminized disciplinary regimes are perpetuated. *Obsession* perfume becomes the cultural obsession with feminized bodily constraint, and the aesthetization of waiflike thinness is irrevocably tied to the practices that its idealization demands.

In trading on this bulimic moment, *Adbusters'* "Obsession for Women" exposes the irreconcilable demands of contemporary consumer culture. Voracious consumption is coupled with valorized self-containment, painfully mediated by the repetition of the binge/purge cycle. *Adbusters'* satirical retort synthesizes Bordo's (1993) articulation of bulimic identity: this modern personality construction "embodies the unstable double bind of consumer capitalism," not as an either/or scenario but as an enmeshment of contradictory cultural demands (201). *Adbusters'* manipulation of the Klein image re-reads its cultural iconography through a critique of contemporary practices of consumption. Where the waif aesthetic of heroin chic reifies the thin feminized ideal, *Adbusters* exposes the often unseen reality of attempting to achieve this ideal, or at least of attempting to negotiate the contradictory demands of contemporary feminized subjectivity. Put another way, *Adbusters'* representation of a purge makes these discursive tensions explicit.

The co-option of this satirical statement by pro-anas was an unintended outcome of the *Adbusters'* spoof. Though the magazine liberally shares images, the editors did not approve its use on pro-anorexic webpages.[5] Instead, the pro-anorexic use of *Adbusters'* "Obsession for Women" represents another rearticulation in this process of mimetic sedimentation. Its reiteration as thinspiration extends the constitutive instability of the image's meaning, signalling the relevance of the *Adbusters'* critique to "Ana." On the one hand, *Adbusters* used the image to exemplify its condemnation of the waif aesthetic; on the other, the pro-anorexic mimesis speaks precisely to its role in the cultural discourses that inform pro-anorexic struggles. The dismissal of such pro-anorexic usage as dangerous and illegitimate by mainstream culture forecloses on important forms of cultural criticism. *Adbusters'* inversion of the Klein ad is read as an exposure of the disciplinary regimes embedded in heroin chic, but its pro-anorexic rearticulation is read as a corruption of this critique, an assumed re-inversion from critique to valorization. Yet, as the meanings of "Ana" are unstable, the seeming re-inversion of this cultural criticism is ambiguous.

This mimetic cultural sedimentation and interpellative resignification continues in another thinspiration image of a crouching woman, again turned away from the viewer, bony back, ribs, hips, and spine juxtaposed against a gaping toilet.[6] Here, Moss's heroin chic is at once closer, in the grimy reality of a dingy bathroom, and more distant in its mimesis of the *Adbusters'* inversion. But while *Adbusters'* spoof may be read as satire, this pro-anorexic image does not evoke parody. This image is harsh: no soft lighting or angles diffuse the realities of sitting on the floor by a toilet to evacuate the contents of an unsavoury bodily struggle.

One final image extends this mimetic trace further still: the staging now irrelevant, the crouched figure of the woman swirls in the toilet. No longer separated from the binge by arms, legs, walls, and floor, she is the binge. "Ana's" interpellation has collapsed across these reiterations, materialized now in a fully formed fetal position, a binge fully realized. While the initial source of the image is lost in its pro-anorexic reproduction, as is the artist's intent, this last image reveals a provisional and disappearing self subsumed by these struggles.

While critics condemn such images as dangerous, their interpellative resonance echoes back to the disciplinary prompts of contemporary femininity. Pro-anorexic thinspiration, trigger, self-interpellation, and erasure under the sign of "Ana" are similarly unstable. It is difficult to determine whether it is this instability that prompts mainstream censure of pro-anorexia or, instead, its (mis)appropriations of familiar cultural narratives. Rebecca Arnold's (1999) analysis of heroin chic is useful on this point:

> Our society is saturated with imagery, and fashion is frequently seen as inhabiting only a commercial, escapist sphere, a trivial froth that floats upon the surface of culture. But this belies the role it plays in defining and redefining our bodies. Our attitudes to gender and sexuality, and concerns about the decay of the body, are inevitably illuminated by this constant scrutiny. So-called heroin chic needs to be questioned, not only because it raises issues about attitudes to drugs in art and popular culture, but also because this imagery encapsulates contemporary anxieties and desires: the myriad of identities that have developed in this fragmented period, a nihilist aesthetic that finds escape by retreating from conventional morality and conventional beauty. If this is the case, should the image-makers be censured? Are they creating role models for the vulnerable that speak of desolation and self-abuse? Or are they creating a means of expression for those who feel disenfranchised? (280–1)

Over a decade later, these same questions emerge within and about the interpellative struggles over "Ana," femininity, and cultural control. As it is articulated in both material and virtual space, the pro-anorexic body comes into view as what Perreault (1995) calls a "locus of tension about identity" (19), a co-authored autographic project that paradoxically conjoins transformation (freedom) and reiteration (normalization).

The visceral, often moralizing reactions to such pro-anorexic representations signal a slippage in the cultural admonitions they prompt. Of the 1990s heroin chic photographs, Hickman (2002) suggests that they are "not primarily about drugs, addicts or clothing. Instead they offer a powerful evocation of ourselves, of our *own* longing. They attract the viewer, producing an irresistible sensation of voyeuristic dread, composed of equal parts fear and desire. They externalize a force that for most of us lies hidden, repressed or redirected" (136, original emphasis). The cultural sedimentation of these images in pro-anorexic thinspiration lays bare the double bind of contemporary culture, forcing a confrontation with its unstable but constitutive significations and its nebulous negotiations of embodied struggle. As Lisa Arndt (2003), webmistress of a pro-ana support/recovery page, states, "*Wanting* to have an eating disorder is a part of an eating disorder, *wanting* to be unnaturally thin is a part of living in the current climate ... our culture is pro anorexia in every sense" (original emphases). This "*wanting*," reiterated in the recycling of an image beyond its prior meaning(s), exposes not only the unstable autographic significations of feminized subjectivity and "Ana" identity, but also a nexus of identity, desire, revulsion, and fear that permeates contemporary culture.

NOTES

1 As they are routinely shut down, I cite pro-anorexic websites by original date accessed.

2 See Bell (2009) for additional analysis of reverse triggers and the grotesque, a discussion that is substantively extended here.

3 For more on Linda Williams' notion of "body genres," see Simon Strick's chapter in this volume (130).

4 Faigley (1999) notes that *Adbusters* also produced a thirty-second television advertisement, in which a thin, naked woman vomits into a toilet. In conjunction with several women's groups, *Adbusters* attempted to buy

advertising time on the CBC and CNN television networks, but was refused by both (191).

5 In personal communication with *Adbusters* staff, I determined that they were not aware of this usage by pro-anas.

6 Thanks to Kathryn McNeil for bringing this image to my attention.

4 Big Judy: Fatness, Shame, and the Hybrid Autobiography

ALLYSON MITCHELL

Hi, I'm Judy and I'm eight years old. I am standing in the Sears dressing room doorway and my mom is looking at me and she is looking at the way my burgundy chords are stretched across my belly and at the gaps between the buttons on my shirt. She's looking at me and I'm thinking, what's gonna happen now?

"We are going to have to get you a bra soon," she says.

I'm eight years old and I want my pants to be snug, but not like this. Not so when I take them off my belly is all red and scarred and maimed looking, and I don't want to wear a bra. She's staring at me now, ready to go for it.

"If you don't get some exercise, you are going to have to start shopping at Penningtons." She knows that the threat of the fat lady store is enough to break me although I try to eat only half my supper. Today I try on some girls' jeans, some boys' jeans, a bunch of t-shirts, a ruffled blouse and an ugly dress with a dropped waist and a high neck and long sleeves and a coat that wouldn't button.

"We are going to weigh your food," she says as she pats my stomach in front of the sales clerk. "You know you can't have anything that tucks in, or has short sleeves or that has a belt or anything that comes in white or bright or pastel."

The sales clerk says, "But she's young, let her wear bright clothes."

My mom says, "She's young and fat, we don't have to announce it to everybody."

I'm standing there in the Sears change room doorway, looking at my mom look at me.

So we are introduced to the story of Big Judy, a young woman we follow from age 8 to 31 in a performance piece by the Toronto fat activist collective, Pretty Porky and Pissed Off (PPPO'd), of which I was a member.[1] As the twenty-minute performance unfolds, the audience meets Judy at several landmark events in her life, interactions that have punctuated (if not explicitly shaped) Judy's coming of age. The narrative trajectory is organized unambiguously around Judy's body – one that by many accounts is considered overweight, out of bounds, and is visually "witnessed" through the actual bodies of the performers in PPPO'd. Tellingly, the story emerges not from Judy's own observations, but from the interactions that her body precipitates; through the way others see and react to her. It soon becomes clear that this is the way that Judy learns she's fat, too.

Narratives such as Judy's – narratives of fat subjectivity – are not as rare as they were even a decade ago. Judith Moore's *Fat Girl* (2005), Jen Lancaster's *Such a Pretty Fat* (2008), Stephanie Klein's *Moose: A Memoir* (2008), and Donna Jarrell and Ira Sukrengruang's *Scoot Over, Skinny: The Fat Nonfiction Anthology* (2005), are just a few of the semi-autobiographical accounts of "plus-sized" life that have found large readerships in recent years. This proliferation can be attributed in large part to the feminist strategy of evoking the micro-narrative (Hewitt 2010). The early 1990s in particular saw the emergence – or, some may argue, the re-emergence – of the autobiography as a capable analytical tool, a way of situating the self politically. Zines, anthologies of personal writing, independent music, and, more recently, online journalling and blogging have been some of the primary vehicles of young feminist political action since the 1990s. Some of the collected and printed versions of this work include: Barbara Findlen's *Listen Up: Voices from the Next Feminist Generation* (1995); Rebecca Walker's *To Be Real: Telling the Truth and Changing the Face of Feminism* (1995); Jennifer Baumgardner and Amy Richard's *Manifesta: Young Women, Feminism and the Future* (2000); Ophira Edut's *Body Outlaws: Young Women Write about Body Image and Identity* (2000); Lynn Crosbie's *Click: Becoming Feminists* (1997); *Fireweed*'s "Revolution, Grrrl Style" issue (1997); Lara Karian, Lisa Rundle, and myself with *Turbo Chicks: Talking Young Feminisms* (2001); the 2001 *Canadian Woman Studies'* issue on young women and activists; Daisy Hernández and Bushra Rehman's *Colonize This: Young Women of Color on Today's Feminism* (2002); Danya Ruttenberg's *Yentl's Revenge: Young Jewish Women Write about Today's Feminism* (2002); Vivien Labaton and Dawn Lundy Martin's *The Fire This Time: Young Activists and the New Feminism* (2004); and Anita Harris' *Next Wave Cultures: Fem-*

inism, Subcultures, Activism (2007). Feminists have invested widely in the importance of their life experiences, and their individual stories collectively tell the tale of larger social phenomena (Siegel 1997).

Fat politics, in particular, has benefited from this focus on the autobiographical given the relative infancy of size-focused politics. While other marginalized communities have benefited from the development of shared politics and collective organizing for decades, size has been historically under-recognized and under-theorized as an axis of identity. The nexus of narratives that has begun to form in recent years is a key component in the galvanization of politicized fat communities and the complex set of fat politics that attend them.

Yet, the conceptual, analytical, and political contributions that autobiographies of embodied experience have made are not without their limitations. While links can (and indeed are) made across individual narratives to engender a broader understanding of embodiment, these accounts are deeply vulnerable to readings that isolate fat experience as an individual phenomenon, glazing over the social, economic, and cultural structures that create and sustain fat identity. Indeed, hegemonic readings of fat subjectivity are generally organized around individual discipline – eating and exercise habits, poor self-esteem or self-control, and so on – rather than the shared cultural, structural, and interpersonal dynamics that constitute embodied life.

Big Judy's narrative was an effort to reorient readings of the fat body away from the individual and towards a localized community. In 2004, after eight years of collective work, PPPO'd wrote, choreographed, and performed Big Judy's story at Buddies in Bad Times Theatre in Toronto. While Big Judy was given a singular moniker (named after the "plus-sized" dress mannequin), hers is a more complex identity: she is the collective story of PPPO'd, stitched together from experiences that our members had, in whole or in part, shared. *Big Judy*, then, was an attempt to re-imagine the fat autobiography beyond the sphere of the individual, locating it in a broader sociocultural realm without sacrificing the importance of the personal. We deployed this strategy for its ability to open up a portrayal of fatness that avowed the abject. In Big Judy, we foregrounded narratives of anger, body dysmorphia, sexual harassment, and dreams deferred – often too painful to be presented on individual terms – by drawing on a community of voices rather than locating them on or through the individual. The performance of the piece, through the differently sized although all fat bodies of PPPO'd members, worked to present a collective fat body but not a homogeneous one. The bodies of

PPPO'd members ranged in weight, shape, fat distribution, and scale; and the visual effect, in turn, was to give the character of Big Judy a small rump, fat bum, big stomach, flatter belly, pear shape, apple shape, slender arms, plump arms, chiselled cheeks, and double chins all at the same time. By embodying fatness in the way that Big Judy does, we generated a shared life story of PPPO'd members told through a kind of anti-monolith of the fat body. This visual political strategy resonates with Sayantani DasGupta's discussion, in this volume, of collective autobiography as a mode of mobilizing what Judith Butler (2004b) has called the "critical promise of fantasy" (Butler quoted in DasGupta 45). DasGupta's analysis of *POP!*, an online art project that envisions male pregnancy, sheds light on the imaginative corporeal possibilities that the construction of a group autobiography can produce. In this chapter, I discuss this strategy of "hybrid" autobiography in terms of its significance as a feminist performance strategy in which the personal – or, more specifically, the corporeal – can be invoked as a political site without collapsing into individualization or the re-staging of trauma. Further, I explore this displacement of focus from the subject of origin onto a nexus of subjects for its ability to create a strategic monolith of the unruly body without devolving into false universalism.

Hi I'm Judy, and I'm 11 years old. I want to be a pop star. I mean, who wouldn't? All the singing and dancing – life would be so exciting. Parties, fancy food, fancy friends, a perfect life filled with pink and purple neon lights. I am Boy George, I am Diana Ross, I am Madonna. The Mini Pops inspire my soft heart to be everything and every body that I want. Music makes my even softer body move to my own special beat. I'm a superstar waiting to be discovered. My hunger for fame grows so that my sister, our friends, our foes, and our pets perform recitals in the backyard, dance routines on the porch, circus acts on the swing set – anything for an audience.

Last year in grade four, my favourite music teacher, Ms. Mumford, directed a school musical called "The Great Garden." I decided this was going to be my big break. I was going to get the lead girl role. I auditioned with my favourite song from Sunday school, "All Things Bright and Beautiful," singing every note with certainty and flare. I knew I was the best girl to audition, I knew the part was mine.

A few days later the list of roles was posted. I was nervous, excited, and really anxious to get rehearsing. As I approached the bulletin board, Ms. Mumford pulled me aside. She told me that my audition was outstanding, that I had a real talent, not to mention such a pretty face. But I was simply too fat to play the lead role. I learned pretty quickly that pop stars aren't chubby. They're slim and tall and pretty in the way only skinny girls are pretty. No, pop stars are not chubby, and I have always been at least chubby.

Representations of fat bodies in North American popular culture are limited at best. Where there has been space for fat bodies, it has been in the field of comedy, and often as the butt of a joke. Both fat male and female bodies find a place here, as exemplified by well-known (if occasionally tragic) personas such as John Candy, Jim Belushi, Roseanne, Margaret Cho, Dawn French, Rosie O'Donnell, and Tom Arnold (Bernstein and St John 2009). Fat also frequently appears as a comedic prosthesis, a sight gag: consider Gwyneth Paltrow in *Shallow Hal* (2001), Robin Williams in *Mrs Doubtfire* (1993), Tim Allen in *The Santa Clause* (1994), and Eddie Murphy in several movies. The success of these films points us towards the broader cultural position of the fat body: funny at a distance, particularly when it is latex rather than flesh – hyperbole, not reality. When fat bodies are portrayed in "real" contexts, it is frequently in the context of sensational news stories and documentaries about the "obesity epidemic," in which fat people are caught unaware, moving about their daily life, captured on film from the neck down. The headless and arguably "subjectless" fat body has become a well-recognized trope in broadcast television (Kent 2001).

As Joan W. Scott writes in her landmark essay, "The Evidence of Experience" (1991), the affective impact of representation is not to be underestimated. It is a powerful, often liberatory experience to see oneself reflected in culture. Scott talks about experience as a goal of producing historical knowledge. Aside from the immediate impact of identification, cultural exposure also provides a sense of community, history, and political possibility (Mohanty 1992). In a fat context, this has resulted in a particular kind of celebratory politic, resituating the fat body in public places and spaces as a way of upsetting hegemonic representations of abject fatness. These cultural productions are strategic moves that insist on a valid and visible fat subjectivity defined by and for fat women, rejecting the abject or externally defined pathological subjectivities otherwise attributed to fat bodies. Some of the most exciting, innovative, and adventurous work in this field is being done by feminist performance artists such as Cindy Baker and performance troupes such as the Padded Lillies, a fat synchronized swim team out of San Francisco; Big Burlesque, a fat erotic dance ensemble also out of San Francisco; Big Moves, a fat hip hop dance troupe that has franchises in Chicago,

Brooklyn, and Philadelphia; Big Dance, a professional fat dance troupe out of Vancouver; and the fat drag king troupe, King Size, and Big Appetyte (formerly the Fat Femme Mafia) in Toronto. The work done by these groups is generally about performing the fat body as beautiful and/or sexy despite or because of its fatness (Cooper 2009; Kuppers 2001).

Pretty Porky and Pissed Off similarly began as a strategy for making fat bodies public. The intention was to flaunt our fat bodies in the face of the negative representations so prevalent in popular culture. Initially, this meant that our performance work was overwhelmingly celebratory of the fat body. We wore tight, loud outfits and danced outrageously – in ways that flattered and highlighted our bodies. The "fat is fabulous" public persona was a source of strength both for ourselves and for our audiences. However, this was often at odds with how we experienced our bodies privately.

I'm Judy and I'm 14. My tight t-shirts and tight pants show off the sometimes embarrassing size of my boobs and butt. The girls in my class are my friends; the boys call me bubble, blubber, sausage, and Big Judy. They also call me "bruiser."

I play intramural floor hockey at lunch. They say when I run that my boobs are so big that it must give me two black eyes. That's how they came up with the name bruiser. They say, "I bet when you look down you can't even see your feet." I tell them to drop dead and I don't prove it to them because they don't deserve it. But you can bet that as soon as I get home I check to make sure that I can.

Three sleeves of saltine crackers, half a block of cheddar cheese, after school reruns and a Seventeen *magazine article that says, "If your boobs are perky enough, you should be able to hold a pencil between them." I'm bored out of my mind.*

The next day at school Trevor and Bruce pass me a note in science class. I'm supposed to check one of the boxes. There are three of them: they say 1) Will you make out with us? 2) Will you suck us off? 3) Will you do it? I crumple up the note and throw it back at them but secretly I feel special inside. That day after school, I cut through the deserted fair grounds. Trevor and Bruce are waiting in the empty snack shack. They know what happens next. I let them feel me up and try a few rough kisses. But I want more. They say don't tell anyone the next day at school because it will be totally embarrassing. They say fat chicks are like merry-go-rounds, everyone wants to ride one, but no one wants to tell anybody. I tell them to F.O. I'd never tell anyone I was making out with losers like them anyways.

I go home and I feel hungry, and I'm not sure if it's the empty grope or because it's almost dinnertime.

After years of cake dances, girl gangs, and free bake sales, the members of PPPO'd began to question our tactics. We came together as a group on an almost weekly basis to take care of one another, share our stories, talk about fatphobia, and discuss ways of resisting it in the practice of our everyday lives. We read and wrote theories of fat liberation and then tried to figure out how to realize them through our cultural productions. The shame we may have felt about our size, the frustration with not being able to find clothing to fit us, our individual and collective experiences of fatphobia, and all of the other trying facets of fat existence were writ large in our private conversations, but ultimately divorced from our public personae.

PPPO'd created a particular context that allowed us to share personal narratives – one based in trust, self-care, and consciousness-raising. As we became an activist hub, it meant that stories came to us through others as well. We became connected to other fat activist groups and began to see the importance of sharing the full spectrum of our stories publicly. We had experienced the joy of playful dances in public and recognized the powerful effects that these moments had on audiences and on our immediate community. However, we knew fat to be more than just this. We knew fat was also difficult, sad, and shameful at times – not simply all pleasure and power. Some of us had also experienced feelings of ambivalence around the disjuncture between our public personae as fat activists and the guilt or shame we felt for not being able to overcome internalized fatphobic judgments about our own bodies. As activists, we found ourselves in a position of privilege: we had publicly claimed our fat identities and bore, in turn, a responsibility to elevate the discourse around fat bodies beyond the "obesity epidemic" and into productive, humanized territory. While "fat is fabulous" was the thin edge of the wedge – audiences can handle critique when it's bundled in fun – it began to feel as though this work was creating a straw figure: if being fat is so great, what's the problem?

The problem is that fat isn't always great. Sometimes it's difficult, sometimes it's confusing, and sometimes it's even awful. For these reasons, Elspeth Probyn (2000) has called for a reintegration of shame and disgust into corporeal politics. She speaks of "disgust and shame as the hidden face of body pride" and warns of the dangers associated with attempts to erase shame, which can result in individuals and cultures in which "disgust, blame and resentment seethe under the surface of a sanitized veneer of acceptance" (128). Indeed, this veneer can wear thin quite quickly. As the members of PPPO'd spoke to one another behind closed doors, we came to realize that our trajectories of embodiment, of coming into being as fat subjects, shared remarkable – and often distressing – similarities. Our introduction to Big Judy at age 8, for example, seems at first glance a simple (if loaded) exchange between mother and daughter under the watchful eye of a salesclerk. However, most members of PPPO'd had had a moment like this as a child, one in which an everyday exchange marked us, hailed us into being as fat, and made clear that such a becoming was not a source of pride. So, too, did we locate similar experiences of not being able to find clothes that fit, being sized up by new lovers, and a host of complicated relationships between food and family. Accordingly, the members of PPPO'd made a conscious shift towards being another kind of activist, choosing to employ strategies that would firmly place the revolt/ing in fat politics (LeBesco 2004). Simultaneously looking to revalue and/or celebrate fat while maintaining an insistence on its disgusting properties may be difficult, but it's a project that pays tribute to the complicated realities of fat embodiment.

I'm Judy and I'm 23.

I'm standing on a familiar dance floor with half a gin martini in my hand. I'm single for the first time in four years and I'm looking around the crowd trying to pick out an old friend whose email had said, "Now that you're not married, are you finally gonna kiss me?"

We haven't seen each other in two years. The myth about moving to a big city and having to schedule in your friendships came true.

Our emails had been really hot and heavy. I see her walk into the bar, she goes right by me and orders a drink. So I walk up to her and tap her on the shoulder. She turns to me and gives me a look I've been getting used to lately: vague confusion, and then embarrassed recognition. She gives me two hard hugs and then says, "Hey baby, you look different, you look really, um, great." The truth is, I've gained about 50 pounds and even though I was a fat activist, fat ally, and a feminist, I didn't really realize how being skinny was a privilege until now.

So at 23 gaining weight meant I had to learn to talk to people, I had to learn how to push through the invisibility that being fat created. If walking through a room wasn't gonna get me noticed I was gonna have to learn to say something that would.

To publicly acknowledge collective experiences of shame is to move towards the complexity of fat experience, of acknowledging that fat *is* great and can be an important position from which to move through the world, but that it can also embody some less wonderful dynamics. The potential in this kind of affective reconfiguration of fat and fat politics is what Eve Kosofsky Sedgwick (2003) formulates as the performativity of "transformational shame" (38). But the difficulty in sharing narratives of disgust, trauma, and internalized fatphobia, of course, is how personal they can be. Fat people navigate the world in isolation, repeatedly subjected to the shame that fat embodiment can engender. Our concern was that we not re-stage these moments uncritically, situating individual actors as targets and asking them to bear the weight of their individual stories. Collectively, we made a decision with Big Judy to tell the story of a fat woman moving through the experience of learning she was fat and what that meant in terms of life limitations and challenges, including changing body sizes. In order to create the play, we practised writing exercises at our meetings. We each came up with significant moments in our lives that had formed our identities as fat, and the stories fit together nicely as a life narrative of Big Judy. Over a span of seven years of working together, we cumulatively came to the point where we felt safe enough to workshop these kinds of complex stories together. The combination of this feminist context of self-care, linked with a political understanding of consciousness-raising and a reliance on personal narrative, is what allowed for the performance of *Big Judy* as a shift in our collective politics.

As individuals and as actors, the importance of this multivalent narrative was that we were able to stitch our personal stories together into the collective story of a fictionalized fat girl. All of us had lived our lives as fat people from childhood to teenage years to adulthood. While we had not lived the same life, we recognized shared experiences and moments. Being able to tag my story onto the monumental, public figure of Big Judy was cathartic. In a kind of "do over," my isolated experience became attached to a fat girl who could be a role model, someone who would have understood and could have talked to my kid or teen self and let me know that I wasn't alone and that I could have community. She would have made a big difference to my own life narrative.

The performance of *Big Judy* created more space for discussion about fat bodies, fat experiences, and the visuality of fatness. Delivered through differently sized and voiced bodies, the collective narrative established a support system so that no one person's story had to take the stage alone. Simultaneously, there was no doubt that these were personal stories, life moments experienced by the actors. Between the monologues that wove the story of Big Judy's life, we performed group dances that interrupted the chronological narrative and allowed for a different expression of physicality and visuality. The dances not only served as reminders of the real, lived, and living bodies that were telling the stories – bodies that held histories and could dance them out in highly physical and ignited ways – but also allowed for a changed visual context in which to regard fat bodies. Memory was not just cerebral; it was in the bodies that changed costumes, leapt, and jumped to various sounds. The dance numbers also interrupted the often solemn mood of the narratives. They were the defiant interstitials reinforcing that, while these bodies had experienced trauma, they now existed, in the moment, on a stage with others who admired and celebrated them – and who could see them.

Hello my name is Judy.

In case you were wondering, this is not the size I used to be. I've been part of Pretty Porky and Pissed Off for about eight years now. One of the things we like to do is go into schools and talk to students about body activism and size acceptance. One of the questions we get asked a lot is whether or not we, as Pretty Porky and Pissed Off, hate skinny people? Whenever I hear this question it makes me think about the war between the fatties and the skinnies, whether or not there will ever be one. I hate to say it but I think if there is going to be a war between the fatties and the skinnies, I think the fatties will win. When you're a group force – force equals mass times acceleration – the more mass you have, the better off you will be. I partially know this because when I was in grade school, I was the Red Rover champion. I could burst through any line, and I would never let go of my friends' fragile wrists. It was the only thing I was ever champion of in grade school that involved movement.

Sometimes I think the war between the fatties and the skinnies is an internal war. Inside every fat person there is a skinny person, and believe it or not, inside every skinny is a fatty. Size isn't just relative; oftentimes I think it's misleading. That's why we have the word, "Pretty," in "Pretty Porky and Pissed Off." It's about more than just what's in style. It's about how size can be personal. I have a friend her name is … let's say Claire, and she has recently "ballooned" to a size eight and won't wear anything that has pockets in the front anymore, or stripes … anything with this sort of motion (motions to horizontal line). She says it makes her look fat. In the meantime I'm thin now; I am a size 10, I'm skinny. So how can there be a war between the fatties and the skinnies if nobody knows who is who?

Big Judy is an example of a politic of "we" created through hybrid autobiography. This was accomplished in part by pushing the generic limits of autobiography and expanding the possible meanings of the feminist mantra, "the personal is political." Rather than existing in the isolated singularity of the personal narrative, *Big Judy* tells the story of a community of women. This strategy shifts the viewer's focus away from the subject of origin and towards a nexus of subjects, creating a strategic monolith of the unruly body without devolving into false universalism by performing fat in a way that makes visible its ambivalent manifestations. In *Big Judy*, our autobiographical self-representation attests to the radical potential of hybridized testimony and experience. Seeing fragments of one's own life in pages, on the screen, or on the stage can generate a sense of the creative possibilities of political affiliation: "we underline the inimitable potential for autobiography and its renovations to address the life of the individual, the lives of groups of individuals, or some self-representational aspect of the individual or her group" (Perreault and Kadar 2005, 1). The life story told in *Big Judy* moves from the politics of individualism to a story in which the "I" blurs with the "we" (5) – one in which both similarities and differences are highlighted. We strategically evoked identity politics and shared experiences in order to make community and the *identity*, rather than simply the physicality, of fat visible, suggesting the possibility for fat culture and politicized fat individuals to try to change oppressive and otherwise negative lived experiences. The fat that is performed in *Big Judy* reveals the performativity of fat.

Sherrill Grace (2005) explores how auto/biographical plays stage Judith Butler's notion of performativity. She writes, "By this I understand Butler to be allowing the potential for stage performance of identity (gendered or any other kind) to be performative and, thus, capable of exposing essentialism as false (as a role) and of challenging the scripts that prescribe our identity acts" (70). Building on Jill Dolan's work on performativity in the theatre, Grace attends to how Dolan invites us "to see if we can locate ways in which live theatre performance can '*reveal* performativity' [and] challenges us to look for theatre performances that show, 'with gestic insistence, that we are not ... self-same individuals'" (66, original emphasis). Grace elaborates:

> Elin Diamond puts it this way: "As soon as performativity comes to rest on *a* performance, questions of embodiment, of social relations, of ideological interpellations, of emotional and political effects, all become discussable. ... Performance is precisely the site in which concealed or dissimulated conventions might be investigated" (5). I believe that this performance site is all the more open to discussion *as performative* when the subject of the play is auto/biographical because in these kinds of plays self-identity is performed, whether by the author as actor or by another actor, before both the author and the audience (understood as both individual and collective). (70, ellipses in Grace, original emphases)

The environment of the performance stage or space for the embodied life narrative creates a complex audience engagement with the performativity of identity – or, in this case, fat identities. Prior to *Big Judy*, much of the PPPO'd performance work happened on the street or in a cabaret bar space where audience attention can, at times, be fleeting compared with the demands of the theatre setting where social conventions insist that an audience sits in chairs in a dark room, silently observing the performance on stage. In part, the suspension of time and space that a theatre creates mandates an attentive audience from beginning to end. In the context of autobiographical installations such as the ones that Sarah Brophy and Janice Hladki refer to in the introduction to this collection – including my own *Ladies Sasquatch* and Mona Hatoum's *Corps étranger* (the subject of Kim Sawchuk's chapter in this volume) – spaces of viewership literally set the stage for the audience's engagement with the work (15–19). In order to share the difficult stories of *Big Judy*, the performers of PPPO'd needed the safety of immediate audience responses, including laughter, respectful silence, and, finally, applause. The layered affective relationships between performer and audience assisted in expanding the fat body under investigation and articulated through performance – an expansion that allowed a sharing of subjectivity through the creation of a collective Big Judy.

Hi, my name is Judy and I'm 31 years old.

Right now I am thinking about my career and where I want to be five years from now, and how I'm going to manage to have a place in the city and a country house. It doesn't have to be big; it doesn't even have to have running water. Just somewhere I can go, and be alone. My vision involves a lake, and a hill that I can stand on and look at nothing and hear silence. I would be wearing something sexy, and probably something shiny, and depending on my mood I would either be wearing heels, or be barefoot with a sweet, fresh pedicure.

I started my career in publishing eight years ago at a Canadian fashion magazine. It was fun, glamorous, and completely devoid of any politic on any level. That was until the day we put Iman – Mrs David Bowie – on the cover. The amount of reader mail that poured in congratulating us on a "different" look made it clear that it had been quite some time since we had had a woman of colour on the cover. I couldn't very well expect the magazine to have a fat politic. And although they were very complimentary – liked my garage sale finds, thought my painter pants were so Helmut Lang – I couldn't help but hear a little amazement in their voices. Like, "how can a fat chick be so cool?" and if she was so cool, why was she fat? I took my tentative compliments and moved to a solid editing gig at a teen magazine. I wasn't in the Fashion department but I was hip to the trends and had a sparkly polished finger on the pulse of teens across America. I had manic panic hair, wore four-inch platforms and I was good at what I did so it didn't matter what I looked like.

Lately though, it feels like it really matters. For the past five years, I've been getting chubbier, rounder, fatter. I've lost the manic panic hair, the four-inch heels, and the tattoos are barely visible. I am a professional fat woman, wearing professional fat clothes. They have no colour, no pattern, are made of horrible fabric, and are cut to fit the generic fat body, which none of us has. I have a sneaking suspicion that, as my ass gets bigger, my chance of promotion gets smaller – pushed aside for a raise, overlooked for exciting opportunity. I wonder if I was thinner, would I get the corner office and be able to make it home in time for a nice dusk swim?

The enactment of the auto/biographical play called *Big Judy* allowed for a deeper exploration of fat subjectivity than had the previous work of PPPO'd. In writing, practising, producing, performing, and processing the work, the members of PPPO'd were able to collect our individual experiences and create a hybrid auto/bio that was embodied in those experiences, along with a figure in and through whom those moments could cohere. *Big Judy* was an active attempt to create social and individual change. In performing the work, we "became" fat activists, for, as Kathleen LeBesco (2001) claims, drawing on Butler's work, "the doer is constructed in doing the deed/political act, not the other way around" (81). Performativities in activist becomings are about understanding what you have to be "doing" in order to "be" an activist. Grace writes, "The point of performing performativity may not be to change the gendered identity script of the actor in real life, but it most certainly may be to show an audience member how to do so" (2005, 70). In this regard, Big Judy is an example of the social uses of autobiography, the ways in which turning the interiority of shame outwards through performance can work to transform shame, not by eradicating it or slapping a happy face on it, but by making it public – keeping it alive in social spaces where it gets to dance in the collective light rather than festering in an individual's psyche and gut.

NOTE

1 *Big Judy* was developed for Mayworks – Festival of Working People and the Arts, in the spring of 2004. The script (Huffa et al. 2004) was co-written by the members of Pretty Porky and Pissed Off: Joanne Huffa, Abi Slone, Mariko Tamaki, Tracy Tidgwell, Zoe Whittall, and Allyson Mitchell. All of the italicized sections in this chapter were drawn from this script.

PART TWO

Rupture and Recognition: Body Re-formations

5 Sex Traitors: Autoethnography by Straight Men

RICHARD FUNG

Recent feature films *Brüno* (2009) and *Humpday* (2009) foreground the mix of repulsion and attraction that characterizes a common obsession that heterosexual men have with homosexuality. As an über-fag screaming across the screens of suburban cineplexes, *Brüno* amplifies to absurdity the swish and salaciousness in the enduring tradition of straight men playing at gay. The widespread knowledge that actor Sacha Baron Cohen is partnered with a woman provides young straight male viewers – especially those in groups – the necessary insurance to risk the queasy pleasure of publicly revelling in queer excess. Though watching *Brüno* was perhaps not entirely risk-free, since it seems that once word spread that the butt of the film's humour is homophobia and not giddily randy queens, ticket sales dwindled (Corliss 2009; Gray 2009). Meanwhile, at art house cinemas, critical praise was drawing respectable audiences to US indie movie *Humpday*, in which two straight buddies contemplate starring in their own gay porno as an art project. But despite their flirtation with queer theory, the film's producers wimp out and the protagonists stay limp, leaving Mike and Jim safely at the straight end of the Kinsey scale. Playing at gay has its limits.

Those on the hegemonic side of social power relations often have an ambivalent attraction to those defined as their opposites: the rich to the poor, the white to the coloured, the straight to the queer. There is a reverse fascination, too. Take, for example, the drag performers in Jennie Livingston's documentary, *Paris Is Burning* (1990), who look across difference from the minor side of power. In the "executive realness" competition category of the New York ball scene of the 1980s, poor Black and Latino gay men perform middle-class heteromasculinity in business suits and with briefcases. But, in general, dominant subject positions remain unmarked and apparently universal; heterosexuality and heteronormative masculinity are submitted to an analytical lens only rarely and in marginal contexts. The curtain of mystery is the device that provides the Wizard of Oz his fearsome patriarchal authority. In this chapter, I consider the work of three artists who use video to lift the curtain on heteromasculinities. Louis Taylor, Evan Tapper, and Robert Lendrum have different preoccupations and draw on diverse artistic strategies, but their work is informed by feminism and queer theory, and they share the use of the self as a way of exploring the larger psychic and social processes that shape the production of straight men, an approach that is best described as autoethnographic. As a mode of autobiography, it clears a space from which straight men can speak individual narratives of collective concern.

Tamy Spry (2006) defines autoethnography as "a self-narrative that critiques the situatedness of self with others in social context" (187). "Autoethnographic methods," she continues, "recognize the reflections and refractions of multiple selves in contexts that arguably transform the authorial 'I' to an existential 'we'" (188). Sidonie Smith (2002) also refers to the "we" in "I" in relation to an "autoethnographic signature" whereby individual narrative and sociopolitical implication are "mutually constitutive" (146). As straight signatures for queer signs, the video works of Taylor, Tapper, and Lendrum offer "an alternative field of the visual" (147). Autoethnographic film- and video-making is a "confounding of genres" (Visweswaran 1994, 4) that goes by many names. For example, Laura Rascaroli (2009) uses terms such as "subjective, first person" cinema (1) and the "self-portrait film" (170). Michael Renov (2004) identified trends in independent documentary in the early 1990s as "new autobiography" and "domestic ethnography" – films that take the maker's family members as their subjects, thus "playing at the boundaries of inside and outside in a unique way" (218). In her writing on autoethnographic film and video, Catherine Russell (1999) makes reference to its close relatives and antecedents, "diary films" and "personal cinema." In this work, the author is speaker, seer, and seen; the first person narrator is "the origin of the gaze" as well as the "body image" (277). A strand in my own work in video has been described as autoethnographic, and tapes such as *My Mother's Place* (1990) and *Sea in the Blood* (2000) undoubtedly display the characteristics described by Spry, Renov, and Russell: they are first person narratives that use stories from my Chinese Trinidadian Canadian family to open up larger questions about colonialism and postcolonialism, diasporic identities, queer sexuality, and vectors of social power including race, class, and gender (Muñoz 1995). Beginning with the first work in this series, *The Way to My Father's Village* (1988), I set first person voice-over against other storytelling modes to tease out discourses of history and memory and to undermine notions of documentary objectivity.

Discussions about ethics in documentary media and social science research are often premised on the assumption that the filmmaker/researcher is shooting or studying "down"; that the investigator is in a position of social power in relation to the filmed/researched subjects, whose interests must therefore be protected. This is generally the case, in fact, and filmmakers such as Michael Moore, who shoot "up," are the exception. This situation does not result simply from the powerful having the means to control their public presentation through physical inaccessibility and the threat of punitive action over unfavourable images – or images, period, as in Madonna's successful suit over a British newspaper's publication of photographs from her 2000 wedding. It is also the case that power, when normalized and hegemonic, is not generally considered "interesting." Fascination with Madonna derives from the exoticism of the flamboyantly wealthy and eccentric, but while even middle- and upper-middle-class lifestyles are available to a small and shrinking North American demographic, they form the customary setting for films and television programs watched by people of all classes. This holds true for most mass media cultures around the world.

So what is immediately attractive about autoethnography is that it seems to sidestep such messy power relations, not just for the maker and subject, but also for the viewer/critic who may feel implicated and compromised watching a film organized around an exploitative gaze. But difficulties remain. Videotaping a subject as close as my mother did not release me from the ethical risks of manipulation or sensationalizing; minoritized people are not immune from reinscribing stereotypical or exoticizing discourses about themselves and others. These were issues I wrestled with as I was making these tapes. But what strikes me today, in reconsidering my own work in this genre, is the fact that the subject-object in autoethnographic film and video is the same classically ethnographic object: the Other of colonial discourse and the Other of dominant social discourse. Even in this emerging genre, the dominant subject position, masculinity included, remains beyond scrutiny.

Calvin Thomas (2008) argues that "to leave masculinity *un*studied, to proceed as if masculinity were somehow *not a contingent* form of gender/sexuation, would be to leave it naturalized, and thus to make it *necessary*, to reproduce contingency as necessity, to protect masculinity from change" (20, original emphases). But speaking from a position of hegemonic power carries its own risks, namely, that of appropriating, delegitimating, and/or displacing the speech of the Other. The men's movement and the fathers' rights movement have certainly been hostile to feminism (and often to gay men), and even though it was developed to oppose these reactionary tendencies, the field of masculinity studies has had to navigate around and through such dangers as well. Michael Awkward (2006) advocates the autobiographical "I" as one way to approach the problems of male speech: "In male feminist acts, to identify the writing self as biologically male is to emphasize the desire not to be ideologically male; it is to explore the process of rejecting the phallocentric perspectives by which men traditionally have justified the subjugation of women" (69). From this perspective, autoethnographic film- and video-making can be seen as a self-reflexive practice in which modes of visual self-fashioning produce cultural critique.

The artists I discuss in this chapter use overlapping and divergent methods for clearing a space from which to speak as men. All experiment with the language of the moving image to find fresh ways of articulating straight masculinities, and all employ self-directed humour that evades the earnest self-flagellation of the privileged, a stance that absorbs energy and space and ultimately serves to re-centre power. Both Taylor and Tapper address women's perspectives directly while simultaneously positioning their own experiences within minoritized masculinities: Taylor as a Black man, Tapper as Jewish. Lendrum's tack is to radically foreground the performance of gender and to deconstruct the speaking subject, recasting identity, in other words, as a visual "'staging of subjectivity'" (Russell 1999, 276) through which both relations of dominance and alternative ways of being come into view. By performing straight masculinities through practices that illuminate the psychic, social, and cultural processes that produce them, all three artists not only map unequal and naturalized operations of power, but also make room for imagining more ethical, relational heteromasculinities.

Louis Taylor

In *Esther, Baby and Me* (2000), Louis Taylor's chronicle of his mental journey leading up to and beyond the birth of his first child, Taylor's self-portrait of Black masculinity is entangled with a legacy of representations of Black men's sexuality and fatherhood. Combining a series of direct-address performance tableaux with playfully recreated scenes – recreations in which his partner of ten years, Esther Pflug, collaborates – Taylor orients his confessional style towards the creation of an emphatically relational family portrait. *Esther, Baby and Me* exemplifies what Soyini D. Madison (2012) describes as a "combination of emotion, poetics, and contemplation" through which the "'auto' ... moves us towards the 'ethnographic' in order to name, deepen, extend, and complicate the world around and beyond the researcher's grasp" (198). Self-reflexively staging the uneasy incorporation of "fatherhood" into his "I," Taylor grapples with the discursive and visual histories that have violently defined the intersection of paternity and Black masculinity.

Taylor – in his own words, an "ex-stripper, ballet dancer, car runner, convicted felon, and most recently an unemployed actor and hardened dreamer" – begins by outlining the many ways in which he is "not the stuff of fatherhood." He wonders, "What would I have to offer a child?" Taylor's confessions about mood swings and relationship tensions are recounted with clownish exaggeration, but candid revelations underlie the humour. "Any time I think of having sex with Esther I feel like a pedophile," he declares, and the screen is plastered with a newspaper headline blaring, "Black daddy buggers baby while baking!" As the couple's sex life diminishes, masturbation and pornography re-enter Taylor's life as he hopes to keep the "inner bow wow" in check. As the point-of-view camera tilts down the swollen breasts and distended belly of his pregnant partner, Taylor muses, "I'd always thought about a woman's body as something to enjoy, nothing really more than an object existing for my pleasure. But as Esther grows, I can no longer blind myself to the fact that genetically I'm a parking lot attendant to her big tent of procreation, and that outside of the ooh-baby-baby-squirt-squirt, I no longer have a biological function."

Most sensitive of these confessions are the anxieties of the Black father-to-be about having a mixed-race child. Taylor's concerns about what that might suggest about his identity – an externalized inner voice whispers, "You always thought Barbie was cuter than Black Skipper" – unfold into a parodic negotiation of the visual economy of white supremacy. While he has been with Esther for ten years, they have not married, a situation that allows him to justify their relationship as transitory. In time, he reasons, he would naturally find and marry a Black woman. The impending birth threatens that eventuality. If cultural race nationalism is a defensive response to white supremacy, then, in *Esther,*

Baby and Me, Taylor refracts imagined accusations of self-hatred and selling out for being with a white woman through the "visual vomit" of D.W. Griffith's *Birth of a Nation* (1915). The film that legitimized cinema's claim to be art, and an inspiration for the filmmakers of the Soviet Revolution, *Birth of a Nation* is also a deeply racist text, the hero of which is the Ku Klux Klan, with the mulatto as the villain. It is a diatribe less against Black people (provided they stay in their subservient place) than in opposition to miscegenation, and it established in cinema the figure of the sexually threatening Black man. With blond wig and blackface, Esther and Taylor re-enact the ex-slave Gus' pursuit of Flora Cameron. But, in their version, Flora does not have to die to save her virtue, and the dirty deed is consummated – followed by a post-coital cigarette.

Save for the Griffith parody, *Esther, Baby and Me* comments only obliquely on stereotypical representations of Black masculinity, but, with self-belittling humour, Taylor creates a unique self-portrait of the abject straight Black man. None of Taylor's occupations rate high on the respectability scale, and, on the masculinity scale, car runner and convicted felon sit at the opposite end from stripper and ballet dancer. Dancer, stripper, and actor invert the gendered hierarchy of looking identified by John Berger (1972) and Laura Mulvey (1975). The male stripper, like the male athlete, exemplifies male physicality; but whereas an unstated sexual desire may underlie the appreciation of the sportsman's performing body, the stripper's routine is explicitly about being looked at and sexually consumed.[1] Playing up and playing with gendered racial stereotypes, as Taylor recites his CV in voice-over, he depicts himself stumbling around a desert wilderness in fedora, overcoat, work boots, and kilt: a mismatched mélange of ethnic and gender codes that de-essentializes the racialized male body.

The parodic and ironic visual strategies through which Taylor composes his self-portrait can also be read as attempts to negotiate the fraught constructions of fatherhood in North American discourses about Black men. In 1965, American Senator Daniel Patrick Moynihan published *The Negro Family: The Case for National Action,* commonly known as the Moynihan Report. The government paper took as its starting point that "three centuries of injustice have brought about deep-seated structural distortions in the life of the Negro American," and that the legacy of slavery manifests itself in families that are "unstable and in many urban centers ... approaching complete breakdown." Moynihan identified absent fathers, female-headed families, and rising rates of children born out of wedlock as a "tangle of pathology" threatening African American urban life. Although he, in fact, identified two groups – a rising middle class and a sinking underclass – the report helped to establish, in policy circles and in the public imagination, a causal link between a generalized Black male paternal irresponsibility (along with emasculating Black females) and the host of problems affecting African American urban communities.[2] Even as it was criticized by African American civic leaders at the time for its assumptions based on normative, middle-class, white family structures, the report's central themes, in fact, echoed and drew from contemporary African American writers and activists (Horowitz 1997, 427). As feminist writer bell hooks (2004) notes, "The Moynihan report did not create gender warfare in black life; it simply validated the sexist beliefs among African American men and to a grave extent legitimized their effort to subjugate black females" (13).

These tensions endure in Black politics across North America and shape attempts to recuperate Black masculinity in Black popular culture. Take, for instance, the mission statement of Louis Farrakhan's 1995 Million Man March, which states, "We should accept the responsibility that God himself has imposed on us as heads of families and heads of communities" (quoted in Harris 1999, 60), a frame of reference opposed by Black feminists and their allies. As Luke Charles Harris (1999) contends, "By implication, many of Black women's problems are a result of the failure of Black patriarchy, rather than the results of patriarchal structures within the Black community – which is to say that they are problems that could be eliminated if Black men would only *take control* of the situation" (60, original emphasis). Stella Bruzzi (2005) points out how African American independent films such as *Boyz in the Hood* (1991), *Jungle Fever* (1991), and *Deep Cover* (1992) reiterate the notion that "subscription to the hegemonic patriarchal norms is the only way out of the cycle of drugs, violence and death that otherwise awaits the contemporary Black male" (169). Rinaldo Walcott (2003) makes a similar critique of the Canadian film *Rude* (1995) for reiterating these conventional discourses of the hood film: "Such narratives invent, centre and stereotype black masculinity, arguing that it has become impaired or flawed because it lacks the necessary resources to produce good patriarchs. The repetition of these narratives has come to occupy a sacred place in contemporary black popular culture, foreclosing the possibility for much more interesting imaginative works" (94). Navigating the complex representational terrain between the sexually threatening Black man and the irresponsible paternal figure conjured by the Moynihan Report, Taylor refuses to shore up his heteromasculine identity at the expense of Black women and Black feminisms.

This refusal can be discerned in the structural choices that shape *Esther, Baby and Me,* namely, in Taylor's decision not to end the film with the birth of his daughter. At the three-quarter mark of the film, the new father greets Simone Afeya Pflug-Taylor with the line, "She has defined my future with her first breath of existence." But *Esther, Baby and Me* continues to catalogue the shared elation and relationship difficulties that unite and tear new parents apart. Taylor notes a shift in preoccupation: "I still wonder about the world, but in terms of what it will do to her … What racism, rampaging capitalism and neo-con political shifts will forge her into." Ending the film at Simone's birth might have suggested that what matters most is the fact of fatherhood, the proof of a man's virility. By continuing the narrative beyond this obvious milestone, *Esther, Baby and Me* evades falling into patriarchal pedagogy, but neither does it pander to social anxieties about delinquent Black fathers. The film is, as its title suggests, a relational portrait, a collaboration between Taylor and Esther in which their recreated scenes sit in productive tension with those of a more straightforward documentary nature. The result is a hybrid product un-tethered from narrow ideas of authenticity – one that "attend[s] to how our subjectivity *in relation to others* informs and is informed by our engagement and representation of others" (Madison 2012, 10, original emphasis).

Evan Tapper

If, in *Esther, Baby and Me,* Louis Taylor chronicles the ups and downs of a heterosexual relationship pushed to crisis, then Evan Tapper builds an archive of failed heterosexuality. In a substantial body of short videos and live performances, many about a failure to connect romantically to women, Tapper tackles the burden of ethical responsibility to the Others of the heterosexual male: women and gay men. Tapper draws on what Russell (1999) formulates as the autoethnographic strategy of offering oneself up for inspection, but he "do[es] so ironically, mediating [his] own image and identifying obliquely with the technologies of representation" (279). Like Taylor, Tapper attempts to come to grips with difficult inheritances by routing his investigations of Jewish masculinity through meditations on the predicament of the artist: religious and artistic legacies of sexism and Tapper's own embodied subjectivity become the recalcitrant materials with which he works.

Like Taylor, Tapper offers an extended self-portrait of abject hetero-masculinity. Always performed by the artist himself, whether live action or animated, Tapper's protagonists are self-doubting and sexually unfulfilled, pictured alone and complaining of loneliness. In *Self-Portrait as a Teletubby* (2003), the artist shaves a square on his hairy chest to mimic the popular television characters aimed at toddlers, and uses a black marker to write a series of self-lacerating questions on the shaved spot, among them: "Do you do silly things and call them art?" and "Do you use art to justify being alone?" Produced three years later, *Artist Seeks ...* (2006) features a recorded telephone message addressed to "Evan" by "Kristin," who has evidently met him through a dating service or personal ad. Kristin's voice is that of a well-educated and level-headed woman, and her tone expresses concern: "I think you're right that we wouldn't necessarily click as a couple, but I just think you're wrong not to keep yourself open, and I think it's really sad that you are taking your email account apart and closing everything down ... You have to try a little more. You can't just put yourself lightly out there once." The image field is composed of a montage of snapshots taken from online dating profiles in different degrees of intimacy, including flash frames of erotic scenarios. In each picture, one person – sometimes the subject of a portrait, sometimes one in a group shot – is digitally removed, leaving behind a white silhouette. The meaning of the deletion is undecidable: whether an act of reprisal, as when an ex is literally cut out of the picture, a gesture of protection that renders a participant unrecognizable, or a symbolic erasure of self, Tapper inscribes an absence in the visual field that points to missed, lost, and possibly mourned connections. Through this visible/invisible tension in the relationship of represented subjects, Tapper's device of autoethnographic indeterminacy recalls the uncertainty of "absent presence" (Smith and Watson 2002b, 34) and the fragility of "connective tissue" that Sarah Brophy and Janice Hladki explore in their chapter in this volume (264–6).

Sheh-asani Kirtzono (2008), which incorporates a commissioned performance at the Jewish Museum in New York, extends this investigation of failed connectivities by situating Tapper's relationships to women in the context of religious mediations of gender relations. Videotaped against a wall of cardboard and behind a bouquet of fresh flowers, Tapper shaves a bushy beard, combs his hair, applies deodorant, and dons a white shirt and black jacket. Prompted by a question from a man off-screen, Tapper explains that the concept of his performance is that he is preparing for a date, and that in the finished video the space to his right will be filled with blurred photographs of women posted on JDate (which advertises itself as "the leading Jewish singles network").[3] A later conversation with an off-screen woman engages both parties in an extended conversation about Tapper's understanding of misogyny in Judaism. The dialogue is passionate and honest, and one searches for signs of chemistry between them. But their parting words are unmistakably final. Tapper takes up the flowers from the vase and drinks the water left in it. He stares blankly into the camera before walking off the set. The planned series of specifically blurred photographs and the relegation of his female interlocutor to the space beyond the visual frame anticipate the failure of a date to materialize from this elaborate preparation.

The rare reference to a love relationship in Tapper's work is offhand and mocking. *Untitled (Self-portrait in Blue)* (2001) is a faux music video built on a sliced and truncated appropriation of Billy Ocean's 1984 pop hit "Suddenly," a favourite choice for first dances at weddings. As the singer croons lines such as "Suddenly, life has new meaning to me" and "Each day I pray this love affair would last forever," the video reveals lushly layered and blue-tinted footage of a long-haired, coyly nude Tapper striking languid poses on a rumpled bed. The two and a half minute video is book-ended by excessive on-screen text. Opening titles pompously announce that this is "an art film by Evan David Tapper, dedicated to anyone who has ever been in love," and cites "Michel Foucault, 1972 – Voila!" The video closes with a disproportionately long credit sequence attributing everything from producing, directing, editing, and starring in the video, to catering, hairstyle, makeup, and financial support to Evan David Tapper. However, what might otherwise be read as a mere send-up of hubris and kitsch in romance and art takes on a darker, more personal meaning with the one role in the lengthy list not credited to Tapper: "camera by a former lover of Evan David Tapper (name withheld)." Even as he draws attention to the gaze that organizes the spectator's access to his body, Tapper, echoing the white silhouette cutouts in *Artist Seeks ...*, inscribes his former lover as an "absent presence" (Smith and Watson 2002b, 34). The bracketed "name withheld" recalls the title of the piece – *Untitled (Self-portrait in Blue)* – suggesting that the refusal to attribute the camera work to a proper name has rebounded on and undone, or un-titled, Tapper's self-portrait.

If *Untitled (Self-portait in Blue)* intimates resentment, then it is most likely directed at the artist himself. Tapper's body of work suggests that his protagonists' inability to connect with women derives from the fact that they are so burdened by the weight of misogyny that they cannot act. The videos repeatedly return to the topic of male violence against women and its roots in art, culture, and religion. In *Graphic Material* (2003) and *I Teach Young Men How to Make Art* (2008), Tapper confronts his responsibilities and his limitations as an artist attempting to undo sexual exploitation. In the former, the hero of a sexually violent comic book that Tapper finds in the trash feels trapped in his role. So the artist digitally animates the comic in the hope that by fragmenting the drawings and altering the chronology of events he can offer the hero other options. But the nature of the source material is ultimately unchangeable, and he fails to engineer a different outcome. In the latter, a student submits a paper detailing how he used the occasion of a class assignment to visit an art exhibition as an opportunity to seduce a woman. Tapper struggles in vain to confront the student on this delicate matter, which falls outside the terms of the normal academic relationship. The accompanying montage of classical drawings, paintings, engravings, and sculpture, all aestheticizing rape, suggests that the problem runs deeper than the art teacher's immediate dilemma. Recalling Taylor's complex reworking of the rape scene in *Birth of a Nation*, Tapper presents himself as a male artist struggling with and constrained by the legacies of sexual and gender violence that are sedimented in visual culture. Autoethnographic self-reflexivity allows him not only to consider how these legacies have shaped his identity as a man, but also to unsettle the traditional division of artistic labour that imagines the male artist-subject as giving shape to pliable, feminized material.

While the pedagogy of misogyny is manifest in the history of art and popular culture, Tapper locates its origins in religion. *Sheh-asani Kirtzono* begins with words presumably addressed to Jewish women: "You see my Jewishness as a test that I've passed; I see it as a wall between us." He then cites the Orthodox Jewish prayer in which little boys are taught to thank God for not making them female, while the girls thank God for making them according to His will. Tapper also describes the story of Yiftach who, in exchange for victory in battle, promises God that he will sacrifice the first animal that he sees, which turns out to be his daughter running to greet him: "What kind of God would want him to have kept that promise?" Yet, rather than suggesting that misogyny is a specifically Jewish phenomenon, Tapper contemplates it as a Jewish man, his videos building complex associations between his psychic and emotional disconnection from women and a history, to which he indirectly but repeatedly refers, of negatively racialized and feminized constructions of the Jewish male body.

In contemporary North America, the body of the Ashkenazi Jew is simultaneously white and racialized, but this was not always nor everywhere the case. In eighteenth- and nineteenth-century Europe, Ashkenazi Jews were seen as "black," and in *The Jew's Body* (1991), Sander Gilman catalogues the various ways in which European anti-Semitic discourse attached physical traits – from the Jewish foot to the Jewish nose – to both account for and detect Jewish "difference." As justifications for Jew-hatred shifted from religious to scientific, physiognomy came to full prominence in the Nazi era. In an essay about Kafka, Gilman (1995) describes how "circumcision came to be seen as the exterior sign of the inherently different nature of the Jewish male" (178). This body stood outside of dichotomous terms of male and female, as well as the newly invented categories of homosexual and heterosexual: "the Jewish male body is also – if only in the rhetoric of the time – not a truly male body; it was the analogue to the body of the homosexual" (180). These ideas were pervasive, and, as Raz Yosef (2004) notes, "The categorization of the Jewish male as a sort of woman appeared not only in the anti-Semitic discourse and in Christian medical scholarship, but also in the writing of Jewish scientists and medical doctors" (17), including Sigmund Freud.

While the stereotype of the feminized Jewish male in nineteenth-century Europe seems the antithesis of the hyper-macho Black male in contemporary North America, they both represent an intersectional gendered racism. Tapper's search for an ethical heteromasculinity thus resonates with Taylor's: where the latter attempts to refuse sexist recuperations of Black masculinity through patriarchal power, the former struggles against potentially misogynist reclamations of the male Jewish body as hypermasculine. Yosef describes, for instance, how Max Nordau set out to create a "new muscular Jew" inspired by the combination of physical culture and nationalism in German gymnastics: "Zionist leaders such as Theodor Herzl and Max Nordau believed that a creation of a new modern male Jew body would solve the physiological and psychological 'complexes' of the Eastern European Jews that were imposed on them by anti-Semitism. Zionism was understood to be a cure for the Jewish gender illness, as well as the economic, political, and national problems of the Jewish people" (19).

Tapper's response to this legacy is whimsical and rather cryptic: throughout his body of work he builds an idiosyncratic, polysemic lexicon of symbols that includes an intermingling of the horn and the Hebrew letter Shin. A proliferation of markings and protrusions, then, operates as a visual counterpoint to the gaps and absences through which Tapper represents his vexed relationships to women. The horn has both celebratory and anti-Semitic connotations. In Jewish practice, a shofar – usually the horn of a ram – is blown on Rosh Hashanah to mark the beginning of the New Year, while in medieval anti-Semitic discourses Jews were imagined to have horns, the sign of the Devil. In more general terms, the horn is a sign of the cuckold in a European context, and of course, it also has phallic associations. Tapper's first reference to the horn is in the mixed media drawings titled *Unicorn Men* (1996–99), which, according to his website, "obsessively piece together diverse icons of masculinity in order to examine and deconstruct codes of gender representation within high and popular culture."[4] In the animated short, *Tumor* (2001), the protagonist is struck by a rock with a note that marks his forehead with the Hebrew letter Shin, out of which sprouts a single horn. The artist himself relates the horn that grows out of the Shin to the mark of Cain, as according to oral tradition in Judaism the mark of Cain was a horn or pair of horns.[5]

In *Lot* (2001), as in *Tumor*, branding with the Shin marks the protagonist as a Jew, visually implicating Tapper in narratives that weave together masculine submission to authority with the sexual violation of women's bodies. With the word Shin superimposed on his forehead, Tapper recounts two stories. The first is the biblical story in which Lot offers up his daughters to lascivious townsmen in lieu of the visiting angels whom God has sent as a test. The second is a narrative about how, as a boy, Tapper's grandfather is asked by soldiers arriving at his village where the prettiest girl in the town lives. He tells them immediately, thus sealing her fate. In Judaism, Shin is used to signify one of the names for God and is inscribed on the mezuzah affixed to the doorframes of homes and businesses. In both *Tumor* and *Lot*, it becomes a bodily imprint that, since the Holocaust, conjures the Nazi practice of tattooing prisoners. Significantly, both the Nazi tattoos and the mark of Cain represent survival, though a precarious and contingent one, as the Nazis only tattooed those who would not be killed immediately, and God gave Cain a mark as a warning for others not to harm him (Mellinkoff 1981). *Lot* thus sets the stage for the questions about Judaism, misogyny, and masculine identity and survival that Tapper continuously poses across his diverse body of work. From animated shorts to confessional videos, he unfolds an extended self-portrait in progress, fashioning – perhaps inventing – a Jewish, masculine self that attempts to be answerable to others.

Robert Lendrum

Robert Lendrum also explores the social production of subjectivity and gender, but where Tapper's videos stage or re-enact narratives in which gender constructions and politics become visible, Lendrum deconstructs the very technologies through which subjectivity, including gender, is perceived. In comparison with Tapper's aesthetic dexterity, these works are, for the most part, deliberately spare and un-cinematic. Compared with Tapper's gentle humour and sincerity, Lendrum's work is blunt and confrontational. And while Tapper's videos advocate political change based on identification and empathy, the impetus behind Lendrum's work is more theoretical than interventionist. Lendrum's *Imposter: A Self Portrait* (2006–08), exemplifies how "autoethnography is a vehicle and a strategy for challenging imposed forms of identity and exploring the discursive possibilities of inauthentic subjectivities" (Russell 1999, 276). In the essay that accompanies the *Imposter* series, Lendrum cites a "tension" between Judith Butler's notion of performativity and Pierre Bourdieu's concept of habitus as formative in the development of the project. In short, he was drawn to the agency but bothered by the seeming lack of social context in Butler's work, and attracted to Bourdieu's attention to the social but resistant to his apparent determinism: "To navigate these ideas, I arrived at a figure that is acutely aware of these opposing influences: the impostor. The impostor demonstrates weaknesses in both of these theories" (Lendrum, 2006–08, 8). A series of four videos made in the context of graduate programs at Concordia University in Montreal and Ryerson University in Toronto, *Imposter* makes heteromasculinity visible and open to critique by refusing to allow it to cohere into recognizable forms.

In the first volume of *The History of Sexuality* (1976), Michel Foucault famously argues that, in the Western tradition of "scientia sexualis," sexuality is understood as revealing the "truth" about the individual. Beginning with *The Audition* (2008), a tape that accompanies the *Imposter* series, Lendrum represents the "truth" of the subject as a kind of endlessly receding horizon. The project begins with the use of market research tools to develop an "objective" self-portrait: "In 2006, I created an online survey asking over 50 questions about my physical, social, subjective and political identity. Over 75 people responded to the survey. The information gathered was used to create a market-research style report. This report was then sent out to actors responding to a casting call for the part of 'Robert.'" These words in on-screen text introduce *The Audition*. Six Montreal actors vying for the role, including three women, interpret the research data they are given and create the character of Robert in wildly different ways, from charming to awkward, and from smooth heterosexual player to gay effete. Lendrum conducts the interviews in disguise, lest the actors connect him to the profile, and we only hear his disembodied voice coming from somewhere outside the locked-off camera shots. It is striking how often the conversations in *The Audition* return to the matter of Robert's sexuality, either spontaneously due to the actors' comments or prompted by Lendrum's questioning. Underscoring Foucault's argument, it is as if by pinning down his sexual orientation, they can discover his essence.

The incoherent, perhaps even failed, impersonation at the centre of the *Imposter* series intensifies the instability that *The Audition*, by refusing to settle the question of Lendrum's sexuality, introduces. To portray himself, 27-year-old Lendrum ultimately selected 47-year-old Jacqueline van de Geer, recently immigrated to Canada from the Netherlands, and, as he explains on his website, different from him in "body, sex, gender, nationality, language and age."[6] The four *Imposter* videos feature van de Geer wearing Lendrum's clothes, sporting a short red wig in imitation of his hairstyle, and attempting to reproduce Lendrum's mannerisms and voice despite her strong Dutch accent. These attempts to sum up and mimic Lendrum's physical presence only underline the impossibility of the attempted substitution. In *My Commonly Used Phrases* (2006), van de Geer stands before a dark curtain and reads a list of expressions such as "Fuck," "No way," and "OK, I'm out," repeating each line four times with different intonations. Her delivery suggests that she is not always aware of what these phrases mean. In *Chipmunks* (2006), shot in the barn at Lendrum's family farm, she recounts in first person how "I" was given a BB gun at the age of 7. The "I" simultaneously registers Robert's presence and, in a performative echo of the psychoanalytic account of the subject's emergence through language, substitutes for him, splitting him from himself. In *My Favourite Jokes* (2006), van de Geer stands against a fake brick wall and tells a series of corny jokes in an approximation of a stand-up comedian, but the clumsy delivery and absence of a laugh track render her performance funny only because it is so badly executed. Finally, *Dudes* (2008), subtitled "Rob's pronounced traits in situations with only heterosexual men (based on survey results)," features van de Geer with three young white men, one of them Lendrum (identified as such only in the credits), in a bare white set decorated with a case of beer, posters of naked women, and a Montreal Canadiens banner. Van de Geer and the actors perform a series of sketches based on traits selected from Robert's personality profile. Van de Geer interprets the space of exclusive heteromasculinity with rough play, excessive swearing, and exaggerated sexual – and sexist – humour. On his website, Lendrum admits, "Jacqueline's performance of me is at times uncomfortable for me to watch, it is out of my character, unpredictable and intensely strange. Her performances were always improvised and never tempered by me." What we see in *Dudes*, then, is actually a woman's (worst) fantasy about what straight men are like on their own. Beyond simply offering himself up for inspection, Lendrum allows himself to become the "material" for a performative substitution, shedding light on heteromasculinity by vacating his subject position so that it can be inhabited by another – or, more accurately, an Other.

In contrast to the "realness" criteria used to judge the drag performers in *Paris Is Burning*, Lendrum uses the purposeful failure of van de Geer's impersonation, as he explains on his website, as a tactic to "create the 'conditions for critical reflection' and to find new knowledge by courting the absurd." He writes, "In fact, the videos offer no point of reference between my doppelganger and myself. The project is not about comparing how close van de Geer's performance comes to reality, rather the 'subject' of the project becomes *the* performance."

In the introduction to *Female Masculinity* (1998), Judith Halberstam argues that what we think of as "dominant" or unmarked masculinity belongs to white male bodies; excessive, even monstrous masculinities are linked to Black, Latino, and working-class men, and "insufficient" masculinities to Asians and upper-class men. Hence, "masculinity ... becomes legible when it leaves the white male middle-class body," and performances of female masculinity are exemplary in achieving this legibility (2). Halberstam writes: "Far from being an imitation of maleness, female masculinity actually affords us a glimpse of how masculinity is constructed as masculinity. In other words, female masculinities are framed as the rejected scraps of dominant masculinity in order that masculinity may appear to be the real thing. But what we understand as heroic masculinity has been produced by and across both male and female bodies" (1).

The tension in authorship and gender between Lendrum's and van de Geer's multilayered, cross-dressing performance pries masculinity from the male body and serves to denaturalize and lay bare the social production of categories that undergird the status quo of gender and sexuality. As Judith Butler (2004b) theorizes, "Sexual difference is not a given, not a premise, not a basis on which to build feminism; it is not that which we have already encountered or come to know; rather, as *a question* that prompts feminist inquiry, it is something that cannot quite be stated, that troubles the grammar of the statement, and that remains, more or less permanently, to interrogate" (179, original emphasis).

By offering up their heteromasculine identities and identity formations for examination, Louis Taylor, Evan Tapper, and Robert Lendrum advance both the interrogation and the dismantling of sexism and heterosexism. Their response to feminist and queer critique is not to refuse masculinity in favour of supposed gender neutrality. Instead, within the limitations and possibilities of their chosen genres, they strategically perform their heterosexual masculinities – and femininities – to draw attention to how gender and sexuality function intersectionally with other vectors of power, including age, religion, class, and race. Their autoethnographic videos create progressive pedagogies that help us imagine, and yearn for, different ways of being.

NOTES

Thanks to the editors and especially to Sarah Trimble for thoughtful assistance and support of this chapter.

1 The ballet dancer, too, is stereotyped as the antithesis of normative masculinity, although Cynthia Weber (2003) identifies how, in films such as *The Full Monty* (1997), *Strictly Ballroom* (1992), and *Billy Elliot* (2000), "men suffering from masculinity crises often engage with dance in order to once again make a credible claim to their masculinity."

2 bell hooks (2004) notes that the report was released at a time when the American military was actively attempting to enlist Black men: "Ironically, the imperialist white-supremacist capitalist state which claimed the black family would be healthier if black men headed households, had no

difficulty taking men away from households and sending them far away from families to wage war, to sacrifice their lives for a country that was denying them full citizenship" (13).

3 http://www.jdate.com/

4 http://evantapper.net/html/Lot_UnicornMen

5 Evan Tapper, conversation with the author, Oct. 2009.

6 http://www.robertlendrum.com

6 Looks Can Be Deceiving: Exploring Transsexual Body Alchemy through a Neoliberal Lens

DAN IRVING

I remember vividly my discovery of female-to-male transsexual (FTM) artist Loren Cameron's work. I stood in a bookstore perusing his internationally acclaimed *Body Alchemy: Transsexual Portraits* (1996). Spellbound, I met the gaze of Cameron's FTM photographic subjects, whose images represented life on the other side of sex reassignment. My gut reaction was not jubilation; instead, I panicked, threw the book down, and bolted out the door in what would be a last attempt to escape my increasingly inevitable transition. This recollection is a useful preface to my critique of Cameron's visual representations of trans men because it points to the arduous task facing artists constructing transsexual imagery. If I had such a visceral response to Cameron's work, how would broader audiences react?

In their introduction to this volume, Sarah Brophy and Janice Hladki speak to the increasingly prevalent conditions of "optical scrutiny" that shape bodies and citizenship status in the current neoliberal moment (Hesford quoted in Brophy and Hladki, 5). In this chapter, I apply a critical political economy framework to critique three photographs in the "Fellas" series published in *Body Alchemy*: a self-portrait of Cameron entitled "Heroes," as well as portraits of "Chris" and "Chase." Though I am wary of economic reductionism, I believe it is critical to pay particular attention to the political impetus underlying visual depictions of trans men as "deserving" neoliberal subjects who properly "belong" to the United States.

Cameron's "ph/autography" is a pedagogical and political project (Halberstam 2005, 114) that explores the potential of "the regime of visuality, particularly photography" (Smith and Watson 2002b, 18), for autobiographical representation through both self-portraits and portraits. As Susanna Egan (1999) argues, such "dialogic" autobiographies are "not simply dialogues because they involve pluralities but are often also dialogic – in terms of their dynamic and reciprocal relations" (23). Taken as a group, the photographs in *Body Alchemy* can be read simultaneously as visual biography, as a kind of relational self-portraiture, and as an exploration of the "frames" that govern FTM representations. Recalling Judith Butler's (2009) analysis of the frames that organize the visual field, attributing recognizably human life to some bodies and not to others, we can ask what kinds of "life" – or "bio" – possibilities do Cameron's (auto)biographical portraits secure for trans subjects? Cameron's approach enacts a relationality whereby the construction of a life is implicated in and by the "bio" dimension of the portraits, which is complexly shaped by a neoliberal biopolitics that delineates what it means to be a "good" biological citizen (Rose 2006).

Portraying transsexual masculinities as normative subjectivities affirms and empowers FTMs by reflecting pieces of their biographical narratives. By depicting the ease with which FTMs fit into hegemonic masculine categories as, simply, "fellas," the photographs in *Body Alchemy* challenge biological determinism and defy the pathologization and vilification of transsexual lives. Cameron's artistic contribution to politicizing transsexual male embodiment works on multiple levels. The "Fellas" series captures the pressures from within certain FTM milieus to occupy a space of normalcy rather than to perform counter-hegemonic gender expressions. Viewers are called to witness a claim that is foundational to transsexual communities: Cameron and his masculine subjects *are* men. For some audiences engaging with Cameron's photographic subjects, which include both Cameron and others, difference gives way to the familiar and makes the achievement of social recognition for trans identities – an essential step towards formally addressing the debilitating consequences of social marginalization (Juang 2006) – more plausible. Such ph/autography is in tune with trans activists lobbying for political rights (e.g., the enshrinement of "gender identity" within human rights and hate crimes legislation), employment rights, and social rights (e.g., access to trans specific and general health care).

Yet, as Simon Strick explores in another context in this volume, surgical denaturalizations of hegemonic ideas about gender can be, and often are, undermined by the visual "reiteration of a normative, naturalizing, and painful notion of gendered self-conduct" (132). Framing FTMs as valuable citizens depends on producing visual auto/biographies that are coherent according to governing rationales, including and especially neoliberalism. As the dominant regime of capital accumulation for over a quarter of a century, neoliberalism celebrates the free market and maintains social order through increasing securitization and surveillance mechanisms. Neoliberal logics are articulated at a micropolitical level through the shaping of the subject as a market wo/man, or an entrepreneurial, autonomous, and self-sufficient being whose democratic freedoms emerge from participating in competitive free market labour and consumer relations (Foucault 2008; Harvey 2005; Read 2003; Rose 2006). Discourses of belonging are securitized such that the ability of individuals to perform as normative subjects determines the response to the question implicitly posed to members of society: "Are you authorized to be here?" (Muller 2004, 287). This chapter thus builds on the work of queer theorists, anti-racist scholar-activists, and feminist political economists who have demonstrated that securing social intelligibility as an active neoliberal subject also hinges on garnering legitimacy according to the imperatives of whiteness, heteronormativity, and nationalism.

Cameron's (self-)portraits of FTM subjectivity valorize FTMs by contextualizing them in terms of neoliberal common sense: as deserving citizens who exemplify proper masculine attributes of autonomy, strength, and a willingness to work hard. This deployment of untroubled normative categories to frame visual models of transsexuality risks further marginalizing individuals who do not fit the neoliberal model of the worthy subject: those who are impoverished, un(der)employed, incarcerated, living with HIV/AIDS, and/or working in criminalized economic sectors. In Cameron's "Fellas" series, trans men located beyond the borders of respectability are not part of the picture.

More than simply mirroring existing social dynamics, art as a cultural institution emerges from multiple sites of power and plays a pivotal role both in forming governable subjects and in reproducing commonsensical discourses that legitimize existing power relations. Furthermore, cultural production can contribute to the construction of beings rendered abject by the logics of capitalism, colonialism, and imperialism (Slaughter 2007, 3, 8). My purpose in critiquing Cameron's (self-)representations, then, is not to suggest that Cameron is a conservative artist. Located within trans and queer communities, Cameron's presentations of alternative visual depictions of manhood through naked self-portraiture have been celebrated for their candour, earning him a reputation as a "gender outlaw" (Whittle 1995, 128). In *Body*

Alchemy, he reveals scars from his mastectomy and body modification through tattooing and weightlifting, injects masculinizing hormones, and breaks down sobbing with a gun held to temple. His work demonstrates that "'gender is always posthuman, always a sewing job which stitches identity into a body bag'" (Halberstam quoted in Whittle 1995, 212). Sex and gender are socially produced and embed norms within the body. Cameron's work has been extolled among progressive artists and scholars for its fluidity and refusal to submit to the dictates of sex/gender power relations as imposed by the observer (Jones 2007; Singer 2006; Whittle 1995). Nevertheless, reflecting on the ways that queer politics have often morphed into approaches that accentuate the normative (Duggan 2005; Puar 2007), it is important to critically inquire into contemporary representations of sex/gender fluidity.

Cultural production is entangled within governing sociopolitical and economic relations that, in turn, influence artistic expression (Schaffer and Smith 2004). My argument here is that even groundbreaking artistic work like Cameron's can inadvertently concretize the market actor as the deserving citizen. As human rights discourses have gained ascendancy within neoliberal contexts, various Indigenous groups, racialized populations, and sexual and gendered minorities have positioned themselves as "activated victim[s]" by crafting personal narratives that often take the form of testimonies (3). Autobiographical accounts of suffering are commodified by, circulated within, and consumed by Western audiences. They elicit the responses necessary to mobilize for rights claims and for the recognition on which the success of those claims is based. But individualizing narratives too often serve to contain what could result in a more radical political trajectory (25–6). As I have discussed elsewhere, this has been the case with transsexual autobiographies that cater mainly to non-trans audiences (Irving 2009).

Acknowledgment of one's existence does not translate directly into social tolerance. Cameron's representation of himself, Chris, and Chase as "regular" people is partially strategic. These clothed trans men posed in routine scenarios stress the relative ease of their assimilation into "normal" life. Continuous reports of violence perpetrated against trans individuals whose sex/gender alterity can be visually detected demonstrate that some of the other portraits in *Body Alchemy* – including the naked self-portraiture and photos of post-operative FTM chests and genitals shaped through hormone treatments, surgeries, or both – would not likely garner widespread acceptance. How do the looking relations among visual artist, image, and viewer shape and negotiate the terms of recognition? How does Cameron, who works not only to counter the invisibility of trans men, but also to compel audiences not to avert their eyes out of fear, anger, or disgust, negotiate the dilemmas of intelligibility?

Contrary to the liberal democratic and universalist notion of humanity, in order to be eligible for rights, one has to be intelligible according to sexed, gendered, heteronormative, imperialist, and racialized power/knowledge relations. Those "deserving" of human rights are individuals and communities who are deemed able to be assimilated into broader power structures. Some difference will be tolerated and, in some cases, celebrated under the moniker of diversity, as long as the individual is understood as non-threatening to governing logics. Consequently, the transsexual as an outlaw who poses a visible and unrelenting challenge to heteronormative gender roles (Stone [1991] 2006), as a "monstrous" identity (Stryker [1994] 2006b), and as an individual who embraces queerness and fights steadfastly against the real "gender terrorists" – defined as defenders of disciplinary regimes of sex/gender (Bornstein 1994) – can be eclipsed, even by trans artists within subcultural spaces, in favour of portraits that emphasize sameness and regularity.

Historicizing *Body Alchemy*

> For the longest time, transsexuals and especially transsexual men (females-to-males) have been virtually invisible ... Marginalized ... transsexuals have occupied no real space of our own. In the last decade or so, more and more transsexual people have been ... beginning to represent ourselves for the first time and develop our own voice. Body Alchemy is the first photodocumentation of transsexual men from within our community.
>
> Loren Cameron, Preface to *Body Alchemy*

Until the early 1990s, the trans struggle for voice was configured in terms of transsexual people challenging their objectification by non-trans "experts." Yet, this fight for subject-hood obscures differences within transsexual demographics. Who are the visible transsexuals on the front lines of the struggle for recognition? Or, to pose the question negatively: Why do the significant number of transsexuals who are incarcerated, impoverished, disabled, and/or criminalized not constitute the public faces or voices of transsexuality, especially in trans-produced representations of sex/gender alterity intended for a popular audience?

The historical development of the term "transsexuality" reveals the complex negotiations transsexuals undertook to move from obscurity towards social integration, which would provide grounds for accessing the rights that citizenship entails. In North America, transsexuals were defined primarily by the medical and psychological professions as mentally ill because our desire to embody our sex/gender identities challenged the dominant understanding that biological sex – determined in utero – is immutable (Meyerowitz 2002). Challenging the pathologization of transsexuality remains the fundamental task of intellectual and political resistance, and efforts to gain legitimacy for transsexuality as a valid sex/gender identity are often articulated through the rhetoric of self-determination. According to this logic, transsexual men are simply living true to our spirits, which are hidden by the two-sex/gender system. Achieved through technological, legal, and social processes of reassignment, the de-pathologization of transsexuality not only demonstrates the validity of the sexed body and gender performance, but also reflects the liberal individualist foundations from which such efforts emerged.

Scholars engaging with transsexual subjectivities and politics as material processes ought to examine the cultivation of reifying approaches to sex/gender self-determination (Irving 2009). Medical and psychological professionals' definition of transsexuality as a physical and mental defect was shaped by more than concern for the health of their patients; this definition also channelled broader anxieties regarding transsexuals' ability to contribute to the wealth of the nation (Irving 2008). The major question determining a transsexual individual's eligibility for medicalized transition has been and still is to a large extent whether or not that subject would be able to contribute, post-transition, to the development of society, or whether the disorder would relegate them to social parasitism (Cauldwell 2001).

Medical discourses of sex/gender pathology were also produced and circulated through visual depictions. One of the most telling images comes from a pictorial representation of a transsexual man published in *Sexology Magazine* in 1949 and entitled "Psychopathia Transexualis." We see a two-headed, two-bodied monstrous creature whose masculinized top half appears to be choking its feminized bottom half out of existence. The wavy shape of this caricature and the tensor bandage recognizable as a method of binding denote a warping of the (gendered) image. Resembling a genie emerging from a bottle, the trans man is positioned as threatening to normative sex/gender relations. If the image was inverted, the viewer would be looking at a victim of sex/gender carnage; however, when looking at the image right side up, one bears witness to an unfamiliar and violent entity: the transsexual "psychopath" (see figure 6.1).

Intersecting relations of governance influence this image of trans masculinity. The sketch was published in the immediate aftermath of the Second World War, when the state and social institutions aimed to reconstruct a heteronormative gender regime that positioned men as primary breadwinners and women as reproductive labourers. In this context, representations of the transsexual as an enemy lurking within helped foster the social anxiety necessary for "(re)making normal" (Brock 2003). In the postwar rhetoric of sexology, the transsexual man becomes visible as a delusional entity that chokes the life out of the properly feminine citizen and renders her un(re)productive. Extending these observations to the current moment, the ongoing subordination of FTMs makes sense in the context of neoliberalism. As a political rationality, neoliberalism requires "a specific and consequential organization of the social, the subject and the state [that involves] the explicit imposition of a particular form of market rationality on these spheres" (Brown 2006, 693). Discourses that emphasize personal responsibility for one's well-being through the exhibition of financial, mental, and physical fitness exemplify neoliberal common sense. One's value – indeed, one's humanity – is measured through labour, consumption, and other (economic) contributions to society.

The discourse of the return of the working-class hero has played an important role in justifying hyper-exploitative labour relations. This heroism is connected to hegemonic masculinities that are historically tied to the image of the heterosexual, white, blue-collar male labouring in the manufacturing sector. The decline of this sector in the global North and the rise of (feminized) service sector jobs have created a crisis of Euro-American masculinity (Halberstam 2005, 137–8). By no means does this crisis render hegemonic working-class masculinity obsolete. Rather, it indexes the social anxiety created when material conditions and social relations no longer cohere with symbolic ideals – in this case, the vital role that labour plays in the making of a man. Anti-welfare sentiments exemplify the clash between hetero-/homonormative masculinities and men's actual social locations. In 1996 (the year *Body Alchemy* was published), in the United States, the Clinton administration passed the Personal Responsibility and Work Opportunity Reconciliation Act, which contributed to an increasingly hostile

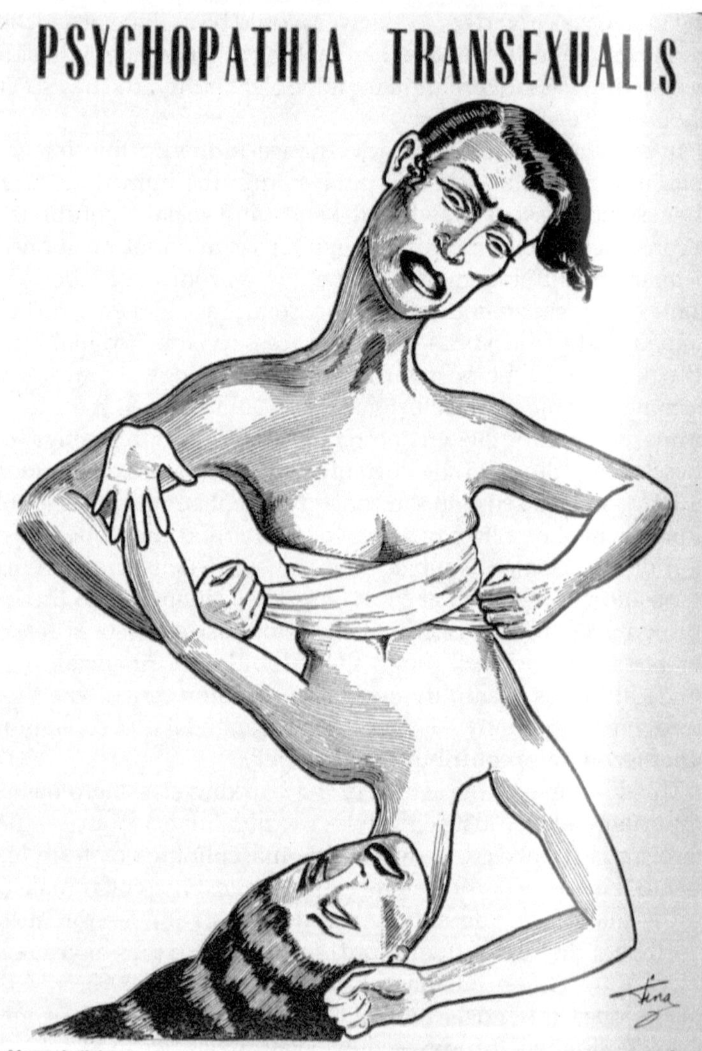

PSYCHOPATHIA TRANSEXUALIS

Many individuals have an irresistible desire to have their sex changed surgically. Some females want to become males, some males want to change into females. These persons are not necessarily homosexuals. Our surrealist artist vividly illustrates the case of a young girl who violently insisted to become a male. She wore only male clothing and in a desperate effort to change her sex she bound her breasts so they would take on a more male-like appearance. The dual personality is shown in the two figures, merged into one. The top represents the "masculine" female, the bottom the real-recessive female. Individuals of this type are psychopathic, i.e., sick persons. This condition is by no means rare. Many medical men have had such cases.

274 Sexology, December, 1949

6.1. "Psychopathia Transexualis" (*Sexology Magazine*, 1949). Used by permission of the Kinsey Institute for Research in Sex, Gender, and Reproduction.

climate wherein poverty was repositioned as an individual defect and the un(der)employed and poor were blamed for their socio-economic locations.

What is more, (economically) normative masculinities are inseparable from processes of racialization. Configurations of racialized bodies as criminal, pathological, and threatening to national security have proliferated under neoliberalism (Cohen 1999; Puar 2007; Razack 2008). As I will explore in my analysis of "Chase," below, for racialized FTMs, their monstrosity is not rooted entirely in their embodied avowals of the mutability of sex; rather, the public perception of their sexed bodies and gender expressions as dangerous also derives from the predominance of whiteness (Noble 2006).

Various transsexual networks have challenged the pathologization that excludes many transsexuals from the logics and practices of national belonging. However, a paradox exists. Trans activists, including those, like Cameron, who produce visual representations of trans lives, seek to expose the binary system as a narrow biocentric fallacy. Yet, even as their resistance efforts open up spaces for recognizing a multiplicity of sexes and genders, this recognition is located firmly within the class-based and nationalist logics that mediate sex/gender categories. In other words, it is by occupying a privileged position within these governing systems that transsexual male subjects become palatable.

Snapshots of FTM Lives

Consider the photographic representation of embodied trans masculinity entitled "Heroes," which features Cameron standing upright with both hands wrapped around an American flagpole. Showing his slightly furrowed brow, this self-portrait signals a steely determination. Cameron's confident gaze is fixed forward in a way that defies challenge. His relaxed jaw and slightly raised chin do not, however, suggest a cheeky adolescent defiance. This is not an image of an unsure boy; rather, we witness a proud man (see figure 6.2).

In terms of the positioning of the artist-activist holding the flag, "Heroes" resembles freedom-fighting iconography that can be interpreted either as part of a militant subversive politic or as part of a patriotic military masculinity that contributes to a wider imperialist order. In his artist's statement, Cameron discusses participating in one of the first Trans Pride marches in San Francisco. The strength that trans demonstrators mustered to participate in the march, where they were subjected to the sometimes hostile gaze of onlookers, is a strength that

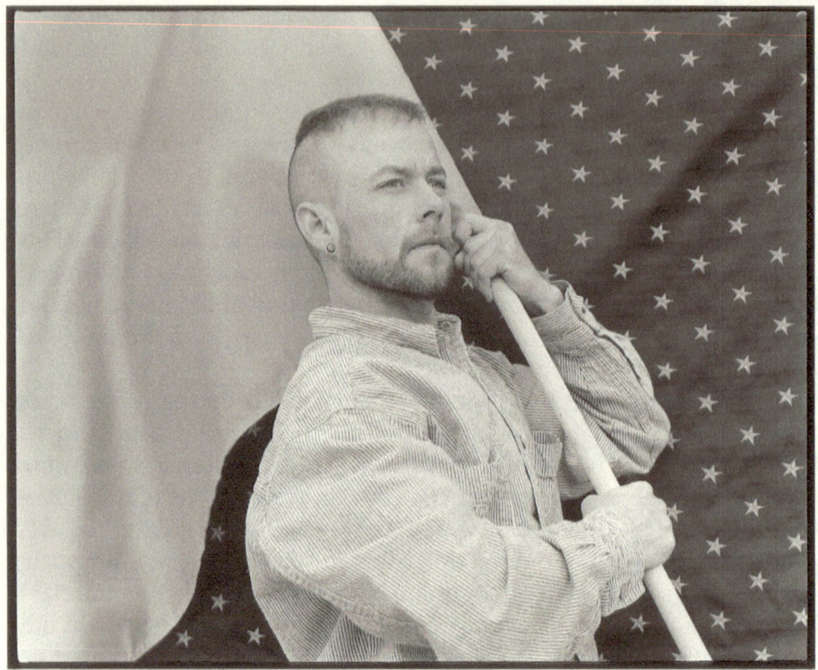

6.2. "Heroes" (Loren Cameron, *Body Alchemy: Transsexual Portraits*. San Francisco: Cleis Press, 1996, 19). Used by permission of Cleis Press.

his photographic subjects share. Cameron states, "I marvel at their strength: like tempered steel, it is the kind that propels armies and liberationists … When I *look through my lens at them*, I *recognize the power of such willfulness*. I want the world to know the *force* of their beauty" (1996, 19, emphases added). Here, it is more than the lens of the camera that structures the photographer's view. Cameron shares the commonsense perspective of the witness whose vision is discursively shaped. For those outside of FTM communities, the man seen here is not known as Loren Cameron, FTM artist/activist. He appears as an attractive, young, able-bodied American male. He passes as a white working-class man, a soldier perhaps – a patriot. As such, his rightful place within the nation is unlikely to be questioned.

What is the "*force* of [this] beauty"? "Heroes" was taken in 1996, five years after the first US-led invasion of Iraq. This self-representation of

FTM masculinity thus participates in dominant constructions of American nationhood. The American male as a symbolic ideal generates images of primarily white, able-bodied, working- or middle-class masculinities. These desirable attributes unite individuals occupying a vast territorial space by fostering a sense of familiarity. The label "stranger" is reserved for those on the outside of the psychic and physical borders of the nation. In this context, what norms, if any, is this transsexual self-portrait transgressing?

How would this visual text be read differently if, for instance, an FTM of Middle Eastern descent were pictured holding the "stars and stripes"? Since Orientalist and imperialist frames already render such racialized bodies monstrous (Puar and Rai 2002), such a depiction of FTM masculinity would reveal more than the social construction of sex/gender. In the strategic battle for trans rights that presents FTMs as assimilable subjects, a trans man of Middle Eastern descent holding the American flag would have denoted a "stranger within" (Phelan 2001) well before September 11, 2001. This racialized body cannot pass as normal within the context of American imperialism and, as a result, would be a dangerous FTM identity to foreground in the struggle for legitimacy. Cameron's patriotic masculinity enables him, and other FTMs who are read as white, to be associated in the public imaginary with relative economic and national security, as well as physical and mental health. This translates into easier assimilation into normative relations of power in spite of our transsexuality.

As he represents himself in "Heroes," Cameron is not a casualty of the war on sex/gender variance. There is nothing visibly queer about him to denote his participation in the battle for gender and (trans)sexual freedom. This begs the question: to which or from which battle is this hero (re)turning? This line of inquiry is crucial given that US and Canadian imperialisms – and the Orientialism, xenophobia, and racism that attend them – have been reconfigured and further entrenched in the post-9/11 era. Moreover, given that conceptualizations of sex/gender transgression are structured by Western dualisms, Cameron's representation of the white working-class transsexual male as heroic is rooted in the colonial histories that continue to animate contemporary imperialisms. The erasure of sex/gender variance in many Indigenous societies was part of the genocide perpetuated by European and, later, US and Canadian colonial powers. In contemporary settler-colonial societies, while there is some acknowledgment of Two-Spirited and/or trans people within wider trans communities, they remain marginal. The oppression of Two-Spirited people is not fully articulated when framed solely in terms of rights to "gender identity" and its expression. After all, the reverence for sex and gender alterity within various Indigenous cultures stems, in part, from economies that differed drastically from the capitalist private property form. Decolonizing struggles that include emancipating Two-Spirited subjects reject the fragmented liberal democratic model of rights claims. Expressions of sex and gender are intrinsically embedded in questions of land, language, history, and Indigenous sovereignty.

Viewed through such long historical lenses, the "Heroes" photo aligns itself with the settler-colonial imagination. A complex web of colonial relations comprises, in part, the "force" of the beauty of these portraits of heroic transsexual subjects. When the gaze of the FTM patriot meets that of the already acknowledged, "proper" US or Canadian citizen, what "hegemonic bargain" is struck, rendering the photographic subject beautiful at the expense of the colonized Other (Chen 1999)? Would a visibly Indigenous trans man holding the flag of the American Indian Movement be considered a hero? Would his struggle for Indigenous self-determination and land, along with his non-normative sex/gender, be construed as a threat to US and/or Canadian national security rather than as an image of forceful beauty belonging within its rubric?

Recall that the introductory statement accompanying this self-portrait begins with Cameron's memory of marching with an "FTM Trans Pride" banner. With his body and identity exposed, he recalls, "I wanted to watch people's reactions to us, and more than anything, I wanted to walk with dignity" (Cameron 1996, 19). All sex/gender variant people are familiar with the exhilaration and relief that comes with publicly expressing one's sex/gender identity, as well as with the fear that this entails. The withholding of social acceptance is deadly for many trans people. I have been arguing that, historically speaking, this refusal is based on systems of dominance that intersect with and go beyond the sex/gender binary tout court. Today, the political dangers of ph/autographic productions of and by trans people reside in their potential complicity with these overlapping systems of domination.

"Chris" aims to achieve the same goal as "Heroes" – to assure viewers of the subject's normality. The portrait emphasizes working-class masculinity, calling to mind the iconic image of the rugged worker. Chris sits clad in a hard hat, work clothes, and steel-toed boots, the sun shining on his weathered face as he takes a break. Perched on top of the metal pipes with which he presumably works, he exudes confidence as he gazes, brow furrowed, directly into the camera. The play on phallocentricity that informs the positioning of Chris on top of long steel rods is obvious. Unless the observer was informed of Chris being a FTM, he passes undetected as just one of the guys, a regular, working-class stiff. Framed by the masculinized industrial setting, this man is on top of his game.

The politics of passing that shape the construction of Chris' image resonate with the tensions inherent in neoliberal labour relations. The photo obscures the actual gendered, racial, and national composition of the American working class. By using capitalist logic to frame the transsexual as a productive body, this visual representation of FTM masculinity undermines solidarity among the working class, working poor, and un(der)employed. Again, we must inquire, at whose expense? Neoliberal economic restructuring has significantly reduced the number of blue-collar manufacturing jobs in the global North. "Chris" functions unmistakably to reinforce the dominant representation of the typical American worker, which remains the blue-collar, heterosexual, masculine, white, able-bodied male. In addition to obscuring shifts within employment sectors as part of global economic restructuring, this visual representation masks the location of a significant portion of the transsexual demographic. The few empirical findings available concerning working-class transsexuals locate many within the service sector comprised mainly of precarious, low-paying, part-time "McJobs" with little or no benefits (Hirschman 2001).

Cameron's artist's statement points to tensions in Chris' life, but, in keeping with the neoliberal discourse of self-sufficiency, it suggests that Chris is prevailing under adverse conditions. We are informed that he works two shifts daily at two factories in order to survive. He is a single parent whose girlfriend resides hundreds of miles away and who travels frequently to maintain his relationship. As a result, he "doesn't sleep too much" (Cameron 1996, 64). The message conveyed by the composition of the portrait, though, is that Chris is managing these stresses. Here, neoliberal discourses of strength and autonomy are mediated by gendered roles and expectations. Taking it like a man, Chris sits in the sunlight on a much-deserved break, rejuvenating before returning to work.

Chris' transsexual embodiment is shrouded in protective clothing. Similar to the hard plastic and steel that armour his body, his outwardly coherent appearance operates as a shield protecting him from the unsafe working conditions that might result from his transsexuality. Like women, as well as effeminate and/or racialized men, visible transsexuals are at serious risk of workplace discrimination, harassment, and assault. The probability of this happening to Chris is low as he is portrayed as a relatively normal guy (single parenthood notwithstanding) to whom many non-trans people can relate. The point here is not to dispute Chris' self-identification, but to pose questions about the political and conceptual implications of the reproduction of this particular image in Cameron's collection of trans (self-)portraits. For example, how does Cameron frame the ph/autographical subject to generate what Brophy and Hladki, in the final chapter of this volume, theorize as ethical encounters with embodied difference? And what is at stake, politically and pedagogically, in Cameron's intersecting representations of transsexual embodiments? Again, we have to interpret "Chris" within the broader context not only of heteronormative sex/gender dichotomous relations, but also of neoliberal discourses that celebrate the labourer even as neoliberal capitalism generates conditions of hyper-exploitation that harm the body, mind, and spirit. Not many people are getting much sleep these days.

The photo entitled "Chase" features a Black FTM, one of two racialized men in the "Fellas" series (see figure 6.3). Chase is an extremely muscular man whose physique results from being a "disciplined, competitive athlete" (Cameron 1996, 68). Chase's body is under significant stress despite being photographed in a seated position. He is straining to lift unseen objects (presumably weights), his muscles taut, the chords in his neck bulging, his face grimacing, and his head tilting upwards. Cameron is working towards an inclusive understanding of FTM diversity through his depiction of "Fellas" from different class and racial locations. But the meanings derived from these diverse representations vary due to the social contexts, including neoliberal and subcultural ones, that frame audience perceptions.

As with the first two images, Chase's manhood must be seen within the contexts of whiteness and the ongoing capitalist (re)constructions of the economy and nation. Black male viewers and other racialized and colonized FTMs may see themselves and their own struggles in the obvious stress that pains Chase's body. However, white audiences may read this image in ways that reinforce their personal investments in white supremacy. In his analysis, in this volume, of Black Canadian filmmaker Louis Taylor's family portrait, *Esther, Baby and Me*, Richard Fung illuminates the ways that Taylor's autoethnographic video navigates the abjection and hyper-sexualization of the straight Black man

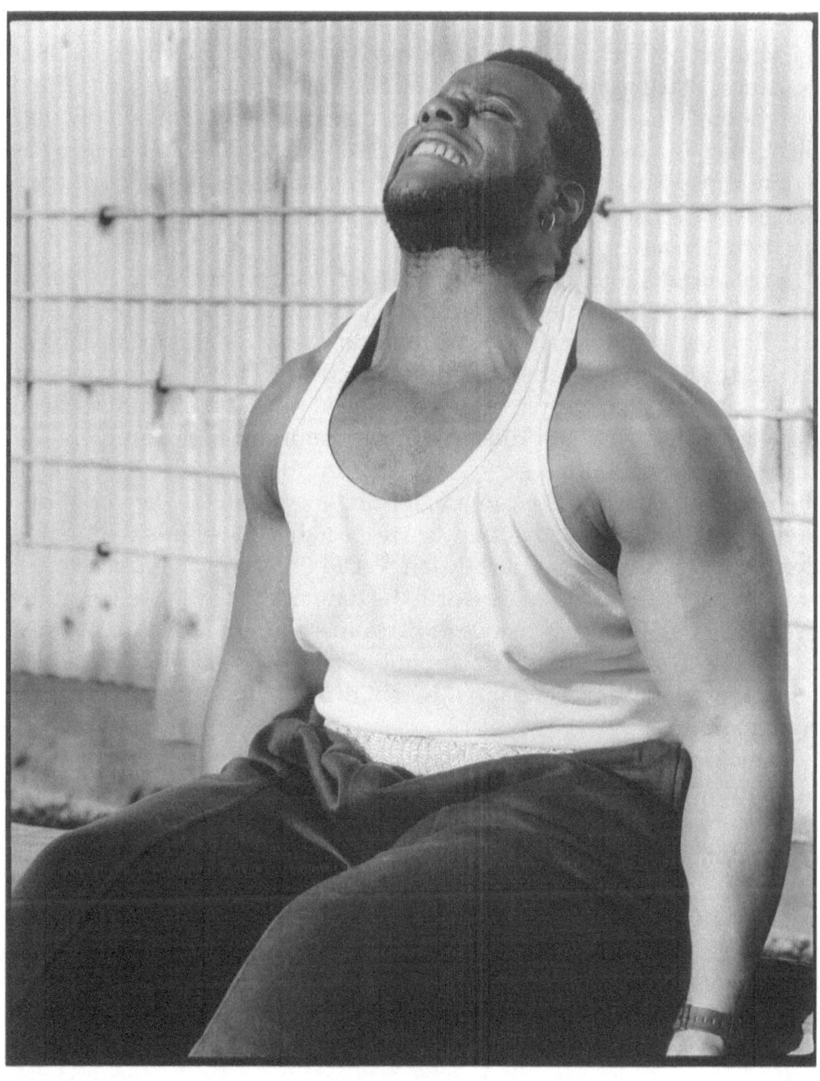

6.3. "Chase" (Cameron, *Body Alchemy*, 68). Used by permission of Cleis Press.

(84–8). Building on Fung's analysis, I am arguing here that the bid for recognition of Black FTMs involves more than battling forms of pathologization that render transsexual bodies monstrous: a portion of the weight that Chase bears inheres in the discursive construction of "the" Black man as a hyper-sexualized aggressor (hooks 2004, 67). Passing as a non-transsexual man will not necessarily translate into the inclusion of Chase as a "normal" social subject; instead, his passing threatens to position him as a sexual predator.

A racialized body, Chase is framed in terms of deviance. His status as an FTM further removes him from the parameters of social belonging, and the mental, physical, and spiritual suffering that this exclusion entails is written on his body. We witness his pained facial expression, his teeth gnashing, his body working, his eyes shut. Chase, with his head cast upwards, projects a different image from those of Cameron and Chris, whose masculine expressions are performed partially through their defiant gaze into the camera, locking eyes with the viewer. While they must demonstrate that they are respectable, the efforts required to do so are not the same as the burden placed on Chase. Even as he must work constantly to prove his worth, he dare not look the viewer in the eye. The palatable performance of Black masculinity is one that, as bell hooks (1992) has argued, is compatible with a visual field in which white masculine subjects claim the right to look and, in turn, refuse that right to others.

Cameron's statement regarding Chase's industriousness vis-à-vis bodybuilding is also significant given the ways that race, class, and gender are enmeshed in neoliberal society. Like many Black men, Chase can garner some degree of respect as a man by harnessing patriarchal discourses of competitiveness via athletic performance (hooks 2004). Yet, his embodiment of the fit neoliberal subject will not elevate him to a straightforwardly privileged position. The fact that he displays an entrepreneurial spirit as a "self-employed fitness trainer" (68) will challenge racialized notions of the (un)deserving neoliberal citizen. While Chris can be shown relaxing, Chase's quest for recognition as a legitimate subject needs to be much more convincing. Not only does he have to be depicted as working, but he also struggles against racist notions of irresponsibility, ineffectiveness, and mental inferiority (hooks 2004; Jackson 2006). Chase's large and muscular frame does not translate into heroic masculinity, nor will it necessarily translate into a labouring body. Yet, Jasbir Puar (2007) explains that the "ascendancy of whiteness" can interpolate "appropriate multicultural ethnic bodies" within the fold of the nation (25). It is possible for Chase to be included in the national body as an "exceptional patriot" provided that he exercises "fitness within capitalism" (26). For some racialized subjects, this translates into having access to material and cultural capital, usually by occupying a highly skilled position within the labour economy and being able to actively participate as consumers. Chase will be recognized as a citizen via his "market virility" (26). To ease the anxiety projected onto the body of this racialized and transsexual Other, Cameron explains that Chase is also pursuing a university degree and is interested in political science and finance (68).

Conclusions: Towards Radical Democratic Representations

Ongoing struggles to achieve legitimation for transsexuals confront social terrains rich in complexity. As the relational self-portraiture in Cameron's "Fellas" series demonstrates, there is significant pressure for FTMs to perform hegemonic masculinities. These visual representations and the statements accompanying them resist the decades of pathologization that have situated transsexuals as unintelligible beings. As Egan (1999) suggests, in "dialogic autobiography," "the politics of autobiography are more than personal and extend into the desire for change beyond any individual life in question" (225, 229). But Cameron's ph/autographic resistance to pathologization capitulates, in "Fellas," to the individualizing logic of heteronormative, colonial, and racist liberal-democratic and capitalist relations. The individual worth of some trans men is demonstrated, but to the detriment of others.

To recast the challenge for cultural producers, we might ask: How can the visual arts strengthen the interventions already made by many community-based trans activists to link sex/gender oppression to other power relations? There are significant examples of trans visual artists such as Del LaGrace Volcano who are creating images that test the limits of power in order to rekindle our political imaginations. With respect to the pedagogical and political role of visual art in the framing of radical democratic politics, these artists' methods serve as significant counterpoints to the normalizing impetus of Cameron's (self-)portraiture.

According to Susan Stryker (2006a), a transgender method is one that "disrupts, denaturalizes, rearticulates" – that places visual portrayals of transsexuality in direct engagement with "the operation of systems and institutions that simultaneously produce various possibilities of viable personhood and eliminate others" (3). Like the effect that double-exposure has on film, there is a ghostly presence that lurks in the background of transsexual imagery. What critical interventions result when visual images are created to illuminate this entity and enable audiences to listen to apparitions, to hear the unspoken and see its invisible workings (Halberstam 2005, 60–1; Puar 2007)? The ghost lurking behind images of recognizable transsexual men is a "social figure, and investigating it can lead to that dense site where history and subjectivity make social life" (Gordon quoted in Halberstam, 60). This ghostly presence serves to illuminate the multiple socio-economic, political, and cultural forces that suture the identities of FTMs into coherent form.

Both Sandy Stone (2006) and Stryker emphasize the phantasmal underpinnings of transsexual subjectivities. Stone channels the spectre of a more militant, post-transsexual subjectivity – one whose non-normative trajectory towards sexed embodiment and whose commitment to challenging hegemonic gender performance must be(come) visible. Stone thus challenges transsexual individuals to create counter-discourses by speaking from beyond the boundaries of gender (230). This entails engaging in celebratory proclamations of our difference and striking repeatedly against the systemic power relations that comprise the transsexual "empire" (Stone 2006). Likewise, Stryker (2006b) conjures the transsexual monster as an unrelenting storyteller whose sutured body confronts an audience's fears of inauthenticity. The monster is not a recognizable entity and does not speak in terms of "I am"; rather, this assemblage signals what has been done to, through, and by "us" (Stryker 2006b).

Visual representations of transsexual subjectivities that are attentive to the ghoulish, ghastly, and monstrous demonstrate that the individual photographic subject does not, in fact, emerge onto the social and visual scene alone. Viewers are implicated in these visual landscapes because they are not put at ease through the invocation of the familiar. They are forced to confront sex and gender as it is mediated by other systems of power in ways that trigger their anxiety, fear, anger, and curiosity. The images confronting them cannot easily be contained through rationality; the wider audience is also haunted.

This relational approach to transsexual (self-)representation lends itself to radical politics through the construction of a "transgendered gaze" that fosters a critical re-conceptualization of sex/gender relations through the lens of neoliberal power relations. In his critique of the visual work of Del LaGrace Volcano, T. Benjamin Singer (2006) argues that Volcano's approach to trans (self-)portraiture is linked to the "sublime" as an alternative mode of interpretation and knowing. Singer defines the sublime as "*'reason (being) forced to confront its incapacity to deal rationally with the infinite'*" (616, original emphasis). Relating ethically to visual representations of non-normative bodies requires a shift from the aesthetic notion of beauty to that of the sublime. This shift addresses the ways that beauty is shaped by governing relations shared by artist, photographic subject, and audience. Within this logic, transsexuals who reflect back to the audience aspects of themselves can be inscribed as beautiful. FTMs whose masculine personae coincide with neoliberal discourses of nationalism and virility will not likely be dismissed as grotesque.

In contrast to the hegemonic bargains struck by Cameron's "Fellas," Volcano's work exhibits the revelry of disobedience and the refusal to be disciplined for being "unreasonable." Posted on his website, his "Selves" and "Gender Optional" series provide useful examples of Volcano's resistance.[1] His ph/autography refuses to abide by neoliberal discourses of maturity and financial fitness that "make the man" in late capitalist society. The titles of some of his photos in the "Gender Optional" series eschew the modernist temporal progression from boyhood to manhood. He insists on referring to himself affectionately as "Del Boy." He photographs himself clad in attire and in poses that queer his masculinity. Other photos, such as "Andro Del," confront the relationship between gender and race in contemporary society through his embodied construction of hyper-whiteness as the context in which gender is produced (Singer 2006, 613–14).

Volcano's work is disruptive, unsettling, and provocative. When placed beside "Heroes," "Chris," "Chase," and other normative depictions of FTM masculinity premised on worth and patriotism, Volcano makes it clear that he is no ordinary "Fella." The ghosts he stirs within the viewer transport us to the sublime. We are moved. To feel the sublime is to feel overwhelmed as one confronts the terror of boundaries "collaps[ing] at the edge of the limitless" (Singer 2006, 616). Trans visual self-portraiture need not emphasize the normal to win forms of recognition that will benefit only a few. It must implode all of the systemic barriers that leave the most marginalized out of the picture.

NOTE

1 The "Gender Optional" series is best viewed as a sequence of images, and can be accessed via Volcano's website: http://www.dellagracevolcano.com/genderopt.html#1

7 Visceral (Auto)biographies: Plastic Surgery and Gender in Reality TV

SIMON STRICK

Today's "wound culture" (Seltzer 1998) abounds with confessional presentations of one's innermost conditions. In fact, as Dieter Mersch (2003) has put it, we are only subjects insofar as we make our selves visible and insert them into the visual and narrative frames of the present cultural condition. The television genre known as "reality TV" (McCarthy 2007; Biressi and Nunn 2005) is one of the most popular and controversial arenas for the fabrication of public selves. In shows like *Survivor*, *Big Brother*, and *The Apprentice*, reality television employs modes of representation that foreground personal trauma, stress, and the testing of a person's psychological, physical, and social limits. Ahmed and Stacey (2001) have argued that the selves presented in these shows are not only largely (auto-)biographically produced, but also that these biographies rely heavily on revealing a person's trauma and pain. In this view, the successful narration of the public self is largely dependent on a person's ability to disclose his or her traumatic experience. One is only able to produce a public self if one articulates it within the rhetoric of personal hurt or grief, and, eventually, the successful transformation of trauma into life-changing experience. This chapter examines visual narrations of transforming selves as they are produced in the particularly spectacular and controversial reality show, *The Swan*, which depicts women undergoing plastic surgery. As these women commit to plastic surgery in order to "change their lives," as the show's slogan announces, the program (and the women themselves) fabricate a particular form of visual (auto)biography, taking medical procedures as turning points to narrate a "before" and "after" self. This seemingly basic model of narration (before/after) raises two complex critical questions: How is the notion of change/rupture produced narratively within a technology that has been described as a tool of gender coercion and the mutilation of female bodies (Blum 2003)? And, second, how do these narrations of a cosmetic self relate to both plastic surgery (K. Davis 1995, 2003) *and* autobiography as practices of agency and self-empowerment?

Plastic Surgery's Double Edge

Feminist critics have for a long time called attention to the simultaneity of emancipative programs and modes of self-disciplining. Among them, Sandra Lee Bartky (1988) has analysed feminine beauty practices as being complicit with an internalized male gaze, while at the same time related to *jouissance*, self-expression, and the articulation of self-empowerment. Following this argument, Elizabeth Grosz (1994) has written:

> The line between compliance and subversion is always a fine one, difficult to draw with any certainty. All of us, men as much as women, are caught up in modes of self-production and self-observation; these modes may entwine us in various networks of power, but never do they render us merely passive and compliant. They are constitutive of both bodies and subjects ... Its enmeshment in disciplinary regimes is the condition of the subject's social effectivity, as either conformist or subversive. (144)

In this perspective, cosmetic surgery and other "technologies of gender" may instantiate both disciplinary and self-empowering programs via the female body. Kathy Davis' (1995, 2003) empirical and theoretical work on consumers of plastic surgery procedures has stressed that any feminist critical approaches to this technology must engage with the double force implicit in the production of a gendered body: the production of an "embodied female subjectivity," on the one hand, and an "objectified female body," on the other (Davis 2003, 85).

While this simultaneity of empowerment and discipline is vital to understanding late capitalist technologies of the body, the visual, bodily, and self-fashioning strategies at work in *The Swan* complicate this dichotomy. By exploring narrative strategies of self-transformation, this chapter opens up the rigid binary of oppression versus agency and navigates the increasingly complex area between empowerment and normalization, agency and disciplinary apparatuses, which has been created by contemporary bodily technologies. Addressing the narratability of the cosmetic self, I argue, with Maasen (2005), that technologies only become meaningful – where emancipation and oppression denominate two possible meanings – through their enmeshment in discursive networks and social narrations. Approaching the *narratability* of subjects produced by beauty technologies allows us to engage with the discursive framing of technology, to shed light on its complicity both in the production of gendered bodies and in their assessment by an audience as, for example, "empowered" or "oppressed." How cosmetic selves and cosmetic technologies are narrated will therefore be my key question in addressing *The Swan*. The surgery show, which sees female candidates competing for the "greatest personal makeover,"[1] illustrates the ambivalence of cosmetic surgery discourses as it oscillates between the production of "successfully made-over" femininities and narratives of personal improvement and empowerment. My reading of the series specifically addresses the corporeality of cosmetic technology and its relation of the physical and visceral to the narration of subjectivation, thereby leading to an understanding of cosmetic surgery as a somatic technology of the self. By analysing the visceral aspects of *The Swan*, I propose that narrative moments of pain, crisis, and trauma function as tropes that allow for the narration of plastic surgery procedures as technologies of embodiment. Pain and trauma are staged as instances where the material body (the object of surgery) and the female subject (the consumer of surgery) meet, thus enabling viewers to imagine plastic surgery as a technology to "make over" not only the body, but also the self. Through the exhibition of pain, trauma, and bodily states of exception, plastic surgery shows represent cosmetic procedures as technologies that can produce an embodied, radically gendered, self.

The Swan

The Swan is an internationally distributed format, produced and broadcast in countries such as the United States (Fox Television) and Germany (Pro 7). The German format features fourteen candidates competing against each other for the title of the "Swan pageant"; the women go through a series of cosmetic and surgical procedures, fitness drills, and psychological counselling sessions. Each episode culminates in the evaluation of two candidates by a team of "experts" consisting of cosmetic surgeons, fitness trainers, and psychologists who decide which of the women has gone through the "greatest transformation" and may advance to the Swan finals. Each time, the narrative of personal change or improvement constructs the women as having transformed from ugly ducklings to beautiful swans. The controversy surrounding the program at the time of its airing resulted from the double meaning implicit in this narrative: health politicians and many newspaper critics, while largely failing to address *The Swan*'s preoccupation with the normalization of femininity, saw it as an uncritical and potentially dangerous promotion of plastic surgery. Others – including people writing in the show's online forums – regarded *The Swan* as an incentive for women to take charge of their own bodies and to become the woman they always wanted to be, even if that meant replicating normative views of the female body.

The narrative structure of each episode reflects these aspects of the gendered self – normality, performance, and agency – and recreates them in the language of trauma. For example, in episode 3 of the German series, we see contestant Annette with her partner and daughter, joking and hugging in their living room. This image of the happy family is contrasted by the voice-over:

> Annette feels insecure and miserable. The reason: she was abused in childhood. Her mother left her father, but her new stepdad also put his aggression on little Annette. For sixteen years now she has been living with Frank. For him, Annette is the love of his life, but Annette is scared to marry him. She's scared of the final step. The trauma of her childhood overshadows her whole life.

From the start, the candidates of *The Swan* are marked as wounded women who, for various reasons, fail in their proper gender performances; for example, they have been abused as children and fail to marry, they work as motorbike mechanics and are no longer regarded as women by colleagues and husbands, or they have simply been "punished by nature" (episode 4) with a non-normative body. Following these introductions that diagnose each woman as traumatized or wounded, every episode then depicts the women confessing their psychic and bodily traumas to the camera, always in tears. Annette: "When I look into the mirror, I hate what I see. This is just not who I am … I am ready to change, so I can live a new life" (episode 3). These introductions not only present the candidates as feeling ugly or wishing for an improvement in their appearances, but also invariably suggest that the women experience a split between their imagined identities as women and the identities represented by their bodies – a split that the show's experts translate into a diagnosis of "living in the wrong body," thereby appropriating a trope from popular narratives of transgender identities. The therapeutic narrative consistently links personal trauma and the desire for change to surgical procedures and the male expertise of the surgeons and fitness trainers. For example, when the candidate is brought into the operating room to be greeted by the surgeon, the voice-over formulates the *biographical* operation about to commence: "Will Annette succeed in overcoming her childhood trauma?"

After the surgical procedures, the causal relations of "trauma–gender failure–refusal of body" are narrated backwards, thereby presenting the material processes of surgery as psychological therapy. Over images showing the candidate in agonizing post-operative pain, the voice-over announces a video message from her family: the bandaged Annette then watches Frank propose to her on videotape and is shown, once again, in tears. The voice-over confirms the therapeutic success of the operation: "Annette is overpowered, and for the first time lets her feelings take over." The traumatic arrival in the new body is narrated as the beginning of a new and successfully gendered personality. The restitution of gender culminates in the show's finale, in which the candidates, now styled and in full evening dress, see their new reflections in a mirror for the first time and are subsequently returned to their now happy families as restored women.

Biographical Work / Body Work

The Swan presents the correction of body sculpture as a means not only of restoring female gender performance, but also of bringing back the lost integrity of the gendered self. The biographical sketches featured in the individual episodes replicate a therapeutic discourse, an understanding of which, Kathy Davis (2003) argues, is vital to the feminist evaluation of plastic surgery. In her reconstruction of the notion of agency in what she calls "surgical stories," Davis suggests that women turn to plastic surgeons for reasons of feeling "not normal" (73). This encompasses experiences of being limited, discriminated against, and feeling alienated by and for their bodies. According to Davis, these women are positioned in a "trajectory of suffering" (79) that prevents them from leading normal lives and that can only be ended by a symbolic dissociation from the pathological self. Davis comments on a case:

> The trajectory begins with the recipient's realization that something is seriously amiss with her body. Gradually she comes to see her body as different, as uprooted from the mundane world ... As she discovers that she

> can't do anything to alleviate the problem, she is overcome by hopelessness, despair, and, finally, resignation. Her body becomes a prison from which there is no escape. In this context, cosmetic surgery becomes a way to "interrupt" the trajectory. (79)

In Davis' view, the cosmetic intervention functions primarily as a symbolic break with the old self, which is necessary for the application of the therapeutic narrative. Plastic surgery is, for Davis, not so much a technology of female oppression as a therapeutic device that can help to distance oneself from a somehow "wrong" self-image. It allows patients to achieve a self-willed interruption – in both a corporeal and a biographical sense – and enables them to frame their selves within a temporal narrative of "before and after," and thus to do biographical work (80). For Davis, this work makes the notion of an autonomously chosen self, of agency, plausible. In this vein, she argues for the recognition of surgery as a means of biographical-therapeutic agency that enables women to take control of their gendered selves and life narratives.

The dramatic setup of *The Swan* reinforces this conceptualization of plastic surgery as a technology of biographical rupture. The show removes the candidates from their social environments (families, jobs), which the narrative presents as a dissociation from false habits and roles. Simultaneously, the surgical and therapeutic experts confront the candidates with their respective "trajector[ies] of suffering" (Davis 2003, 79) and challenge them to do the necessary biographical work in order to shed their failed gender identities. In every episode, the contestants are interpellated in terms of this rupture: "You have to take this step now! These are the most important weeks of your life!" On a bodily and visual level, the women undergo a further depersonalization: they don grey, indistinguishable fitness clothing and are screened by surgeons, who divide their bodies into "zones of intervention" (teeth, tummy, breasts, hips, and so forth). The show's exposition narrates an abandoning of the failed gender biography and the emergence of the candidates as "bodies" ready to be operated on, both by the women themselves ("You must work harder," says the fitness instructor) and by the medical experts. *The Swan* thereby constructs a biographical state of exception in which the gendered self is suspended and can be (re)aligned within a therapeutic narrative of "change" or, as Davis puts it, "an intervention in identity" (2003, 82).

Cultural critics, including, in this volume, Dan Irving, have situated narrative programs that conceptualize the gendered self as a biographical-therapeutic project in relation to specifically neoliberal governmental technologies of the self, which both supply new modes of self-narration and facilitate the commodification of identities (100). Reality TV, especially, has been viewed as an agent in producing forms of self-governance by formulating knowledges that prescribe the permitted, desirable ways to perceive and live the self (Biressi and Nunn 2005; Palmer 2003). Framing plastic surgery within a therapeutic narrative of "before/after" thus generates a model of self-conduct in which the technologized manipulation of the body according to gender and beauty norms becomes narratable as a way of (re-)discovering and fashioning an authentic self.

But how does this biographical-therapeutic technology of the self become a somatic one? That is, how is the transformation articulated on the bodily level? Biressi and Nunn (2005) have stressed the central role of representations of extreme trauma and bodily states of exception in reality programs – that is, representations of bodies on the limits of (self-)controllability (6–8, 131–43). The visceral-affective moments in reality television range from the revolting *Big Brother* or *Survivor* challenges to the manifold bodily and emotional breakdowns in shows like *I'm a Celebrity – Get Me Out of Here!* (in Germany: *Das Dschungelcamp*). *The Swan* incorporates these primarily affective narrative modes in two ways: first, through the successive reduction of the candidates to "mere bodies" that serve as the material and fleshy arena of change; and second, by repeatedly and relentlessly capturing images of the women crying, moaning, hurting, suffering, and breaking down. These images supplement the therapeutic narrative with an excessive – and excessively visual – representation of bodily and emotionally painful conditions: the women cry as they relive their trauma in psychological counselling, describe their contempt for the old body, suffer from panic attacks before the operation, ache in the gym, and cry, bandaged, in the post-operative hospital bed. The mise-en-scène presents the individual phases of the transformation as the candidates' walk of sorrows, as their personal passion, thereby recreating the biographical dissociation from the old self on a bodily level.

Can such pains – framed in the context of biographical work – be understood as a somatic technology of the self, or *body work*? The experts' final evaluation of the candidates suggests as much, for the "Swan pageant" title is explicitly not given to the candidate looking the most beautiful. Rather, as each finale proclaims, the winner is that contestant "who has been through the most profound transformation" –

that is, the greatest degree of pain. The relentless representations of pain therefore effectively produce the candidates' sufferings as active investments in the new self, and thus as acts of agency. This pain-work serves a double function: to explicate the narrative "incorporation" of the new self, its articulation on the bodily level, and to authenticate the technologized women as "embodied subjects" (Strick 2008).

Gutting Out

The Swan narrates a governmentalization of pain – a cosmetic self produced through acts of bodily self-conduct. This economy of pain and hurt can, in fact, be regarded as an important step in the authentification of the cosmetic body, not only for the spectator, but also for the women themselves. As Davis (2003) explains, by investing feelings of pain into the new bodily self, women reconstitute themselves as "sentient and embodied female subjects" (115), thereby reclaiming their bodies as sites of experience where identity can be negotiated anew. In *The Swan*, however, the narrative of the sentient, suffering corporeal self as a site of personal experience leads to the dramatic climax of the show: the operation, which stages the contestant's body in a zero state of subjectivity that I call "gutting out" (Fournier 2002, 57). I argue that this narrative, symbolic, and material effacement of the female subject undergoing plastic surgery profoundly complicates the notion of body work. The show establishes the narrative climax as a bodily state of exception that – in analogy to the biographical rupture – marks the turning point between before and after. In its narrativization of surgery as a bodily technology of the self, the show's mise-en-scène is complex enough to merit a close reading, and essentially breaks down into two dramatic steps: schematization and eradication.

Schematization

As the candidates move into the "Swan Camp," they shed their social gender identities. This pre-operative phase discloses the gendered body as just that, a body, which from here on can be subjected to medical and technical scrutiny, evaluation, and measuring. The surgeons analyse the candidate's body, marking it with curves and lines foreshadowing the cuts and implied new shapes, thereby fragmenting it into various "crisis areas." In this narrative sequence, the women are already reduced to mere bodies on display, while the surgeons seize interpretational authority by writing and drawing their artistic vision onto the skin with felt pens. The next sequence translates these inscriptions on the skin into schematized images that present the candidate's body as a technical and medical project: in front of a nondescript background, the free-floating patient body is superimposed with pink arrows and circles delineating the individual procedures and measures to be performed (liposuction, rhinoplasty, and so on). A list of manipulations appears on the right side of the screen as the voice-over names them, resulting in a technical checklist of the gendered body as technological project.

This transitional stage before the operation scene is essential to the narrative in several respects. First, the explicitly sloughed and expressionless bodies caught in mugshots anticipate the patient's literal formlessness during surgery, in which the former bodies emerge as unfeeling masses of flesh that are worked on and given shape. Second, the circles and arrows depicting the various "zones of intervention" produce the body as a gathering of construction sites and crisis areas. The voice-over simultaneously describes the surgeries as "an individually fitted program of improvement," thus furthering the displacement of the embodied patient by a technical discourse. The individuality of the program of improvement substitutes for the identity of the candidate, and the body emerges as a tailored, "personalized" object to be worked on, devoid of any personal or emotional reference.

Eradication

After both social and individual gender have been subtracted – or, indeed, amputated – from the body, the cosmetic narrative now enters the climactic operation phase (usually after the second advertising break). Evoking splatter movie aesthetics, this sequence primarily consists of depictions of the surgeon's work: the rhythmical probing of the needle during liposuction, the handling of flabby breast implants, the cutting open of noses and bellies. While the surgeons comment on and explain the procedures they are performing, the women have ceased to perform as autonomous subjects. Their bodies serve as mere raw material in a technological apparatus and are represented as purely formless masses – feeling-less masses of flesh subjected to a *Formgebung* (shaping).

On the bodily level, the breaking point between "before" and "after" is thus not narrated as a patient's bodily state of exception, but as the complete eradication of self and the reduction of embodiment to raw matter. Thus, where Davis conceptualizes surgery as a necessary rupture in "trajector[ies] of suffering" (2003, 79) and, as a result, perceives an affirmation of agency, *The Swan* presents a fully and completely objectified body turned to sheer formable matter – a zero point of subjectivity. In effect, while the biographical rupture can be tied back to the candidates' decisions and experiences, the somatic turning point is by no means framed within emancipative or personal terms. Rather, it is narrated as the eradication of the embodied self and the subsequent insertion of the bodily material into a masculine technical apparatus geared towards resignifying the abject mass of flesh.

Valérie Fournier (2002) has convincingly argued that this figuration of the body as "abject mass" is at the very core of constructions of femininity. In her essay entitled "Fleshing Out Gender," Fournier asks how the inscription of gender norms is thinkable on a bodily level. Extending the theory of a negative constitution of femininity, she argues that the construction of female corporeality should also be conceptualized as negative – that is, as a reduction to overpowering pain, fleshiness, and de-signification: "gendered mechanisms do their work of inscription on women's bodies by hurting and injuring, and more specifically ... by gutting out or emptying out" (57). With reference to Bruno Latour's actor-network-theory, Fournier thus argues that femininity is the result of processes of de-signification, a dissociation and severing from significant materials and relations. In her view, the non-referentiality of pain epitomizes these processes: "the very constitution of womanhood works through fracturing the connections that make us into something, that give us 'ontological security.' The gutting out of materials that count in the making of the self, like pain, serves to detach womanhood from connections to networks, attachments to materials that would fill and give substance to, the self" (64). As mere fleshy matter, the gutted out body represents the necessary zero point of subjectivity, a negation of self and being. It figures as a completely abject "tabula rasa" through which the construction of womanhood becomes possible:

> We could think of gendering as something involving the distribution of pain and embodiment. The constitution of woman through her effacement or immateriality ... involves a stripping of materials that count in the making of the self, a process of evisceration that is done and experienced in the body, and that hurts. By drawing on the symbolism of pain, I [suggest] that becoming woman involves a sense of being emptied out and reduced to a mass of abject ... flesh. (62)

The Swan, which narrates the technological production of female embodiment, makes this form of construction explicit. While the women's dissociation from social and material networks narrates the biographical rupture, the bodily breaking point is produced by gutting out, eradicating, and effacing the candidates' subjectivities. Insofar as the instalment of a new gendered self therefore passes through a symbolic negation and, indeed, annihilation of subjectivity, it guts out any possibility of agency or autonomous decision. The narrative framing of a cosmetic femininity produces the moment of self-change as a point not only of powerlessness, but also, ultimately, of non-existence. Femininity is not something that *The Swan* contestants claim, perform, or do; it is, rather, done to them as male experts (re)model them into proper feminine bodies.

Visceral Relations

Fournier (2002) argues that the symbolic connection of pain and womanhood furthers the authentication and materialization of female gender norms inscribed on the body: "substantiating and 'making real' involves the disassemblage and reassemblage of bodies" (69). How is this re-signification narrated, or, how do unfeeling masses of flesh become embodied cosmetic subjects? In *The Swan*, this process of reconstituting a gendered subject involves several steps, which I will only briefly point to: first, the surgical procedure in itself serves to give meaning through shaping, in that it produces a "body sculpture" – a term that both experts and candidates use repeatedly throughout the show – made up of augmented zones that literally express a sexualized and intelligible femininity. Second, the candidates are restored as successfully gendered subjects by being framed within different situations organized around their now functioning female bodies. Among these framings is the final (roughly Lacanian) mirror scene, in which the camera intercuts the now sexualizing gazes of the medical experts and surgeons with frontal shots of the candidates scrutinizing and – again in tears – evaluating their new bodies. After this self-recognition as a gendered and sexualized subject, the successfully gendered body is further rewarded by the gazes of an overtly happy husband and laughing children, compliments from the show's female host, and envious looks from the defeated contender. By establishing looking relations around the new cosmetic body, it is re-signified as desirable, happy, and successfully gendered.

Yet, the cosmetic narrative of *The Swan* offers another level of interpretation, which is vital for the successful embodiment of femininity. As the narrative steps of the show suggest, *The Swan* incorporates different topoi that Linda Williams (2003) has described as characteristic of what she calls "body genres." In her systematic approach to these genres – horror, melodrama, and porn – she argues that each of them is connected to a particular notion of bodily excess. All of these excesses and bodily exertions can be found in *The Swan*. The show employs narrative patterns and arrangements from melodrama, including emotional breakdowns or confessions made in tears and signifying "primal … emotions" (269). Further, the bodily and visceral pains evoke the horror genre and its figurations of flesh, wounds, and fear. Pornography, finally, is called on in the show's finale, when the hypersexualized bodies are displayed to the aroused gazes of experts, husbands, and viewers as objects of desire.

The Swan thus presents a spectacular amalgamation of "sex, violence and emotion" (Williams 2003, 268) that offers identification to the viewers primarily on a visceral level, via the basic emotions of "pleasure, fear, and pain" (270). The acts of pain that I have discussed can therefore be understood as identificatory moments demanding the viewer's visceral reaction: sympathy, compassion, or repulsion. In turn, spectators accept the technologically produced body as sentient and therefore vulnerable; that is, as livable. Further, the massive displays of blood, the acts of cutting and wounding, produce a sort of community of shock, which articulates a mutual bodily experience between candidate and viewer. As in horror films, where our pleasurable identification with the victim works through a gut reaction to his or her woundings and lacerations, *The Swan* constructs identification via the visceral. Shocked by the brutal images, we suffer *with* the cosmetic body.

Visceral identification therefore does vital symbolic work in narrating the technologized body of plastic surgery as authentic, especially in light of the problematic figuration of zero subjectivity during surgery. The viewer's involuntary, sympathetic reaction, in fact, transfers a basic capacity for sentience, pain, and vulnerability onto the post-operative body. In other words, it projects an embodied subjectivity on what figures as sheer de-signified flesh. Judith Butler (2004b) describes this reciprocity of bodies and processes of recognition as a mechanism that is both violent and necessary:

> A vulnerability must be perceived and recognized in order to come into play in an ethical encounter, and there is no guarantee that this will

> happen ... [W]hen a vulnerability is recognized, that recognition has the power to change the meaning and structure of the vulnerability itself. In this sense, if vulnerability is one precondition for humanization, and humanization takes place differently through variable norms of recognition, then it follows that vulnerability is fundamentally dependent on existing norms of recognition if it is to be attributed to any human subject. (43)

Williams' "visceral ... manipulat[ion]" (2003, 271) of the viewer by excessive displays of violence and pain results in the powerful projection of embodied subjectivity in the very moment when the narrative of the cosmetic self passes through the annihilation of subjectivity. The recognition of pain and vulnerability thus produces the sentient body in the moment of its eradication. This happens according to what Butler describes as "existing norms of recognition"; the de-signified abject is restored as a gendered body through the viewer's visceral recognition. Recalling Fournier, this dramatic arrangement fixes suffering, powerlessness, and eradication as preconditions to the possibility of female embodiment.

Before/After

Conceptualizations of both reality TV and plastic surgery as modes of self-narration that endow subjects with agency and may enable acts of self-empowerment are highly problematic. The autobiographical modes employed in both confessional TV formats and discourses that frame surgery as a therapeutic device promote a notion of the gendered self that requires the symbolic effacement of subjectivity in order to construct a narrative of "before and after." It is therefore difficult to follow critics like Kathy Davis, who posit pain and suffering as moments of self-decision and subversion of existing norms of gender and subjectivity – or, in Foucauldian terms, technologies of the self. For these moments are inevitably caught up in teleological programs of self-making and self-narrating that reiterate existing norms of recognition, regardless of whether these narratives focus on empowerment or oppression.

Therapeutic self-narrations, such as those staged in *The Swan* or those discussed by Davis, presuppose the construction of a zero point of subjectivity in order to produce the idea of change. But where the construction of a breaking point is regarded as an act of empowerment, my discussion of the female cosmetic subject reveals that this precise act implies that the construction of successful femininity demands what Fournier has referred to as negation or immateriality. The construction of "before and after" thus appropriates and powerfully overrides experiences of pain and suffering, instrumentalizing them in order to produce successfully gendered subjects. Since shows like *The Swan* actually pursue the project of narrating the totally technologized production of female bodies as a therapeutic uncovering of the "natural" self, the relevance of visceral and corporeal visuals becomes clear: the display of exceptional states producing embodiment are essential to the naturalization of the cosmetic subject. They function to mask the cultural and technological apparatuses that plastic surgery, and femininity, are. Through displays of suffering for the self, agency is simulated in that particular site where gender is reinscribed as natural through technology. In other words, the technologization of the female body masks itself by narrating its processes of gendering as autonomous decisions for renaturalization (i.e., "becoming the woman I really am"). If, following Donna Haraway (1991), one perceives the cosmetically enhanced body as cyborgian and as a cultural production, then the hegemonic function of "before/after" narratives becomes even clearer: the temporalization that therapeutic and self-narrations impose effectively arrests these alternate views of the cosmetic body as a cyborg, as a cultural and technological artefact, and as a representation of a thoroughly denaturalized notion of gender. The trope of "before/after," and the therapeutic notion of self-realization that it supplements, thus undoes the de-ontologizing or transcategorial effects that the cosmetic body could enact. It reterritorializes the cultural artefact in a narrative of the gendered and heterosexual subject recovering itself and its nature. The potentially disruptive inhumanity of the cosmetic cyborg is thus surrendered to the reiteration of a normative, naturalizing, and painful notion of gendered self-conduct.[2]

NOTES

1 All quotations are taken from the German series of *The Swan*, which aired on Pro 7 in 2004; all translations are my own.

2 French performance artist ORLAN's work crucially undermines the processes of subjection and gender production exhibited in *The Swan* because the artist decidedly refuses to submit to surgery's annihilating "gutting out." As I have argued elsewhere (Strick 2008), instead of having herself subjected to the zero-point of subjectivity like the show's contestants, during her "surgery performances" (*La Reincarnation de Sainte*

ORLAN, 1991–99), ORLAN remains conscious, active, and crucially in command thanks to local anaesthesia. When she directs surgeons, dancers, and cameramen, and reads various texts during the operations on her body, ORLAN performs a sort of "inhuman" paradox – namely, the disembodied woman as author/artist who is in control of the cultural technologies that brutally shape her body. In my view, ORLAN's painless body work thus offers important critical perspectives on cosmetic procedures, embodied subjectivity, and gender.

PART THREE

Interior Lives: Conditions of Persistence and Survival

8 My Life as a Museum, or, Performing Indigenous Epistemologies

PETER MORIN

The world has no name, he said. The names of the cerros and the sierras and the deserts exist only on maps. We name them so that we do not lose our way. Yet it was because the way was lost to us already that we have made those names. The world cannot be lost. We are the ones. And it is because these names and these coordinates are our own naming that they cannot save us. That they cannot find for us the way again.

Cormac McCarthy, *The Crossing*

Language and Changing the Nature of Learning from the Museum

In an Indigenous epistemological practice, the museum is not a building; it is a place, a location for potential learning, in the landscape. As a Tahltan Nation person, I can travel to this place to gather knowledge and bring that learning back to our community.

In my time of learning about community art practices from the Kaska Dena Elders at Frances Lake, Yukon Territory, they shared with me an important Kaska Dena philosophy about the value placed on learning, knowledge practices, and personal and communal histories. I would like to acknowledge the wisdom and guidance of these teachers, including Mary Maje, Mida Donnessy, Anne Maje Raider, Leda Jules, Aggie Maggum and her sister Phoebe, Alice Broadhagen, and Charles Magum. They said you had to work – contribute to the community – in order to earn knowledge in the form of stories from your Elders. This has become a guiding principle for my work as both a visual artist and an educator working with urban Indigenous youth.

I had the privilege of participating in a Kaska language learning camp in the summer of 2005. At the start of the camp, Leda Jules explained that it was mandatory for us to work on something with our hands if we were going to learn the language. Leda said, "This is how we learned our language, we were always sewing or making something when our Elders were teaching us." I keep this teaching about the transfer of knowledge present in all of my work. Our language is tied to the community's material products: words represent the action, the praxis, of our community epistemology. Leda Jules told us to remember that our community objects also speak our language and that we can turn to them when we need to be reminded of our language and values. Indigenous hands have held these objects. Indigenous hands have held these objects out to younger Indigenous learners.

Physical objects are connected to spoken language, and spoken language is a system of organization for ideas and philosophies that shape new ideas. There is spoken language connected to the transference of knowledge connected to the making. And the object itself has a spoken language: a basket speaks basket language and communicates philosophies connected to the practices of weaving. It was a summer in the north when we started learning Kaska Dena language and philosophy at Frances Lake. There were about thirty of us. Many of the participants were Elders and older Kaska Dena people who either had fluency in Kaska Dena or had had conversational fluency at one point in their lives. Some had lost their language because of the residential school system and were at the camp because they wanted to return to their first language. And some were younger, like me, and trying to find a stronger sense of community. When I visit the First Nations collections of Western museums, such as those at the Royal British Columbia Museum or the University of British Columbia Museum of Anthropology, the story of my experience at Frances Lake stands beside me. It is because of this story that I am able to hear the laughter in the museum. The objects are teaching me language. The museum is filled with drumming, singing, speaking, smoke tanned hide, and laughing. There is no silence.

If I was going to apply the English word "museum" to the experience of Tahltan epistemologies captured in my story, then the museum is a place of movement and sound. And my remembering of this place is a ceremony. But "ceremony" is an English word just like "museum." In this case, I want "museum" to encompass everything before the making of an object, the act of making, and everything that follows the making of that object. I want the word also to include the act of remembering the transfer of knowledge embedded in the object. We need to organize our collective ways of knowing, a project in which the Western museum *can* play an important role. Indigenous ways of knowing are fluid; they are about process. Knowledge is the articulation of this fluid process of knowing. If I am a basket maker, then my first basket informs my second basket and every subsequent basket. It becomes my responsibility to remember and celebrate that first basket. This is the embodiment of knowledge. My practice as a performance artist informs my work with youth at the museum. When we are finally able to reflect on these ways of knowing and on the ways in which Indigenous communities have organized this knowledge, then we can rebuild the museum together.

In this chapter, I choose to employ narrative therapy style questions, which will allow me to embody Tahltan epistemological practice concerning the Indigenous body and the museum. Narrative therapy has its roots in New Zealand with practitioners David Epstein and Michael White. I would describe it as a practice that organizes the exchange of language and stories. It is an ongoing conversation, prompted by the therapist's questions, that keeps creating new spaces for more stories and more questions. In some ways, the therapist becomes a bridge between stories. While this is a very brief synopsis of the practice, I choose this approach as a means of engaging the emotional and historical trauma that is connected to the impact of the museum on the Indigenous body. One teacher whose question I bring forward here is Vikki Reynolds. Vikki taught me about "witnessing" in the activist tradition. She asks, "Who do you people the room with?" Another teacher I bring to the creation of these questions is educator and activist Ga Ching Kong. She asks, "Who do you bring to witness my story?"

The Western museum helps us to remember a version of history. The organization of this history aids in its promotion. This is purposeful organization. Inside any Western museum, you witness, participate in, and experience knowledge that has been collected, organized, evaluated, and deemed significant. There are also opportunities to contribute your own acquired knowledge to the museum. For example, you can donate your grandfather's collection of Salish baskets to the museum, and it will be considered a legacy of your family to the history of the nation. My purpose here is not to explicate the history of the museum in the West, but to illustrate alternative ways of engaging with this collected knowledge. One of the critical assumptions that will continue to inform our collective engagement with this style of organization is that the museum has a highly developed purpose in relation to the dissemination of Western epistemological praxis.

Narrative Therapy Question 1: When you go to the museum, who do you bring with you? (Going into the museum as a site of Indigenous learning)

> It is through these disciplines [Enlightenment knowledge projects] that the indigenous world has been *re*presented to the West and it is through these disciplines that indigenous peoples often *re*search for the fragments of ourselves which were taken, catalogued, studied and stored.
>
> Linda Tuhiwai Smith, *Decolonizing Methodologies*

When I go into the Western museum, I bring the Tahltan Nation territory with me. A relationship to the land is inherent in the continued development of Tahltan epistemology. The Tahltan land is an epistemological tool that has developed knowledge and ways of articulating that knowledge for our community. The land is an archive of acquired knowledge. In this volume, Kim Sawchuk writes about how our identities, our *selves*, are inherently connected to our ability to read and move through space (164–5). This idea leads us back to the land as an archive and reminds us how that archive supports the survival of the community. Hunters return from the land. Medicine comes from it. And our stories of return, return from travel on the land, continue to develop the nation of ideals we called Tahltan. Hawaiian scholar Manulani Aluli Meyer (2008) writes that "land is more than just a physical space. It is an idea that engages knowledge and contextualizes knowing. It is the key that turns doors inward to allow us to reflect on how space shapes us. It is not about emptiness but about consciousness" (219). The ability to articulate this knowing through a created visual record acts as a form of truth that reflects on and challenges dominant epistemologies. At one time, this acquired knowledge was communicated and recorded through story, song, objects, and ceremony. This exchange continues to develop, though it was directly hindered for a significant amount of time by the Canadian government through legislation like the Potlatch Ban, which was in place from 1884 to 1951.

The museum is a place on the land. We travel on the land.

When I go to the museum, I bring my experience as a maker of objects that are defined by Tahltan epistemological practice. I am a Tahltan Nation artist. Cultural objects tell me stories; they are grandmothers and grandfathers. Tahltan objects speak Tahltan to me, and I witness their rich histories. I witness their embodiments of Tahltan cultural identity and Tahltan cultural practice. Indigenous community members feel inherently connected to the objects on display in the museum. We can't help but feel our hands moving through the beaded stitches, woven wool threads, shaped wood boxes, and hide drums. We can't help but envision our aunties as the makers of the moccasins that are behind the museum glass. I carry this connection in my heart when I am in the museum. I bring my ancestor-makers to the museum with me. I acknowledge that the objects have a maker, a maker with a name and a history. I acknowledge that there is a forced silence in the museum. This can cause a rush of blood to the heart. My breath is rushed. I rush through the collection. I rush through the system of organized meaning to find the word that means the most to me. I look for "Tahltan." I search out my Tahltan-ness in the museum because it is exciting to see my *material* history. And to be excited by history is a miracle. This excitement overshadows the colonial awareness that happens when I cross through the museum doors.

Yet, the awareness of colonial history remains. Indigenous viewers carry trauma and spiritual pain into the museum. Trauma has a connection to the colonial project. It is articulated in our spiritual bodies and deeply embedded in our spirits. Trauma recurs as a result of the loss of the relationship to the objects within the museum. This is also a loss of connection to the makers and the teachings inherent in the objects' materiality. The objects are meant to be held. This relationality is at the heart of Indigenous pedagogical practice. Cree scholar Shawn Wilson (2008) writes, "The shared aspect of an Indigenous ontology and epistemology is relationality, or that relationships form reality. The shared aspect of an Indigenous axiology and methodology is that research must maintain accountability to all the relationships that it forms" (137). The physical connection reinforces our connection to the history of our communities, as well as the subsequent connection to the land of our traditional territories. Our aunties would have held these objects out for us to hold. The colonial project purposefully silences this performed history of objects.

Indigenous epistemologies shaped the process of making these objects to include exchanges between knowledge keepers and knowledge learners. The objects are keys that enable this intergenerational exchange. An experienced maker speaks with authority about how these objects fit into the history of the community. This is an important aspect of maintaining the community's ways of knowing. After a period of time, the master carver or master basket maker will make their best work available to the student. The student will have acquired the appropriate learning to be able to read the object and share the story of his or her learning from this object. This does not happen on the first day of working with a master; it may take years to earn that privilege. During our brief time together at the language camp, the Kaska Dena Elders impressed upon me the necessity of apprenticeship. Kaska Elder Mary Maje stated: "Young people think you just get your stories whenever you want, but we had to work for our stories, get up, chop wood, pack water, help out, make sure chores are done, and then, before bed, dad will tell you a story. You have to work for your stories." Mary's philosophy reminds us about the commitment to learning.[1] You see this same ethic within most traditional stories. In the Tahltan story of the light, our Tsesk'iye Cho (Crow) is reborn as a baby boy to a family living on the land. This baby grows very rapidly. He grows and he learns about where the man is keeping the light. Crow plans and gets ready to steal the light, and since there are different forms of it, he starts with the smaller lights until he is strong enough to carry them all at once. Eventually he is strong enough to hold all of the light and escapes with it out of the smoke hole to give it to the world. The story demonstrates that work, along with spiritual, mental, and physical growth, are required in order to create. As noted Tahltan/Tlingit artist Dempsey Bob says in relation to button blanket robes, "In order to interpret the designs, you have to know the stories, yourself, your people, and nature. To be an artist, you have to know all those things. That is why our people say our designs and blankets are very special" (quoted in Jensen and Sargent [1986] 1993, 6).

When I go to the museum as an educator, I often bring Indigenous children and youth with me. In my time with the children, we talk about grandmothers and grandfathers and their teachings. I remind them that our grandmothers and grandfathers are good teachers because they have patience for all kinds of questions. They have patience without judgment. We talk about Elders as people who are able to speak with authority on a subject – so children can be Elders, youth can be Elders, and Elders can be Elders. It's about carrying the knowledge. It's about how you use that knowledge. I tell them that the objects carry knowledge also. We talk about the kids' lives, and how some of them have never met their grandparents. Some have never had the opportunity to be with Elders to listen to the knowledge of their community. Most of these kids have never had a relationship to the objects of their community. We do all of this both before we go into the museum and while we are there. So, reimagining the museum involves travelling to our home communities. We go there to visit with our grandparents. The objects speak as a grandparent would speak when we cannot otherwise connect with our traditional territory. They speak of our land, telling us stories in our Indigenous language. We want to hear these Elders speaking to us, and they want to be heard.

During one of these visits, I asked kids who had never been home, and who were from ocean-going cultures, to identify and name the different paddle types. And with a little help from their grandparents (the objects), these youth showed me the different paddle types and how they were used – the larger paddles for the ocean-going canoes versus the shorter paddles for smaller canoes. Over the years, with the support of the Royal British Columbia Museum and its staff, our group has had the privilege of connecting youth to the ethnographic collections that are not on display. The ethnographic collections manager has met with us, explained his or her job, and taken us on a tour of the collections that stay in storage. I've explained to the conservator that these visits are about visiting grandmothers and grandfathers from our home communities. Kids get to look at collected objects from their communities of origin – objects that speak to them in their language.

Narrative Therapy Question 2: Reflect upon a time you were able to perform Tahltan epistemological practice in the museum. Was the museum changed? Were you changed?

Hunting still happens.

And stories are still created from those hunting trips, and these stories still return home.

As a Tahltan Nation person, I know that there is still knowledge being produced that contributes to the well-being of the community. This drive to acquire new learning is a tradition in most Indigenous communities. As an Indigenous person you can enact this epistemology within the museum. The story of your trip to the museum, the story of your learning while in the museum can, in turn, shape community-centred knowledge practices. In 2003, the Museum of Anthropology at the University of British Columbia hosted an exhibition of Tahltan artworks called, *Mehodihi: Our Great Ancestors Lived That Way*. The opening of the exhibition was scheduled to coincide with the 93-year anniversary of the Tahltan Declaration of Independence. This document, which outlines our desire to be responsible for the resources housed within our traditional territories, was presented to the provincial government in 1910. Community members still talk about *Mehodihi.* More than one hundred Tahltan people attended the opening. They sang Tahltan songs and danced Tahltan dances. The object in the museum still has a history; it has a way of inserting itself into the intellectual history of the community through its production. We still have access to that history.

In 2005, the University of British Columbia Museum of Anthropology invited me to create a performative intervention within their visible storage. A unique feature of the Museum of Anthropology is that the majority of their collected objects are on display within large glass storage cases. These cases are a significant aspect of the design and experience of the museum. My intervention was featured as the opening of the New Forms Festival. The goal of the work was to reach through the glass, to reach to the object. The performance was called *I grieve too much,* and the idea was to create a space for Tahltan epistemology and my Tahltan body to exist as one in the space of the museum. With this piece, I was hoping to subvert the glass barrier. I wanted to recreate and reflect the violence of this mediation to viewers who were not Tahltan. The performance action took place beside the Tahltan collection in the visual storage area, and we decided to broadcast the action to the audience that was waiting in the museum's lecture theatre. For the duration of the performance I was blindfolded. I brought several objects that embodied Tahltan epistemology and history into the museum with me and planned to interact with them alongside the museum-collected Tahltan objects. During this artwork, I washed my face with water from an enamel bowl, poured tea into tea cups, wrapped eagle feathers in red cloth, listened to a portable CD player, sang a song, and brushed my teeth. I wore a T-shirt that said, "Tahltan Nation." For the performance I created a Melton wool jacket that I covered with red iron oxide that I had harvested from our traditional territory.

Performance Notes

I began the performance by acknowledging the Elders and youth from my home community who were arrested earlier that year near Klappan in our traditional territory. They were blockading Shell Canada from moving into the Sacred Headwaters because they didn't want the test-drilling for natural gas in this area. The Sacred Headwaters is a spiritual site for our people, and the Skeena River, the Nass River, and the Stikine River all flow underneath this place.

Afterwards, I told the story of Essie Parrish, a healer from the Pomo Nation. Essie Parrish was one of the last "sucking doctors" and she allowed some anthropologists to film her performing her healing ceremony. She told the anthropologists that she would allow this if they promised to never show the film anywhere. They lied and showed the film across the country. Her community members felt that this film, and the showing of this film, impacted Essie's life and led to her early death because she allowed these anthropologists to record the ceremony.

After telling the story, I washed my face in the enamel bowl that I had brought and I wrung out the water in a glass jar. I brushed my teeth and spit out the foam into a glass jar. I held sweet grass and then put it into a glass jar.

When I was finished these cleansing tasks, I pulled out the drawer that contained the Tahltan community objects. Inside the drawer are beadwork objects such as moccasins, a belt, leggings, and necklaces – all things that don't exist in the community anymore. I acknowledged that it was my aunties who made these things, and I spoke about how my aunties love their tea. So I pulled out four bone china cups, placed them on top of the drawer, and poured them tea.

After I finished pouring the tea, I stood up and went to a strategically placed bent wood box that the museum lent to me for the duration of the performance. A bent wood box is very special because, traditionally, communities on the northwest coast would use these boxes to store their regalia. From inside the box, I removed four eagle feathers. These eagle feathers were wrapped in red cloth like the ones in which you would wrap tobacco ties. I placed them by the teacups. I did this to honour my aunties again, to honour the makers of objects. The feathers represented the bodies of past makers and became my prayers for them.

After I placed the eagle feathers, I went to the bent wood box again. This time I took out a Discman. I wanted to sing a song for my aunties, for the Elders and youth who were arrested, and for Essie Parrish. It needed to be a specific song. So I chose Richie Havens' version of "Fire and Rain." I sang along with Richie.

I ended by removing the blindfold.

The entire performance intervention took less than twenty minutes. I wanted it to be captured by a camera because, as Essie Parrish's story demonstrates, the camera, like the museum, has played a role in colonizing Indigenous knowledge. There is a history of capturing Indigenous performance, just as there is a history of collecting Indigenous objects and putting them behind glass. I also didn't want the audience to have easy access to my grief. The camera breaks this connection. I didn't want the viewer to directly experience the connection that I was making to the history of the objects. The camera broadcasted the work. The viewers in the lecture theatre at the Museum of Anthropology watched. It was hard to be near these collected Tahltan objects, made by my relations, talking to them through glass. So, too, the viewers saw my performance through glass. You want to touch. You want to smell. You want to hold. It is close but not close.

During the performance, I heard these Tahltan objects singing and this singing was beyond my reach. Afterwards, I realized that I had always heard them singing. I wanted to participate in the making of these objects. I imagined community members sitting together, telling stories, laughing, gossiping, crying, drinking tea, and sewing these objects that connect to Tahltan epistemological history. The museum has a tendency to lose the singing. The voice connected to the objects becomes hard to reach. In her ground-breaking book on Western-based research in Indigenous communities, Maori scholar Linda Tuhiwai Smith (1999) writes about how certain structures are necessary for colonizing practices of Indigenous knowledge: "The cultural archive with its systems of representation, codes for unlocking systems of classification, and fragmented artefacts of knowledge enabled travellers and observers to make sense of what they saw and to represent their new-found knowledge back to the West" (60). The challenge to the museum is how to shift this Western paradigm to allow for enough Indigenous epistemological practice to alter and co-create the space inside the museum. These artists sat together to work on beadwork, they shared stories, they shared tears, and they shared much laughter. These artists collaborated with each other to create this work. These artists collaborated with me to create a new artwork. The silence in the museum needs to shift if we are going to hear the laughter.

Narrative Therapy Question 3: How does witnessing Tahltan epistemological practice in the museum continue to change your relationship to the museum?

We are travellers on the land. There is a need to remember where we have gone and how to get back home. If we return for a moment to the claims with which I began this chapter, about the links between learning and *doing*, and apply this to our travels, then we can develop a clearer picture of the need to organize and structure learning. Travelling on the land is messy; there are kids crying, and people are hungry. The challenge to developing Indigenous epistemological practices is to create a structured environment that nurtures and supports continued travel on the land and helps calm the kids. There is always a need for practical thinking. If we apply this idea to the museum as it currently exists, we will recognize that there is a much longer history of the museum embedded in North American epistemologies. There has always been a need to keep meaning and meaningful objects safe. The need to structure knowledge enfolds itself in structured creative practices. Kaska Dena Elder Leda Jules says, "We were always making something with our hands when we were learning language." This reflects these much older practices of knowledge.

In *Red on Red* (1999), Creek Nation scholar Craig Womack writes, "Without Native American literature, there is no American canon. We should not allow ourselves, through the definitions we choose and the language we use, to ever assume we are outside the canon; we should not play along and confess to being a second-rate literature. Let Americanists struggle for their place in the Canon" (7). What is useful here is Womack's sense of redress of Indigenous epistemology and the ways that Indigenous knowledge unfolds within its communities of origin. A question arises about why an engagement with an Indigenous canon is not more apparent in Western styles of mapping space and history, including the museum. When Womack writes that "there is no American Canon," he is challenging us to prove him wrong. And his statement helps us to see the fallacy of overdependence on colonizing knowledge. What if Indigenous objects, and the Indigenous history of knowledge to which they are connected, were defining the museum first – as an Indigenous space?

As a Tahltan Nation person who still travels across this land, I suggest that the phrase "there is no American Canon" is also useful in my work within museums. I am a traveller in the tradition of travellers within the history of my community. This puts me in a very unique position to acquire new learning that can be included in the history of Tahltan ideas. The things, places, and people that I engage with during my travels can inform the development of new Tahltan knowledge. The older artworks inform the creation of my new artworks. In order to put Womack's theory into practice when visiting the museum, I go to connect to the history lessons held within the objects themselves. I name the Tahltan objects as speakers of Tahltan history. It is my job as a younger Tahltan person to work for the development of Tahltan history. I have to re-imagine our connection to the land in which the museum is situated because this is also a Tahltan practice of knowing. I have to re-imagine my connection to Tahltan ways of knowing. I have to re-imagine the museum as a site within a wider context that encompasses a global range of ideas, and I have to re-imagine my relationship to the museum as a place of experience. I am not able to hold the Tahltan object, but I can still see the maker. The maker is still talking. And I can share what I am hearing the maker say. In travelling, we honour and acknowledge our learning by leaving offerings, creating stories, and contributing these experiences to the greater community of ideas.

In my last visit to collections of the Royal British Columbia Museum, I took a young Indigenous man through their First Peoples exhibit. We were looking for ceremony and power in the objects. I said to him, what if the objects were, themselves, museums housing the community's memory? We thought of ceremony as the purposeful enactment of collective Indigenous knowledge, the history of community ideas, and respectful engagement with a material process. We named Indigenous aesthetics as a form of spiritual power for the community and we articulated the components of this aesthetics as a balance of knowledge, materials, language, and a history of ideas. This power reflected a truth of Indigenous knowledge. We decided that artists are philosophers, historians, inventors, and scientists who are constantly trying out theories that put Indigenous epistemology to the test. Together, we searched and found that ceremony is directly connected to articulating power, the truth of experience, and spiritual knowledge.

This trip was unique because there were only two of us there. We started our visit by understanding the history of the Western museum: what it does, what it does not do, and what it has only begun to do. We were looking at the story of the Western museum, and we were looking for the Indigenous story of power. The Royal British Columbia Museum's First Peoples exhibition is on the top floor of the building. The style of the space is modern, with designed walkways, levels, and viewpoints throughout. The museum does a lot in a small space. On the upper level, there is a guided tour of images and objects from Indigenous nations. The museum uses the British Columbian landscape as a method of organization. This upper level has a view of a larger open area in which there is a display of totems and Northwest Coast house fronts. This is the one larger area within the exhibition space. The poles are backed by a house front with an entrance hole that allows you to move further into "traditional" space. But, of course, this is all what Jean Baudrillard (1981) would call a simulacrum – a hyperreal representation. The placement of the objects in this space has become an interesting addendum to the experience of the museum because, often, the youth who accompany me have been inside "traditional" Indigenous spaces in their home communities. These kids tend to move comfortably through this manufactured experience. The museum is a mash-up of these two spaces and their associated epistemologies, and can become like a version of home because Indigenous-defined spaces give the Indigenous body a sense of safety.

There is a view within the Royal British Columbia Museum of totem poles. This space is outlined by smoked glass vitrines. Some of these vitrines are oriented to face the totem poles and some outline a corridor that encircles the open space. In one of these three-sided vitrines, there is a frontal view of a replica Haida Nation village, complete with miniature representations of Haida Nation people. I have always imagined this vitrine to be purposefully located for the visitor to see through the glass, over the top of the miniature Haida Nation village, to the life-sized poles arranged in the open space beyond.

The young man and I were talking about power – about spiritual power connected to the objects at which we were looking. We were talking about the goal of our learning being the ability to articulate the acquired learning of our community. (Well, mostly I was talking.) The power of artists resides in the ability to organize their ideas about the history of knowing in order to reflect on the history of ideas for their specific community. The works either represent their learning or build upon their learning through the making. Artists are historians of their community; they create vehicles for the living memory, and their works create new experiential philosophies connected with the history of ideas for their communities of origin. I think the kid was mostly with me as we talked through these concepts. In looking through the glass container at the totems, we could see a strong practice of Indigenous aesthetics and understood that the makers had the ability to articulate powerful connections to their knowledge. This articulation is a valued tradition.

In some ways, though, the key to making this conversation one of learning was a vitrine containing objects created for sale by artists during a post-contact period. In the vitrine there are Nuu-chah-nulth woven teacups, Salish woven tables, Salish woven baskets, and beaded wall hangings. There is a version of this vitrine in every museum across Canada. In the Royal British Columbia Museum, the design of the museum allows for a perspective on both the objects made for sale and the objects made for communal use. You can see across time from a period of economic abundance (totem poles, in this case) to a period of economic poverty (baskets made for sale to feed grandchildren). This viewpoint, looking through time, illuminated a strong tradition of articulating community-based knowledge. These objects were unapologetic and profoundly shaped by the history of ideas in each represented community. The totems were strongly Haida or Tsimshian. The woven teacup, made for sale to European settlers, strongly articulated a Nuu-chah-nulth world view. We saw a continuity of Indigenous ideals and knowledges, forces that continued to exist through and beyond periods of economic pressure. This continuity, this history of knowing across Indigenous art movements, is not easily defined either by the shared nation or the museum.

During our visit to the museum, my young friend and I wondered about the words and philosophies that would work to articulate the artistic and material choices embedded in these objects, and how well these choices represent the history of Indigenous ways of knowing. These ways of knowing have helped us to live well on the land. They have helped us to see the strength of Indigenous epistemologies throughout history. The act of articulating these significant aspects of Indigenous knowledge production can benefit our shared community. It's time to ask: What are the words that the Indigenous people used to describe their artistic material production? What are the words?

The Last Question: Should the Museum Move on the Land?

These reflections are about practice, about a movement through ideas, materiality, and history. Travel still happens on the land; for Indigenous travellers, the land has just become larger. In order for Indigenous epistemologies to enact their meanings inside the museum, the collections must reflect how voice is connected to material processes. I am not suggesting that we burn down the museum and start again. What I am trying to highlight is our ability as a society to enable and engage with multiple meanings; a major component of the Indigenous epistemological tradition is based in adaptability and transformation. The challenge is the re-creation, re-enactment, re-establishment of the unique epistemological possibilities created by Indigenous communities beside the objects that are on display. The questions now are: If singing is a marker of Indigenous epistemological practice, and Indigenous objects are included in museum collections, how do we include the singing with the collected object? (You should sing when you are making a drum. A good song to sing while making a drum is a song about travelling.) How do we reorganize so that information flows within the museum, so that these flows can create a river inside the building, and so that this river allows for more than one stream of knowledge to make itself felt?

The created object, shaped by Indigenous epistemological practice, exists as a historical document for the history of the Indigenous nation. There are also the specific performance aspects of objects, which are never addressed within museum collections. The object performs Indigenous meaning within the community, which is complementary to the performed meaning involved in the making of the object. There is an ongoing need for this performance of Indigenous meaning within the museum. We need to understand how the performance can change and still reflect the importance of Indigenous thought. My own performance in the museum – my created space for grieving the loss of connection to Tahltan objects – helped me to learn that the basket is also a prayer; it is also a ceremony, an historical document, and someone's grandmother or grandfather. In fact, I have never seen a basket in the museum. I have only seen the land reflected back to me.

In the Kaska language camp, many of the older people in camp were conversationally fluent speakers of Kaska. The spoken Kaska is closely related to the spoken Tahltan. I am a Tahltan Nation person. I am also a committed Tahltan language learner. It takes a lifetime to speak your language well. So, when we would gather for our lessons, the Elders would be speaking Kaska to each other, and the language would fill the space with warmth. Then, the lesson would start and the fluent language would stop, and English would creep into the space with us. Yet, the rhythm of their language – the pacing of silences and the places for laughter – created a space that developed the experiential learning connected to our spoken language. You can't teach language without laughing. It seemed to me, as a non-speaker of Kaska and as a learner of Tahltan, that there was a sense of calm because no one was struggling with English. Within the spoken Kaska language there was no need to struggle with the ghosts of colonialism, residential schools, educational systems, racism, and so on. Of course, I can't truly remark on what these fluent speakers of the Kaska Dena language were feeling in the moment, and I am not trying to deny that these conflicts were there with us, for they are always present. But these contemporary experiences weren't standing in the way of our community practices. The community practice, or praxis, happens whether we are in the museum or on the land. The space needed to acknowledge that community praxis is important to the experience of objects.

The development of a system that supports Indigenous-based knowledge – and the development of new structures to support and organize these collective ways of knowing – depends on the continued practice of existing Indigenous epistemologies. In the next museum, we need to privilege the idea that a basket is also a spoken prayer, that the basket maker is performing a spiritual act. We need to do this so that the next basket makers can carry on this tradition. At the front door of the museum, there needs to be a space for ceremony. Indigenous people have to feel supported to continue this practice. We can't leave our history, even if the silence within the walls of the museum is overwhelming. The museum, and travel to the museum, is about practice. The artwork inside the museum is about practice. It is not about visiting the past but, rather, acquiring and creating new meaning. The structures to support such practices need to be built into the larger organizational systems, including the museum, so that the transfer of knowledge can continue. This is an act that opens up ideologies and spaces. This transfer can be felt, even if not fully grasped, across cultural border zones. The process of learning and the process of connection to Indigenous knowledge can develop over time.

The objects held within the silence within the museum tell the story of the people. The story of the people is also the story of the land. These objects are forced into silence. The history of the object, and of its maker, are forced into this silence that compartmentalizes our experience and ways of knowing.

The objects can help our voices to heal.

NOTE

1 Mary Maje also spoke about doing chores at the camp. She said that there were often many chores but she did them without complaining because she knew at the end of the day that there would be a story from her grandparents. I remember this teaching because of Mary's participation in the creation of the story. She saw her work, along with the story, as two parts of the experience of participation within the Kaska Dena epistemological matrix.

9 Gut Reactions: Mona Hatoum's *Corps étranger*

KIM SAWCHUK

The critical power of art, or any cultural form, may not be perceived universally, but if it is perceived, it hits you in the gut.

Susan Buck-Morss

Mona Hatoum's award-winning video installation, *Corps étranger*, is comprised of a large cylindrical tube, approximately twelve metres high, which visitors enter and exit through two narrow vertical openings. Sounds emerge from speakers carefully placed inside the walls: a heartbeat booms at a bass register and gurgling noises immerse the listener in the body through sonic amplification. When the projection starts, a series of images unfold. Entryways into orifices are enlarged in scale and scope, revealing inner surfaces dripping with gastric juices. Within the pinkness of this fleshy interior, bilious yellow tones glisten. The effect is beautiful, yet grotesque – a version of Edmund Burke's ([1756] 1990) sublime as "agreeable horror," or perhaps the very definition of "the abject," which Julia Kristeva (1982) conceptualizes as an involuntary revulsion that is aroused when the body's boundaries are violated. When I finally experienced *Corps étranger* in 2004, I wanted to flee the room. Yet, I was immobilized, transfixed. I left but returned several times.

At first glance, *Corps étranger* dramatically highlights the seductive, pervasive operations of the medical technologies that mediate our relationships to our bodies, rendering inner space into a landscape for virtual travel through technological means (Sawchuk 2000). First conceived in 1980, while Hatoum was a student at the Slade School in London, the installation was not produced until 1994, at the invitation of the Centre Georges Pompidou in Paris. Hatoum collaborated with a surgeon to "scope" her corporeal landscape in three ways: by using endoscopy, which detects cervical abnormalities; by using colonoscopy to illuminate the intestinal tract; and by deploying ultrasound to capture the rhythmic pulsations of her heartbeat. Yet, the impact of the exhibition deepens when we understand this immersion into Mona Hatoum's body – its staging of an encounter with the insides of her bowels, vagina, and esophagus – as revealing a small segment of a multiscalar story. Through the use of visual tropes and through a strategy of engaging viewers at a gut level, *Corps étranger* offers autobiographical details, a "synecdoche of subjectivity" (Smith and Watson 2010, 179) that links Hatoum's "bios" to history.

Not only does *Corps étranger* immerse exhibition visitors in Hatoum's very guts, in a move that powerfully troubles medical intrusion and surveillance, but it also brings us, viscerally, into a key historical moment for Palestinians known as Al Nakba, "the catastrophe" (Ankori 2006). During the period of 1947–48, Israeli military and paramilitary forces waged a campaign of terror, widely documented yet often denied, in a bid to consolidate the Israeli state within Palestinian territory. In a matter of months, hundreds of Palestinian civilians were killed in the villages of Deir Yassin, Saliha, Lod, al-Dawayima, and Abu Shusha (Morris [1988] 2004, 256–7; Pappé 2006, xiii). In the ensuing months, it is estimated that 531 villages were destroyed and eleven urban neighbourhoods evacuated. Those who were not killed were forced into neighbouring Arab states, where they lived in refugee camps. Over 750,000 Palestinians were exiled during this time, and those who remained lived under an intense regime of surveillance (Bloom 2001; de Reynier 1969; Finkelstein 2005; Hammami 2004; Hasso 2000; Morris 1990; Said 2000; Sayigh 1979, 1994). Mona Hatoum's parents took part in this exodus.

Hatoum has said that her works are not directly autobiographical but, rather, inflected by her personal history:

> There isn't a conscious effort on my part to speak directly about my background and history. But the fact that I grew up in a war-torn country; the fact that my family was displaced, a Palestinian family that ended up living in exile in Lebanon, has obviously shaped the way I perceive the world. It comes into my work as a feeling of unsettledness. The feeling of

> not being able to take anything for granted, even doubting the solidity of the ground you walk on. (Quoted in Spinelli 1997, 134)

This chapter situates *Corps étranger* as a work of difficult inheritance, where inheritance, as Sara Ahmed (2006) writes, is both a gift and a responsibility that is passed on through "*the work or labor of generations*":

> The "passing" of history is a social as well as a material way of organizing the world that shapes the materials out of which life is made as well as the very "matter" of bodies. If history is made "out of" what is passed down, as the conditions in which we live, then history is made out of what is given not only in the sense of that which is "always already" there, *before our own arrival*, but in the active sense of the gift. (125, original emphases)

Hatoum's artworks, then, are inflected by a story of migration and exile that is written across bodies, written into her body. This is communicated not only through her use of visual tropes, but also through a powerful mobilization of phenomenological aesthetics. As art historian Gannit Ankori (2006) asserts, Hatoum's representations of the viscera are deliberate; they act as "signatures" through their persistent thematic presence. My focus here is on Hatoum's strategies for provoking a "gut reaction" that references both autobiographical detail and a collective history of occupation, migration, and exile. Hatoum's phenomenological aesthetic strategy employs "somatic cognition" (Buck-Morss in Kester 1997, 43) to foreground remembrance as a part of living memory.

Foreign Bodies

As art critics have said of Hatoum's work, it is imperative to pay attention to her titles: "The play between the literal and the figurative is an important aspect of Hatoum's artistic process. She enjoys the multiple meanings of words and often favours punning and allusive titles" (Harper 1998, 2). While the title plays on chains of association, what is experienced in *Corps étranger* is, arguably, not merely a metaphor for the unwanted entry of foreign elements into the vulnerable space of the body. Metaphor implies that we understand by comparing one thing to another. Yet, rather than engaging in a comparison, here we participate in a performative enactment through Hatoum's staging of a situation.[1] The chains of intellectual association that the title sets in motion invite new meanings after we experience the artwork, highlighting a second vector of political critique instigated by an initial visceral reaction.

Herself a trilingual subject in exile from her homeland, displaced by war and violence from invading forces, Hatoum fashions titles that often work across linguistic boundaries. For example, the French term for body, "le corps," puns on the linguistic interplay between the dead and the living body, the corpse and the "corps." This clever pun also signals an elision in the English language, which has only one term for the body. The German language, for instance, distinguishes between *leib* and *körper*, the former signifying the lived, processual, and animate body, and the latter reserved for the body when it is understood as mere physicality and matter. The phrase "foreign body," the English translation of Hatoum's French title, is, like the body itself, polysemic. It refers not only to the installation we see before us and experience – the inner body usually hidden from view – but also to the spectator's entry into the space. It may indicate the camera as well, a foreign technological body.

The term "foreign body" is also a colloquial expression used to single out others who enter into the nation state from outside and elsewhere. In politics, one speaks of the body politic, indicating a long tradition within political philosophy of depicting nations in corporeal terms. Thomas Hobbes' *Leviathan* (1651) is the most obvious example of this analogy. Depicting the borders and boundaries of the body in political terms, or politics in corporeal terms, suggests a history of deep identification between an individual subject and a larger entity that often demands a sacrifice of its subjects' bodies in the name of the state. From within this discursive framing, the nation state is figured as a body that must be protected from foreign invasion and unwanted intrusions that may "infect" its inherent and "natural" purity. It is also significant, then, that "corps" is a military term for a group of soldiers.

Hatoum's chosen title for the installation, *Corps étranger*, the foreign or outside body, speaks to elements of the artist's autobiography as a Palestinian exile living in England, whose family has directly experienced war, invasion, death, and displacement. Hatoum observes that, at the time that she began to focus on the body in her work, she "was perceived as this isolated incident, a person coming from nowhere and trying to disrupt a respectable intellectual environment" (Antoni 1998, 57). Yet, as she has also added, this relationship between her body art and her experience of exile is not straightforward. While Hatoum was involved in activist groups during the making of *Corps étranger*, at the time of its conception she saw art and activism as different realms, insisting that she works in an intuitive way that deals with "an environment that is hostile and intolerant and eventually those feelings began to pervade the work – and still do" (Archer 1997, 14). These feelings do not leave. They form a crucial, if fragmented and partial, part of Hatoum's intergenerational visual autobiography.

In a leaflet published by Hatoum to accompany her first performance tour in Canada in 1983, Hatoum included excerpts from an interview in which the interviewer, Sara Diamond, asks the question: "Do you visit your parents often?" In response, the artist tells a story:

> It's a nightmare when I do. I went to Beirut looking for my parents and in the wreckage of their home I found two plastic boxes – a pink one and a blue one. I opened the blue box and it was full of tiny toy soldiers that exploded out into the air around me becoming a cloud of flies that took on the shape of a black gravestone – "We were only obeying orders!" I heard them say. There were two names on the stone, but as I strained to read them they began to pulsate in a rhythmic heartbeat that faded away. I struck out at the black gravestone, trying to smash it as agonizing screams rose up around me. When I turned back to the pink box, the lid was open disgorging human entrails in an endless stream. I heard my mother's voice saying, "They were disemboweling pregnant women, that's why we had to leave." (Archer et al. 1997, 122)

The tale that Hatoum recounts entangles personal biography with a history of the forced exodus of Palestinians during the war of 1948. At this time, paramilitary groups such as the Irgun used terror, intimidation, and the murder of civilians to drive the exodus. Key to the implementation of this terror was the use of leaflets informing civilians that they would be severely punished if they refused to leave (de Reynier 1969). And, as feminist historians of the period contend, the tactical targeting of women, including pregnant women, was a critical aspect of territorial conquest through a forced evacuation (Bloom 2001; Hasso 2000).

Like so many of Hatoum's artworks, *Corps étranger* contains autobiographical inscriptions of Al Nakba, traces that link past with present. In a reading of Palestinian artists living in Palestine who continue to depict their understandings and remembrances of homeland, Olga González (2009) writes:

> For Palestinians, the Nakba is not a historical circumstance that resides in the past, only to be commemorated once a year with events that include

> art exhibits, among other things. The Nakba is experienced instead as the uninterrupted process of Israeli domination that was given continuity by the 1967 occupation, and that pervades every facet of Palestinian daily life. Several markers of the occupation that infringe upon Palestinian rights and freedom are the eight-meter-high wall that spans 403 miles across the Palestinian territory, the hundreds of checkpoints and roadblocks, and the illegal Israeli settlements and outposts. The occupation is thus an all-encompassing experience in Palestinian life from which artists are not exempted. (203)

Experiences of migration and exile materialize within specific corporeal, temporal, and spatial coordinates – moments and situations that may resonate with the experiences of others, but which have their own particular histories. Places and memories are connected, although for the exile what links them, as Ahmed (1999) writes, is the "impossibility of return" (343). It is impossible to fully return to a place that was home because "home is not exterior to a self": "The movements of selves between places that come to be inhabited as home involve the discontinuities of personal biographies and wrinkles in the skin" (343). The experience of migration, writes Ahmed, produces a feeling of perpetual discomfort in the body, which feels "out of place" (343).

In *Corps étranger* this sensation of being "out of place" is doubly articulated. The use of a flow of images of her inner body space allows Hatoum to speak to anybody who has a body. Yet, these images also mobilize a set of references that speak another story to spectators who either know of, or have been affected by, this history of forced migration and occupation. As Hamid Naficy (2001) writes of Hatoum, "These works are both autobiographical and corporeal, for they involve not only her history but also her body – the height of exilic indexicality" (149). Crucially, more than simply pointing, Hatoum's mobilizing of corporeality as autobiography stages the *effects* of an inheritance of exile. Rather than directly depicting massacre and death, *Corps étranger* unfurls – and places visitors to the exhibition – directly within the contradictions and tensions inherent in practices of monitoring, surveillance, and violence common to political systems of domination and territorial control that name some bodies as "foreign" and in need of expulsion. It is an artwork that, in the words of Susan Buck-Morss, "hits you in the gut" (quoted in Kester 1997, 43), even if you are not fully aware of the historical referents.

From Representation to Situation

In an illuminating examination of Hatoum's artistic trajectory, Guy Brett (1997) notes that there are three phases to her work: "An early period marked by free experiment; then the years of 'issue-based' works, roughly 1982–88, which mainly take the form of performance and video; and third, a period beginning in 1989 with *The Light at the End* and drawing on many ideas first proposed in her student days" (36–7). The shift that Brett discerns in 1989 coincides with Hatoum's critique of the limits of *directly* representing the politics of the Middle East, including the 1947–48 displacement and the subsequent massacre of refugees at Sabra and Shatila in September of 1982, as well as her foregrounding of issues of race and racism (*Them and Us ... and Other Divisions*, 1984) and homelessness and unemployment in Britain (*Unemployed*, 1986). For Brett, the extraordinary video, *Measures of Distance* (1988), based on an exchange of letters between Hatoum and her mother during the bombing of Beirut, marks the end of this period of politically based work (Baert 1993, 109–23).

Brett's assessment perceptively identifies a shift in Hatoum's practice towards object-based minimalism and conceptualism. While this distinction helpfully tracks the development of one aspect of Hatoum's aesthetics, Brett's discussion of the artist's turn away from a direct representation of political issues to an emphasis on "spectatorial self-awareness" (1997, 59) hints at continuities between the "issue-based" works of the 1980s and Hatoum's post-1989 artistic production. The key is her use of the viscera and her interest in both materiality and phenomenological "situation." Hatoum states that by 1986 the production of her artwork had shifted towards a phenomenological approach that was increasingly attentive to materials and to the performative potential of installations to trigger visceral, instinctual reactions in viewers. As she explains, her practice moved "from a situation of representation to a desire to create an actual and real situation that the audience could experience directly for themselves. I wanted to explore the phenomenology of the space and materials to create a kind of gut reaction to the situation before the process of questioning and associations begins" (quoted in Spinelli 1997, 134). Hatoum's use of the term "gut reaction" is both telling and deliberate. While her overt reference to the political potential of phenomenology is clear, the significance of this critical premise is rarely examined in readings of Hatoum's oeuvre. The political potential of this turn from representation to situation becomes clearer still if we consider feminist readings and appropriations of phenomenology, which conceptualize embodied politics through emphases on orientation, situation, and approach. What follows, then, considers the feminist and postcolonial politics of phenomenology in order to formulate a critical context that can illuminate the visceral force of Hatoum's work.

Phenomenological Encounters

From the classic works of Maurice Merleau-Ponty (1962, 1964, 1968, 1973a, 1973b) to the more contemporary post-phenomenological writings of feminists such as Vivian Sobchack (2004), Elizabeth Grosz ([1994] 2008), and Sara Ahmed (2006), phenomenology stresses the relationship between consciousness and corporeality, emphasizing the distinction between the body and embodiment. Sobchack explains: "Embodiment is a radically material condition of human beings that necessarily entails body and consciousness, objectivity and subjectivity, in an irreducible ensemble. Thus we matter and we mean through processes and logics of sense-making that owe as much to our carnal existence as they do to our conscious thought" (4). In emphasizing "sense-making" through "carnal existence," a phenomenological approach does not just "examine" the body as it exists in discourse or representation, but frames and understands it as having a capacity for movement, sensing, and perceiving; it is alive, lived, living to the core.

Merleau-Ponty asserts that for subjects to take up positions in the world, they must be able to situate themselves in the space occupied by their bodies, an ability that is acquired through an engagement with the world from the moment of birth. In Merleau-Ponty's framework, the anchoring of subjectivity in our sensing bodies, conceived in terms of these spatial orientations, acts as a pre-condition for finding some semblance of a coherent identity – one that will constantly evolve, based on our interactions, through the multifarious ways that we come to mobilize and nurture all of the senses, somatically. This understanding of our ontological condition as embodied subjects and the corresponding relational nexus of body-space-senses provide a powerful template that identifies form and size, direction, centredness, location, depth, dimension, and orientation as integral to our navigations through the world.

Writing in the wake of liberation struggles in the postwar era, postcolonial thinkers such as Frantz Fanon ([1952] 2008), Albert Memmi

(1965), and Aimé Césaire ([1955] 2000) famously used phenomenological readings of the racialized embodied subject to critique the dynamics between colonizer and colonized. Building on both this tradition in postcolonial thought and on Merleau-Ponty's insights, Sara Ahmed (2006) draws attention to the colonial and postcolonial implications for understanding *situation* and the capacities for different bodies to act in the world, where actions create both distances and proximities. Ahmed thereby emphasizes relative relations of power that are grounded, quite literally, in the complexities of movement and direction. Merleau-Ponty writes: "My body appears to me as an attitude directed towards a certain existing or possible task. And indeed its spatiality is not, like that of external objects or like that of 'spatial sensations,' a spatiality of position, but a 'spatiality of situation'" (quoted in Ahmed 2006, 134). If one of the hallmarks of phenomenology is its attention to the way that bodies are oriented and situated spatially, then Hatoum's work stages a "situation" that, by disorienting those who experience it, operates as a sensorial, political, and phenomenological aesthetic.

The performative event that is *Corps étranger* implicates the embodied spectator in the scene of a visceral drama. Visitors do not merely look at a representation of the surface of the skin, or the inner folds of the viscera, or the walls of a vaginal canal. Rather, they are brought into uneasy contact with the installation, which creates a disturbing kinaesthetic experience in which the gallery-goer is swallowed up within the bowels of Hatoum's visual and sonic assemblage. The installation is built to augment and optimize the sensorial capacities for heightened reception. In order to destabilize our relationship to space, the videos and sounds are not projected onto a wall, but into a larger circular structure. Two narrow slits on either side emit light and sounds from within and create an opening that is just large enough to squeeze through. The curious must come closer, overcoming any initial reticence or fear and step inside. A circular image is projected onto the floor, from above, almost to the edge of the walls. Visitors see what looks like a pink tunnel that pulsates on the ground at their feet.

Corps étranger is not organized in a way that assumes that visitors will encounter the video from beginning to end. Yet, if one does view the piece in its entirety, one of the first images shows the exterior space of the body in an establishing shot that orients and then disorients the spectator. *Corps étranger* thus immediately breaches the boundaries of the individual body perched at the edge of this circular visual vortex, violating social norms of propriety and comportment. In turn, the circular projection subtly shapes the movements of visitors, who gravitate towards the walls, but, because of the circle's spatial limitations, are forced into close proximity with each other. Spectators are brought uncomfortably close not only to the hidden recesses of the body's interior, but also to the very edges that demarcate the inside and the outside of the flesh. The videotaping of these liminal zones reveals the fine line separating exteriority from interiority. Rather than a body contained by the skin as a kind of impenetrable barricade, what is uncomfortably depicted is its folding, and the subtle reversal between inside and out.

Sound is a central component in the creation of a full kinaesthetic corporeal experience of disturbance and destabilization in the space that is *Corps étranger.* Pulsating echoes of a heartbeat reverberate off the walls of this semi-enclosed chamber, intensifying the claustrophobia of immersion within the folds of a technology that gives us what we want: knowledge of our intimate insides, the ability to penetrate what is hidden. Visitors enter into both the technological assemblage and into a body – one that is brought close up in order to enhance a fusion between bodies. Along with the volume, the viewers' forced proximity to the walls – achieved through the use of the projection on the floor – makes the skin act as a resonance chamber, a vibrating membrane that becomes part of these audio-phonic rhythms. The amplification of sounds, coupled with the sight of this miasma of pulsating cavernous orifices at your feet, augments the sensation of having entered into the body of the artist via the resonance chamber that encloses those who dare to enter within. Visually and sonically, the chamber also acts as a mediating force, creating a deeply visceral, affective connection to the *Corps étranger*. At the same time, one's senses of form, size, directionality, centredness, location, depth, dimension, and orientation are destabilized. The piece is a turning away from what we habitually know or encounter. It makes strange that which is most familiar.

Amplification and magnification of this "situation" force a relational proximity to the sounds and sights of inner body space, a phenomenological re-creation of travel into the body, and our collusion with the machine, into which we must enter in order to participate. Visitors may desire to move away from the light source and towards the safety of the walls. But, if they do, then the sound is overwhelming. If the next step is taken towards the miasma "churning" at your feet (Brett 1997, 70), then you risk entering into the shaft of light in this darkened space. If you do, your body creates a shadow on the image. You become a shadowy, dark presence in this beam of light; you become the invading object, the invading force interrupting the image. Onto your figure, a fragment of her image is now projected, creating a new comingling of forces, another corporeal connection: a dis-orientation and re-orientation of relations of power.

Hatoum's phenomenologically informed artistic practice foregrounds a "relational" contact with these hitherto hidden recesses, a contact that plays with proximity, distance, and the "strange encounter" (Ahmed 2000) to initiate a corporeal response that is integral to the process of aesthetic criticism as political critique. An encounter, writes Ahmed (2000), is "a meeting which involves surprise and conflict" (6). The dis-orienting strangeness of *Corps étranger* exemplifies Ahmed's (2006) contention that "Orientalism" – Edward Said's (1979) term for Western representations of the East as Other – has not only discursive but also embodied implications. As she explains,

> the word "orientate" refers both to the practices of finding one's way, by establishing one's direction (according to the axes of north, south, east, and west) and to the east itself as one direction privileged over others. We must remember in pointing to this non-incidentality that the etymology of the word "orientation" is from "the Orient" and, indeed, the East as "the horizon" over which the sun rises. Everyone, one might say, has an east; it is on the horizon, a visible line that marks the beginning of a new day. There are multiple horizons depending on one's point of view. (122)

For Ahmed, Orientalism is a form of "world facing," which she characterizes as "a way of gathering things around so they 'face' a certain direction" (118), a seemingly automatic process that takes on a veneer of normalcy and common sense – and one that, through how we carry ourselves in the world and conduct ourselves in relation to others, organizes space according to race. Spaces, Ahmed writes, "become racialized by how they are directed or orientated, as a direction that follows a specific line of desire. It shows us how the Orient is not only imagined as 'being' distant, as another side of the globe, but also is 'brought home' or domesticated as 'something' that extends the reach of the West" (120–1).

In this analysis of Orientalism, then, whiteness is a function of distance: "When distance is embodied, as whiteness, it becomes the starting point for orientation. What is here, is the 'line from which the world unfolds'; what is there, becomes the other side" (Ahmed 2006, 125).

Those who are on this "other side" come to embody distance, and, for Ahmed, it is this "embodiment of distance" that produces whiteness as "proximate," giving a particular skin colour the unacknowledged place as *the* "starting point" for all forms of subjectivity, all orientation, norms, values, and ways of "facing" the world. "Whiteness becomes what is 'here,' a line from which the world unfolds, which also makes what is 'there' on 'the other side'" (113).

Ahmed's reflections on Orientalism and diaspora offer a rich vocabulary and analytical framework for understanding Hatoum's material, visceral aesthetic, which is predicated on the idea of "situation." Given Hatoum's references to lost and damaged objects in the experiences of refugees, exiles, and migrants, Ahmed's writing on the role of objects within diasporic cultures is vital. Domestic spaces, she argues, are not only shaped by bodies, but by the "object histories" (149) that form part of our everyday worlds and give our environments, even our most intimate ones, shape and meaning:

> The gathering of objects at home takes a different form; objects scatter "along with" the scattering of bodies into spaces, as a scattering that makes an impression. When bodies and objects resurface they acquire new shapes. For diasporic communities, objects gather as lines of connection to spaces that are lived as homes but are no longer inhabited. Objects come to embody such lost homes. (149)

If our subjectivity is shaped by the objects with which we come into contact, then it is also, presumably, shaped by those objects that we lose – losses that we also inherit. For those who are forced to flee from their homes, objects, or memories of objects, carry sensory memories, complexly mingling comfort and pleasure with pain. Within Hatoum's sculptural world, objects from the home – a crib, a heating fan, a household grater – are re-sized and reconfigured as reminders of what is lost. Forgetting, as Ahmed (2004) suggests, "would be a repetition of violence or injury" (33). The task is "'to remember' how the surfaces of bodies (including the bodies of communities, as I will suggest later) came to be wounded in the first place" (33).

Ahmed's corporeal, political, and profoundly relational understanding of Orientalism and phenomenology exemplify what Elizabeth Grosz (1994), following Merleau-Ponty (1968), calls the chiasmatic "intertwining" of spaces and embodied subjects (96). We come into being not as isolated individuals, but through contact with an environment;

space is not empty but, rather, inhabited by a multitude of lives, including those of people, objects, animals, and plants that are deeply interconnected and that come to play a role in how we experience "home." Perceptions of space depend on the relations that we establish to these others. Grosz's reading of the body-space-senses nexus in Merleau-Ponty's work emphasizes a sense of space that is lived – that comes into existence through the way we live in it in concert with others, in our experiences of comfort and discomfort as we move about the world.

If we think about embodiment, bodies, home, place, and displacement, we are confronted with a visceral reminder of how the body remembers: the food we eat, the objects we take in with our eyes, the smells we sniff, the traumas we experience. History and place are not only written on the body's surface; they are also ingested. Inner corporeal space is linked to lives lived, both perceptible and imperceptible. This understanding of inner space as a series of continuous folds, connected to everyday life, interrupts facile notions of interiority and exteriority of the epidermis. What lies below is not a void, but a complex intertwining of tissue that carries memory. Likewise, every internal organ has its own skin, its own surface; just ask someone with a bleeding ulcer, or recall the last time you scorched the roof of your mouth with hot soup. At this liminal point, where the exterior surface of the skin folds back and over to become coterminous with the interior, one experiences a disorientation and dislocation that is particular to one's life narrative and embodied memory.

Gut Reactions

Hatoum's fascination with the visceral and concern over the increasing surveillance of her every orifice result in a poignant comment on cultural attitudes towards embodiment, leading to a commitment, on her part, to an exploration of how we can learn through the senses, but also to asking how we remember. As she comments in an interview, "I have always been dissatisfied with work that just appeals to your intellect and does not actually involve you in a physical way. For me the embodiment of an artwork is within the physical realm; the body is the axis of our perceptions, so how can art afford not to take that as a starting point? We relate to the world through our senses" (Archer 1997, 8). To instigate a visceral response through an aesthetic experience indicates a desire to initiate a respect for intuition and instinct as integral to the reasoning process. What is important from this perspective is that embodiment does not preclude reasoning; one is bound up in the other. The evocative colloquial expression, "gut reaction," used by Hatoum in an interview with Spinelli, conjures the etymological and historical links between the visceral and the viscera in relation to both knowledge and forms of truth telling (Hillman 1997, 92).

Historically, the intestines have been connected both with the instincts and emotions and with reason (Hillman 1997; Sawday 1995). David Hillman writes that in the pre-modern period leading up to the Renaissance, the idea that important truths lay hidden within the body's recesses was prevalent, truths that early anatomists such as Vesalius were at pains to expose. Based on Galenic medicine, the early modern understanding of physiology included detailed categorizations and interpretations of each specific organ and their links to the character of a subject: for example, the viscera, a part of the region of the torso that included both heart and stomach, were linked to courage and fortitude. Penetrating the hidden visceral depths offered the possibility of knowing the other and overcoming scepticism: "if entrails are where the other's innermost truth is imagined to be located or guaranteed, the skeptic appears to be searching out the ulterior truth within the body, beyond the veils of its surface" (Hillman 1997, 82).

While *Corps étranger* may be Hatoum's most graphically "realistic" representation of entrails and orifices, it was neither her first nor her last engagement with the world beneath the skin, with the surveillance of bodies, and with the disturbance of liminal boundaries. A history of work focused on intestinal exploration and visceral engagements precedes *Corps étranger.* In *Look No Body!* (1981), a video monitor in the exhibition space was connected to a live camera in the toilet. Hatoum drank cups of water, offering every second cup to the audience to incite them to use the facilities. Throughout the performance a pre-recorded voice read out a scientific account of "micturition," or urinating. As she explains, "With *Look No Body!* I was considering the body in terms of its orifices and how some of the orifices and activities associated with them are considered socially acceptable and some not" (Archer 1997, 10). *Don't Smile, You're on Camera* (1980) mixed live video images of the audience displayed on a monitor and synchronized with images of bodies without clothes, giving the impression that Hatoum had "X-ray vision" or the ability to see through people's clothing (Archer 1997, 10). Clothed bodies were superimposed over naked bodies and genders were mixed. Hatoum recalls that these early works, created while she was a student in London, aroused controversy because they were seen as aggressive and invasive. But this was entirely her point. By exaggerating the act of surveillance, Hatoum's intention was to "make people aware of the fact that we are constantly subjected to some mechanism of surveillance – the invasive look" (Archer 1997, 12).

Hatoum's persistent fascination with orifices and entrails is also evident in *The Negotiating Table* (1983). In this powerful, political performance of endurance, Hatoum lay on a table for five hours, wrapped in gauze covered with animal entrails and plastic sheeting, while the disembodied voices of recognizable politicians spoke of peace. Brett (1997) describes the table: "The artist lay motionless on it, wrapped in plastic and gauze, covered with entrails. Just breathing" (43). Featuring a body that barely moved, the performance space conveyed the idea of the artist on a sacrificial altar, whose status as a living body (a corps) or a dead body (a corpse) was shrouded in ambiguity. And, in later conceptual work, Hatoum used visual signs of viscera to promote a gut reaction – and a desire to touch – even in those cases where the body is only obliquely referenced. For instance, *Socle du monde* (1992–93) covered the surfaces of a magnetic cube with magnetic filings, whose positive and negative charges created a twisting surface in an intestine-like form that, as Brett (1997) comments, "corporealized" the modernist form of the cube (70). In a later work, *Entrails Carpet* (1995), a snaking silicon red rubber rug – a direct reference to inner body space – was produced at Philadelphia's Fabric Workshop. However, unlike the above-mentioned pieces, *Corps étranger* is the only installation that re-created the sensation of a potential line of flight *into* Hatoum's body, transplanting clinical and extremely private information from the laboratory into a public art gallery.

The Visceral and the Visual

In her discussion of *Corps étranger*, Laura Marks (2000) suggests that what is at stake in the installation is a distinction between embodied visuality and a vision that enters the body. *Corps étranger*, she says, is perplexing, for it depicts vision as violently entering the body, making our bodies "objects to us" (190). Marks' distinction between embodied visuality and a vision that enters the body emphasizes the violence of these visualization practices. However, *Corps étranger* is about more than a biomedical entry into the body. It also stages our forced entry into the machine and into a collective historical nightmare – one experienced by an entire people forced into exile and that continues to be lived and experienced in the present, but the story of which is often out of sight (Fiske 2002, 2005).

Once we enter it, *Corps étranger* forces us to look, recreating the conditions for the experience of the embodiment of vision at the same time as it depicts the penetration of the body's orifices by scientific vision machines. To borrow Hamid Naficy's (2001) turn of phrase, Hatoum engages in a form of "tactile optics" whereby "the human body is experienced from both sides of the phenomenological divide" (29, 28). On one side of the divide, one is subject to external forms of visioning, to external forms of mediation that include "the mediating gaze of others" (29). On the other side of the divide, internally, we experience vision by means of our own senses of vision, balance, and proprioception. Hatoum's installation dwells in this interstice, not only to destabilize the visitors to *Corps étranger*, but also to reverse traditional relations of power in the field of vision – a reversal that is embedded in the design of the installation space itself. As Paula Harper (1998) has observed, *Corps étranger* practises an ocular inversion. Her placement of the video image on the floor, so that spectators can walk around it, suggests a reverse oculus that turns the architectures of looking within Greek and Roman culture upside down: "A feature of ancient domed buildings such as the Pantheon in Rome, the oculus, or round opening at the top of a dome, served as an eye to heaven, but here we seem to be looking down into the seething bowels of the earth" (4). Rather than accessing an eye to the heavens, we stand at the threshold of a light source that seems to rise up from the floor. In staging this ocular inversion, Hatoum reminds us that the eye is both an organ for sight and an integral part of a body, a duplicity that is also deeply unsettling: who is watching – or penetrating – whom?

The paradox of seeing is that if one is either too close or too far, one's vision is obscured: obtaining the "proper" distance is necessary. In the words of Merleau-Ponty (1964), which recall Ahmed's (2006) analysis of the spatial extensions of whiteness, "to see is to have at a distance" (166). As Hatoum herself comments, despite one's closeness to the body in *Corps étranger*, it is difficult to know what one is seeing. Is it the vagina? The colon? The only certainty here is the feeling of instability. As Hatoum has mused, this image projected onto the ground, rather than above, has a directly feminist reference in its invocation of "a wonderful paradox between woman as victim and woman as devouring vagina" (quoted in Berger 1994, 149). What is conveyed is the sensation of a potential fall into a moist, enlarged, threatening, inviting abyss – a feeling enhanced by the camera movements that draw our attention, through our eyes, into this unnamed territory, at once familiar and yet distant.

To see others and to possess the technological means to augment vision is an integral part of the monitoring that does not merely open up a space but, as Foucault's ([1975] 1995) reflections on the panopticon and the relationship between power, truth, and vision underscore, also transforms it into a territory under a particular kind of jurisdiction. These territories are not simply *there*; they are constituted through acts of claiming and controlling space (Said et al. 2000). Here, Foucault's emphasis on the surveilled body resonates with the work of postcolonial and feminist phenomenologists. Like the panopticon, colonization is a process through which, as Frantz Fanon ([1952] 2008) so cogently put it, territorial violence transforms subjects into objects in a dialectical hierarchy of power and enslavement to the will of the colonial master. From this perspective, visibility is not merely akin to an act of seeing that leads to recognition, but is also understood as potentially leading to domination. Stepping into *Corps étranger*, visitors are brought into an uncomfortable, disquieting spatial proximity to Hatoum's foreign body (the viscera's strangeness, but also the familial and political histories of having been made strange, other, and forgotten) through an act of surveillance in which they become complicit with an all-seeing, probing "eye of power" (Foucault 1980) that not only monitors subjects but also produces conditions of subjectification.

Inheritance, Uncertainty, and Complicity

In *Corps étranger*, as in all of Hatoum's other visceral visual work, autobiography and personal experience become a resource for the re-staging of a historical event that unsettles. Playing with the dynamics of attraction and repulsion, uncertainty, and the doubling of both movements and of bodies, Hatoum presents an intimate portrait of the territory of exile and death by presenting a disturbing, yet compelling, journey into the recesses of her visceral environment. In providing a moment of uncertainty between the seductive pleasures of looking and the repulsion felt by what is being looked at, she offers a powerful critique of the affective pull of our investments in these imaging practices, and of our complicity in systems of surveillance and the monitoring of "foreign bodies."

Standing within the territory demarcated by the *Corps étranger*, we step into a landscape where we potentially become the foreign body; as such, a critique of biomedical imaging also becomes an examination of the de-territorialized status of the Palestinian in exile. It brings us into this inheritance. *Corps étranger* reclaims this inheritance through a phenomenological/aesthetic critique that does not directly reference these historical events, but is, instead, dedicated to "creating a situation which would hopefully trigger those associations in the spectator's mind" (Spinelli 1997, 135). In this sense, autobiography and history are embodied and embedded in the very materiality of Hatoum's installation-assemblage. She does not tell, she shows. She shows, we experience. We experience, we question. Scenarios are put into place wherein we are invited to actively make connections. Her work sets off a chain reaction of associations, beginning with the senses and perception, a "gut reaction" that brings us into the interstices of our tacit acceptance of technologies of surveillance, instigating a visceral awareness of our condition in a world of violence, forgetting, and trauma.

NOTE

Thank you to Tamara Shepherd for her incisive editorial assistance and phenomenological insights; to Sarah Brophy for her comments and suggestions; and to Peter Van Wyck for his close reading of this text.

1 Merleau-Ponty critiques the notion of metaphor on similar grounds. As he states in the Working Notes from *The Visible and the Invisible* (1968), both thinking and thought involve "a quasi-locality that has to be described" (222). In other words, knowledge is situated.

10 "Please Don't Let Me Be Like This!" Un-wounding Photographic Representations by Persons with Intellectual Disability

ANN FUDGE SCHORMANS
AND ADRIENNE CHAMBON

Oh God, I don't want to be like this, oh God, please don't let me be like this!

Donna, responding to a photographic image of a man with an intellectual disability in a national newspaper

Roland Barthes (1981) writes that when we pose for the camera, we want the photograph to present us as we really (think we) are, or as we would most desire to be seen, and not as the self that the photographer and the moment capture. But what happens when you have had absolutely no control over how you are represented, over the visual images presented to viewer(s) that define, delimit, and determine how you are seen and thus known? As a group, people with intellectual disabilities (ID) have had little, if any, influence over the making and use of public photographic images of people so labelled. This is troubling, given the enormous power of photographic images, as "scenes of instruction" (Mauer 2005, 96), to shape the understanding and expression of self and Other in contemporary culture (Derrida 2001).

The necessity of, right to, and recognition of the ability for self-representation and autobiography – both personal and collective – by people with ID, in any form, have only recently begun to be acknowledged within the academic disciplines of disability studies and ID, as well as in the disability service sector (Fudge Schormans 2005). Long silenced, the voices of people with ID "are the ultimate 'lost voices' in terms of auto/biographical records" (Atkinson and Walmsley 1999, 203). This can be traced to tenacious assumptions that theirs is a biological, and not a biographical, life (Fudge Schormans 2005). These are bodies believed to be without history, or with only a very limited or arrested one beyond that of biology. Most non-disabled interest is concerned with what these bodies have (i.e., a diagnosis) or do not have (i.e., intelligence, reason, thought – characteristics understood to constitute the human) (Fudge Schormans 2005). Reduced to their labels, there is little incentive to learn *from* persons with ID who they are, their ways of being, and the meanings they attribute to their experiences. This reveals an elemental disbelief in their capacity for insight, memory, and reflexive personal and collective understandings. Beyond an assumed inability to articulate their stories, they are presumed devoid of the capacity and means of knowing, and understood as objects of knowledge instead of as knowing subjects (Atkinson and Walmsley 1999; Fudge Schormans 2005).

Reflecting Judith Butler's (2004a) and G. Thomas Couser's (1997) concern with what counts as a life, along with Jacques Derrida's (1998) interest in whose stories do/do not get told, by whom, and how, we argue that people labelled intellectually disabled are conspicuously underrepresented as creators of and commentators on their own lives. Theirs are the missing autobiographies, missing because perceived to be non-existent or impossible to access. Socially produced as non-viable speaking subjects (Butler 2004a), they are spoken for and by non-disabled others, who, in writing dysfunctional narratives onto the disabled body, write away the stories, meanings, and signatures of labelled people. The knowledge they possess is excluded, made irrelevant, and our knowledge *of* them is both disabled and disabling.

In this chapter, we discuss a project that creatively engages with the ethics and politics of self-representation as a group of people labelled intellectually disabled critique, re-image, and re-imagine public photographs of people so labelled. We take as our points of departure Derrida's (1998) writing on "the right of inspection," our "right to look" at photographs, as well as his focus on re-imaging outside of conventional representation, in order to learn from labelled people how they address the (non-disabled) viewer's entitlement to "take" a photograph (2) – to tell (or mis-tell) the story of ID in and through the photographic image. Is this the right of inspection or the invention and/or possession of the "Other"? We ask, too, what happens when labelled people are, themselves, granted the right of inspection – the right not only to critique how they have been visually (mis)represented, to interrogate the stories told about them, but also to engage in practices of visual autobiography? How would they visually represent themselves, and how would they use visual autobiography to trouble our understandings of ID and to address non-disabled producers and viewers of existing disability imagery?

Seeing People with Intellectual Disabilities

In tracing the historical emergence of the disabled subject in northern Europe, Tim Stainton (2004) comments on the transformation of representations of persons with disability that coincided with the advent of a rationalistic, secular world view in the early Renaissance. Examining comparable scenes in works by two Dutch artists – fifteenth-century painter Hieronymus Bosch and sixteenth-century painter Pieter Bruegel – Stainton argues that no fixed concept of disability existed in the early Renaissance. By contrast, later works such as Bruegel's included figures depicting specific and realistic physical and intellectual impairments. Such figures were increasingly rendered as creatures of un-reason, representatives of a distinct kind of person whose gestures and facial expressions were understood to reflect negative moral traits that Stainton characterizes as signs of depravity. By the end of the Renaissance, the "Other" was created.

Moreover, with the advent of photography in the nineteenth century, a new order of reality was claimed. In his social history of photographic practices, John Tagg (1988) demonstrates that photography seemingly provides unmediated access to truth: "A photograph can come to stand as evidence" (4), as "a kind of proof" (67) that acquires a legal and scientific status. Through this technology, persons with disabilities were no longer merely depicted; they were identified, classified, entered into records, and photographically displayed to the broader public. Indicative of what Sarah Brophy and Janice Hladki, in their introduction to this collection, describe as forms of visual representation and "optical scrutiny" (Hesford 2000) that support regimes of biopower (9), people with disabilities came to be shown as specimens, as a "sort" of individual that can be traced to specific categories of being. Privileging ability, this type of photographic portraiture was used to assist medical practitioners in identifying pathologies and creating taxonomies of difference critical to the invention of what we now term "intellectual disabilities." Despite increased awareness that "the image is often determined before it is made" (Starr 2005, 101), with the technological ease of reproduction, photographs have become conduits of generalized representations that are taken as objective facts: "they pretend that they are showing us the thing itself" (Derrida 2001, 45). As an act of stark objectification, the taking of a photograph establishes new forms of subjection of the persons thus classified.

The connection between disability and the camera has often been a violent one. Visual images are critically important to people with disabilities who are, most of all, conceptualized in terms of how they are viewed (Darke 1998; Newbury 1996). Reflecting inequalities in power and the control of knowledge operating in public spaces, the marginalization of people with ID is revealed by their re-presentations in public photographs – images created almost exclusively by non-disabled others. Most disability imagery relies on hurtful stereotypical representations that present ID as tragedy, disaster, and lack, and people with ID as victims of their impairments. Alternative images are rare. As images of excess, photographic representations of people with ID selectively exaggerate impairment and distort the subject to the uses of the makers of the images (Hevey 1997); they publicly construct a seemingly dysfunctional and incommensurable subject, which perpetuates disability as a sign of extreme Otherness that distances labelled people both from non-disabled viewers and from themselves. Kaja Silverman (1996) notes that the determinative force of the cultural (in this case, ableist) gaze reflected in the photographic capture of labelled persons may profoundly influence understandings of the disabled Self. How we see ourselves is less important than how we are seen by others. For the person with a disability, "personal experience is over-determined by its social context" (Newbury 1996, 356). Or, as Eli Clare (2001) powerfully writes, "The pernicious stereotypes, lies, and false images can haunt a [disabled] body, stealing it away as surely as bullets do" (363).

Paradoxically, these reductive images virtually eliminate the distances among disabled people, creating a collective iconic identity that encompasses all labelled people, denying individuality and disavowing the diversity existing within this community (Carlson 2001). A single story of impaired and dysfunctional biology serves for all labelled people. There is, then, no reason to seek another story, or an other's story.

Public photographs of people with ID are structured so that *we* treat *them* as objects of our non dis-abled gaze, and not as subjects who return our gaze. In this respect, they share in what Susan Sontag (2003) identifies as the photographic conventions shaping the exhibition of colonized human beings: "for the other, even when not an enemy, is regarded only as someone to be seen, not someone (like us) who also sees" (72). Rosemarie Garland-Thomson (2009) extends this point to consider the act of staring at people with disabilities. She suggests that staring is different both from looking and from the oppressive disciplinary gaze; as an "intense visual exchange" between starer and staree, it is involved in meaning making and identity formation for people with disabilities (9). She proffers that "being stared at demands a response" (3). But this notion of exchange is perhaps troubled by conventional ideas about ID. The thinking seems to be that if, as a result of impairment, people with ID are unable to understand themselves, neither will they be sensitive to, nor wounded by, the ways we look and stare at them, or to the violence of the visual representations and stories that we (non-disabled others) show and tell. We do not expect them to be able to look at an image, to express an opinion, value, or moral judgment on representations. We do not expect them to have knowledge about society, to notice or care about events and situations outside of themselves – or to have associations *from* and *to* public images. We do not expect them to be able to create their own representations of themselves. Relationally, we do not expect them to be able to have a shared interest or to be aware of a group identity. Interpersonally, we do not expect them to be able to exchange, discuss, or listen to one another. Finally, and importantly, we do not expect them to have the ability or wish *to make an address* to *their* Other(s). Imagined as neither able nor desiring to respond to public looking, staring, or (mis)representation – individually, collectively, socially, or politically – people with ID are neither seeing nor seen. They, we tell ourselves, do not stare back.

These normative and powerfully durable discourses make disability a static, a-temporal, and dysfunctional characteristic. The lived experiences, informal discourses, and individual and collective identities of people with ID remain unknown, and the structures and forces inherent in these pathologizing discourses remain unveiled. These photographic conventions convey to viewers that whatever the circumstances, nothing has changed or can change – that the scripts of ID that have always existed will endure. Such assumptions shut down unsettling questions about our ability to reach out and know labelled persons, and about our reasons for not doing so.

Judith Butler (2004a) eloquently argues that practices of representation engage the fundamental question of the humanity and/or dehumanization of lives. Proposing an ethics of vulnerability that requires a redefinition of responsibility, she writes:

> Each of us is constituted politically in part by virtue of the social vulnerability of our bodies – as a site of desire and physical vulnerability, as a site of a publicity at once assertive and exposed. Loss and vulnerability seem to follow from our being socially constituted bodies, attached to others, at risk of losing those attachments, exposed to others, at risk of violence by virtue of that exposure. (20)

Butler engages with Levinasian ethics to consider how the face of the Other is admitted into public representation, how public re-presentations efface what is most human about the "face."[1] The face of the Other, being faced *by* the Other, is the means by which the Other addresses and makes an ethical demand on us, a demand to assume responsibility for the Other. It is the trace of our already being in an ethical relation with the Other (Perpich 2008). Being rendered faceless, or a de-humanized other, absolves *us* (the non-disabled) of responsibility for *their* well-being and, instead, authorizes violence against them (Butler 2004a). But, as Wendy Kozol asks, in this volume, how can visual practices be used to engage the viewer to do more than just voyeuristically look at images of trauma and oppression – to engage, rather, in an "ethical spectatorship" that entails a recognition of complicity and a movement towards critical awareness, action, and responsibility? Garland-Thomson (2009) argues for the political and ethical possibilities of staring when understood as a productive exchange, a relation of mutual beholding that allows the starer to acknowledge and accept the staree as a fellow human being who also stares back. Taking up Garland-Thomson's notion of "beholding," in the final chapter of this volume, Brophy and Hladki note that while it cannot guarantee a particular pedagogical or political outcome, visual autobiography has the potential to disturb, to trouble rather than confirm, that which we thought we knew (245). Questioning the limits and consequences of a public field of appearance, Butler, like Garland-Thomson and Derrida (1998, 2001), wishes to trouble the boundaries of what can and cannot appear in public spaces, asking why and how dominant forms of representation and practices of looking can be disrupted: "Certain faces must be admitted into public view, must be seen and heard for some keener sense of the value of life, all life, to take hold" (Butler 2004a, xviii). Self-representation is critically important to disrupting a visual field that differentially allocates recognition, value, and "life":

> When we consider the ordinary ways that we think about humanization and dehumanization, we find the assumption that those who gain representation, especially self-representation, have a better chance of being humanized, and those who have no chance to represent themselves run a great risk of being treated as less than human, regarded as less than human, or indeed, not regarded at all. (141)

The PhotoChangers and "What's Wrong with This Picture?"

We wish, now, to share some of the work created as part of what came to be known as the "What's Wrong with this Picture?" project. Ann Fudge Schormans conducted this research project towards her doctoral degree in Social Work; Adrienne Chambon was Ann's thesis supervisor. One purpose of the project was to better understand the ways that photographic images represent, mis-, or dys-represent, people with ID, which influences how and what we come to know – and what we tell others – about them. It was an inclusive,[2] arts-informed interpretive inquiry into how labelled people would see and respond to these cultural representations as means of knowing. It also aimed to explore how they could use photography to problematize these (dis)abling representations, trouble non-disabled knowing, and enable forms of self-representation. The goal was not to reach the "right" or "correct" representation but, rather, to illuminate the challenges, and consequences, of representational practices (Butler 2004a; Newbury 1996).

Approaching a local self-advocacy group of people with ID, Ann provided information about the project and invited interested persons to participate. Sam, Bob, Donna, and Robin enthusiastically agreed to be involved. They ranged in age from their early 20s to mid-50s, and had different although strikingly similar backgrounds in terms of experiences of marginalization and stigmatization. (They insist upon the use of their own first names in this publication; however, keenly aware of the risks of media representation, they are reluctant to have their full names circulating in the public sphere.)

The invitation to participate, along with the positioning of these four adults as the ones entrusted with the right of inspection, was no small thing for Sam, Bob, Donna, and Robin; they had never before been asked for their opinion on visual representations. Soon after beginning the work, they began to identify as a group (and included Ann as a member), naming themselves the "PhotoChangers." The intent of the project was not only to invite and give voice, but also to support the group to have as much control over the process as possible. At the start of each meeting, they would examine a selection of public photographic images of labelled people, supplied by Ann, and they – not Ann – would then decide which image(s) to work on (individually and/or collectively) that day. Ann drew an array of images from newspapers, charity advertising, service agencies, medical journals and magazines, social documentary, and, more rarely, photographic art – the most typical forums for photographic images of disability (Evans 1999; Garland-Thomson 2001; Hevey 1997).

Meeting one to three times per week for three months, the group first engaged critically with the images. By responding at first to questions posed by Ann, and, later, in conversations they themselves initiated and led, Sam, Bob, Donna, and Robin addressed what they did or did not like about the images; the stories or messages they read within them; and how they felt non-disabled viewers would interpret these images. Over the next two months, the group then transformed the images (with support from Ann and a consultant photographer using Photoshop to visually realize their desired transformations), or directed the taking of new ones, to reflect their critique and put forward images they preferred. The images were then exhibited to different audiences at a series of community exhibits that they curated. Here, we discuss their work with one particular image.

Seeing and Responding: Opposing the Imposition of Other(ed) Stories and Identities through Visual Autobiography

> Oh God, I don't want to be like this, oh God, please don't let me be like this. I do not want to look like this. I do not want to live like this. I think this is the most depressing picture I ever saw in my life. Do you find it upsetting? Like you're ready to cry or something, you know.
>
> Donna

Shaking her head, her gaze shifting between the image and the faces of the other group members, Donna's entire being was engaged in looking and responding to the photograph she held tightly in both hands. Drawn from a national newspaper, it is an image of a man with intellectual and physical disabilities. The image is bare/barren; little has been included, and what is there is bleak. The man's body has been similarly staged. Photographed almost completely naked, he wears only a diaper; he is exposed to the camera, to the viewer. He lies alone on a thin blanket that partially covers a plastic-protected mattress placed on a carpeted floor. The black and white image is dark – the bits of light contained within pushed by its dark walls towards the centre of the image, concentrated on the mattress, the diaper, and the man's body. He is very thin. His knees are held tightly together, his arms drawn close to his body. His face is averted from the camera. From his appearance, the group correctly surmised that he was unable to physically care for himself. His averted gaze tells them he is embarrassed to have been photographed this way.

Struggling with what she saw, Donna was troubled that by virtue of her label, "intellectually disabled," and as a consequence of this visual representation of ID, she, too, would be and had been identified by the non-disabled viewer as similarly incapable, equally dependent – the *same* as the man in the image. She worried over the consequences this might entail for her; she worried about how, in standing for her, this representation would delimit the possibilities for her own life and her ability to tell it, as well as for the lives of all similarly labelled people.

What the PhotoChangers saw in this image are the rules governing its production and the non-disabled viewer's reading of it – a reading that, in Derrida's (1998) words, must "remain within these limits, this frame, the framework of these frames" (1). The ableist gaze haunts the image, determines who can and cannot look, what can and cannot be seen, and what biographical story is or is not told. Sontag (2003) notes that public photographic images created from the hegemonic perspective foster the illusion of consensus among all potential viewers, which, in this case, depends on the shared belief that people with ID are excluded as viewers. The PhotoChangers understood this image as intended only for a non-disabled audience. The disabled body the viewer is given-to-be-seen (Silverman 1996) is understood, erroneously, as representative of all people with ID. The destructive and self-enhancing ableist gaze writes dysfunctional narratives onto the body of the labelled person captured within the image's frame (and "captured" is how they understood it). This gaze writes away the stories, meanings, and signature of this particular person and of labelled people more generally. This is not the man's story, nor is it theirs.

In what they perceived to be a stubborn reliance on disabling tropes and normative schemes of intelligibility that frame disability, one-dimensionally, as something tragic that nobody would ever want to be, the PhotoChangers felt the staging of this image, in Hevey's (1997) terms, enfreaked and de-humanized the photograph's subject. This was accomplished by the focus on the man's body. As Sam noted, this is what the viewer's eye is drawn to first: "I mean, like, because, um, how the way, because he's like all crippled, and then he's like crinkled with his hands and arms and even his feet is not steady … his body length is very crooked." Garland-Thomson's (2007) notion of how, for the non-disabled viewer, "shape structures story" (113), works well to explain the PhotoChangers' understanding of the image. By accentuating and attenuating the impaired body, the photograph supports the tenacious belief that "the configuration and function of our human body determines our narrative identity, the sense of who we are to ourselves and others" (113). As a site of publicity, the differentness of this body, combined with how the man is photographed alone, with no evidence of sociality, exposes and determines his to be an un-lived and un-livable life (Butler 2004a). For a life reduced to body and biology, autobiography becomes impossible.

For the PhotoChangers, the violence of this image lies in how it forecloses other narratives of ID: both those of the man in the image and their own. According to Robin, "[the image] does not explain it [what it means to have an ID]. It just tells you the picture is sad." This static and reductive construction was not regarded as reflective of the very livable lives of the group members and of other labelled people. Instead, this image was little more than, in Derridean (1998) terms, an invention of an other – one imposing a pathological and iconic identity upon *all* labelled people. Yet, this identity was often at odds with the PhotoChangers' sense of self.

Here, we present two of the ways in which the PhotoChangers visually responded to this image, practices that function as an expression of critique and/through autobiography. The first was a re-imaging of the original photograph (directed by Bob); the second was the taking of a new image by three group members (Sam, Bob, and Donna).

Bob worried over the man in this photograph, a man who (like some, but certainly not all labelled people) he understood to require a great deal of support and care. He would gently hold the image in his hands, lay it carefully on the table, and wonder if anyone was taking care of the man. While Bob understood that non-disabled viewers would likely find the man frightening, his own response was different. For Bob, the man was vulnerable; lacking human contact, he was not in the world as much as in an empty, impersonal space: "he's locked in this dark room alone, by himself." Bob fretted over the vulnerability created by the photographic exposure of the man's body – over the absence of markers of care, including material provisions such as clothing, and of caregivers. Opposing this empty and seemingly non-human landscape, along with the lack of care it signified, Bob's remedy was to ask us to use the computer software program Photoshop to cover the man with a blanket; the touch of the blanket signified protection and the extension of human(izing) care to the photographic subject. In that the original image represents the man as approaching, if not beyond, the limits of the human, Bob recognized how the image worked to de-humanize the man in Butler's sense of the word: unable to see the human in the image, the human life existing beyond the image's frame, the viewer has no reason or responsibility to respond. Bob, however, did see the life beyond this image – a life that appears in all of its precariousness (Butler 2004a) – and felt some responsibility to the man. His re-imaging was his response to this vulnerability. In Bob's transformation, the dark blanket looks soft and warm; it drapes over the man's body, snugly but not tightly. The shape of his body underneath is still visible, but his thinness and the diaper are covered. The light in the image is no longer focused on the man's frail and exposed body, but on the blanket enfolding him in a care-full embrace.

What made this transformation autobiographical was Bob's own history of un-care. In re-imaging this photograph, Bob was speaking not only to what he saw, but also to his own life – to what he has experienced, and what he would have preferred. The transformed image both rendered visible his own treatment by non-disabled others and came to represent histories of un-care shared by the rest of the group. Over the course of the project, all the group members recounted numerous incidents of hurtful treatment couched in the language of care, as well as the pain ensuing from such mistreatment. This image thus evoked personal feelings of vulnerability. As Donna explained, "I couldn't see myself walking around the street like that, and have people look at me, make fun of me, and laugh at me – no thank you!" Bob added, "Sometimes when people look at these pictures they give them [the people in the images] dirty looks, like [they do] at me." Articulating their belief that the stigma of ID coexists with the experience and/or threat of rejection, teasing, abandonment, and bullying, the group members proffered that the original image reveals that, because of impairment, people with ID are not wanted, that, as Robin put it, "people don't care."

Bob's identity is strongly rooted in his sense of independence, but he is generally accepting of his ongoing need for support: he lives in his own apartment and a social worker helps with tasks he identifies as difficult. For Bob, his transformation of this image spoke to and against the lack of care-for, and caring-about, labelled people – to and against his and the other group members' experiences of hurtful "care." The blanket worked to repudiate assumptions that nobody could or would care for, or about, a man as disabled as this – that somehow such caring-for was unnecessary, such caring-about impossible. It was also an expression of Bob, himself, as caring. It was designed to challenge understandings of ID in terms of individual pathology and to, instead, place responsibility – for the image, for the (mis)treatment of labelled people – squarely in the hands of the non-disabled other. It sharply reprimanded those who would believe the man undeserving of dignity and respect. Beyond just telling, Bob used visual autobiography as a means of addressing the non-disabled other and providing a way of re-viewing the persistent de-humanization of labelled people – of evaluating the present, re-evaluating the past, and anticipating a perhaps different future (Cotterill and Letherby 1993).

Let us now turn to the second visual response to this image of the man in the diaper: Sam, Bob, and Donna's taking of a new picture. Garland-Thomson (2001) writes that photography provides non-disabled "viewers with an immediate yet distanced way to contemplate the disabled body without actually having to expose themselves to visibly disabled people" (338). What assumed tremendous importance to the group members – who are keenly aware of the aversion of many non-disabled others towards labelled people – is the realization that it likely never enters the consciousness of the non-disabled producers of these images to consider the perspectives *of* people with ID *regarding* the images: to seek consent for the taking of their photograph, to give credence to their critique, or, perhaps most importantly, to let them use photography for the purposes of autobiography. In this way, viewer and viewed, able-bodied and disabled, are each kept "in their place." The PhotoChangers were aware of their positioning as non-viable actors, non-viable speaking subjects (Butler 2004a). They understood that their subjugation as knowers underpinned their disenfranchisement as authors of their own stories, their deliberate exclusion from the processes of creating and critiquing visual re-presentations of ID. Speaking again to the image of the man in the diaper, they did not believe that he had any control over how he was visually presented. Donna asked, "Whose permission was it to take this picture? ... Who decided, who gave permission to take this picture ... that's my concern ... I don't want people taking pictures of me without my permission. I have had that experience. Believe you me, it's no fun ... Because I want to know what it's used for. It's my right." The issue of consent to photographic representation was a very important consideration in the construction and operation of this project. Control over the use of their own images rested entirely with the group members. The project did not require this; it was their initiative, their decision, and one they chose to exercise politically as a form of "visual activism" in response to this (and other) images (Garland Thomson 2009, 193).

The PhotoChangers were unequivocal in their opposition to how the man in the diaper had been visually represented. Seeing themselves in the image and refusing this identification, they made it clear they would have represented themselves differently:

> How come the pictures don't show people with disabilities as part of a family, or as having friends? – Bob
>
> Yeah, or as people who have jobs or who help others or who are in the community? How come they don't show us as people who join groups like self-advocates or church groups or as people who make presentations at conferences? – Sam
>
> We like pictures of people with disabilities all together as friends. These pictures have the true meaning of disability – people together as a group. They are not ashamed of their disability, they want to get the picture out and be recognized. It shows they can be independent. – Bob

The group photograph that they created is an autobiographical one (see figure 10.1). It is their collective visual telling of the story of their friendship. Reflecting their thoughts as to what was missing from ID imagery, they took charge of the scene (Garland-Thomson 2009), taking this photograph, in part, as a counter-image. Demonstrating their long-standing relationships with each other, they wished to convey, too, their connection to others in the community, and included in this image Ann's daughter, with whom they had developed a reciprocally caring relationship. Their caring is demonstrated by the holding of hands, arms gently lain across shoulders, and relaxed poses. Smiling faces register their happiness. In contrast to the black and white image of the man in the diaper, this colour image is bright; the viewer immediately sees the blue of the sky, the green grass, the colourful clothing. Seated on a bench in a public park, buildings and other people are visible in the background. Sam, Bob, and Donna are not segregated, not alone, neither abandoned nor hidden away. Instead, they have portrayed themselves as being within the community, as part of each other's lives and of the world around them.

While adhering to conventions of typical portraiture, the setting of the park, the jacket tucked behind Bob's back, the paper in his hand, and the figure of the boy walking by, suggest the spaces and motion that "are the coordinates and the context of 'real life'" (Garland-Thomson

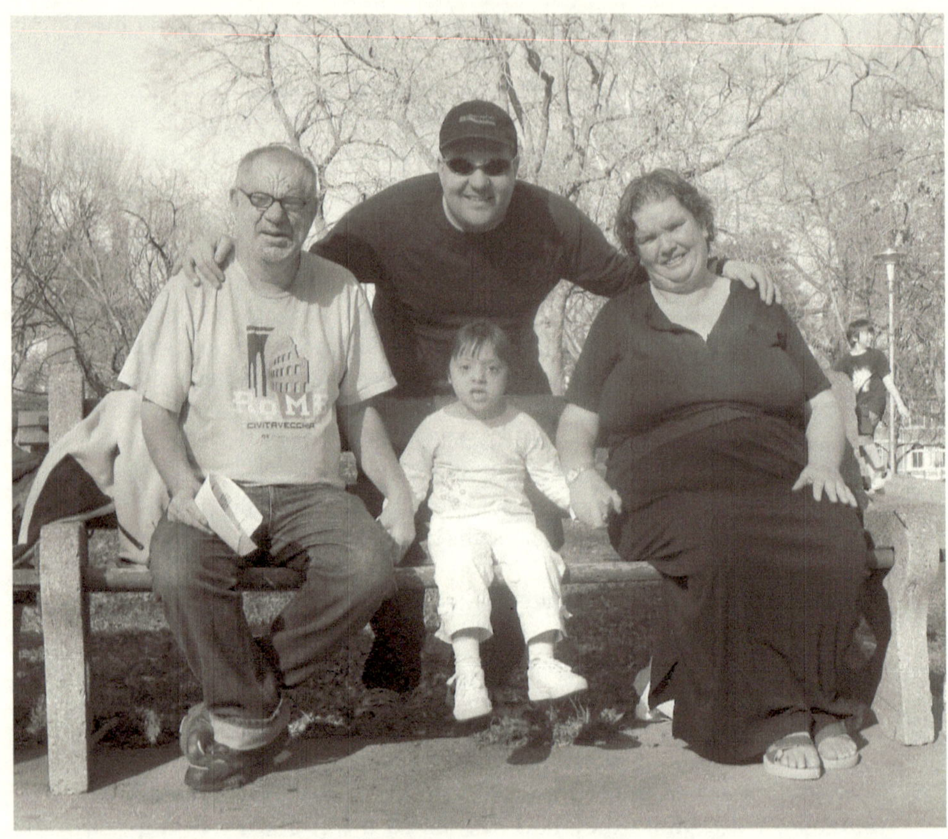

10.1. Personal photograph created by Sam, Bob, and Donna (PhotoChangers, 2007). Courtesy of Ann Fudge Schormans.

2001, 336) – the human(izing) beyond of the image. They reveal to non-disabled viewers that the group members, in many ways, have a good life. The group here is concerned with the necessity of the non-disabled viewer's seeing more than what typical representations of ID will let us know. They also use traditional portraiture as a means of trying to engage the viewer, staging the image such that their eyes seem to reach out of the image, calling the viewer to look back and to get to know *them* rather than stare at a stereotypical misrepresentation. Garland-Thomson (2009) suggests that, because non-disabled viewers are unaccustomed to being stared back at by those typically understood to be unable, this relational strategy is surprising in that it confers authority, thus troubling conventional understandings of disability by demanding a response. Returning to Kozol's term, "ethical spectatorship" (this volume), the PhotoChangers' looking-back acknowledges the simultaneously ethical and voyeuristic gazes that visual practices of autobiography entail. What is at play, then, is a reconfiguring not only of whose eyes determine what can and cannot be seen and told, but also of whose eyes are looking back: a new viewer who is seeing, responding, and telling.

As visual autobiography, Sam, Bob, and Donna's image counters cultural practices that objectify disabled subjects through the group members' re-authoring of their life stories (Gillman, Swain and Heyman 1997). Juxtaposed with the original image of the man in a diaper, this image further subverts dominant conceptions of ID and acts as a record of marginalized and neglected stories that speak not only of social isolation and derision, but also of inclusion, participation, community, and achievement (Gillman, Swain and Heyman 1997; Goodley 1996).

The Act of Visual Autobiography, the Call for Responsibility

Paul Darke (1998) wonders if we, the non-disabled, are ever able to *see* a disabled person or if we see only the stereotypic icon for the construct "disability"? Jessica Evans (1999) argues, further, that it is this "whole language of 'seeing them' which is the problem precisely because the oppression and inequality of disabled people is not caused by their bodily impairments but by the social arrangements which allow those impairments to become disabilities" (335). As Hevey (1997) notes, "Once again, the entire discourse has absented the voice of those at its centre – disabled people" (335). The PhotoChangers would seem to concur with all three critics. They make plain that, whatever they might be, public photographic representations are resolutely not autobiographical. Denying both the right and the ability of labelled people to create visual autobiography, such photographs are dysfunctional misrepresentations that act as a form of social erasure of individual identities and write over the authoring of lives. These are not their stories, and they are not even the stories of the disabled subjects of the images. They do little more than reduce labelled people to "others" – easily encapsulated by a fixed frame, relegated to the very margins of humankind, or frozen into non-humanness altogether. Without evidence of lives lived, the images reveal an absence of caring – either caring about or for them, or recognizing their own ability to care, in turn. The implication is that one cannot be both vulnerable and caring, needing to be cared for and about and simultaneously able to care.

The PhotoChangers' work critiques the void that is photographic representations of ID. Characterized by both physical and metaphorical bareness, the original photographs used in the "What's Wrong with This Picture?" project suggest only emptiness. For the subjects in the images, theirs is a bareness *of* and *in* life; reduced to their biology, they are exposed. Sam, Bob, Donna, and Robin also understand the catalogue of images of ID, as created by non-disabled people, as a void – an archive that is missing the perspectives and lived experiences of labelled people that are otherwise found in photographs of daily life. While these subjects may be *exposed* in these dysfunctional public images, they are not *revealed* (Wagner 2000). Further, this exposure makes them vulnerable to hurtful inspection, but not available to knowing. The images thus wound in that they delimit how non-disabled viewers know labelled people, what we do and do not know – and tell others – about them, and what we do with, for, and to them. They wound in that they affect both how people with ID come to understand themselves and how they experience their lives and relations with the world. And they wound because the radical othering of people with ID that photographic images foster actively discourages non-disabled movement towards – attempts at respectful relationship or knowing – this Other.

The PhotoChangers interpreted the images they viewed as dehumanizing. In the limited field of appearance constituting public photographic images of ID, they saw not the face of the individual within the frame, but what Butler (2004a) might term the production of the face of ID, a framing that de-faces the labelled person captured within the image and authorizes the violence that they and the group members experience in their own lives. Rendered faceless, people with ID are reduced to non-living objects. But, in speaking to and telling disabled lives and cultures, the group's work connects humanization to self-representation, to visual autobiography. Challenging assumptions that people with ID "can't think, can't understand what's going on" (Robin), the project reveals their ability to express their opposition to these images; their wish to demystify and undo the harm that such images perpetuate. Invited to visually narrate their own lives, their re-imagining of existing photographs and putting forward of original counter-constructions simultaneously undo representations of certainty and multiply the meanings of ID, differentiating across personalized autobiographies in relation to a collective re-creation.

The group image created by the Photochangers that we addressed in this chapter, then, is an important visual autobiographical move; an image the group *chose* to make and one not part of the initial research plan. For the PhotoChangers, it was not enough to redress the circulating images of ID through the creation and exhibition of their transformed images. They extended their telling into a more powerful autobiographical strategy in which they became not only viewers and directors of – and commentators on – the visual performance, but also "actors." In this image of themselves in daily life, they are performing themselves as they see themselves and as they want to be seen. Seeing and performing, they have shifted beyond critique to take part in the cultural production of their everyday lives. Politicizing the body, the PhotoChangers use visual autobiography as a means of acting and speaking against the imposition of a dysfunctional biography and challenging the inscription of ID as dysfunction in conventional public images. In their work, no longer does "shape structure story"; rather, as visual autobiography, "story structures shape" (Garland-Thomson 2007, 113). The stories told in and by these self-produced visual representations work towards new understandings of people with ID.

Visual autobiography is a means of ensuring that the group members are both seen and recognized as seeing, and, in the case of images they create of themselves, understood to be both staree *and* starer. Inviting non-disabled staring at their images, they simultaneously stare back. This "is not a plea, but rather an assertive outreach towards mutual recognition across difference," a mutual beholding (Garland-Thomson 2009, 94). Creating new spaces of self-representation, the PhotoChangers address a non-disabled audience through a range of un-wounding counter-images. This returns us to the connections between (self-)representation, response, and responsibility. Garland-Thomson (2001) posits that public photographic images of disability require no response from the non-disabled viewer. Butler (2004a) argues, instead, that the non-disabled viewer, the *normal* human, in their placement outside of the image's frame, is not captured *by* the image but is, rather, charged with capturing and subduing the image, with possessing the non-human other within the frame. Therefore, if we can look beyond the image at the precarious lives that the image does not permit us to see, we can see the face of the Other. This, Butler claims, is what calls one to an ethical relation with and responsibility to the Other. The group members clearly concur: their visual autobiographies function as an address, a call to response and responsibility – a demand for "ethical spectatorship" – on the part of non-disabled others (Kozol, this volume). Exemplifying Derrida's concern with "the intrusion of the unexpected and the unanticipated," these counter-images – if seen, heard, and believed – touch the non-disabled viewer (2001, 5; Derrida 1998). They do so by troubling what non-disabled viewers think they know, creating an opening to the Other (Simon 2000) and to new knowledge, and holding them accountable for taken-for-granted assumptions about ID. Garland-Thomson (2009) suggests that in disturbing the visual status quo one can also disturb the ethical status quo. Counter-images shift the gaze; they reintroduce connection, relatedness, and responsibility, and, in that manner, they educate.

NOTES

1 We rely on Butler's (2005) use of the signifier "other" to denote the human other in its specificity (be this a non-disabled or disabled other), and "Other" in the Levinasian sense as a "placeholder for an infinite ethical relation" (x).

2 It is important to note that the Bob, Sam, Donna, and Robin were not involved in the writing of this chapter. As a group, Ann and the *Photo-Changers* determined a number of different audiences for the work and made decisions as to who wished to be involved in the various dissemination strategies identified. The PhotoChangers have made numerous conference and community presentations – with and without Ann's participation – and together have given lectures to social work classes. Two of the members are in the process of writing a co-authored article with Ann. However, the group members are content to let Ann (and Adrienne) write for academic publication. Similarly, at the outset of the project they were made aware that, to complete her doctoral requirements, Ann would be required to write a dissertation. Ann showed examples and explained the purpose of such a document, how it would be used, and who might read it. While wanting to help Ann with the writing – to help her "pass" – they understood the reasons why this was not possible.

11 "Why Should Our Bodies End at the Skin?" Cancer Pathography, Comics, and Embodiment

LAURA McGAVIN

Midway through his acclaimed graphic memoir of cancer experience, *Stitches* (2009), David Small invites readers to "step inside your mouth with me" (182). Here we are asked to participate in a fantasy of embodied self-knowledge predicated on our ability to see; in a series of five panels, the narrator reveals to us the inside of a mouth and throat and explains that the function of the vocal chords is to "[make] the sound of your voice, your curses and your prayers" (183). The first three images show a tiny figure climbing through teeth, over a tongue, and peering downwards into the esophagus towards the vocal chords, which resemble a large eye. Through this fantastical seeing, interior bodily knowledge is momentarily imagined to be possible – for both David and the reader, both "me" and "you." Taken together, these panels invite us to ponder the impossibility of viewing the inside of our own bodies in real time. The images confound distinctions between subject and object, interior and exterior: the mouth could be your mouth, or mine, or David's; and because we cannot see his face, the boy could represent you, or David, or me. Through the staging of an impossible visualization – that of being inside of, and seeing, one's own mouth and throat – these images transgress the boundary between the interior and exterior body. For Small, this means "returning" to the site of his cancer, which was operated on when he was 14 years old, to view the vocal chords that were damaged during a traumatic surgical procedure.

In graphic cancer pathographies, the ill body is frequently drawn as becoming its surrounding environment or disintegrating into smaller constituent bodily parts or processes. Small's *Stitches* and Joyce Brabner and Harvey Pekar's *Our Cancer Year* (1994) visualize bodies in which metastatic cell division, surgery, or responses to chemotherapy and radiation render boundaries between the inner and outer body strange or incoherent. In both form and content, these graphic cancer memoirs undermine the "seeming visual self-evidence" (Barad 2007, 155) governing what constitutes healthy or normalized bodies. However, the texts' respective depictions of unbounded cancerous bodies are drawn using inside-out visual motifs. In *Stitches*, images of David's body are directed inward through Small's use of bodily close-ups, fragmentations, and truncations; in *Our Cancer Year*, dissolving, integrative depictions of Harvey's body show its contours radiating outward into his surroundings. These conversely inward- and outward-pointing images of the body parallel different autobiographical strategies that seek recuperation from cancer's threat to self-identity and order. Small's introspective memoir returns through memory to the site of his cancer in order to repair the traumas of illness and estrangement from an abusive, neglectful family. In contrast, the collaboration between Brabner, Pekar, and illustrator Frank Stack explores the meanings of illness through the act of situating shared cancer experience in intersubjective contexts of personal, community, and even global narratives. Although both texts depict the ontological instability of the cancerous body's boundaries, *Stitches* and *Our Cancer Year* respond to and recuperate the suffering of cancer experience using inverse graphic representations of unstable embodiment.

Serious considerations of graphic pathography[1] serve as necessary and timely interventions into understanding alternative literary genres that address cancer experience. As graphic narrative scholar Hillary Chute (2008a) has observed, "Increasingly, the complex representation of illness and its effects is finding a home in the medium of comics" (413). Certainly this is the case with cancer narratives. The majority of cancer comics, whether serialized or printed in long-format graphic narratives, have been published within the last decade or so. These include Stan Mack's *Janet and Me* (2004), selections from Alison Bechdel's *Invasion of the Dykes to Watch Out For* (2005), Miriam Engelberg's *Cancer Made Me a Shallower Person* (2006), Marisa Acocella Marchetto's *Cancer Vixen* (2006), Brian Fies' *Mom's Cancer* (2006), Tom Batiuk's *Lisa's Story: The Other Shoe* (2007), and Small's *Stitches*. While not all of these comics are autobiographical (the character with breast cancer in Bechdel's *Invasion of the Dykes*, for instance, is fictional), and some are written from the perspective of a caregiver (*Janet and Me*; *Mom's Cancer*), each thematizes the psychological and physical suffering of cancer diagnosis and treatment.

But what kinds of embodiments are rendered in graphic cancer pathographies, and why is the comics medium so appropriate and so widely used for representations of cancer and its treatments, as well as the dissolution of stable or self-contained bodies? Discussing the significance of comics for the field of literature and medicine, Susan Squier (2008a) suggests that "in their attention to human embodiment, and their combination of both words and gestures, comics can reveal unvoiced relationships, unarticulated emotions, unspoken possibilities, and even unacknowledged alternative perspectives" (130). As Will Eisner (1985) and Scott McCloud (1993) have theorized in their respective studies of comics, the medium combines gestural forms, represented pictorially, with written narrative. Since they juxtapose gestural images and text, graphic narratives are generically equipped to depict embodied conditions of illness and disability, including neurological impairment and chronic pain (Squier 2008a, 2008b). Yet, scholarship in the medical humanities, cultural studies, and literary studies is only beginning to consider the ways in which the hybrid visual-textual properties of comics illustrate what it means to "be" ill.

It is illuminating to bring together two emergent fields in order to explore how *Our Cancer Year* and *Stitches* represent cancer experience: the study of comics or graphic fiction, and post-humanism, which reconsiders the category of "the body" by showing it to be enmeshed with seemingly exterior agents and processes. These cancer memoirs reveal an embodiment that resembles Karen Barad's (2007) post-humanist understanding of material entanglements, wherein internal bodily processes are mutually constituted with both the self and the world outside the body. I am concerned with how the ontological instability of the cancerous body's boundaries is articulated through the politics and ethics of writing graphic pathographies, which seek to repair the corporeal and psychic harm that serious illness poses for its sufferers. Graphic narratives are a formally inclusive genre: that is, they work through the integration of words and images, panels and gutters, speech and gestures. For this reason, they are able to show the somatic and material self as it is conjoined with the speaking and sensing self. Graphic pathographies portray subjective, affective, and politicized dimensions of cancer experience, and simultaneously show the ongoing relationship between bodies and worlds – a material-discursive joining that is, crucially, "agentive, not a fixed essence or property of things" (Barad 2007, 137).

Barad's "Intra-action" and Bodily Boundaries

Our Cancer Year and *Stitches* use visual and gestural cues to suggest bodily disorientation. Both Stack, the illustrator of *Our Cancer Year*, and Small, who painted his own images in *Stitches*, employ an often stark black and white palate, combining this with artistic techniques that create a sense of visual inseparability between the self/body and its interior or exterior. Stack's repetitive use of cross-hatching, for example, which radiates outwards from Harvey's body and into his environments (home, hospital, neighbourhood), or even into other characters, suggests not only bodily disintegration and pain, but also a merging between Harvey and his physical surroundings. In *Stitches*, Small uses complex visual motifs to suggest conjoined sociosomatic relationships between the interior, cancerous body, the self, and the family. Recurring images that resemble the inside of David's cancerous throat visually suggest ongoing processes of memory, cognition, and affect: the circular image of the vocal chord that we are invited to view is repeated elsewhere as a seeing eye, as spirals depicting his loss of consciousness under anaesthetic, and as a puddle of tears.

Post-humanist theorizations of embodiment offer a framework for explaining how, why, and to what effect these graphic memoirs distort the contours of the cancerous body. The term "post-humanism" has come to be associated with scholarship in science studies and cultural studies that aims to destabilize the notion of an exceptional, closed, and autonomous human subject.[2] Defined, in part, by an ethical and ontological commitment to both humans and non-humans, both nature and culture, "posthumanism doesn't presume the separateness of any-'thing,' let alone the alleged spatial, ontological, and epistemological distinctions that set humans apart" (Barad 2007, 136). Although post-humanism may seem to want to announce the end of the human, I am interested in how it, in fact, seeks to re-conceptualize humans as situated in "the intimate relation of the living present to its outside, the opening to exteriority in general" (Derrida quoted in Wolfe 2009, xxi), as well as how its theorizations of embodiment are significant for our understandings of illness and disability.

In *Meeting the Universe Halfway: Quantum Physics and the Entanglement of Matter and Meaning* (2007), Barad argues for a post-humanist understanding of embodiment that is constituted by endless, dynamic, and "intra-active" human and non-human processes – what she describes as "ongoing reconfigurations of the world" (141). Proposing that "things" and "words" are not objects with intrinsic meanings but, rather, that both exist in perpetual and "agential" relation, Barad offers a "naturalcultural" understanding of material relations that are "produced and productive, generated and generative" (137). Central to her conception of the body is a destabilization of the margin between interior and exterior. Bodies are always materialized in ongoing relation with what appears to be outside of them, for

> all bodies, not merely human bodies, come to matter through the word's iterative intra-activity – its performativity. This is true not only of the surface or contours of the body but also of the body in the fullness of its physicality, including the very "atoms" of its being. Bodies are not objects with inherent boundaries and properties; they are material-discursive phenomena. (153)

Bodies are differentiated from one another and from non-human things and processes through an enactment of boundaries that relies, in part, on "visual self-evidence" (155). This self-evidence depends on our faith that we can visually distinguish the coherent body from its apparently separate surroundings. The skin is a seeable barrier appearing to separate the body from everything that surrounds it, and everything that the skin itself surrounds. Barad echoes Donna Haraway (1991) in asking, "Why should our bodies end at the skin?" – a question that prompts us to reconsider both the body's interiority and its exteriority as intra-active sites of becoming (Barad 159).[3]

Barad's concept of post-humanist performativity is situated in a lineage of feminist theory, sometimes referred to as "the new materialism" (Ahmed 2008; Hird 2004), which argues that post-structuralist or "social constructionist" theory fails to account for the ontology of biological matter.[4] The field does not take as its point of entry an engagement with historical materialism; rather, it begins with "the critique of past feminism for not engaging with matter, as such" (Ahmed 2008, 32). Elizabeth Grosz (2004), for example, writes that cultural feminist theory "[has] forgotten the nature, the ontology, of the body, the conditions under which bodies are encultured, psychologized, given identity, historical location, and agency"(2). Similarly, Elizabeth Wilson (2004) charges post-structuralist feminism with being firmly "anti-biologist" (13), disavowing the functions that sustain biological life by prioritizing political and cultural dimensions of embodiment. Barad is clear that her concept of agential realism "is not an invitation to turn everything (including material bodies) into words; on the contrary … [it] is precisely a contestation of the excessive power granted to language to determine what is real" (133). Material feminism's focus on what Barad calls "onto-epistemology" is valuable because it requires us to rigorously interrogate interactions between language and the agency of biological matter. However, there is room to expand Barad's comments on intra-active corporeal boundaries in order to address ways in which embodied selfhood is negotiated during serious illness, and how these negotiations become "*textured*" through autobiographical representation (Titchkosky 2007, 16, original emphasis). Tanya Titchkosky emphasizes that the "appearance" of disability – and, by extension, of any non-normalized form of embodiment – is enacted and then encountered through the reading and writing of texts (17). She argues that texts bring into being culturally contingent and politically inflected norms that regulate the normalization of embodiment. Crucially, "insofar as the meaning of disability is actively produced from our daily relations with texts, there are ethical, political, and practical reasons for the analysis of this phenomenon" (16).

Although Barad does briefly discuss the significance of bodily intra-activity for disability studies, her work does not account for the contingent and individual ways in which the instability of bodily boundaries is experienced due to disability or illness. As Margrit Shildrick (2002) suggests, "The healthy body … far from being consistently present to us, is scarcely experienced at all"; but "once it … is broken – that is diseased, damaged or otherwise unwhole – the body forces itself into our consciousness" (49). Like Barad, Shildrick argues that ostensible lines of separation between body and world "are realised quite literally in the material of the body" (51), and that this separation is visibly marked by the skin-boundary. But she emphasizes that the construction and maintenance of bodily boundaries "is not … a matter of material practices alone, but is fully imbricated with the discursive mechanisms that constitute psychic identity" (55). As the stigmatizing metaphors associated with cancer and HIV/AIDS make clear (Sontag [1978] 1990), unstable, "leaky," or "monstrous" bodily boundaries threaten individual and collective senses of order and control (Shildrick 2002, 48, 55). The contingency of the "normal" body – which is never a neutral or value-free entity, but which is materialized through boundary-drawing practices – calls attention to the ways in which "the disruption of corporeal integrity and the open display of bodily vulnerability is always a moment for anxiety" (Shildrick 2002, 53). Such moments of anxiety are affectively, politically, and ethically recuperated through the acts of writing and reading pathography.

The self-evidence of bodily containment becomes untenable "when the body doesn't work – when the body 'breaks down'" (Barad 2007, 158). But for women and men with cancer, the signs of illness are often mysterious or unapparent because cancer's initial, molecular stages of growth are invisible to the person in whose body they occur; metastasis remains in the realm of what Susan Sontag (1990), in her discussion of cancer metaphors, calls "the interior décor of the body" (28). Jackie Stacey (1997) points out that carcinogenesis, which begins as a mutated form of the body's own tissues, "is produced by the body, is of the body, and yet it is a[n invisible] threat to the body" (77). Cancer's "deviancy" is not immediately detectable; cancer "hides" and "impersonates the subject" (Stacey 1997, 78). Most often, medical visualization employed during the diagnostic process – including ultrasound, CT scan, or MRI technologies – "reveals" cancer to both physician and patient by creating an image of the interior body. Moreover, a patient's felt experiences of painful or unpleasant bodily sensations primarily arise from the effects of cancer treatments, including surgical intervention, chemotherapy, radiation, or alternative therapies. As Stacey argues, after diagnosis, suffering partly arises from a fundamental disturbance to one's identity – from realizing the presence of the other (the cancer cell) within the self. In their respective theorizations of "monstrous" bodies, Stacey and Shildrick both appeal to Julia Kristeva's (1982) concept of the abject in order to argue that the instability of bodily boundaries causes "persistent unease occasioned by corporeal difference" (Shildrick 2002, 53). The abject is a category defined by Kristeva as neither subject nor object, neither body nor un-body. Stacey observes that a malignant cell has qualities of the abject because "it is of the body" but "a threat to the body" (77). Cancer causes the disturbance to identity that abjection marks: "the horror of not knowing the boundaries of distinguishing 'me' from 'not me'" (78).

Cancer experience involves at least two embodied processes, both of which make apparent the body's open-endedness or intra-activity: apprehending interior cellular metastasis and negotiating the body's interactions with exterior interventions of treatment. In each case, "having" cancer means re-conceptualizing the embodied self as existing in ongoing flux with the internal cellular body, external interventions into that body, and somatic changes that result from medical treatments. This involves the opening of the body to what Sontag (1990) has called the "non-self": "cancer is understood," she explains, "as the overwhelming or obliterating of consciousness[;] you are being replaced by non-you" (67). As Renée Van de Vall (2009) argues, both interior and exterior threats to the contained body also constitute threats to selfhood, for "[the] dominance of the modern concept of the body as a self-contained entity is closely connected with notions of individuality and identity as somehow being located in our bodies, the skin forming the boundary between 'self' and 'other'" (11). The threat to identity accounts at least in part for why graphic cancer pathography often troubles – even dissolves – the skin-barrier that seems to separate the body from its internal and external environments. Bodies always already exist in fluctuating, agentive relationships with what we deem "other"; however, the experience of cancer reveals, often in unsettling ways, the instability and vulnerability of the self/body's apparently absolute boundaries.

Stitches: Bodily Duplicity

Recounted in retrospective first person narration, David Small's autobiography of his childhood and adolescence in Detroit, Michigan, is an account of betrayals, secrecies, and silences. Early in the memoir, we learn that David's father, a radiologist, exposed him to multiple X-ray treatments in order to "cure" recurrent sinus problems (Small 2009, 21). At the age of 14, David endures two surgical procedures to remove a tumour from his throat, thyroid gland, and vocal chord, waking up to find that he has lost most of his ability to speak and that his neck is covered in a large vertical scar. The narrative becomes a working-through of both familial trauma and the trauma caused by cancer, surgery, scarring, and the partial loss of David's voice. The memoir's title resonates not only with the recurring vertical image of his scar, a "crusted black track of stitches; my smooth young throat slashed and laced up like a bloody boot" (191), but also with the process of stitching together, using visual memory, revelations that unveil familial and somatic secrets: what David thought was a benign "growth" in his neck was actually a malignant tumour; surgery would leave him scarred and nearly voiceless; the doses of radiation prescribed and administered by his father, in fact, caused his cancer.

Structurally and thematically, silence pervades *Stitches*. There is little dialogue, and the images often appear cinematic. "Born anxious and angry," with sinus and digestive disorders, David quickly "learn[s] a way of expressing [himself] wordlessly ... Getting sick" (18–19). These early sicknesses are both his loneliness and his "language" (19). As he convalesces in bed, we see him receiving a spoonful of medicine and the gift of a discarded, lifeless teddy bear. His mother speaks rarely and gruffly; she mostly communicates by coughing – "KNH!" (15) – and slamming kitchen cupboard doors: "WHAP! WHAP!" (15). Further panels, reminiscent of film noir, weave together snapshots of invasive medical treatments and sinister hospital scenes. For example, in a series of forty-seven images, we see David exploring a laboratory in the hospital where his father works and finding several stored fetal specimens. Using close-up images of his increasingly incredulous and terrified gaze, these panels narrate his fantasy that "the little man in the jar" (45) pursues him down the hallways of the hospital. In this manner, much of the text's embodied meaning accumulates using visual associations rather than words – a track of surgery scars resembles dark hallways and stairs; a whirling ridged tornado shape is differently figured as Alice's rabbit-hole, a stomach into which David descends in a childhood dream, the back of his throat, or cavernous hospital space. Family secrecy and evasion eventually become manifest in a horrifically ironic silence: after David's second surgery, having had one vocal chord removed, he can only muster a breathless hacking sound. Isolated on the page, an image of his mouth as a black cavern, disembodied and disarticulated, contains a declarative speech bubble reading only, "ACK" (184).

Visually rendering memories of embodied distress thus becomes a means through which Small can understand and contextualize his cancer, surgeries, and the loss of his vocal chord. Using the visual associations of memory and imagination, artistic images throughout *Stitches* not only return to sites of domestic history, but also to the bodily site of David's cancer, which can itself be read as a "domestic subversion" of the internal body (Sontag 1990, 105). *Stitches* pieces together the story of his tumour's causation, diagnosis, and treatment, and, in several panels, Small recalls his earliest, nascent understandings of cancer. Skimming through his father's medical textbook, 6-year-old David finds a photograph of large lumps in a man's neck, which are explained by his brother as "[a] growth ... something that grows. It's unnatural" (Small 2009, 55). His mother's friend, Mrs Dillon, sees the lump on one side of his neck, which she also calls "a growth" (116). And, while aboard a yacht, a colleague of his father's palpates his neck and diagnoses him as having "a cebaceous cyst" (129). In this way, the *Stitches'* narrative revisits and re-apprehends two betrayals: the biomedical and psychosomatic abuse by his father and mother, and the interior malignancy of cancer. It is important that both are understood only retrospectively; David is as oblivious to his cancer's metastasis inside his body as he is to its secret causation.

The revelation that David has had cancer comes when he finds a letter from his mother to his grandmother. Significantly, his response is to fantasize a collapse of the distinctions between seeing/sensing, inner/outer, and subject/object: "At home, late at night," he explains, "I began to have the sensation that I was shrinking down ... and living inside my own mouth" (216). In a series of images that echo his earlier invitation to "step inside your mouth with me," we see David curled into the fetal position, holding his head, and sitting on his own tongue. The inside of his mouth is claustrophobic, he tells us, a "hot, moist cavern, in which everything I thought, every word that came into my brain, was thunderously shouted back at me" (217). In a close-up of his shoulders and face, David cowers inside his own mouth, his individual teeth bigger than his head. Meanwhile, the jagged scar of his surgery remains visible on his neck, suggesting that this is not a fantasy of return to a post-operative self but, rather, a difficult coming-to-terms with the reality of cancer, surgery, and loss. The seeing eye of the vocal chords, represented in the first series of mouth images, is replaced here by a dark gaping blank at the back of his throat. These pictorial representations of the self/body can be read as an allegory of autobiographical expression: the artist returns into himself, into his embodied memories, as a means of acknowledging and resisting perpetuated suffering. I would suggest, too, that the images of David inside his mouth tell us something about his ontological experience of cancer.

Reflecting on her ovarian cancer diagnosis, Stacey describes distrusting her body's ability to recognize signs of internal disease. For Stacey, the absence of visual signs of cancer prior to diagnosis constitutes a kind of bodily duplicity. "How could one look so healthy and be so ill?" she asks. "How is it possible that after the very first malignant cell division the body did not send out warnings?" (141). While Barad argues that the "self-evidence" of bodily boundaries is called into question "when the body 'breaks down'" (158), both Stacey and Small are unaware that cancer cells are multiplying inside of their bodies until the moment of diagnostic revelation. The sense that bodily boundaries are neither static nor inherent arrives in retrospect. After the realization that cancer is present inside of their bodies, Stacey and Small become aware that their body's interior is, in fact, materially agentive – that their bodies are not discrete objects ending at the skin but, rather, that bodily processes are co-constitutive, open-ended, and unpredictable. Furthermore, these processes have been happening without their conscious recognition or awareness; the molecular growth of cancer has been silent and invisible. In *Stitches*, this disturbing cellular growth parallels the secrecy of the Small family.[5] For Small, imagining that he can live inside his own body, viewing his teeth, tongue, tonsils, and vocal chords, enacts a double encounter with what he imagines to be underneath his skin, both in the initial (and terrifying) adolescent fantasy that he can "[shrink] down" and enter his mouth (216), and in the autobiographical re-presentation of that fantasy. These encounters with the interior body, or what Kim Sawchuk, in this volume, formulates as the "continuous folds" of "inner space" (165), are imagined returns that seek to resolve duplicity – as both damaging family secrecy and as the interior body's silence during cellular cancer growth – by inverting David's insides and collapsing boundaries between interior and exterior, unknown and known, invisible and visible.

David's difficult discoveries of his illness and its cause are eased through revisiting, visually and verbally, the years of his sicknesses and of life in the family home. Psychoanalytic therapy and artistic expression allow him to regain mental health and to regard his mother in a more embodied, relational manner. The afterword of the narrative shows a photograph of her as a young woman, and the accompanying text quotes the poet Edward Dahlberg: "Nobody heard her tears; the heart is a fountain of weeping water which makes no noise in the world" (327). Small learns that his mother was "born with her heart on the wrong side of her chest" and "also had only one functioning lung" (327). In adulthood, he is able to relate his mother's cruelties to her own health problems and to her hidden lesbian sexuality. Likewise, the cynicism or horror of inward-turning, truncated, and fragmented images in *Stitches* is assuaged by the addition of family photographs in the text's afterword featuring a 6-year-old David and his parents. Where Small's drawings of his mother's and father's faces are pinched, skeletal, or glaring, his insertion of these photographs shows their vulnerability and suggests a retrospective forgiveness. In a departure from the estranged and sometimes demonizing images throughout the narrative, the indexical nature of the photograph anchors Small's mother and father in history and allows us to see them as comparatively complex, if still mysterious, figures.

Our Cancer Year: Bodily Inseparability

If *Stitches* is a narrative of secrecy, duplicity, and silence, then Joyce Brabner and Harvey Pekar's *Our Cancer Year* conveys a different experience of illness – one that emphasizes community and interconnectedness, and that contextualizes Harvey's lymphoma within layered narratives: the onset of the Persian Gulf War in 1990; the ongoing financial and creative demands of Pekar's comics series *American Splendor*; the gentrification of the Cleveland, Ohio, neighbourhood where Joyce and Harvey share an apartment; and the correspondence into which Joyce enters with seven students whom she meets at a peace conference and then travels to visit in New York and Tel Aviv (Squier 2007). As Susan Squier (2007) remarks in her comparison of *Our Cancer Year* to Brian Fies' *Mom's Cancer* (2006), Brabner and Pekar "[shift] the conception of the patient from individual and normate to non-normative, intersectional, even collective" (343). This collectivity is reflected in the memoir's narrative voice – *Our Cancer Year* is a co-authored and multivocal text that moves between Harvey's and Joyce's first person accounts – and in the authors' visual-textual collaboration with illustrator Frank Stack. While Small's memoir opens with silent images of an empty house, *Our Cancer Year* immediately situates Harvey's illness within the scope of domestic and worldly relationships. "This is a story about a year when someone was sick," Joyce narrates on the opening page, "about a time when it seemed that the rest of the world was sick, too. It's a story about feeling powerless, and trying to do too much … Maybe doing more than you thought you could and not knowing what to do next. It's also a story about marriage, work, friends, family, and buying a house."[6] Here, the accompanying image shows Harvey and Joyce walking together through a neighbourhood park. Their mostly opaque bodies visually merge into a single dark shape; we cannot make out where his body ends and hers begins.

Conjoined bodies and objects in *Our Cancer Year* also trouble bodily boundaries, although in a markedly different manner than we see in Small's *Stitches*. Throughout *Our Cancer Year*, the outlines of Harvey's body are depicted as merging into a carefully detailed mise-en-scène, suggesting interconnections between Harvey's embodied self and the world(s) of which he is a part. Stack's portrayal of Harvey is, in this way, quite different from Small's self-portraiture in *Stitches*, in which images of David's body appear zoomed-in, truncated, or cropped. We often see David's body *parts* – legs and feet climbing stairs, his mouth making the wordless "ACK," or a single eye widened in terror – which portrays isolation, alienation, even horror. On the contrary, in *Our Cancer Year*, Stack usually represents Harvey's body in intimate relation with details in the panels' frames and with other characters: Joyce; Harvey and Joyce's apartment manager, Slim; Joyce's friends, Kimmie and Saroem; Harvey's doctors and nurses; and Delores, Harvey's home care aide.

It is important to note that Harvey's most intense moments of confusion and pain are also the moments when his body is illustrated as disintegrating into his surroundings. Reading these images is complicated by the co-production of image and text in *Our Cancer Year*. Because Stack acted as the artist for Brabner and Pekar's memoir, it is difficult to know the extent to which these drawings render Harvey's felt experiences of cancer, Stack's interpretation of those experiences as described to him in retrospect, or, simply, Stack's realist drawing style, which uses line shading even in those images that do not show bodily merging. Stack did approach the project with a documentary eye; the afterword to the book explains that he spent one year drawing the illustrations for *Our Cancer Year* using photographs and videotapes as inspiration, during which time he also lived with Joyce and Harvey. Still, the illustrations of Harvey's body merging with its environments, his corporeal contours radiating outwards, should be at least partially attributed to Stack's visual imaginary. Stack's illustrations reinforce the sense that Harvey's cancer is, in part, something outside of himself.

In the middle chapters of *Our Cancer Year*, in which Harvey undergoes chemotherapy and radiation and suffers severe pain caused by herpes zoster, Stack renders physical suffering, disorientation, and even hallucination using stark visual lines and shapes that emanate outwards from Harvey's face and body, troubling the ostensibly absolute margins between him and his surroundings. Rather than fantasizing, like David, that he can see or move inside his body, Harvey appears to feel as if he is merging with things outside of himself. In a series of panels in which he lies on his bathroom floor, depleted and disoriented by psychoactive pain medication, his features are indistinct and the contours of the right side of his body are shown melding into the floor. "I'll lay on the bathroom floor and die," he thinks. In another scene, driving home from the hospital with Joyce, he begins to "hallucinate": "God, what's happening to me?" he thinks. "I can hardly hear Joyce talk. I've got this picture in my head of two rectangles, a grey one inside a colorful one. There are figures in them, but I can't make them out." Here, alternating thick and thin lines blend the space where Harvey begins and ends between panel gutters. The middle panel of the page shows two circles encasing Joyce and Harvey, their bodies joined by splotches of white and heavy black cross-hatching. In the second circle, three faces (Harvey, hallucinating; another smaller and more cognizant Harvey; and a profile of wide-eyed Joyce listening to Harvey) meld together to show his panic. His feeling that "I'm talkin' and ... I don't know what I'm saying," visually corresponds to his spatial disorientation and to the reader's sense that the previously defined contours of his face are simultaneously disintegrating (see figure 11.1).

A series of five panels midway through the narrative that depict Harvey rising before work is one of only a few that show him alone. The bottom triptych of images, joined down the middle by a wave-shaped gutter, exemplifies Harvey's sense that his embodiment feels increasingly tenuous. In a long vertical panel, we see him taking a shower and noticing that he is starting to lose his hair as a result of chemotherapy. "Now it's really starting to go," he says to himself. A small circular inset in this image shows a close-up of the shower drain covered in hair. The inset is ambiguous; we must infer from the splotchy group of black circles that it indeed represents the shower drain, for the magnified circle image also resembles a microscope slide showing cells or microorganisms, or even the inside of a cell with its curly strands of DNA. I notice a curious reversal from the images in *Stitches* in which David self-incorporates, travelling inside himself to the site of his cancer. These panels in *Our Cancer Year* also address loss; Harvey is losing his hair, of course, but his perturbed facial expression, inability to sleep, and self-determination to maintain his working routine also indicate that he is actively coping with threats to his identity and well-being. Rather than visualizing his interior body, however, Harvey focuses on the external: his hair. Meanwhile, the magnified circular inset encourages visual associations among Harvey's hair (outside the body), his cancer cells (inside the body), and his embodied sensations of corporeal change and disintegration. Bodily borders are disturbed not only by physical changes associated with chemotherapy – hair loss and facial swelling – but also by Harvey's corresponding sense that his body's outlines have become strangely indefinite. In the remaining right-hand

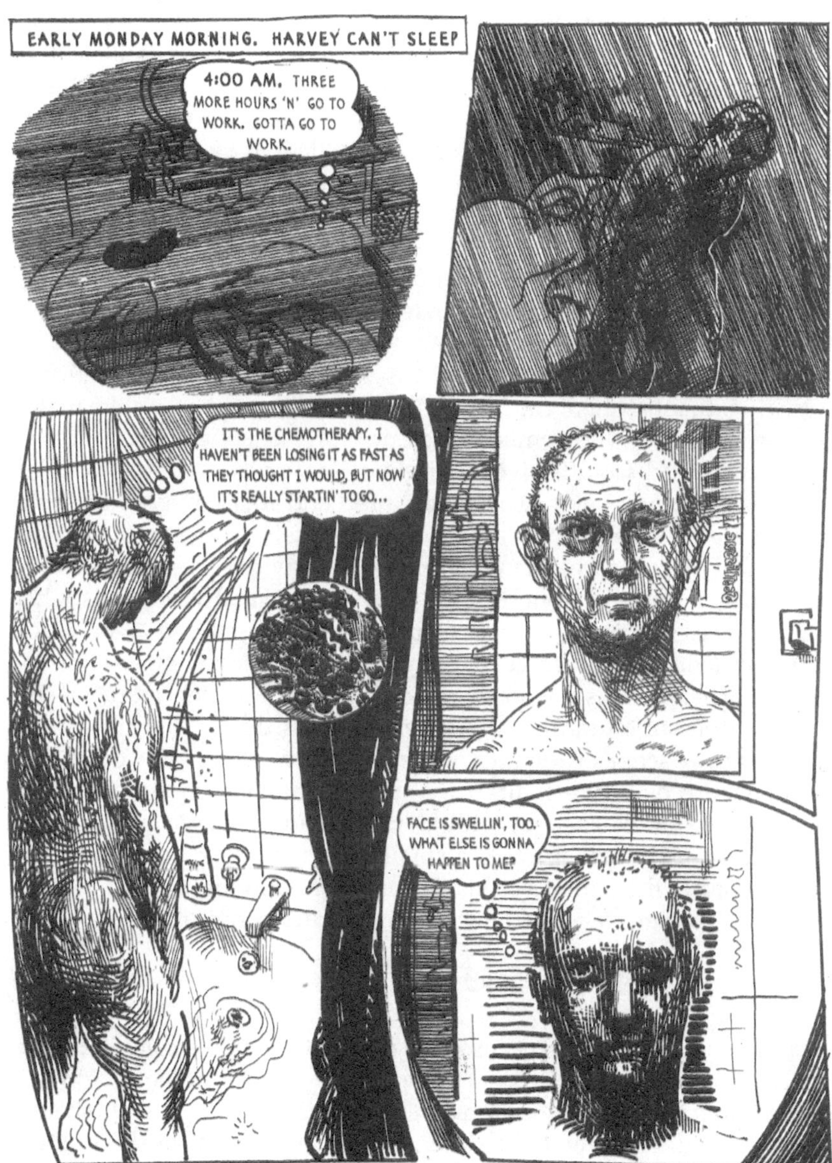

11.1. Graphic novel excerpt from *Our Cancer Year* (Joyce Brabner and Harvey Pekar, Philadelphia: Running Press, 1994, n.p.). Courtesy of Joyce Brabner, on behalf of the Harvey Pekar Estate.

panels in the triptych, he stares at his image in the bathroom mirror, noting that his face has become swollen and regarding himself as literally disintegrating. The top sketch shows Harvey in Stack's characteristically realist use of detail, with dark circles under his eyes, little hair, and a taciturn expression. In the bottom sketch, Stack has drawn Harvey as he presumably sees himself, the darkness of the face intensified, its details now obliterated by thick black vertical lines that radiate outwards from his head and into the background of the frame.

Sketches that show this type of merging or disintegration illustrate Harvey's corporeal and psychic crises throughout *Our Cancer Year*. Although these images certainly demonstrate his affective responses to treatments and side effects (panic, disorientation, or melancholy), the visual-textual nature of the comics medium also emphasizes the material aspects of Harvey's embodied responses. The text not only encourages us to read for affective, subjective, or discursive dimensions of cancer experience, but it also situates affect and subjectivity in multiple and complexly negotiated spaces that themselves appear integrated with Harvey's physical, material self. While David feels alienated from his family home and from his own body in *Stitches*, Harvey senses his self/body as profoundly situated within home, hospital, and workplace environments, as well as in companionship with Joyce, other caregivers, and friends. This relational embeddedness ultimately assuages the anxiety and suffering that Harvey experiences throughout treatment, restoring his sense of identity and calm – and, along with them, the seemingly recognizable limits of his body. At the conclusion of *Our Cancer Year*, as Harvey engages with Joyce's friends, Kimmie and Saroem, and offers to take them to see a small waterfall outside of Cleveland, Stack restores the outlines of his figure using definitive black lines that visually separate Harvey from other things and people in the frames.

Why Should Their Bodies End at the Skin?

Stitches and *Our Cancer Year* use visual-narrative strategies to illustrate embodied incarnations of what it means to "be" cancerous; and, in doing so, both texts portray continual and agentive entanglements shared between bodily matter, individual subjectivity, and the world. In their depictions of cancer and its treatments, both texts make strange the boundaries that ostensibly define the fixity of the body. Reading *Stitches* and *Our Cancer Year* together, we are confronted with different accounts of cancer and disrupted corporeal boundaries. While *Stitches* enacts an imagined return into the interior and cancerous body, fantasizing a collapse of the self into its own insides that parallels Small's retracing of trauma and sickness, *Our Cancer Year* portrays Harvey's body as radiating outwards and into his surroundings, moments of integration that are paralleled in the interconnectedness of Joyce and Harvey's narrative with layered relationships and events. Crucially, by illustrating the body's interior and seemingly disintegrating exterior, these graphic memoirs defamiliarize the border of skin that appears to separate the body from what surrounds it and what it surrounds.

This defamiliarization suggests that an important aspect of both Small's and Pekar's cancer experiences – and, in turn, their autobiographical representation and re-visiting of those experiences – involves coming to terms with the body's vulnerability to an internal proliferation of cancer cells and to bodily suffering caused by surgery, radiation, and chemotherapy. The disruptions to identity, belonging, and well-being that these embodied vulnerabilities pose for Small and Pekar are ultimately negotiated through autobiographical agency. Small recuperates his parents' and his own body's betrayals through memory work and artistic expression, and Pekar resists isolation by working with Brabner and Stack to create a collaborative narrative of shared illness experience. In each case, the innovations of *graphic* pathography afford an imaginative force that might not be possible in text alone. Small's and Stack's visual representations of duplicitous or dissolving corporealities convey the ways in which experiencing cancer is always more-than-discursive. Images of bodily isolation and merging formally reinforce David's and Harvey's respectively introspective and collective experiences of cancer. Although *Stitches* and *Our Cancer Year* use graphic form in different ways and to different ends, the visual-textual properties of both narratives exemplify how the materiality of cancer is crucially conjoined to its subjectivity and to its autobiographical telling.

NOTES

1 A combination of "pathology" and "autobiography," the term "pathography" refers to memoirs of illness. Hawkins (1993) and Frank (1995) offer foundational studies of this mode.

2 See, e.g., Haraway (1991, 2003), Hayles (1999), Latour (2005), and Wolfe (2009). For recent definitions of post-humanism as I use the term here, see the Introduction in Wolfe (2009) and chapter 4 in Barad (2007).

3 Haraway asks this question – "Why should our bodies end at the skin?" – in *Simians, Cyborgs and Women* (1991, 95).
4 See Ahmed (2008) for an important critique of "the routinization of the gesture towards feminist anti-biologism" (23); see also N. Davis' (2009) response to Ahmed, which counter-argues that the new feminist materialism "theorize[s] an entanglement and non-separability of the biological with/in sociality" (67).
5 I do not mean to suggest that David's cancer was somehow caused by repressed emotion or psychological trauma. Although the final section of *Stitches* is, in part, a "therapeutic" recounting of David's adolescent psychotherapy and recuperation, it is clear that radiation therapy, administered by David's father, caused his cancer. This point is an important one because cancer remains culturally associated with a "forlorn, self-hating, emotionally inert" personality type (Sontag 1990, 53). Both Sontag and Stacey (1997) argue, quite rightly, that linking cancer's causation to the repression of trauma is a stigmatizing practice often capitalized on by alternative health practitioners.
6 *Our Cancer Year* is unpaginated, and there are, consequently, no direct page references to the text here. I attempt to situate quotations within the trajectory of the narrative wherever possible.

PART FOUR

Spectatorship and Historical Memory: The Ethics of Critical Embodiment

12 Witnessing Genocide and the Challenges of Ethical Spectatorship

WENDY KOZOL

On 26 July 2010, an international tribunal in Cambodia found Kaing Guek Eav, also known as Comrade Duch, guilty of crimes against humanity, torture, and murder. Duch, the chief torturer at the notorious Tuol Sleng Prison, was the first of five senior Khmer Rouge leaders to be prosecuted for his participation in one of the worst genocides of the twentieth century. International news coverage of the trial frequently reproduced images of victims from the prison's photographic archive, which contains over five thousand pictures of prisoners who died there. For viewers outside of Cambodia, how do we witness these images in ways that do justice to this history of suffering while resisting the voyeurism embedded in perpetrator photographs? Since the 1990s, there has been an increase in juridical and commemorative practices related to human rights crimes, ranging from United Nations tribunals to truth and reconciliation commissions, as well as new museums and monuments dedicated to commemorating the Holocaust, genocides, and other atrocities. These practices have provoked numerous dialogues about the entangled practices of remembrance and accountability.[1] The affective power of visual evidence particularly demands a careful consideration of the cultural politics of gazing at embodied suffering. This essay explores the challenges of visual witnessing for viewers at a temporal and geographical – but not an ethical – distance from state violence through an analysis of *okay bye-bye*, independent filmmaker Rebecca Baron's autobiographical documentary film about US military and political complicity in the Cambodian genocide.[2]

Baron produced *okay bye-bye* in 1998 during a period of international attention to political changes occurring in Cambodia.[3] From 1975 to 1979, approximately 1.7 million Cambodians were either killed or died of starvation or disease under the brutally repressive regime of the Khmer Rouge. In 1979, a Vietnamese invasion pushed the Khmer Rouge from power but ongoing civil war continued for two decades, until 1998, when Pol Pot died and the Khmer leadership finally collapsed (Chandler 1999; Cambodian Genocide Project 2008). In 1997, the Cambodian government requested support from the United Nations to establish genocide tribunals, but it took over a decade to resolve disputes over these proceedings. Confronting the magnitude of this genocide, in which about 21 per cent of the population died, poses ongoing historical, political, and personal challenges for Cambodians. Debates about the utility of the tribunals coexist with memorializing efforts that include the preservation of mass graves and prisons (Chandler 1999; Hughes 2003; Ledgerwood 2002).

Remembering and memorializing this violence has also been a provocative challenge outside of Cambodia (Hughes 2003). In the United States, both government and popular narratives today denounce the Khmer Rouge, although the genocide often appears as a violent aberration unconnected to the history of US military actions in Southeast Asia. For instance, on the US Department of State website (2008), the only discussion of American military involvement in Cambodia is a brief reference to air raids in 1969 and a ground assault in 1970, described as responses by US and South Vietnamese militaries to North Vietnamese and Viet Cong incursions. Such explanations ignore the American bombing campaigns from 1969 to 1973 that contributed massively to the destabilization of the country. Moreover, official narratives do not discuss the financial support provided by the United States (as well as China) to the Khmer Rouge throughout the 1980s. Popular accounts similarly minimize or elide the role of foreign intervention in the brewing political crisis that developed in Cambodia in the early 1970s. Most familiar, perhaps, is the Hollywood feature film, *The Killing Fields* (dir. Joffee 1984), which downplays the US role in the war in Southeast Asia, instead reproducing a Eurocentric gaze that privileges the perspective of the heroic white male news reporters who attempt to save a Cambodian journalist (Goldberg 2007).

In *okay bye-bye*, Baron confronts narratives that elide the prominent role of the United States in the conflict zones of Southeast Asia through an interrogation of the various kinds of visual evidence available to US audiences. For Americans located within normative frameworks – that is, within positions of privilege such as whiteness or citizenship – the act of looking can implicate viewers in a hegemonic gaze at distant suffering (Boltanski 1999). And yet, for human rights activists committed to social justice agendas, to look away from violence is unacceptable. Using an autobiographical frame, *okay bye-bye* explores the ethical challenges of transnational viewing practices.

Transnational feminists and human rights scholars such as Inderpal Grewal (2005) argue that human rights advocacy has been closely identified with Eurocentric claims of universality and individualism, often resulting in representations of Third World people, especially women, *only* as victims in need of rescue. Rights practices have more often relied upon than challenged the paradigm of Third World chaos, primitivism, and violent misogyny that demands Western intervention. Taking heed of these cautions, how can Western viewers and producers of visual culture enact ethical viewing practices across transnational distances that resist imperialist structures of power? How to balance a witnessing gaze with the ways in which viewers are often implicated in hegemonic practices of domination, exploitation, and violence? These questions resonate with Kim Sawchuk's interest in the interstitial tensions between external forces of visioning and surveillance and the subject's own embodied vision – tensions addressed so beautifully in Mona Hatoum's installation art (this volume, 158). In contrast to Hatoum's attention to competing visualities, documentaries about human rights abuses often utilize the camera as a pedagogical tool through which viewers can instrumentally learn about the past. Yet, as Roger Simon (2005) argues, we must consider "what attention, learning, and actions such accountability requires" (5). Simon's call for a pedagogy of remembrance that insists upon a substantive engagement with collective responsibility requires that we do more than just "look." Recent scholarship on affect, empathy, accountability, and spectatorship has begun to explore this urgent question about critical witnessing positions. Along with Sawchuck's work on vision, affect, and embodiment, Jill Bennett's (2005) attention to "empathic vision," Mieke Bal's (2007) emphasis on "seeing for," and Kyo Maclear's (2003) term "ethical vision" all strive to understand how and why certain images affectively move the viewer from the encounter with the sign of violence to a space of critical awareness and action. This cluster of terms signals shared concerns among visual culture scholars about how best to understand the politics of affect and the role of ethics in discourses about trauma and mass violence.

Building on the insights offered by this scholarship, this essay uses yet another term, "ethical spectatorship," in order to trouble the desire to find visual practices of witnessing that could somehow avoid voyeurism or spectacle. The oxymoronic underpinnings of the term "ethical spectatorship" intentionally resonate with feminist theories about spectacle and the gaze in order to address how visual practices contain both ethical *and* voyeuristic gazes.[4] Like Sawchuck, I am interested in how formal elements in visual culture designed to provoke affective encounters work to implicate the viewer in the political complexities of historical processes. *okay bye-bye* provides a pedagogical model of visual witnessing by staging a confrontation between, on the one hand, the spectres of trauma produced by archival and media histories of the Cambodian genocide and, on the other hand, the complicity of the autobiographical subject who gazes at those hauntings.

Transnational Gazes

okay bye-bye is a self-reflexive meditation on historical witnessing that combines fragmentary autobiographical references and documentary visual evidence within the epistolary structure of a "letter-film" (Naficy 2001, 101). The film begins with a female narrator's voice explaining her attempt to write to an absent friend who spent time in Cambodia after the "destruction years." Baron divides the film into segments, or letters, each of which is demarcated by a black-screened intertitle in which a date appears. The reason to speak now, the narrator says, is because Pol Pot, the leader of the Khmer Rouge and the architect of the genocide, has just died. Although the letters move chronologically from 1995 to 1998, the film lacks a unified narrative, instead staging a series of meditative encounters that explore how, as the narrator says, "history weighs down on us." On screen, the film moves between contemporary southern California landscapes and visual evidence such as iconic images from the Vietnam War and the Tuol Sleng archive. Never "leaving" the United States, the film's voice-over monologue instead interacts with archival images to produce a sceptical gaze at official narratives.

In the last two decades, politically oriented independent filmmakers like Baron have troubled the boundaries of film genres in order to explore the role of subjectivity in developing a critical consciousness about traumatic histories (Zimmermann 2000, 53). This is apparent in the film from the outset, when the narrator, in a voice of intimate longing, addresses the friend whose absence creates desires that are inseparable from the desire for historical knowledge. Here Baron links individual memories and traumas to larger national histories. The absent friend could be said to be a witness who could explain the genocide that, the narrator reminds us, she never experienced. And yet, the friend never speaks, so neither the narrator nor the viewer has access to whatever insights into this history the unnamed friend may have. A picturesque ocean view appears as the narrator comments, "I don't even know what you are doing now but I'll always associate you with a place I've never been to." Connecting the genocide to the absent friend exposes the limits of "knowing" another's experience while the ocean scene visualizes a spatial and temporal divide between the present of the filmmaker's gaze and the violent past in Cambodia. As Jim Lane (2002) explains, "Autobiographical documentaries use reflexivity not to eradicate the real as much as to complicate referential claims" (18).

Crucially, personal memories insert an autobiographical subject position into this critique of witnessing practices. Baron's mode of address is a voice-over speaking subject, a "performance of the self" that creates an ambiguous relationship between the perspective of the filmmaker and that of the narrator (Naficy 2001, 35). Along with her ongoing one-way conversations with the absent friend, the narrator describes memories of growing up in the 1960s, her mother's nostalgia for a time when the "war brought people together," and her father's sceptical reactions about her "research ... It isn't for anything." These memories, though, remain fragmentary and undeveloped so that the viewer never learns about the narrator or her relationship to the addressee of the letters. Ambiguity over the "realness" of the autobiographical voice is one of the ways in which the filmmaker foregrounds questions about authenticity, subjectivity, and archival evidence.

Importantly, *okay bye-bye* never visualizes the narrator as an embodied female figure. Departing from essentialist claims of women's opposition to militarized violence or symbolic representations of mothers and children as war's victims (Kozol 2004), the film presents a female voice of longing, but refuses to give the narrator a visual shared space of identification with suffering and trauma. Just as the narrator questions her own motivations, including her "own version of American guilt," Baron provides no visible body with which to identify. Feminist scholars have long raised the problem of speaking for another, or assuming shared understandings because of gender (Alcoff 1995; Mohanty 1991). In keeping with these critiques of identification as a form of appropriation, gender does not provide the narrator of *okay bye-bye* with privileged access to understanding. Instead, disembodiment forces the spectator to share the film's self-referential gaze at the historical record of US involvement in Southeast Asia.

The seemingly incongruous title of the film highlights the issue of complicit citizenship. One of the "letters" focuses on the US evacuation of Phnom Penh as the Khmer Rouge entered the city on 17 April 1975. It was during this process, the narrator explains, that Cambodian children waved and said, "okay bye-bye" to the marines as they left. Baron foregrounds differences in language (and the struggles to acquire the occupier's language) as a trope for the neocolonial relationship between the two countries. Military film footage featuring the last moments before the US evacuation shows a helicopter arriving at the American embassy's landing pad. The footage then switches between scenes of marines running towards the helicopter and a crowd of Cambodians watching the evacuation, including several close-up shots of children. As the helicopter flies off to an aircraft carrier, the narrator reads a letter from Prince Sirik Matak to the US Ambassador to Cambodia, John Gunther Dean. Matak, along with several other political leaders, had refused the US offer to leave. Instead, he condemns the Americans' withdrawal, saying, "I have only committed this mistake of believing in you." The cheerful-sounding phrase "okay bye-bye" belies the emotional and political complexities in this story of abandonment, a juxtaposition that facilitates the film's self-reflexive gaze towards the role of US militarism in the ensuing genocide. The title thus hauntingly reverberates throughout the film to confront the profound divisions as well as historical connections between the Americans and Cambodians.

okay bye-bye is representative of Baron's film oeuvre, in which she has extensively explored the role of visual culture in the production of historical knowledge. Similar to other autobiographical documentarians and "accented filmmakers" like Rea Tajiri (Lane 2002; Naficy 2001), in *okay bye-bye*, Baron examines how public discussions of the war such as official government statements, Hollywood cinema, and news reportage influence both personal and public memories (Lane 2002). Originally, the narrator says, she planned to make a documentary about Cambodia. As she reviews the historical record of colonialism and war, film footage shifts from news conferences of President Nixon and Henry Kissinger to colonial-era films of Cambodians dancing for Europeans to television news coverage of the Vietnam War. Wanting to "trace everything back to its cause," the narrator begins to list factors such as power struggles, religious beliefs, economics, and the psychology of military leaders. Overwhelmed by this list, she then concedes that she'll "never make that film." Similar to how the story of *okay bye-bye* exposes the neo-colonial gaze structuring visual truths about the wars in Southeast Asia, this concession grapples with, rather than dismisses, evidentiary traces of the past (J. Baron 2007, 17).

If, as the film argues, documentary cannot provide transparent access to the real of "history," the filmmaker also does not avoid the demands of the real. Instead, Baron creates a dialogic relationship between visual evidence and a sceptical voice-over. The restlessness of the film, jumping between past and present, as well as the elusive appeal of personal narrative produce both partial insights and frustrating barriers that affectively push viewers towards a critical encounter with the genocide and its aftermath (Bennett 2005). In this regard, *okay bye-bye* operates through what Patricia Zimmermann (2000) calls a "strategy of transaction," formal documentary techniques that rely on juxtapositions and movement across multiple spaces and narratives "to unsettle the very space of politics" in ways that encourage active spectator positions (91–2). As the narrator speaks about the erasure of historical memory in American culture, the film gazes from a distance at the southern California landscape of suburban sprawl, military bases, and impoverished diasporic communities. Baron shot most of the contemporary footage from within enclosed spaces; for example, through a window looking out towards the ocean or upward at the top of trees, or from a moving car looking across the highway towards new housing construction. Enclosure provides a paradoxical feeling of safety and distance, especially since the filmmaker never situates the camera amid these landscapes (Bennett 2005). Zimmermann (2000) argues that independent filmmakers in the 1990s began to turn to the local as a means of countering globalization's seemingly relentless processes of deterritorialization (88). For Baron, the local is not a pastoral landscape but a space of rapacious suburban development and urban decay. At one point in the film, a car drives the streets of the Anaheim Corridor, a poor Los Angeles neighbourhood where Cambodian and Latino gangs had recently engaged in violent conflict. Multiple diasporic histories haunt the film visually as the car drives past boarded-up buildings, small grocery stores, and restaurants in this mixed Latino and Cambodian neighbourhood. By locating the film's transnational gaze at the violence in Southeast Asia firmly within a US cartography, this visual autobiography emphasizes the ethical challenges embedded in the ongoing relationship between past traumas, present social politics, and spectatorship.

As the car travels down the street, the narrator tells a story about a waiter at a local restaurant who stared at her wallet because it had a picture of Astro Boy on it, explaining that as a child in Vietnam he used to watch that television show. The waiter's memories, triggered by the wallet, reference the transnational circulation of cultural practices that themselves encode multiple histories. The narrator concedes, however, that she can do nothing to address or alleviate his painful reverie: "I wanted to give it to him but it was grimy and I was embarrassed." This unvisualized scene refuses to romanticize witnessing; instead, it addresses the ways in which transnational connectivities are as much about cultural and political distances as they are about intersections (Grewal 2005). Rather than seeing the local as bounded or distinct from the transnational, here the focus on the diasporic community exposes the often painful interstitial relationships between local and transnational spaces (Zimmermann 2000, 194).

Switching between archival images of Cambodia and contemporary scenes of southern California visualizes transnationalism as the literal and imaginative mobilities that both link and divide people, cultures, and histories. Confronting the seemingly unbridgeable gaps of war, citizenship, race, gender, poverty, and migration, the narrator questions her own motivations: "I didn't know what I was looking for – it was hard to call it research when it felt like rubbernecking." This reference to rubbernecking calls attention to the scopic desires of documentary traditions wedded to the ideal of uncovering "truths." Locating the war through fragmentary memories while questioning the legitimacy of her own research creates a frustrating affect crucial to the film's self-critical inquiry into the ethics of looking practices.

Embodying Genocide

A century of war photography has made spectacles of death and suffering commonplace for American viewers. Recognition of the problems of spectacle in news reportage has led many to turn instead to the archive for seemingly unmediated visual evidence. *okay bye-bye* engages with this search for visual truth by shifting between media representations and the archive of the dead, but does so in ways that pedagogically demand that the viewer grapple with the ethics of spectatorship. Jaimie Baron (2007) identifies a trend among independent documentary filmmakers like Rebecca Baron who are interested in how the "information age" has destabilized conventional wisdom about archives and knowledge production. As she notes, "Reflecting this historiographic crisis, they inhabit and thematize the desire for a coherent history confronted by the unruly vestiges of its passage" (14). Notably, filmmaker Baron uses formal techniques to interrogate the desire for a traumatized body in acts of visual witnessing.

One of these techniques features close-ups of a computer screen displaying photographs of genocide victims from the website of the Cambodian Genocide Project (2008). This website contains all 5,700 pictures taken at Tuol Sleng, a detention and torture centre in Phnom Penh where over 14,000 people were sent by the Khmer Rouge, and only seven survived.[5] Beginning in 1994, the circulation of the Tuol Sleng photographs in overseas exhibitions has contributed greatly to renewed international interest in Cambodia (Hughes 2003). Moving beyond statistics, the enormity of which can seem incomprehensible, photography exhibitions, documentaries, and websites today continue to publish the pictures as evidence of the horrific violence that the victims endured. Baron, however, resists the use of the Tuol Sleng pictures as unmediated evidence of the genocide, instead asking the viewer to ponder the practice of looking at the dead. Close-ups show the computer screen scrolling through the images, including delays as the computer loads. Positioning the viewer's gaze, with the narrator's, at the screen calls attention to how archival technologies structure strategies of remembrance (J. Baron 2007, 21). Scrolling through the website also references the transnational circulation of information and the accessibility of gazing at trauma, at least for those privileged enough to have computer access. In this way, *okay bye-bye* implicates witnessing in the circulation of trauma photographs on the Internet, which can function as a form of cybertourism.

A crucial aspect of the Tuol Sleng archive, like many archives of torture, is the visual absence of the Khmer Rouge. Considering the politics of reproducing perpetrator photographs, Marianne Hirsch (2002) warns that uncritical circulation of such images can enable perpetrators to remain invisible, obscuring both individual and state responsibility. One question for historical witnessing, then, is how to look at these pictures in ways that disrupt the "genocidal gaze" (Hirsch 2002, 106), a gaze that in this context also risks reinforcing Orientalist imaginings about the Third World. Reminiscent of the work of artists involved with retrospective witnessing of the Holocaust, Baron's film incorporates perpetrator photographs in ways that "clarify the limits of retrospective understanding, rather than make the past too understandable" (Hirsch 2002, 10).

As the narrator searches the website, she pauses at each image to look at shocked and exhausted faces of prisoners who show only minimal evidence of violence on their bodies. As the viewer looks on, the narrator talks about being emotionally unsettled as she looks at this "graveyard of faces." Rather than a "crude empathy," such as sentimentality or pity, however, Baron's self-referential attention to archival practices produces a destabilizing affect intended to explore the politics surrounding the encounter with signs of trauma (Bennett 2005, 19). As the camera scrolls through the website, computer-loading delays force the viewer to stare at faces with distinguishing features like messy hair, or beards, or someone who smiles for the camera. Searching the site can be a means of access for friends and relatives, yet for the narrator (and thus for the viewer) it becomes a site of consumption: "I selected different combinations that produced thousands of results." As the narrator names these combinations, close-ups of each picture align the viewer with the spectatorial gaze, peering with the narrator at the dead for signs of familiarity.

The Tuol Sleng pictures have had a complicated afterlife as they continue to circulate on websites and in documentaries as the "undisciplined envoys of Cambodia's traumatic past" (Hughes 2003, 24). Returning later in the film to the archive, the narrator discusses an American museum exhibition of the photographs that featured an elegant coffee table book, which, she says, "made a profit through images of the dead."[6] Far from offering a didactic criticism, though, the narrator observes that her tastes were similar to the curator's, for they selected many of the same images. The film's insistence on reflexivity implicates an autobiographical spectatorship in this critique of consumption, especially when the narrator comments, "Treating the photos like Hollywood movie stills – it took a long time to disgust myself." Unlike many documentary films that turn to individual survivors in an attempt to rehumanize state-sponsored violence, Baron's emphasis on mediation uses the autobiographical frame to position herself and the viewer as central to the entanglement of spectacle and ethical looking. Staging this encounter with pictures of the dead functions pedagogically "not to console but to provoke" (Rosenberg 2000, 78).

Baron's complex understanding of witnessing recalls Dominick LaCapra's (2001) concept of empathetic unsettlement, which he defines as a form of witnessing that does not appropriate the experience of the other but, through the "radical ambivalence of clear-cut positions," attends to the "problem of the relation between the past and the present"

(20). As he explains, empathetic unsettlement "comes with respect for the other and the realization that the experience of the other is not one's own" (40). By troubling the desire to "know" the other, to be intimate with suffering, Baron produces a radical ambivalence between spectacle and empathy.

Survivors, like perpetrators, are noticeably absent from this film. *okay bye-bye* includes no interviews or ethnographies with survivors who could provide testimonials about the genocide. One concern viewers have raised with me is that this filmic strategy erases Cambodian survivors' agency by not providing testimonial space. On the one hand, the political imperative to give voice to survivors of violence has been one of the great contributions of feminist activists as well as human rights and other social justice advocates. On the other hand, many feminists warn of the dangers of over-identification through social categories like gender while ignoring trauma survivors' agency and the historical contexts that produce gendered, racial, and ethnic violence (Grewal 2005; Hesford 2004). Postcolonial theorist Rey Chow (1996) further warns against too quick a turn to the authentic survivor, the "passive victim on display" (123). She cautions that the search for the authentic figure of oppression motivating the spectacular image, or a search for a better image that restores "true subjectivity," can itself be implicated in the colonizer's gaze. As Chow suggests, the search for the authentic subject may be more about "enriching ourselves precisely with what can be called the surplus value of the oppressed" (124). Baron's refusal to turn to "experience" clearly shares feminist and postcolonial theorists' concerns about speaking on behalf of others.

If the film offers no survivor testimonials, it does address the desire to look upon the survivor, a desire that appears in many forms of witnessing (Kozol 2004). Several times during the film, Baron reproduces a fragment of super-8 film that she found on a suburban street in San Diego (R. Baron, personal communication 2005). The silent filmstrip features an Asian man wearing a watch but no shirt in a room with shelves and an overhead light. He smiles and gestures in what appears to be one of those intimate moments when a person hams it up for the home movie camera, especially because his partial nudity suggests an informal setting and a casual familiarity with the person behind the camera.

The serendipity of this found footage creates an archive of sorts, but one without a context. Who is this man and why is he smiling? The only information on the filmstrip is the words, "Koh Kong," written on the film itself. The narrator recalls that the unnamed friend had sent her a postcard from this western Cambodian province, thus linking this fragmentary evidence to personal memories. This intimate connection fosters the implication that the man is performing for Baron's camera, a suggestion the narrator reinforces when she says, "I tried to pretend I was behind the camera. I invented who he was and why he was there." The found footage promises the "realness" or authenticity of the presumed survivor who at some point found the joy to sing and dance. And yet, the man's unidentified status destabilizes any assumption that he embodies the experience of trauma. Baron pushes this point further in the narrator's comment to her unnamed friend that "most of what I know about Cambodia came from you and the time you spent there. Your horror at the evidence of destruction. And so, it's easier to imagine the footage is yours." Inventing stories here calls attention to the dominant human rights gaze that typically attempts to impose a Eurocentric narrative on distant trauma (Hesford 2011). The personal intimacy suggested by the imaginary ownership of the footage also confronts the authenticating power of historical narratives that promise to "expose" the truth.

At one point, the narrator says that she looked for the man in the film fragment in the Tuol Sleng archive. She comments that she imagines this footage having been taken before the genocide because she cannot imagine him acting this happy afterwards. Baron here addresses the ways in which historical depictions of trauma often freeze survivors within the moment of suffering, as if they lack a past or a future. Leaving the viewer with only questions, is she, are we, watching footage taken before the genocide? Is he even a survivor of the genocide? Such unanswerable questions at the centre of this autobiographical documentary produce a discomforting emptiness in the space where one might expect the narrative to "explain" the trauma. Instead, the lack of information creates what Bennett (2005) describes as a sense memory: "Rather than inhabiting a character … one inhabits – or is inhabited by – a sensation: a sensation that is challenging precisely because it is not anchored by character or narrative" (34). Thwarting expectations that evidence will document the trauma, the filmstrip repeatedly ruptures the solemnity of the narrator's voice-over through the incongruity of its silent and unexplained joy to create a haunting and recurring memory of loss.

As the only Cambodian to appear "alive" in the film, the man performs an embodied identity that visually materializes the instabilities of race, national identity, and gender. The difference in film quality, the lack of sound, and the explanatory comments all position him as the other: the man who may or may not have suffered the genocide, who may or may not still be alive, and who, as a result of the filmic gaze, is positioned only in relation to the trauma. Multiple appearances of the filmstrip keep reinserting the man's face and partial nudity, thus calling attention to two dominant categories of Asian masculinity – that of the unvisualized, hypermasculine Khmer Rouge perpetrator, and the visible but destabilized masculinity of the presumed victim. Not knowing the man's citizenship status, or even if he is part of the diaspora, further implicates race and gender in the complex interactions of national and personal histories whereby the American-born female narrator speaks over the silent and unidentified Asian male "victim." Familiarity and inaccessibility create an affective push/pull that also clearly demarcates boundaries between self and other.

Even as these boundaries are visually explicit, this anonymous performance of joy decidedly unsettles the privileged position of the filmic gaze. Notably, the rupturing effect of the filmstrip refuses the tendency in memory work to turn survivors into emblems of suffering (Rosenberg 2000). With no access to the subjective experience of trauma, the genocide remains a political phenomenon that is both elusive and present as it extends, via the filmstrip, into the lived space of the filmmaker or, rather, into the space of the present (Bennett 2005, 12). A suburban neighbourhood appears on screen when the narrator first talks about finding the film fragment. Scenes of suburbia resonate with a history of white middle-class privilege that contrasts vividly with depictions of the Anaheim Corridor. The space of past trauma is thus located in a complex contemporary landscape shared by both the Cambodian diasporic community and "Americans" living in the suburbs.

Baron's use of the filmstrip, like the scenes of diasporic neighbourhoods, disrupts the tendency in American popular culture to figure Third World state violence as ahistorical and unconnected to processes of globalization, capitalism, and US imperialism. At the same time, normative US citizenship trumps any move towards an "easy" affective affiliation such as empathy, for the narrator's voice speaks over the man's image, echoing the historical silencing of trauma survivors, even as she questions her own desire for a story. Through the use of the filmstrip, *okay bye-bye* repeatedly raises the question not only of who has the authority to speak, but also of which histories are told, and by whom.

Activist Witnessing

Visual images have long been a key tool in human rights activism, and one that has seen increased use in the twenty-first century. Ethical spectatorship provides one means of working with visuality that engages with the "difficult inheritance of those called" to bear witness (Simon 2005, 4). Today, the need to study the politics of visual practices and reception in relation to social justice is as pressing as ever. Along with retrospective witnessing at the Cambodian genocide tribunals, human rights and feminist activists are currently struggling to balance the need for publicity with the problematics of spectatorship in places like Darfur, Afghanistan, and Iraq. As Sharon Rosenberg's (2000) work on the limitations of memorialization demonstrates, rethinking the relationship between remembrance and activism requires configuring witnessing as a political act of historical accountability as much as a practice of mourning. In other words, inclusion within a political community means that, for those of us invested in social justice advocacy, it is imperative that we recognize how our witnessing gaze implicates us in larger historical processes of violence, privilege, and mourning.

Politically committed independent filmmakers today are mapping a shifting visual and political topography of what Zimmermann (2000) calls the "new world image order" (xxii). Innovative documentaries, including autobiographical documentaries like *okay bye-bye*, use multiple film techniques that cross genre boundaries to destabilize hegemonic notions of race, gender, citizenship, nation, and war. Drawing on the lessons of this film, I argue that ethical spectatorship provides a framework for understanding how contemporary filmmakers deploy complex visual frameworks that recognize historical subject positions of complicity and difference. At its best, *okay bye-bye* uses an autobiographical frame to locate the viewer within a shared space that confronts the representational violence haunting human rights, feminist, and other social justice agendas.

One concern I have, though, is the risk of conflating a hegemonic US gaze with a transnational gaze, both because it can reproduce a US-centric spectatorship and because such a gaze often presumes a monolithic American viewer-witness. In terms of the latter concern, *okay bye-bye* does not interrogate the multiple subjectivities of those living in the United States. The film's refusal to represent the narrator visually resists a solipsistic empathy between survivors and witness and also recognizes the narrator's citizenship status in relation to diasporic communities. Yet, perhaps because of its autobiographical frame, the film does not engage with non-normative American viewing subjects. Citizens and non-citizens from marginalized communities in the United States, for instance, participated in military service in Southeast Asia in disproportionate numbers. How might those viewers, or subsequent generations of viewers who carry other historical memories, witness the US role in the Cambodian genocide and its aftermath?

Contexts of circulation significantly impact reception and, in this regard, can potentially disrupt such a conflation, especially in the complex global public sphere of human rights. In 2007, a screening of *okay bye-bye* at the prestigious international art exhibition, Documenta12 in Kassel, Germany, took place in conjunction with Rithy Panh's powerful documentary, *S-21*, about survivors and perpetrators from Tuol Sleng. Panh's film features testimonials by survivors and perpetrators who struggle to narrate their experiences of pain and suffering, as well as guilt and denial (Aquino 2007; Hesford 2011). The two films address very different affective witnessing practices, which potentially mobilize varied critical encounters with trauma. Screening the films together can affectively push viewers towards a more extensive understanding of this history. I am reminded here of Sawchuck's analysis of the formal elements in Hatoum's *Corps étranger* that pull embodied spectators into spaces where visceral and visual elements collide in ways that incite complex affective responses (this volume, 161). Drawing out the implications of her insight further, multiple viewing contexts, like recognition of the diversity of viewer-witnesses, can produce unpredictable conditions that may resist the tendency in Western cultures to conflate personal, national, and transnational gazes.

Returning to the story of the waiter's reverie while staring at the narrator's Astro Boy wallet, this unvisualized scene insists that looking is always a historically contextualized political process. Importantly, Baron locates the waiter and the narrator in a moment of transnational connection and division. Just as the narrator cannot give the waiter her wallet, the filmmaker reminds us of the ways in which human rights, feminist, and other activists always function within contexts of privilege and power that cannot simply be given away. As scholars, critics, and artists grapple with the shifting boundaries of transnational cultures, *okay bye-bye* exposes the ways in which, for American citizen-viewers, the transnational gaze is complexly bound up as much in US imperial military agendas as it is in attempts to recover the histories of other people's suffering.

NOTES

I would like to thank Rebecca Baron both for her richly provocative work and for sharing information about the film with me. Thanks, too, to Rian Brown-Orso for introducing me to Baron's work. Much gratitude to Amy Brandzel, Rachel Buff, Jessica Grim, Wendy Hesford, Pat McDermott, and Rebecca DeCola for timely and supportive critiques and to Sarah Trimble for her editorial work. I am especially grateful to Sarah Brophy and Janice Hladki for their insightful comments on an earlier draft and their work on behalf of this anthology.

1 Schaffer and Smith (2004) note that the 1990s has been labelled both the decade of human rights and the decade of life narratives, observing that "over the last twenty years, life narratives have become one of the most potent vehicles for advancing human rights claims" (1). For related discussions, see Huyssen (2003), Rosenberg (2000), and Simon (2005).
2 I use Lane's (2002) concept of autobiographical documentary to locate the film in the tradition of independent political documentaries that "have become a potent site of American cultural production where private individuals and history coalesce" (5).
3 The film was shown at the Whitney Biennial in 1998, won awards at the San Francisco and Ann Arbor film festivals, and continues to circulate in art venues, including Documenta12 in Kassel, Germany, in 2007. Film schools and cultural studies classrooms also continue to screen the film.
4 See Azoulay (2008), who discusses the ethics of the spectator but does not explore the politics of spectacle in the ways I call for here.
5 The Khmer Rouge photographed all prisoners sent to Tuol Sleng upon arrival and many after their deaths. A non-profit group, the Photo Archive Group, rediscovered, cleaned, and catalogued the photographs in 1993. Yale University currently runs the website, the Cambodian Genocide Project, on which all of the extant photos appear. The stated aim of the website is to make the photographs available for Cambodians to identify missing relatives, and to provide information about the genocide (French 2002).
6 See French (2002), who analyses the social and aesthetic politics surrounding these exhibitions, especially the problems that arise when art museums ignore historical contextualization.

13 Digital Melancholia: Archived Bodies in Carmin Karasic's *With Liberty and Justice for All*

SHEILA PETTY

As a multilayered and contested historical narrative, the Middle Passage, with roots in economically driven and morally justified slavery, has cast a long shadow across American race relations. For African Americans, "chattel slavery's hyperexploitation of labor, multi-scalar expropriation and deformation of place – of bodies, homes, communities, and national status" continue to inform discussions of systemic racism for reasons that remain poorly understood by a mainstream white culture that seems to view the matter as ancient and now redundant history (Kaplan 2007, 512). In a very real way, mainstream white society continues to deny the ongoing legacy of a country founded on justice for some through the dehumanization of others.

Recently, the term "melancholia" has entered the lexicon of Black diasporic theory. Historically rooted in Freudian psychology, the concept of "melancholia emerges as a failure of mourning that originates in a loss that cannot be fully known or claimed" (Kaplan 2007, 513). The term, however, has been reconstituted as a means of describing the process by which subjects of historically situated oppressions internalize the ongoing legacies and subsequent social consequences of those experiences (513). Melancholia thus sheds light on racism, "with its attendant processes of exclusion, subjugation, and bodily and territorial expropriation" and "its continuing national disavowal" as "constituent elements of nation-building in the United States" (514). More specifically, it offers a way of accounting for the ongoing interrelationships among history, loss, and denial that undergird African diasporic subjectivity in America.

The concept of melancholia is fraught with contradiction and controversy, largely due to the fact that most contemporary theory on melancholia is drawn from Sigmund Freud's landmark 1917 essay, "Mourning and Melancholia." As Anne Cheng (2001) notes, Freud's essay outlines two distinct types of grief. Mourning, considered the "healthy response to loss," is a finite process in which the libido first relinquishes and then replaces the so-called lost object (7). Melancholia is grief in its pathological state, and occurs when the griever cannot accept an appropriate substitution (8). The inability to find release prevents resolution of the grieving state, resulting in what Cheng describes as "a condition of endless self-impoverishment" (8). According to this framework, mourning's process of release consigns the psychical trauma to a "resolved" past, whereas melancholia carries the trauma forward as "the past remains steadfastly alive in the present" (Eng and Kazanjian 2003, 3–4).

Melancholia, then, is attractive for theorizing the intersections among histories of slavery, colonialism, and racism in contemporary Black diasporic experience because one of the most difficult aspects of addressing these issues is the persistence of their traumatic legacies over time. However, melancholia's pathological status within the Freudian schema raises a number of potential contradictions. For example, Cheng (2001) notes that the melancholic subject's refusal to release the degraded "lost object" engenders feelings of rage and disjunction, which are then internalized as "self-denigration" and "profound resentment" (9). This is a state that cuts both ways and can account for both racial exclusion and the promulgation of racist frameworks that must rationalize their existence within mainstream cultural parameters (11). If all sides of the argument are using the pathological processes of melancholia to perpetuate the past, how can any satisfactory outcome be obtained? Certainly, given the historic displacement of power disadvantaging those oppressed by racist histories as compared with their oppressors, it seems difficult to argue that their respective experiences of melancholia are either equivalent or driven by similar forces. Moreover, because of the historic dehumanizing of African diasporic cultures by slavery and/or colonization, it is also troubling to argue that the broad categories of oppressed and oppressor have equal access to the position of subject. Thus, it appears that within the context of Freud's "Mourning and Melancholia," melancholia is descriptive of persistent loss but not prescriptive in terms of offering resolution of that loss.

There is something significant to be gained by looking further afield in Freud's work for additional illumination. As Eng and Kazanjian (2003) aptly point out, Freud re-evaluates the separation of mourning and melancholia over a series of writings, culminating in his 1923 essay, "The Ego and the Id." In doing so, Freud fundamentally alters the structure of both concepts (4). Tammy Clewell (2004) argues that the revision was prompted, in part, by the repercussions of the First World War, spurred by an "unbridled optimism for the future, holding out the promise that mourning would enable countless Europeans to consign their losses to the past and start life anew" (58). This is a significant historical context, as the vastness of the event and its far-reaching consequences provided Freud with an example of mourning on a large scale – one that vastly dwarfed his original vision of a self-contained and ahistorical narcissistic subject. From this new perspective, Freud eschews the earlier division between mourning (positive) and melancholia (pathological), and instead comes to view melancholia as an intrinsic part of a continually unfolding mourning process necessary for the formation of the ego (61). Although this is a positive step because the revision largely removes pathology as a primary distinguishing feature of melancholia, it still ultimately fails to go beyond a monolithic notion of subjectivity. Freud undercuts his position somewhat by positing a rivalry between the need to incorporate the lost other into the psyche and a desire to destroy that same identification, returning to mourning some of the pathological aspects of his original concept of melancholia (61–2). With these recurrent contradictions, how can melancholia assist in understanding and explicating the ongoing persistence of culturally traumatic events such as racism, slavery, and colonialism?

Clewell proposes a potential solution when she suggests that the ambivalence grounded in Freud's later construction of melancholia offers the opportunity to reject "the self-punishment" that accompanies melancholia in favour of creating an environment in which it is possible to acknowledge loss while still moving forward (2004, 65). Such a refusal opens up the possibility of resisting the social conditions that engender melancholia, transforming its process into an impetus for change; in other words, the loss may persist over time, but it is also possible to mitigate or overcome its negative aspects. Given this context, this chapter will explore racial melancholia through an investigation of Carmin Karasic's autobiographical digital artwork, *With Liberty and Justice for All*. Created in 1998, this hypertext narrative explores how Black subjects in the late 1950s and 1960s were alienated from the American Dream.[1] Comprised of autobiographical multilinear story fragments and archives of private and public photographs, the artwork offers an interactive embodiment of Karasic's personal engagement as an African

American with American society and its racist legacies. Moreover, the artwork's interactivity provides users with the opportunity to explore the personal roots of Karasic's experience of racial melancholia in a way that encourages them to challenge their own beliefs and arrive at their own conclusions. Finally, this chapter will consider how Karasic compares personal and public memories as evocations of diasporic melancholia, thereby exposing the ironies and resisting the realities of everyday racism.

Digital Space and Race

In the initial quest to code the implications of digital media for cultures, identities, and economies, cyberspace was envisioned as a utopian space where race was as "analogue" as tube televisions or abacuses. After all, we were entering a new "post-human" era in which "informational pattern" was privileged over the "material instantiation" of the body, and in which "there are no essential differences or absolute demarcations between bodily existence and computer simulation, cybernetic mechanism and biological organism, robot teleology and human goals" (Hayles 1999, 2–3). According to this framework, when we sit down at a computer, we cease to be a physical being in a finite world and become, instead, a limitless cyber-being in an infinite space where we can reconstitute ourselves in any way we choose by creating new realities. In short, we become information, unfettered and free to move at will, assuming any shape we desire.

Certainly, new media initially offered the illusion of disembodiment, if only by challenging the notion of verisimilitude. In the beginning, facing a screen in physical isolation, users surfed the global tide of code masked by mathematics and distance. Identity could be hidden in a variety of ways, by myriad ISPs (Internet service providers) or by projecting one's own self in a fantasy form that, lacking the potential for physical validation, could appear real. The promise – or the threat – was that one could not tell the difference between the real user and the computer simulacrum, which led to the notion that binary code was the great equalizer. In this context, "'passing'" appeared to make race invisible and perhaps even irrelevant (Hansen 2004, 108). For some, passing online offered the opportunity to "erase a certain institutionalization of race" by permitting "the radical disjunction between racial identity categories and the singularity of each body whose life is always in excess of any particular, fixed identity" (108). Mark Hansen thus goes beyond the notion of the body as information by introducing the idea of "digital performativity," which "suspends the constraint exercised by the body as a *visible* signifier" (109, 111, original emphasis). In other words, the computer renders the physical body of the user invisible, making it unavailable as a bearer of race (111). Although anonymity has been undermined in recent years by increased use of webcams and by the popularity of online services, such as Skype, which allow for face-to-face communication, there still exists the possibility of donning imaginary identities in multiple online contexts.

There are, however, several problems with the position that race is rendered irrelevant by computer technology. Most users do not experience computers as binary code any more than spectators experience film as a camera. Instead, users experience computers as visual media products and, for them, the primary locus of consumption is the screen, although the software running the computer is as relevant to that experience as is the camera behind the film. As we interact with what we see, computer-generated texts can in no way be considered ahistorical in relation to other visual media, nor do the technological differences between the computer's possibilities and other, earlier visual media necessarily negate the power of those connections. For example, although a white user creating an avatar might pass as a Black user, the visual depiction that results encodes race in the avatar's appearance. This makes the white/Black user open to all the positive *and* negative (racist) stereotyping associated with Blackness, including potential racism from fellow players based on the visual appearance of the avatar.[2] In this fashion, the avatar, despite being an object of digital performativity, becomes invested with all the discourses surrounding race in society. Moreover, although the white user might face racism because of their "cyber-skin," it does not in any way correlate to real-life experience as a person of colour because the user has the luxury of reconfiguring such an avatar at will. Play, or passing, is not an indication of a "raceless" cyber environment but, rather, fosters the erroneous illusion that race is a transitory state.

As Sayantani DasGupta notes in another chapter in this volume, "cyberspace is extraordinarily corporeal" (44) in that it remains invested in bodies as bearers of meaning. Race thus remains a powerful signifier in a digital context principally because contemporary online environments are profoundly visual. Many of the strategies of visual representation prevalent in film, television, and print have been remediated for digital spaces and, indeed, there is an active exchange among these media. This is not to suggest that the digital aesthetics of cybermedia are completely contained within the visual strategies of older media. Yet, to presume that new technology is somehow set apart entirely from the influences of the history of visual media is to fail to understand the complexity and potential of cyberspace. Digital media emerged as leading communication technologies precisely because they are profoundly recombinant, allowing simultaneously for interpersonal and institutional communication as well as entertainment, commerce, political engagement, and a host of other functions that are apparently seamlessly available at the click of a mouse. In the process, there emerges an inevitable flow between new and old technologies – one that results in the embedding of earlier visual discourses, including those of race, in new environs.

Carmin Karasic's *With Liberty and Justice for All* engages such histories through a layered narrative structure that combines a variety of aesthetic approaches garnered from earlier media and remediates them within a digital environment. Archived online, the artwork is comprised of three browser windows.[3] A large window on the left contains Karasic's personal narrative of her experiences growing up as an African American child in the 1960s. To the right are two smaller windows that contain, in various combinations, digitally manipulated images of important historical moments in the Civil Rights Movement and iconic images from advertising and children's primers. Each short passage in Karasic's narrative includes a hyperlink that not only transitions to the next passage but also changes the images in the other two boxes. In this sense, Karasic is in charge of her own story, leading the user through the narrative by delimiting choice in a specific manner. Although a user can certainly view the personal and national historical images independently, it is only by following Karasic's lead that their full meaning is integrated into the narrative. In some cases, however, where more than one hyperlink is provided during a passage, the user is only obliged to click on the last one. As a result, the artwork also allows for a variety of readings, depending on the pathway the user chooses through the work and on the images that are subsequently associated with each hyperlink.

For example, in a section of the narrative where Karasic describes the mobile housing she and her family occupied on the military base to which her father was assigned, two possible hyperlinks are offered. The first, associated with the word, "living room," takes the user to an image of a sleek conversation pit, a style of living room epitomizing California Modern design in the 1960s. The opulence of the space both contrasts with the modest description of the family quarters and evokes the apex of what an ambitious family might strive for. The second hyperlink, associated with the phrase, "garbage cans," brings up two images. The first, of Karasic as a young, exuberant child, has been digitally modified to contain a green garbage can in the background. The second image is of a number of young African American children sitting on the steps of a building. By associating the children with the phrase, "garbage cans," and by including the digital image of a can within her own photo, Karasic seems to be suggesting that the African American children are socially disposable. If the user clicks on both hyperlinks, the images of the conversation pit and the children share the same screen space. This juxtaposition undermines the myth of the American Dream as available to all. However, if a user clicks on only one or the other hyperlink, he or she may leave the section with a very different understanding of the narrative. Ultimately, this structure renders the text both stable and unstable, making the user a partner in reconstructing Karasic's narrative and allowing the artist to create irony and social commentary by playing with and against her own reminiscences. As Sarah Brophy and Janice Hladki observe in the final essay in this volume, the relationship between words and images "cannot be made singular or fixed," resulting in "multiple embodiments" that disrupt dominant epistemologies and histories (255). The digital architecture of the artwork mirrors the social foundations of racial melancholia as the hyperlinks serve to unearth the histories of inequality masked by the phrase, "With liberty and justice for all."

The very design of the artwork plays on this notion of interlinked histories by exploiting the ability of digital media to acknowledge and transform earlier media forms. Framed as a remembrance and related in past tense, the hypertext narrative in the first browser window is situated in the present-day even as the hyperlinks to the second and third windows historicize Karasic's experiences. These smaller windows serve as digital archives for the photographs from Karasic's historical and personal context: originally analogue photographs, now translated into digital images, they link multiple histories of technology back to the hypertext narrative. In addition, because they are placed in specific sequences in response to clicking on the hyperlinks, they establish flows of history between Karasic's personal remembrances and the historical events of her time. As each hyperlink provides new images, users are invited to contemplate – perhaps even to create – the interrelationships between the histories evoked and their subject positions as consumers of the artwork.

With its emphasis on autobiographical and historical photographic images, *With Liberty* challenges the notion of the disembodied (nonracial) cyber-self. In particular, the compare and contrast narrative strategy created by the juxtaposition of iconic images of the 1960s with her own personal images exposes the illusion of American equality without sentimentalizing Karasic's own journey from assimilation to awakening. As Anne Cheng (2001) notes, in order to mobilize racial melancholia as a force of change, "the connection between subjectivity and social damage" must be articulated in a way that does not consign the subject "to the irrevocability of 'self hatred' or denying racism's profound, lasting effects" (7). Thus, Karasic's use of autobiography represents more than the creation of a personalized and racialized fulcrum for debate by referencing a long tradition of African American autobiography, a genre through which many of the first African American voices proclaimed personhood and the right to equality in the public sphere. In the act of digitizing her own personal archive, Karasic builds a bridge between this older tradition and new expressions in cyberspace.

African American Self-Authoring

Autobiography has a special place in African American culture. During the 1840s and 1850s, "ex-slave narrators" and their autobiographies became a powerful force in "support of the antislavery cause" (Andrews 1990, 24). The autobiographies of ex-slaves such as Frederick Douglass (*My Bondage and My Freedom*, 1855) and Harriet Jacobs (*Incidents in the Life of a Slave Girl*, 1861) were more than simple recitations of the authors' experiences of slavery; they were also a testimony to the humanity, intelligence, and worth of all African Americans. Such autobiographies serve as counter-histories of slavery, and although they were undoubtedly shaped in part to serve abolitionist imperatives and to address a white audience, these early narratives sought to recast the racist stereotypes and myths according to which slavery was rationalized (Andrews 1990, 24). As such, they created "a crucial collection of narratives that reshape our understanding of black history, literature, and culture in the United States" (Bergland 1994, 87). Works that are as much acts of political liberation as they are autobiographies, the ex-slave narratives founded an African American literary tradition and brought race and racism to the foreground of American intellectual and political life. Whether it is W.E.B. Du Bois's semi-autobiographical work, *The Souls of Black Folk* ([1903] 1994) or Malcolm X's incendiary indictment of racism in *The Autobiography of Malcolm X* (1965), African American autobiography continues to ask, "Whose country is it? Whose view of history and truth will be heard?" (Bergland 1994, 69). By challenging "the dominant, 'national' picture that we have of ourselves," such autobiographies continue to resist oppression in its many forms by acting as counter-histories to dominant historical narratives (Lionnet 2001, 379).

At the heart of such works lies what Betty Ann Bergland (1994) describes as "the autobiographical 'I'" (78), which is of special concern to African American autobiography. Beginning as a genre of resistance and recoupment, African American autobiography has always had a complex relationship with the notion of authenticity. For example, early ex-slave authors struggled against the restrictions imposed by an abolitionist movement that desired a certain type of simplistic rhetorical style that preserved "a [slave] voice that would sound authentic to his hearers" (Andrews 1990, 24). Although authors such as Frederick Douglass and William Wells Brown soon moved beyond these strictures, the notion of authentic, personal experience as a means of mobilizing political opposition to slavery and racism persisted. When Karasic foregrounds her personal recollections of childhood in *With Liberty*, she is drawing on a much older tradition of oral storytelling that is both intrinsic to the African cultures from which slaves were drawn and the only means they had of telling their own complex and often fragmented histories. Digitally connected to iconic images in American history, Karasic's personal experiences animate a counter-history that contests a dominant culture that continues to deny her equal subjecthood on the basis of race. Over the course of her story she presents three visions of herself: the awakening child who learns from her mother on the first day of school that the pledge of allegiance does not apply to her because, as an African American, she is not equal; the transnational African American who discovers, when her father takes an army posting in France, a sense of nation she does not feel in America; and the disjunctive subject who becomes estranged from her white peers due to an absence of role models from her own culture and, more seriously, because of the racism she experiences in her teenage years. What begins as a process of awakening and accommodation becomes a journey towards conscious resistance. The narrative arc inscribed by the artwork is more than personal recollection; it is an articulation of racial melancholia as a *process* of identity formation.

Melancholia and the Persistence of Racial Discourses

The question of why race remains a powerful generator of discourse in society seems puzzling to some who take the position, in the United States and elsewhere, that slavery and colonialism are *past* histories and can be filed neatly in a historical archive, never to be revisited nor repeated. This position is based on a fundamentally flawed view of national history that assumes that there is one historical through-line in which all members of a nation equally share. However, not all national subjects have an equal stake in the dominant culture's historical imperatives, nor are their histories given equal voice. From an African American perspective, it quickly becomes apparent that slavery persists as a living legacy in a country where, for example, in 2008, two white supremacists were arrested in Tennessee for allegedly plotting an assassination attempt on Barack Obama during the presidential candidate's successful drive to become the first African American president of the United States.[4] As Sara Clarke Kaplan (2007) argues, the persistence of racial division in the United States "can only be understood as a three-century practice of genocide" in which African Americans, despite all the advances that are evident in American society, can still find themselves in a position where they must defend their right to existence during the course of their daily lives (512). Yet, it is a great disservice to characterize African Americans solely as continuing victims of slavery, as this also devalues the advances their communities have fought for and won over the course of time. Striking a balance between acknowledging the power of racism without entrenching African American experience as a form of debilitating victimhood has proven to be a difficult matter. As Paul Gilroy (2005) suggests, racial discourse is powerful because it creates a specific hierarchy and orders social institutions along easily recognized axes of difference (8). Gilroy makes a critical distinction, however, when he argues that the focus should not be on race but should, instead, move towards understanding "the enduring power of racisms" as complex political, economic, cultural, and historical constructs (9). In other words, racism is a *learned process* that entrenches its effects broadly across generations and social systems, affecting both the racist subject and the subject of racism.

In order to characterize the dominant culture's nostalgia for the purity of the historical colonial hierarchy, Gilroy uses the term "postcolonial melancholia" to describe how racist beliefs continue to influence social systems once colonialism has been dismantled (2005, 106). Kaplan extends this argument into the realm of race relations in America by suggesting that African Americans undergo "a *process* and *practice*" of racism that "is internalized as racial grief," resulting in a "racial melancholia" (2007, 514, original emphases). It is important, then, to make a distinction between expressions of racial melancholia. When Freud recognized the historical and cultural importance of the First World War by revising his view of mourning and melancholia, he implicitly acknowledged that the development of the psyche can be affected by external as well as internal stimuli. From this perspective, it is possible to argue that white-based racial melancholia and African diasporic melancholia derive from fundamentally different roots, and that they will, in turn, generate decidedly different melancholic discourses. If one accepts the proposition that the process is dependent upon the loss of a specific love object, then the form that cultural melancholia takes must respond directly to the historical impetuses under which it was first initiated. For example, an oppressed individual in the process of mourning the loss of freedom and equality may feel driven to demand social change or initiate social rebellion. By mobilizing the imagery of the Civil Rights Movement and affectively connecting these historical events to her own autobiographical context, Karasic lends legitimacy to the argument that racial melancholia is not necessarily a passive state. It is thus possible to view internalized racism not as a marker of victimhood but, rather, as a site with the potential for resistance that does not define African American culture but is certainly circumscribed within "structures of black unfreedom" that inform daily life (514). Under such auspices, it would seem absurd to consider digital spaces, formed initially within and through Western technological developments and all that such a history entails, as somehow exempt from, or beyond, these dynamics.

Karasic's Digital "I"

With Liberty and Justice for All explores racial melancholia using a variety of discursive strategies. For example, the first narrative sequence of the project opens with the statement, "When I was five, my mother said to me, 'You don't have to say the Pledge [of Allegiance]. It isn't meant for you.'" This statement, created in a cursive font, is set apart from the rest of the text by a larger font size, bolding, and colour. This simple visual difference draws immediate attention to the words and their statement of exclusion. In the remainder of the section, Karasic explains that the discussion, which takes place on her first day of school in 1959, confuses her as she is uncertain what "the Pledge" is or why her mother is so adamant that she should not participate in taking it. By creating this knowledge gap between an adult experience and a child's level of understanding, Karasic creates a discursive space that allows her to outline the process by which her African American identity is formed (see figure 13.1).

This narrative sequence is coupled with two images presented in the second and third windows. The second window is occupied by a long shot of a quintessential split-level house circa 1950, topped by the caption, "Own your own home." White in colour, surrounded by a white picket fence, the house epitomizes the end goal of the American Dream, ostensibly a goal that could be achieved by anyone with a strong work ethic. The third window features a medium shot of a young African American man in a soldier's uniform, holding a young girl and flanked by a young, smiling African American woman. The family portrait of Karasic, her father, and mother, creates an ironic contrast between the house and the content of the narrative sequence. Headed by a responsible male, Karasic's family unit typifies the family ideals of the time, except that in this case the family is African American. The American Dream, symbolized by the house, should by all rights be a reachable goal. Yet, the mother's explicit statement that the Pledge of Allegiance does not apply to her family signals a disjunction between the prosperity promised by hard work and the experience of being denied.

The narrative surrounding the Pledge of Allegiance unfolds over several short passages that reveal Karasic's struggle to balance her desire to fit in with her mother's wish that she resist. Over the course of these passages, she notes that her father, as a soldier, existed "to serve the indivisible dream" of American nationhood. Because she attended grade school on an American military base, Karasic was expected to pledge allegiance to the American flag every morning. Despite her mother's insistence that she refuse to do so, Karasic bowed to the peer pressure exerted by the "new environment" and the fact that she "had the same dreams, hopes and fears as the other 5 year olds." In one of the final narrative sections in this sequence, Karasic admits that "when the

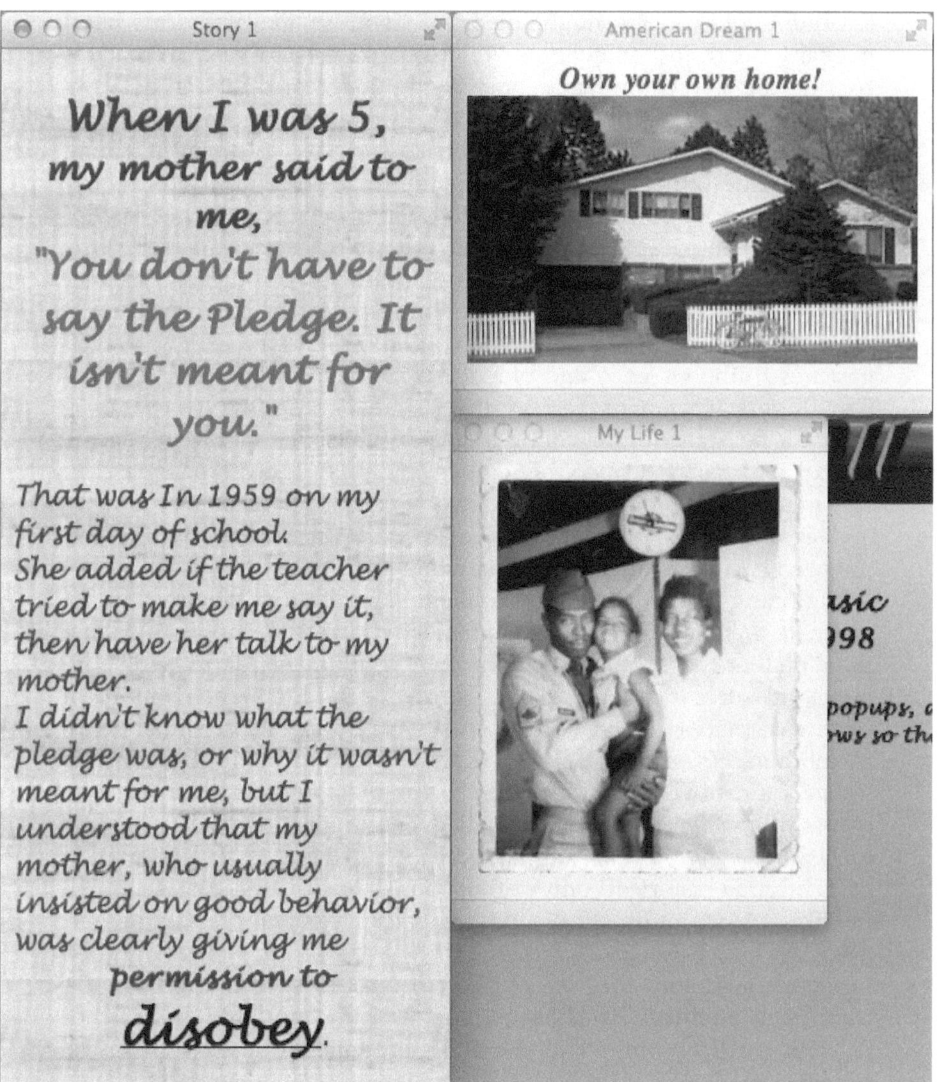

13.1. Screen capture from digital installation *With Liberty and Justice for All* (Carmin Karasic, 1998). Courtesy of the artist.

teacher taught us to recite the pledge, I stood up and placed my hand over my heart, just as everyone else did." The fact that her choice is conflicted is evident in the accompanying image presented in window two. The image is a photograph taken by Vic Cooley of the *Nashville Banner* in February 1960, and it depicts agitators attacking a young African American protester participating in a sit-in at a whites-only lunch counter in downtown Nashville, Tennessee.[5] Karasic has manipulated the photograph, cropping it in order to place added focus on the young African American protester and adding red colouring to the majority of the image, leaving only the protester in the black and white schema of the original photo. The coloration has two effects: first, it gestures to the violence and blood that will spill in the course of the Civil Rights Movement. Second, the visual alteration serves to underscore the resistance of the young protester, whose refusal to leave seems an extraordinary act of courage given the forces arrayed against him. The image thus contrasts with Karasic's conformity in the classroom, and signals the tension that exists between the pressure to conform and the need to rebel against the ruling white authority.

Digitizing the lunch counter image also invites the user to re-evaluate the image as a marker of history, drawing attention to the fact that "neither the photographic nor the digital image can provide adequate measures to account for the horrors of the past: Whoever takes a picture displaces the real and supplants the possibility of authentic remembrance" (Koepnick 2004, 96). Karasic's digital manipulation of the image's meaning draws attention to the instability of historical discourse, the meaning of which is only ever temporarily fixed by specific context. The photograph's digital reconception demands a re-evaluation of its original historical context, thus reconfiguring its status as a transmissible object automatically passed into a contemporary time and place. As Lutz P. Koepnick argues, "the world of digital images, at least in theory, abandons the idea of photographic closure and in so doing transforms an image's relation to time, finitude, mortality, and memory" (2004, 100). By reinventing analogue photos in her work, Karasic renders the photographs as sites of resistance and counter-history.

The personal conflict evidenced in Karasic's sequence entitled "Pledge of Allegiance" also symbolizes the process by which racial melancholia is internalized in African American culture. The tension Karasic feels between the need for rebellion and the desire for conformity reflects what W.E.B. Du Bois (1994) famously described as "double-consciousness," or the pull between remaining true to African American culture and the pressure to assimilate to dominant white culture (2). Forced to straddle both African origin and American culture, these "double aims," from Du Bois' perspective, leave African Americans the unenviable task of asserting subjecthood in a social system that promises equality, on the one hand, and denies it through racism, on the other (3). The ultimate result of this process is a justifiable alienation from and suspicion of American culture, which fuels racial melancholia.

Du Bois is also instructive on the genesis of racial melancholia when he writes that, "Negro suffrage ended a civil war by beginning a race feud" (23). The statement indicts Reconstruction's political and economic failure to deliver on its promise of true equality as a key element of persistent racial conflict in America (23). The rise of segregation in the South subsequently led to the establishment of so-called Jim Crow laws through which the social entitlements of African Americans were heavily regulated, and their contact with white society severely curtailed (Smythe 1948, 46). This betrayal, along with its history of denial of basic rights such as free assembly, the right to vote, and protection under the law from white violence, is fundamental to racial melancholia in African American culture. By placing her narrative within the historical context of the Civil Rights Movement, Karasic not only connects her emerging identity to the social forces mobilizing African Americans to fight back against Jim Crow restrictions, but also connects her personal history to all the past historical conflicts that made the Jim Crow laws possible. Karasic's work thus portrays slavery as a living history because its repercussions have not only shaped her life and America's racial past, but also continue to influence present-day race relations. Racial melancholia is not, as some conclude, a failure to let go of a moribund past but instead represents the recognition of a continuously unfolding history that has yet to achieve any form of closure.

As Karasic's narrative develops, she shares a series of recollections of a move to France necessitated when her father is posted overseas. Here, Karasic develops a sense of herself as an American citizen, an ironic twist given that such identification is denied within the nation itself. Challenged by a ballet teacher who believes Karasic's French is so fluent that she must be concealing an Algerian heritage by claiming to be American, the child proves her nationhood by "pleading" her case in English. The teacher, reasoning that an Algerian child would not speak English as well as Karasic, accepts her as an American. "Suddenly," Karasic recollects, "being American became very special." The incident is ironic on a number of levels. The teacher's insistence that Karasic "must be proud" of her "Algerian heritage" alludes to the Algerian War of Liberation that raged through the 1950s and finally culminated in Algerian Independence in 1962 (Zack 2002, 55–6). As divisive in France as in Algeria, the war "made a profound imprint on a whole generation of people and has continued, to this day, to haunt the political cultures, collective memories, historiographies, and people's psyches in both" nations (56). Although the teacher's statement appears supportive, it also invokes the racism faced by Algerians in France during the time since it simultaneously implies that concealing Algerian identity is desirable to some. Moreover, the use of perfect French as a marker of such identity also raises the spectre of France's program of assimilation forced upon the nation's colonial holdings. Viewed in retrospect, the process of finding pride in being American in the process of liberating oneself from misidentification with another racially oppressed group generates an ironic commentary on the power of racism to structure societies.

Karasic creates a powerful contrast between her idyllic experience of France and Europe and the evolving Civil Rights struggle back in America. In one section of her narrative, she recalls visiting a cathedral in Metz and being impressed by its "awesome energy." Initially, this section of the narrative is accompanied by an advertising image in the second window. An advertisement for Coca-Cola, the medium shot features two comely and smiling young women, identically dressed and sitting under hairdryers. The caption that accompanies the image features the famous slogan, "Things Go Better With Coke!" When the user clicks on the hyperlink associated with the word, "energy," the Coca-Cola advertisement vanishes and is replaced by a photograph of an African American figure standing in front of a bombed-out home. The image has been digitally manipulated to clothe the figure in the stars and stripes of the American flag. This image is also accompanied by a slogan that reads, "They Bombed Homes and Churches," a reference to violence that took place in the American South in the 1960s, including the bombing of attorney Z. Alexander Looby's personal home on 19 April 1960 in response to his defence of Nashville sit-in protesters, and the September 1963 bombing of Sixteenth Street Baptist Church in Birmingham, Alabama, resulting in the deaths of four African American girls who were attending Sunday school that day. The aesthetic reinterpretation of this photograph, which mimics elements found in the Coca-Cola advertisement, suggests that under the bright, idealized exterior of the American Dream, an ugly and far more destructive truth prevails. In particular, the African American figure in the photograph, symbolically wrapped in the American flag, suggests that the violence depicted in the photograph represents the real America.

When Karasic's family returns from France, she experiences repeated disillusionment, and once again becomes alienated from mainstream American society by racism and exclusion. In one poignant section of the narrative, Karasic discusses the difficulties she faced in her pre-teen years because she "didn't have long blonde hair" and had "few friends." The difficulty inherent in the absence of role models is evidenced by the images presented in the second and third windows: the second features a close-up glamour shot of a beautiful, blue-eyed blonde woman; the third shows a picture of Karasic's class at school. She is located just beyond centre right and is surrounded by rows of white faces. Both images emphasize her cultural isolation at a time when, as a young woman, she is internalizing standards of beauty. As Tracey Owens Patton (2006) argues, the "differences in body image, skin color, and hair haunt the existence and psychology of Black women," in large part because white standards of beauty prevail in the advertising, entertainment, and fashion industries (24). Highlighting how her social milieu reinforces "the belief that Black women fail to measure up to the normative standard" (24), Karasic emphasizes feelings of alienation to demonstrate the difficulty of remaining connected to a society that seems committed to surface judgments based on racial difference."

We Still Dreamed of Utopias

With Liberty and Justice for All does not take an entirely bleak view of racial melancholia. Near the end of the narrative, as Karasic enters her teenage years, she begins a process of changing her persona. Assuming the name Carmin, Karasic sets out to differentiate herself from her parents and from the struggle of her early teen years by choosing elements from both African and white American society that suit her needs. Emulating people she admires, Karasic becomes politically active in high school and dons what she describes as a "happy-hippie personality." Her outspokenness and activism result in her election "as one of the class senators." Given this sudden change in direction and popularity, it might be asked if Karasic's choices represent another form of assimilation. The difference between her earlier capitulation to reciting the Pledge of Allegiance and the course Karasic now charts is the element of choice: in the first situation, she was compelled to conform out of a sense of fear, but, in the second, Karasic assumes control of her own identity formation. Racial melancholia may contribute to this process, but Karasic is not necessarily defined solely by its strictures. The autobiographical narrative thus has an open ending, reinforced by the closing words, which read, "In 1969, we still dreamed of utopias and world peace." The words are ambiguous because they do not indicate whether Karasic subsequently recanted that position as many others did after the death of Robert Kennedy in 1969, which signalled an end to the idealism that fuelled the 1960s. The ambiguity is further reinforced if the user chooses to click on the hyperlink associated with the word, "peace." The final image of the work is presented in the third window and is a picture of a teen-aged Karasic in hippie attire, sitting in front of a wall of hand-drawn peace posters. The image suggests that whatever path she has since taken, the cumulative effect of her formative years in the 1960s continues to have power. This situates autobiographical remembering as what Marianne Hirsch (1997) conceptualizes as a transgenerational dynamic of "postmemory," underlining how, for the descendents of slavery, "the traumas of survival and the necessity of remembering and bearing witness to past horrors … are passed down through the generations and reanimated in the present" (Sharpe 2010, 23) and echoing Koepnick's (2004) point about how digitization fosters a new relationship to time and memory (100). This image also exemplifies racial melancholia's generative potential, which, as Sara Kaplan (2007) argues, lies in its ability to formulate "racism's irremediable injury without necessarily constituting an inherently damaged or essentially victimized subject" (514). Karasic's final words and image persist as a point of meditation, inviting the user to take a moment to contemplate the process of racial melancholia and the legacies of the 1960s for race relations. As the ending demonstrates, Karasic's use of digital media for personal autobiography offers an opportunity for the user to experience how competing counter-histories of the same event or period may exist simultaneously. More to the point, the multilayered intersection between Karasic's autobiography and mainstream history reshapes the American cultural landscape by bringing to the fore those social forces that continue to shape African American life to this day.

NOTES

I am grateful for D.L. McGregor's assistance with this essay.

1 The term "American Dream" has been defined in different ways over the course of American nationhood. In this case, based on the era Karasic explores in her artwork, the phrase reflects its postwar incarnation, which promises that hard work will provide the economic prosperity to "move to the suburbs and the ability to own a home, raise a family, send one's children to college, and support oneself in old age" (Starks 2003, 206).

2 For an extended discussion of race and avatars, see Nakamura (2008).

3 The hypertext artwork can be accessed at http://www.carminka.net/wlajfa/pledge1.htm

4 Significantly, the accused men, Paul Schlesselman and Daniel Cowart, first connected with each other online. For more information, see Lichtblau (2008).

5 Andrea Blackman, Nashville Room, Nashville Public Library, Dec. 11, 2008.

14 Connective Tissue: Summoning the Spectator to Visual Autobiography

SARAH BROPHY AND JANICE HLADKI

What will responsibility look like?

Judith Butler, *Giving an Account of Oneself*

Invitation and Negation: Complicating the Affective Dynamic

In our introduction, we argued "that the cultural and political salience of visual autobiographies inheres in how they generate and critically mobilize affect for pedagogical purposes" (6). To complicate our contribution to visual culture studies, autobiography studies, and disability studies along these lines, and to trouble spectatorial engagement with cultural re-configurations of public memory, we conclude with a discussion of visual autobiographies that emphatically *refuse* affective connectivity even as they *demand* it. Why and how, we ask, do these works embed negation? What is at stake, pedagogically, in negation, and what are the implications for understanding visual autobiography and embodiment? When we are summoned as witnesses yet simultaneously turned away, when we are urged to reciprocity yet severed from the autobiographical subject, affective response itself (and not only the represented body) becomes uncertain and disorderly. Through strategies of negation, visual autobiographies recognize the conjoined possibility and impossibility of kinship, reciprocity, and responsibility generated by the spectatorial relationship, opening up new perspectives on the affective encounter, including "empathic vision" (Bennett 2005) and the "touch" to the viewer (Cartwright 2008; Doyle 2013; Simon 2005; Sobchack 2004).

An attention to spectatorial practices and affects is central throughout this volume. For example, recognizing the uncertain complication of reception and witnessing, Wendy Kozol, in her contribution, remarks on "the entangled practices of remembrance and accountability" (209). And, in the context of his analysis of transsexual imagery, contributor Dan Irving explores the potential of the spectatorial encounter as he underlines the "looking relations among visual artist, image, and viewer [that] shape and negotiate the terms of recognition," asking how images "compel audiences" (102–3). Our concentration here, by way of conclusion, on the reciprocal relations generated by visual autobiography also echoes Peter Morin's emphasis, in this volume, on the difficulties of looking, learning, and community building for Indigenous spectators in sites of Western museum epistemology. In this chapter, we contribute a distinct argument to the collection while enriching key ideas about ethical spectatorship woven throughout. Positing the affective dynamic as unfixed, risky, troubled, and contentious, and drawing on Rosemarie Garland-Thomson's concept of "beholding" (2009, 194), we propose that ethical spectatorship in relation to visual autobiography can be understood as an encounter of "tenuous beholding" of and with embodied subjects. We work closely with particular graphic memoirs and autobiographical performances for video, not as illustrative examples, but as the generative and theorizing materials that actualize this argument. Inspired by Mieke Bal's (2010) insistence on not engaging with artworks as "passive objects of inquiry," we suggest that a reflection on the issues at stake requires "learning from the actual practices" (90).

While the cases/texts that we mobilize differ in terms of visual formats and devices, the cultural works intersect through their lines of implication regarding the notion of simultaneous refusal/invitation of affective connectivity. Yet, following from Bennett (2005), we contend that this is "a group of works linked not strictly by theme but by a mode of political engagement ... characterized by an aesthetic of relations ... and conjunctions of affective and critical operations" (21). The works engage empathic vision as a thinking, seeing, and feeling politics. In linking the graphic memoirs and performance videos, our analysis recognizes that there are always already multiple spectators, sites of encounter, and receptions, with "no guarantee" of spectatorial response (Butler 2004b, 43). The visual autobiographies that we discuss here share a concern to explore, critically and imaginatively, spectatorial limits and prospects. They wrestle with Judith Butler's question in our epigraph – "what does responsibility look like?" – by, in turn, examining "precariousness ... at the viewer-image interface" (Ross 2008, 8), engaging the ethics of "beholding" (Garland-Thomson 2009; Rancière 2010), and amplifying the contestatory dynamics that accompany "the right to look" (Mirzoeff 2011). Through both their claims upon the viewer and their negation of such a claiming, these critical visual autobiographies propose that affiliation, kinship, and connection with the spectatorial "other" involve discontinuity and unsettlement. Beholding is fragile. By underlining the incompleteness of autobiography (Gilmore 1998) and by highlighting seemingly incompatible repertoires of memory and meaning, these summoning practices unfix a humanist version of affiliation, which can be understood to assume connection.[1]

We are particularly committed to tracing links across the different embodiments in the artworks through a critical disability studies perspective that focuses on how practices and discourses (and myths) of normalcy produce the conditions of social life for all bodies (Titchkosky and Michalko 2009). Critical disability studies highlights a "mode of corporeality which accommodates not simply the materiality of the body, but the manner in which it is experienced and lived by an embodied subject" (Shildrick 2009, 18). This turn in disability theory to de-emphasize both states of impairment and medical approaches underscores the "instability of all bodies" (35) by conceptualizing embodiment as a process of becoming. Finally, critical disability studies asks us to attend to the significance of intercorporeality, a concept that, in its attention to inter-relatedness and "embodied response and responsibility" (153), is integral to our exploration of self/other relations and the deliberately unsettling spectatorial implications of visual autobiographies.

As Nirmala Erevelles (2011) insists, however, writing from a historical materialist perspective in response to Shildrick's emphasis on multiplicity: "all these becomings – becoming black, becoming disabled, becoming enslaved, becoming poor, becoming un-gendered – become because of the deliberate intercorporeal violence produced out of hierarchical social and economic formations" (47). While Erevelles is concerned about a tendency in post-structuralist-inspired theories of embodiment "to lose clarity about social context" (47), our analysis of critical embodiment in visual autobiography shows that this is not necessarily the case. The particular strength and political importance of visual autobiographies is that they generate critical manifestations of intercorporeality – that is, of relations of looking, feeling, and knowledge production – that can make it possible to remember historical violence and its legacies more vividly, contextually, critically, and empathetically.

Yet, visual cultural production is no panacea, and cultural works that create contestatory spectatorial practices significantly complicate the public roles of art, embodiment, and affect. To theorize these demands and contestations, we take up Bennett's (2005) call for "an analysis of the affective transaction in terms other than those of the identificatory relationship" (10), one that attends to the significance of "how the affective sign unfolds to the viewer" (43). According to Bennett, there are two urgencies at stake in this consideration: the constitution of the cultural artefact or artwork and the generative affective capacity of visuality in relation to ideas. Bennett's conception of art is shaped by a "how does it work" interrogation rather than a "what does it mean" question (41). In this model, affect is understood as a mode of knowledge making rather than as undermining realism or as thought's antithesis (36). Similarly, Rosalyn Deutsche (2010) emphasizes the pedagogical and political function of cultural production and draws on feminist thought to recognize the significance of visuality in relation to personal/political and personal/social intersections. She observes that much contemporary cultural critique is, to its detriment, characterized by "political impatience": it is "impatient not only with the poetic or artistic, ... but also with feminist interrogations of the political," particularly in terms of feminism's insistence "on the inseparability of the personal and political and on a politics concerned with subjectivity" (4). We might also add: with intersubjectivity. Focusing on how political art engages acts of war, invasion, and occupation, Deutsche asks what and how art offers – a critical move that displaces the notion of art as autonomous to instead conceive it as fundamentally constituted by viewing relations (6–7). Drawing on Hannah Arendt, she connects visuality to the social and makes a compelling case for understanding visual cultural production as "deepening and extending" the democratic public sphere (62).

In what follows, we draw together these related perspectives on cultural production, spectatorship, and ethics, endeavouring to "think with" (Bal 2007; Bennett 2005) four visual autobiographies. We consider how graphic memoirs by Marjane Satrapi and David Small and performances for video by Rebecca Belmore and Deanna Bowen enact both an invitation and dis-invitation to the spectator. Occurring through the absence of the body, the voice, the stories, and/or the contexts that would make an auto/biographical subject graspable, the negation of knowing and of affective connection puts the practice of spectatorship under pressure.[2] The displacement of spectatorial knowing and feeling is particularly urgent and consequential in relation to the viewing of disenfranchised subjects who are the embodiments at stake in the cultural works we consider. In the history of visual culture, gazing has functioned as a violent practice, cohering with other regimes of power to dismiss and devalue "others." By interrogating the spectatorial organization of power, the cultural work we interpret in this conclusion warns of the risks of the visual: these visual autobiographies circulate multiple, contestatory, embodied points of view.

Unfixable: Disability and Ethical Spectatorship in Graphic Memoirs

Midway through Marjane Satrapi's *Persepolis 2: The Story of a Return* (2004), the young adult Marji has recently returned to Tehran from Vienna following a failed love affair and several months of living on city streets. She struggles with the feeling that life in what she, from an exilic point of view, experiences as a hypocritically martyr-worshipping Iran, is just as alienating for her as life in Austria. In a chapter entitled "The Joke," Marji attempts to connect her past with her present by visiting her childhood friend, Kia Abadi, who has lost both an arm and a leg in the Iran-Iraq conflict. The visit begins awkwardly. However, by telling Marji a bawdy joke about a war veteran on his wedding night, whose bride discovers that his missing body parts have been re-attached and made functional, though all in the wrong places, Kia assuages both his own and Marji's silent anxieties. Kia's crafting (and Satrapi's re-crafting) of the anecdote – and his enjoyment of the fragmented and mismatched visual images that the story conjures – makes it persist in Marji's memory as an instance not of heroism in tune with state-sanctioned forms of martyrdom, but of resilient, counter-historical rhetorical agency. Here, Kia Abadi performs what Roger Simon (2005) defines as "survivorship," which "is not to be equated with victimization. Rather, survivorship constitutes a structure of recognition, responsibility, and learning" (82).

How do graphic narratives structure learning about embodiment? According to medical humanities scholar Susan M. Squier (2008a), hybrid image-texts put pressure on "the stigmatized categories of cognitive immaturity, impairment, and disability" (130) – and on normative understandings of art, self-representation, and literate democratic participation. Graphic memoirs of illness have "the capacity," she suggests, "to articulate aspects of social experience that escape both the normal realms of medicine and the comforts of canonical literature" (130). For instance, in her analysis of David B.'s graphic memoir *Epileptic* (2005), Squier notes that the "different scales of illness" are "dramatize[d]": the repeated neurological event of the seizure is viewed from multiple angles, "from brain event to macro-drama, from the personal to the institutional, from the individual to the collective, the physical to the psychological" (132). We build on Squier's insights to consider how image-texts mobilize ethical encounters – the possibilities for learning, and learning's fraught qualities – in relation to multiple embodiments. But our interest attaches to what is *unsaid* in these texts as much as to what they "articulate" or bring into meaning and understanding. We are particularly interested in how graphic memoirs, through their unfixing of the meanings of illness, disability, and witnessing, wrest intersubjectivity away from a kind of mirroring that confirms what we already knew, instead testing perception and identification in relation to what is unknown and/or unspeakable.

In "The Joke," Marji has been diagnosed as depressed; Kia uses a wheelchair. They encounter one another in the aftermath of a militant Islamic revolution that has made them each disabled: physical, social, and moral exiles in their own country. Yet, while earlier on, in *Persepolis 1*, the two have been depicted as gleefully acting out a version of the adult world of revolutionary and fundamentalist politics as they develop theatrical childhood games of torture together, in later years the impact of the post-revolutionary Islamic regime on their lives is shockingly dissimilar. Class and gender differences (young working-class men in particular are being propagandized, recruited, and celebrated as martyrs) and specific circumstances (Kia tried to escape the country, but was forced to return and enlist against his will) haunt the scene: and, as a result, Marji's relatively protected status begins to come into focus.[3]

From a material and health perspective, the Iran-Iraq war anticipated the later American-led "wars on terror" in the Middle East by producing "a disproportionate surge in the numbers of children and adults with disabilities as a result of war-related injuries, military torture, civil war, economic scarcities, and psychological trauma" (Erevelles 2011, 144). Situated in this context, where war, physical and mental disability, and gender are disturbingly interwoven, Satrapi's "The Joke" initiates an exploration of ethical learning in relation to embodied politics, flagging this learning as a fraught process – one that does not purport to guarantee any particular pedagogical or political outcome either for the autobiographical avatar or for readers. What Marji learns from the reciprocity she finds in "talking and joking" with Kia appears to be, as she summarizes, that "the only way to bear the unbearable is to laugh at it" (112); however, in *Persepolis* there is no formula for coping with or responding to the "unbearable." By attending to the pressure that embodied intersubjectivity puts on integrative representational strategies, Satrapi's memoir invites readers to dwell in ethically troubling forms of inarticulacy and disidentification. This process is a halting and painful one. For, although it seems that she has had her preoccupation with her own woes effectively challenged by Kia, Marji makes a determined return to health (see figure 14.1). In the feature-length film adaptation of *Persepolis*, Marji's aerobicizing to the 1980s anthem, "Eye of the Tiger," makes her easy to identify with – a figure, like Stallone's Rocky, of fun, vitality, and inspiration. On the page, however, irony is amplified: Marji's self-improvement mantras ("more and more," "strong and invincible," "my new destiny") contrast starkly with her bodily postures, her limbs flying and torso twisting in ways that recall the exploding, falling bodies of her "martyred" male peers (e.g., see Satrapi 2003, 102; 2004, 155). In turn, the ironic gap between this scene and the prior exposure, in "The Joke," of Kia's irreversible bodily trauma suggests that "The Joke" was a false start on a path towards ethical witnessing: Marji's view of herself – of her own rhetorical agency – has not yet taken account of the animating and unsettling dimensions of "remembrance, recognition, and learning" (Simon 2005, 82).[4]

It is not coincidental that Marji's grandmother is the one who attempts to prepare Marji prior to her encounter with Kia's disability (Satrapi 2004, 106). As critics have pointed out, interactions among generations of women are central to Marji's identity formation (Chute 2008b; Miller 2007b; Naghibi and O'Malley 2005). The grandmother's role is not merely to supply an ethical point of reference or even a sense of historical and familial context, but to initiate (again and again) processes of ethical self-scrutiny. In *Persepolis 1*, it is Marji's desire to mitigate her grandmother and other older people's daily experiences of pain that (along with her sense of the unfairness of their house servant not dining with the family) sparks her imagining of a just world – and her childhood fantasy of becoming a prophet who might bring about justice. After "The Joke" and her determined but haunted return to wellness, it is her grandmother who unfixes Marji's self-image again and more profoundly. When Marji laughingly tells an anecdote of a man whom she falsely accuses of harassment in order to escape censure by the guardians of the revolution for wearing lipstick en route to meet

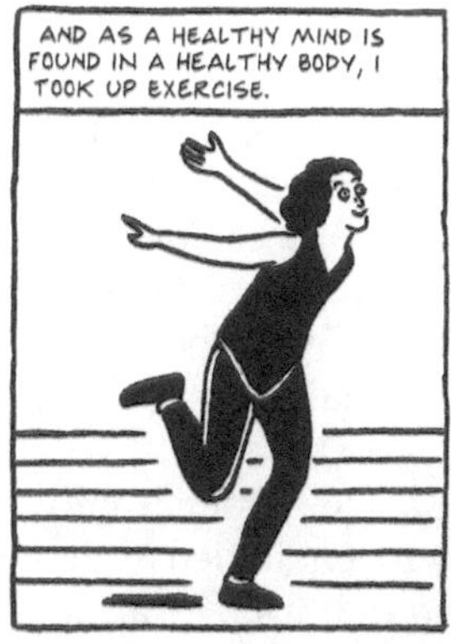

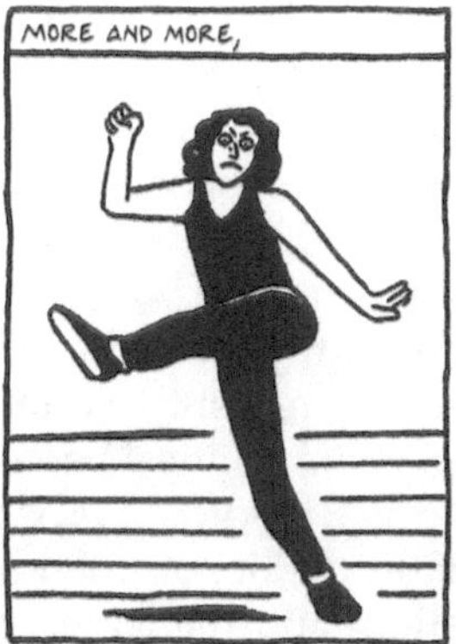

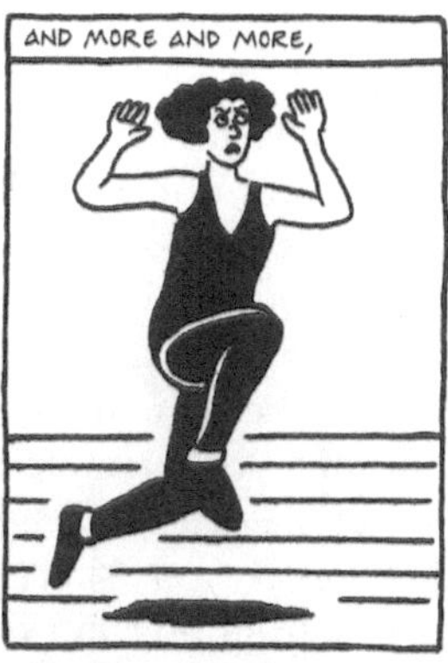

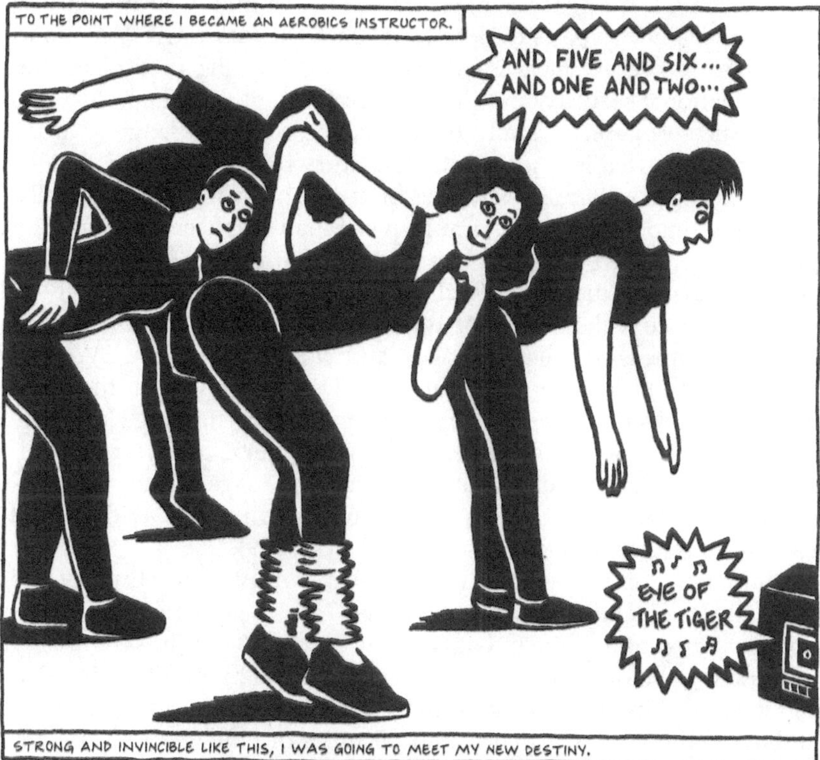

14.1. Graphic novel excerpt from *Persepolis 2: The Story of a Return* (Marjane Satrapi). Translation copyright © 2004 by Anjali Singh, 121. Used by permission of Pantheon Books, an imprint of the Knopf Doubleday Publishing Group, a division of Random House LLC. All rights reserved.

her fiancé, the grandmother calls the laughing Marji a "selfish bitch" who has forgotten about the imprisonment, torture, and murder of politically involved members of her own family, including her grandfather and uncle (137). In the process of casting off her sense of being buried alive (97) and modelling herself on Kia's irreverence, Marji has embraced a hollow agency, devoid of what her grandmother describes as "integrity," that is, of empathy for and accountability to the people around her who have also – or may still – suffer criminalization, mental and physical torture, injury, and political persecution (137).

Like *Persepolis*, David Small's *Stitches: A Memoir* (2009) persistently indexes critical aspects of the politics of embodiment, entangled as they are in troubling kin relations and the larger-scale politics of war and health. Though it might seem, on the surface, a more psychologically than politically driven text, *Stitches* maps what Jackie Orr (2006) and Joseph Masco (2010) have identified as "a collapsing field of mental health, national security, and individualized identity formation across the frontiers of gender, family, expertise, and self-knowledge" (Masco 2010, 145). Situated in mid-twentieth-century middle America, Small's family of origin is literally as well as metaphorically nuclear: medically, politically, and emotionally implosive. Small's cancer pathography performs conflicted, angry, reluctant acts of affiliation by connecting David's cancer of the throat (well-advanced by the time his family finally decides to seek medical attention on his behalf) to memories of his mother's depression, silence, anger, and closeted sexuality. "Whap!" bangs his mother in her silent fury, and David, drawing in the room next door, picks up the non-verbal but nonetheless emotional language (Small 2009, 15). As Laura McGavin puts it, in her chapter for this volume, David's "early sicknesses are ... his 'language,'" and, the "disturbing cellular growth [of a cancerous tumour on David's neck] parallels the secrecy of the Small family" (197, 199).

Ultimately, the text neither simply blames David's mother for the boy's illness and disability nor exonerates her: a possible ethical relation is opened up within and against the "nuclear" family's complicity in pursuing the death of its own members. Along with the magnified significance of non-linguistic sounds, the verbal-visual interplay suggests how the bodies, psyches, and destinies of mother and son intersect. Their fraught coexistence makes them both painfully sealed off from one another and receptive to one another's symptoms. What is eventually described as "the mass" on David's neck is drawn as almost invisible at first, suggesting that this might well have escaped the everyday perceptions of a mother who is absorbed in her own childhood experiences of abuse and neglect and her unfulfilled love for women (Small 2009, 119). Similarly self-absorbed, his radiologist father enacts mid-century scientific fantasies of penetrating and curing all that is strange, and his parents collude in both a do-it-yourself radiation treatment of David's persistent sinus problems (26–7) and, for several years, in the denial of the increasingly evident growth on the boy's neck (160–1). As the memoir proceeds, however, David and his mother increasingly resemble each other in both facial features and expressions. As they grow physically and emotionally alike, they have no choice but to confront one another. When David's mother arrives in hospital offering to grant him a last wish (and following through by supplying him with a copy of the novel *Lolita* to replace the copy she had burned, outraged at discovering her son reading "smut"), mother and son constitute two distinct halves of the same face, dramatically riven (and connected) by a bisecting line (174). Subsequently, losing one of his vocal chords in the long-delayed throat surgery reduces David's voice to a single syllable: "Ack?" (181). An utterance premised on intersubjectivity – the question mark signalling David's interrogation of what is happening to him – "Ack?" also eerily parallels his mother's wordless sounding of frustration (see figure 14.2).

The memoir's final dream sequence, positioned just prior to a phototext epilogue depicting David's mother, extends an ambiguous question: "Who was that sweeping the path from my house to that other place?" This mysterious agentic figure ("who was that ...?") is David's mother. The repetitive sound of her household labour of "sweeping" (a word that contains within it a suppressed "weeping") is neither violent nor static (unlike many of her earlier loud gestures), but leads towards an "other place." This "other place" points towards the ominous prospect of, as the next page suggests, joining his grandmother, who is confined in her later years to the Central State Asylum, a prospect that David refuses with the words "I didn't." The "other place" can also be read, however, as pointing to the site of re-encounter that the text itself creates, and, perhaps, as opening up an emergent empathy for this difficult maternal lineage, particularly for his mother's loneliness and languagelessness, and to those rare road trips on which she did tell him "her family stories" (67).

The paratextual inclusions at the end of the memoir – a photograph of David's mother as a young woman and a short version of her story – tentatively fill in the silence. Small's mother's life comes into view briefly here as what Robert McRuer (2006) terms a "queer/disabled existence" – and as a painful example of the experiential, embodied, and

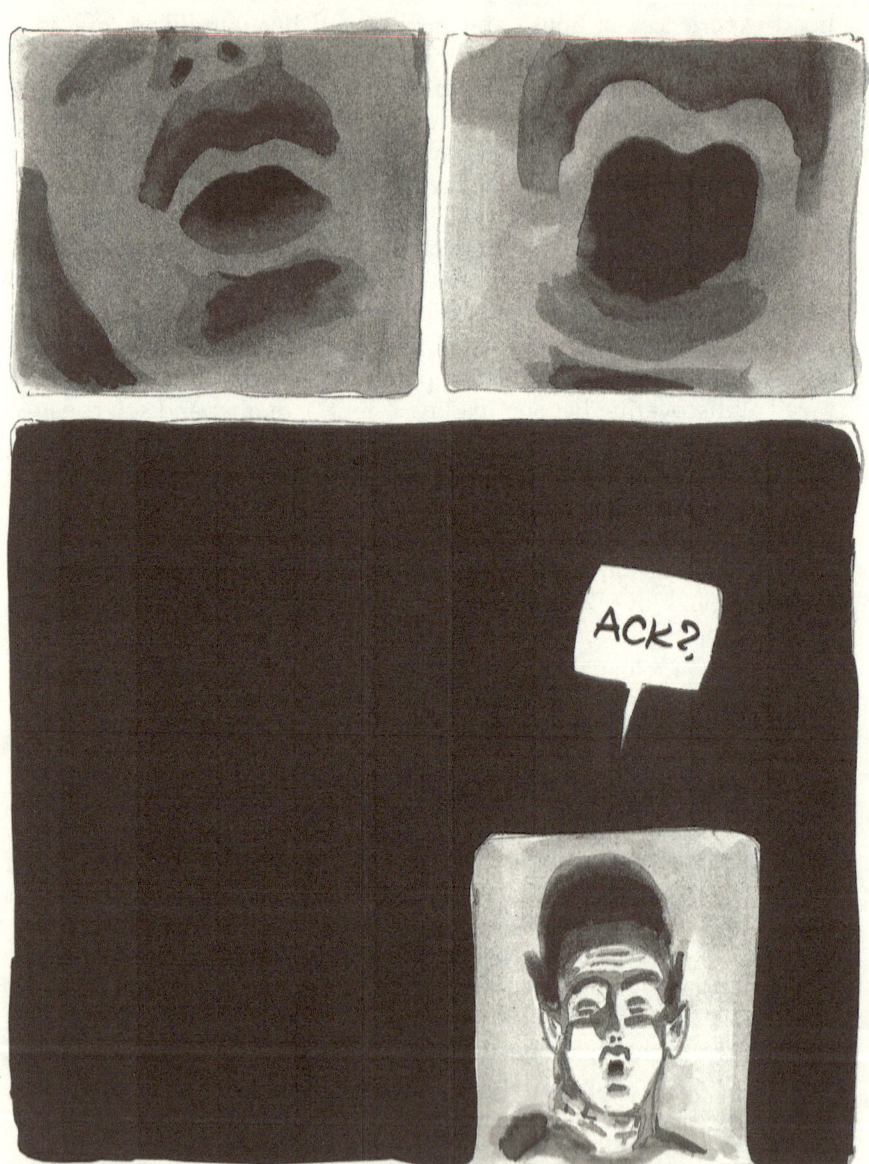

14.2. Graphic novel excerpt from *Stitches: A Memoir* (David Small, Toronto: McClelland and Stewart, 2009, 181). Used by permission of Pippin Properties.

interrelational costs of "able-bodied heterosexuality's hegemony" (31). David's surgeries, hospitalization, and impairment resonate with the medical history of his mother, who, he learned only years after her death at the age of 58, in 1970, had been "born with her heart on the wrong side of her chest, suffered from multiple heart attacks towards the end of her life," and "also had only one functioning lung" (Small 2009, 327). He adds: "If this had been her story, not mine, her secret life as a lesbian would certainly have been examined more closely" (327). Vexed about its own ability to judge what makes a livable life, *Stitches* calls attention to the memoir's orientation towards Small's own survival and escape – and to the aspects of his mother's embodied life that are only minimally registered in this piecing together of a shared past and that strain against its seams.

What is so striking about the witnessing scenarios in the graphic memoirs by Satrapi and Small is the obliqueness of processes of identification, unsettlement, and shame that are triggered by intersubjective encounters with historically and materially specific embodied differences. Gaps in knowledge, discontinuous comparisons, incomplete empathy, and negations or diversions of meaning are constitutive of intersubjectivity in these texts, suggesting both that learning cannot be scripted in advance and that it is characterized by its uncertain, fraught qualities. The relationship between words, sounds, and (drawn, painted, or photographed) images cannot be made singular or fixed: consider Satrapi's evaluation of her own laughter as at first politically and ethically meaningful, and then ethically self-deceiving, and, in Small's text, the wordless sounds that frustrate but become, possibly, a "material route" (Cartwright 2008, 35) to retrospective identification. Multiple embodiments, particularly disability embodiments, and their complex relationships to war, violence, and gender, come into view in these graphic memoirs in ways that make trouble for prevailing definitions of disability as deficit or impairment, as well as for what we think we might know about looking at, learning about, and engaging ethically with the embodied lives of others – and our own.

"I Quit": Video Performance, Embodied Histories, and Spectator Affiliation

Jeans, Jesus T-shirt, and bare feet. Anishinaabe multidisciplinary artist Rebecca Belmore stretches her body across the pavement in a crucifix position. Silent, severe, solitary, Belmore offers her 2010 performance-for-video artwork, *Worth,* in front of the Vancouver Art Gallery. The piece is taped for Internet distribution.

Composed, controlled, cerebral. Multidisciplinary artist Deanna Bowen addresses the viewer in her 2010 video art work, *sum of the parts: what can be named,* as she reads from the record of her Black ancestors.

Minimalist performances created for video, these works of testamentary address interrogate the constitution of trauma in visual artefacts, the representation of embodied knowledges, and the production of ethical spectatorship through an incommensurable tension of inviting and distancing, performative and narrative strategies.[5] Questions about nation, cultural memory, and systemic violence are struggled over in these cultural expressions of what Roger I. Simon (2005) writing with Sharon Rosenberg calls "a pedagogy of remembrance" (85). Belmore's *Worth* examines complexities of occupation, self-determination, and commodification for Indigenous subjects. Bowen's performance video, *sum of the parts: what can be named,* another politically charged work, examines systemic mass violence through a highly detailed, oral history of slavery experienced by Bowen's family. Considered together, the artists' works take up the difficult terrain of trauma and violation, and, by fracturing contemporary and historical allusions and illusions, they gesture towards the unnamable and complicate responsible spectatorship. The power/knowledge statement of Bowen's subtitle is not followed by a question mark, yet we read it as a query. Asking "what can be named" points to questions about what can be articulated and what can be known, by whom, and about which subjects, underlining the unknowable quality both of the spectator's engagement with the artists' namings and of the affiliative consequences. The artist's question also evokes Gilmore's (1998, 2001) sense of autobiography as an indefinite project and, in relation to traumatic and public memory, as an ongoing return that enacts a pedagogical undertaking.

"Insisting on a dialogical process with both history and the viewer" and on witnessing rather than victimization (Zimmermann 2000, 64), the works of Bowen and Belmore relate to other forms of critical contemporary art, or activist visual cultures, that wrestle with the performance and visualization of anguish, violence, and suffering as public memory and that function as critical pedagogical witnessing. *Worth* and *sum of the parts* constitute forms of visual/performance culture that testify about, but do not reproduce trauma (Reinhardt 2007, 14). Ann Cvetkovich (2003) argues: "Especially important is the interventionist potential of trauma histories to disrupt celebratory accounts of the nation that ignore or repress the violence and exclusions that are so often the foundation of the nation-state" (119). The affective and intimate register of these disruptive performance-video body-works is acute – not despite but because of the carefully constructed distancing devices they employ. Mobilizing both invitation and negation for spectators, *Worth* and *sum of the parts* generate difficult witnessing work and testimonial address that confronts a spectator's relationship to injustice.[6]

In the introduction to this volume, we briefly described Belmore's *Worth* and offered it as an animated opening that "brilliantly exemplifies the texts and tactics that animate this book" (3). In this chapter, we return to *Worth* to engage fully with the generative capacity of this arts project in relation to the volume's concern with critical embodiment and with the pedagogical potential of empathic spectatorship. As we described in the introduction, Belmore concludes her performance by presenting a blanket to her friend Daina Augaitis, Chief Curator at the Vancouver Art Gallery. Since 1990, Belmore and Augaitis have had a productive artist-curator relationship, and, in 2008, Augaitis curated the major retrospective exhibition entitled, simply, *Rebecca Belmore*. Belmore does not direct her "I quit" declaration at the end of the performance to her colleague Augaitis, but the curator does stand in for art institutions and institutional practice more broadly. Internet buzz interpreted Belmore's declaration as a decision to quit the art world, particularly given the backdrop to Belmore's performance. Belmore decided to end her contract with the Pari Nadimi Gallery when she was denied payment for works sold. The gallery responded by refusing to return unsold works to the artist and by commencing legal action against Belmore, a potentially devastating consequence for the artist. Beyond the record of Belmore's productive relationship with Augaitis and the Vancouver Art Gallery, it is significant that she includes Augaitis in the performance, given the artist's appalling experience with another gallery. Augaitis' presence at the end of the performance functions performatively and theoretically. Solo and silent throughout, Belmore now makes the performance social and vocal by bringing in another "performer" to whom she relates and with whom she improvises. This development also positions Augaitis as a trusted ally, suggesting the possibility of intersubjective relations, collaboration across difference, and an affiliative future, despite the systemic marginalization of Indigenous artists and the systemic repression of Indigenous subjects more broadly. Belmore's "I quit" pronouncement and her sign, "I AM WORTH MORE THAN ONE MILLION DOLLARS TO MY PEOPLE,"

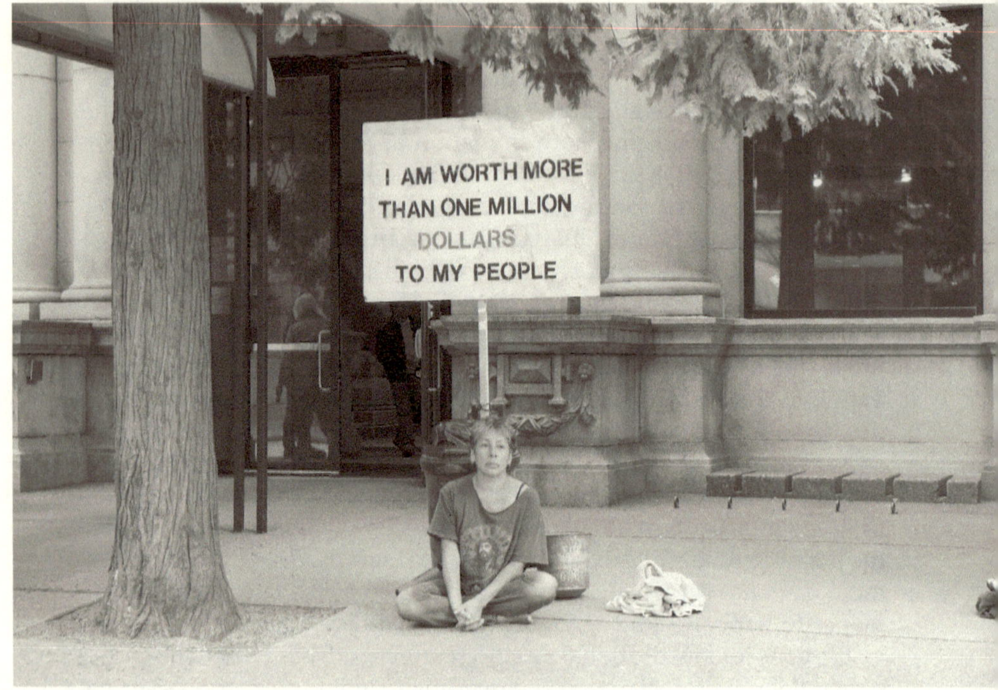

14.3. Video still from *Worth* (Rebecca Belmore, 11 Sept. 2010). Photo credit © Henri Robideau. Courtesy of the artist.

which functions as a backdrop throughout, draw attention to the dangers of political resolve for Indigenous artists making critical political cultural work in a country that continues to exploit and oppress Indigenous subjects (see figure 14.3).

With these language elements, the only ones in the performance, a spectator is spoken to and asked to read a message. She is summoned. When Belmore interacts with Augaitis, and in the previous moment when, sitting cross-legged, she looks around with curiosity, the performance is also one of invitation to and connection with others. Belmore generates a "participatory dimension of performance" (Jones 1998, 85). But she is without an organized audience, and with no evident interaction with the spectators on the sidewalk. The performance functions as a kind of "happening" that spectators will by chance encounter if they are in the vicinity. The "dynamic of posing" (159), which is evident in

Belmore's particular pauses and most evident in her lengthy, immobile, and discomfiting self-crucifixion position, also dis-invites the spectator and creates uncertainty. The combination of spectator appeal and uneasiness is a notable feature of Belmore's art practice: "deliberate ambiguity is characteristic of Belmore's work: the images are beautiful, yet they strongly suggest the body in various states of conflict, struggle or indefinable condition between life and death" (Augaitis and Ritter 2008, 10). Robert Houle (2008) argues that Belmore "creates interiority by pushing the boundaries" (19). Building on Houle's observation, we suggest that Belmore mobilizes interiority as a device, one that she uses to push the boundaries of how a spectator is summoned. Belmore may also be read as enacting an "absent presence" (Smith and Watson 2002b, 34) or creating a "structured absence" (Naficy 2001, 35).

Yet, the negation of the social sphere and identificatory relationship are urgently and profoundly accompanied by the meaningful implications of the performance, which demand responsible spectatorship. In relation to the gallery and within the art-as-product context, Belmore's *Worth* recognizes that worth is measured within the art market, art star, gallery business structure, a system shaped by gendered and raced exploitations and exclusions. In deciding to take authority away from the marketplace, Belmore is punished by that system, by way of the legal suit, which can only measure her worth by what profit she can generate. Belmore's sign, her performance location in front of an exhibition museum, the reference to her exploitation by the Pari Nadimi Gallery, and her "I quit" statement underscore the politics of the museum/gallery as a site that controls the production and circulation of knowledge and that has a highly contested relationship to Indigenous cultural work (Baker 2007; Morin, in this volume; Phillips 2011). As Peter Morin observes, "The challenge to the museum is how to shift this Western paradigm to allow for enough Indigenous epistemological practice to alter and co-create the space inside the museum" (146). *Worth* critiques exploitative gallery and museum practices whereby acquisition, curation, exhibition, and purchase can become perfidious tools contributing to the suppression of Indigenous cultural work and its makers. Belmore's performance art recognizes the ongoing effects of these practices on contemporary Indigenous artists and acknowledges the complexity of shaping an activist art practice given historical and contemporary conditions of marginalization and exclusion.

The performance video *sum of the parts: what can be named* is another counter-historical work that creates "imaginative spaces ... where images, words, witnesses, and history can be resuscitated" (Zimmermann 2000, 64). Visual, performative, and autobiographical strategies mark Deanna Bowen's twenty-minute performed oral history. Bowen voices her research of her family's record, which traces the Bowen family from Clinton, Georgia, in 1815, through multiple locations in the United States, to their migration to Canada, and to Bowen's current home in Toronto. Producing a slavery, post-slavery, and anti-slavery narrative (Sharpe 2010), Bowen complicates histories of Black embodiments, positioning autobiography as a question of self/other relations and as a practice for generating collective futures. Her video mobilizes performative structures to explore struggles for community and kinship in relation to self-recognition. The visual field of this artwork also refers to the complication of identity formation and self-representation. The frame throughout is a head-and-shoulders shot of Bowen, a Black woman in black clothing, in an unmarked and unrecognizable space: an all-black background evoking a black box performance space and underlining non-location. In obscuring and accentuating the Black autobiographical subject, in reproducing and critiquing the background space that Black subjects have occupied in visual culture, and in minimizing and also insisting on Blackness, the black-on-Black-in-black device generates an affective and spectatorial complication. *sum of the parts* interrogates practices of visualizing and situating a self, particularly in terms of gender and race. The first part of the title "sum of the parts" points to the difficulty of securing wholeness: the parts cannot make a "sum" when she has only "some," and the lower case lettering suggests the suppression of Black vernacular – and Black subjectivity – in historical records. Bowen's narrative references Black/white power relations, white domination, and the effort it takes to secure Black selfhood; kinship and collectivity become practices of struggle and contestation. Bowen's video speaks to a Black politics that necessitates claiming community in order to claim a self and to the resiliency this entails given the history of slavery and its still-unfolding effects (see figure 14.4).

Bowen's work intersects with other post-slavery artworks, including the installations of Kara Walker. In examining Walker's Black silhouette figures of plantation life, Christina Sharpe (2010) quotes from Walker's observation about her technique: "It's a blank space, but it's not all a blank space, it's both there and not there" (172). This "absent presence" (Smith and Watson 2002b, 34) that also describes Bowen's use of a blank

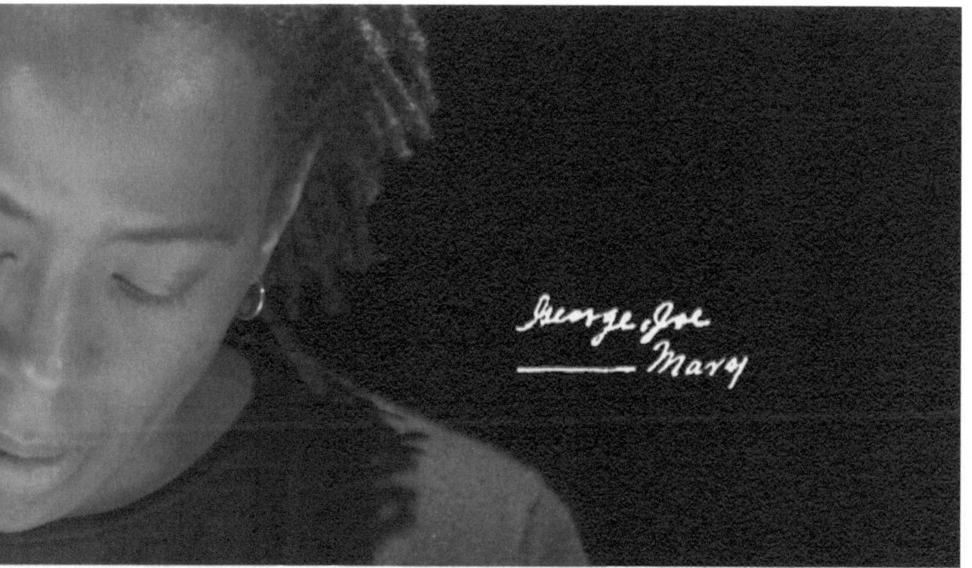

14.4. Video still from *sum of the parts: what can be named* (Deanna Bowen, 2010). Courtesy of the artist.

background is, as we have discussed, a concept for understanding address as negation and resistance. As with Walker's work, Bowen's black/Black visuality also articulates a context whereby "the signifying power of slavery in the past and present is put to work" (Sharpe 2010, 155). The background complicates the representation of and reception to Bowen's subjectivity: as Sharpe argues, the background space is one "against which" the figure of Black difference becomes recognizable (156). "Post-slavery subjectivity" (3) is constituted at the intersection of discursive codes of slavery, health, monstrosity, and perversity. Sharpe's diasporic analysis of cultural texts underlines "monstrous intimacies, defined as a set of known and unknown performances and inhabited horrors, desires and positions produced, reproduced, circulated and transmitted" (3). While Sharpe does not configure racialized monstrosities through a disability lens, we might consider the significance of disability perspectives on embodiments deemed anomalous and threatening (DasGupta, this volume; Shildrick 2002; Snyder and Mitchell 2006) in relation to Sharpe's argument about the traumatic legacies of slavery. As we observed in our discussion, in the introduction to this volume, of Allyson Mitchell's *Ladies Sasquatch* installation and Richard

Fung's video work, *Sea in the Blood*, race and disability need to be thought together to produce a complex understanding of which bodies, when, and how, are constituted as abnormal and expendable (18, 20–2). On these terms, *sum of the parts'* narration of histories of slavery yields an important emphasis on interrogating normalcy, thereby pointing to both the overlaps and incommensurabilities between critical race and disability studies perspectives. Contesting myths of progress and normalcy, the minimal traces of Bowen's and her ancestors' "alternative corporealities" (McRuer 2006, 162) become sites of knowledge production, exerting significant demands on the potential for visual art representation to inaugurate ethical affiliation with others who may or may not understand themselves as materially implicated in African diasporic, plantation, and hemispheric histories of exploitation and erasure.

Let us explain these fraught interdisciplinary linkages and how we see Bowen's visual practice as an intervention in historical legacies of racialized pathologization and enfreakment. As Ann Fudge Schormans and Adrienne Chambon note in their chapter in this volume, the work of critical disability theorist Garland-Thomson (2009) suggests that "in disturbing the visual status quo one can also disturb the ethical status quo" (188). "Extraordinary" and "stareable" bodies, Garland-Thomson writes, can be particularly effective conduits for challenging the idea of viewing as a "one-way act" (11). In *sum of the parts*, a voice narrates and a "staree," an individual who produces an "unfamiliar sight" and reveals "something new" to the starer (Garland-Thomson 2009, 7), confronts the spectator. Bowen is in the visual frame throughout, in close-up as full face or in a head-and-shoulders shot, gazing directly into the camera as she looks up from her book. While multiple positions of the subject's head and torso are clear, movement and expression are extremely minimal, and Bowen is situated predominantly at the margins of the frame. Although the woman narrator is the visual focus in the work, spectatorship is unstable: the lack of subject/background differentiation, the off-centre and almost out-of-the-frame positioning, and the relatively expressionless face, body, and voice unsettle the viewer's attention to and reception of the autobiographical subject. The body is confined and contained by filmic/visualization practices that determine how much of the body Bowen's camera permits the spectator to see and how much space the camera allows the body to inhabit in a non-referential context.

Solemn and non-demarcated visuality and spectatorial tension are matched by the non-emotive verbalization of the script. Throughout the video, Bowen reads from a book about the Bowen family, which highlights histories of slavery in Georgia and Alabama and the migratory experience of Bowen and family members in coming to Canada. The visual and vocal fields are also notable – and starkly unsettling – for the data that are both spoken and printed on screen: names of individual family members, the overall number of slaves in the United States in 1850 (3,204,313), the number of free Blacks in the country (434,495), and the number of free Blacks in Bowen's family's county in Alabama (4). Bowen remarks, "Most of what I have are only names and dates." In underlining research methods, in mobilizing data, surveys, and cultural moments in white normative historicization ("Mark Twain would write"; "Vincent Van Gogh would paint"), and in employing narrative simplicity to convey trauma ("Thigpen owned us"), Bowen's video performance art emphasizes epistemological dilemmas and undermines affective identification. The austere narrative strategies – including the uncompromising accumulation of details about slave histories, about Canada-US racialized border politics, and about multiple homes and numerous families – combine with the visual devices to construct a distancing effect, as Bowen's determined composure both magnifies and manages emotion.

Simultaneously, however, the traumatic substance of the video work invites the spectator to witness and respond, ethically and accountably, to the violences of slavery and to the post-slavery autobiographical subject. The narrative situates Bowen within a complex weave of relations, temporalities, geographies, migrations, separations, and connections. Voiced as a narrative of the past, Bowen's social story would appear to be inscribed in the past. Both Bowen and Belmore consider the past/present as inseparable and share with Kara Walker a performance practice that is "the embodiment of history" (Sharpe 2010, 159). In *Specters of the Atlantic* (2005), Ian Baucom examines cultural, economic, and ethical discourses that shape slave-trade histories, expressing his interest in acts of witnessing that not only counter an imperial past but also, simultaneously, challenge the idea of the past *as* past, thereby interrogating Western notions of time and progress (305). Similarly, in her chapter in this volume, Sheila Petty underlines "slavery as a living history" and as a counterpoint to the discursive organization of historical amnesia whereby slavery and colonialism are conditions of the past "never to be revisited" (239, 234). Bowen's politics of witnessing generates this critique and surfaces additional reflections on witnessing practices, including Zimmerman's (2000) argument that testimonies "propel a process, a movement, between the past and the future" (65). *sum of the parts: what can be named* intertwines private and public narratives that speak to autobiography as constituted in the social and political implications of self-exploration.

Both Bowen and Belmore perform for the camera in their video works, effectively "staring back" and producing counter-discursive narratives of history, nation, embodiment, and viewing ethics. The works address traumas experienced by Black and Indigenous women – bodies that have been wounded, entrapped, denied, and annihilated – and, thinking with these videos, we can question how gendered, raced, and disabled bodies come to be framed as "anomalous," that is, inferior and monstrous (Shildrick 2009, 52).[7] "Still liv[ing] to tell their stories" in the aftermath of lifetimes – and centuries – of systemic violence (Erevelles 2011, 146), these bodies of struggle produce sociopolitical agitation about the constitution of public memory under the continuing injustices of racism and settler colonialism.

Tenuous Beholding

> To be undone by another is a primary necessity, an anguish, to be sure, but also a chance – to be addressed, claimed, bound to what is not me, but also to be moved, to be prompted to act, to address myself elsewhere, and so to vacate the self-sufficient "I" as a kind of possession.
>
> Judith Butler, *Giving an Account of Oneself*

In keeping with Cartwright (2008) and Ahmed's (2004) emphasis on the unpredictability of affect, learning is fraught in the visual autobiographies created by Satrapi, Small, Belmore, and Bowen. "Beholding," according to Garland-Thomson (2009) involves curiosity, "affirmative recognition" (194), "a sense of obligation" (193), and the possibility of "new knowledge and potential social justice" (194). In the artworks we have discussed, beholding is tenuous because affiliative recognition and "empathic identification" (Cartwright 2008, 2) are unravelled even as they are urged. But they are also emphatic. Drawing on Sara Ahmed's (2011) concept of the feminist, raced, and queer wilful subject, we understand the self-representational and summoning practices of these visual autobiographers as political in the sense of "willing to be willful," as "standing against," and as enacting embodiments of "audacity" (250). This wilfulness does not assume affiliation but, rather, insists on "affect, as process" (Bal 2010, 3); the artworks propose unstable connective tissue, a relational uncertainty, what Rancière (2010) describes as an "anticipation of a community to come" (199). This connective tissue, "which rubs the past into the present" (Bal 2010, 3), refers to "a new way of doing politics in art: one that is characterized by an aesthetic of relations" (Bennett 2005, 21). However, we seek, here, to build on theories of empathic encounter and affect: we argue that by insisting on an "ambiguous, precarious, and litigious" (Rancière 2010, 202) approach to an aesthetic of relations, a connective tissue of both possibility and impossibility, the artworks generate new implications for ethical spectatorship in relation to visual autobiography.

The imaginative, intellectual, and confrontational compositions by Bowen, Belmore, Small, and Satrapi that we have been analysing comprise significant interventions for visual culture studies to reflect upon. As Mieke Bal (2007) observes about politically effective art, this work "does not entail a naïve belief in the actual interventionist capacity of art but rather in its potential – precisely due to the role of intelligent imagination – to bring about shifts in public awareness and understanding, both intellectually and affectively, of political issues" (101). Following Bal (2007) and Jill Bennett (2005), we suggest that Bowen, Belmore, Small, and Satrapi deploy autobiographical art as "visual philosophy" (Bal 2007, 98): to explore the complication of summoning spectators to public memory and claiming them for an engagement with critical political art, ethically in relation to others. Underlining the politics of the body as "a lived space marked by events, in which the consequences of violence are felt" (Bennett 2005, 60) through difficult memory work, these video performances and graphic memoirs intimately address the spectator. Yet, the affective identification is both invited and denied. The works generate intensity, but also powerfully call into question the engaged viewer's ability to grasp the significance of the performance, as well as her very right to look at the bodies and historical traumas that the image indexes, and the efficacy of her empathic interest in the autobiographies.

In their strategic mobilization of "absent presence" (Smith and Watson 2002b, 34) incommensurability, and devices designed to unsettle and unfix, the works discussed in this conclusion point the way to new pedagogical possibilities for engaging and understanding visual autobiography. By inviting and refusing connectivity, they illuminate what is at stake in the pedagogical resonances of critical, political visual autobiography; insist on embodiment as a contested terrain marked by temporality, materiality, politics, and affect; and recognize the complex contestation of summoning practices for affiliative possibility. The "connective tissue" of our title applies to the "circuit" connecting the producer of the autobiography, the cultural work itself, and the viewer or reader (Kacandes 1999, 55), with a focus on the potential of the autobiography to disturb any seamless relationship between them. With "connective tissue," we suggest connection and affiliation for spectators that, like the meaning of connective tissue in a biological sense, may bind and support. However, the fibrous nature of tissue evokes the fragility, convolution, distortion, intricacy, twistedness, and disequilibrium of connectivity generated by spectatorial engagement. Connective tissue is a dilemma rather than an answer – a complication to thinking/ feeling embodiment and the relationship of the personal to the social. Visual autobiographies hinge their politics and pedagogy on the possibility and the impossibility of felt, embodied affiliation, in all of this dynamic's necessity, uncertainty, and urgency.

NOTES

1 By "affiliation," we mean critically conscious connections created through culture and developed, ethically, through practices. Writing about ethics and responsibility, Michel Foucault (1988) argues that the development of ethical practices in relation to others depends on self-knowledge and self-care and on the transformation of conduct. Influenced by Foucault, Edward W. Said (1983) also underlines critical consciousness, ethical conduct, the labour of creating social bonds, and social relations practised "affiliatively" (175). Said observes: "To recreate the affiliative network is therefore to make visible, to give materiality back to the strands holding the text to society, author and culture" (175).

2 Smith and Watson (2002b) also inform our consideration of the negated address. They suggest that "absent presence is a central paradox of autobiographical acts and practices," whereby "the processes of represented subjectivity" become a confrontation about embodied presence (34). This paradox is particularly noteworthy with regard to visuality in relation to autobiography, since a range of visual devices, as we point out in our discussion of the graphic memoirs and performance videos, are vital to what Wendy S. Hesford (1999) calls an "aesthetic of impermanence" that is "predicated on ... the movement between absence and presence" (140).

3 The now significant number of critical articles and chapters on Marjane Satrapi tend to focus on how the two volumes of *Persepolis* encode resistance to the Orientalist agendas that have coincided with the global circulation of Iranian women's autobiography in translation (Chute 2008b;

Miller 2007b; Naghibi and O'Malley 2005; Whitlock 2007). Our own reading in this collection of essays enriches critical discussions of Satrapi's circulation/reception by foregrounding the works' ongoing engagement with multiple embodiments (disability, aging) and their ethical implications.

4 "The Joke" was not included in the film adaptation of *Persepolis*.

5 Conceptually, theoretically, politically, and aesthetically, performance by women, including a particular concentration on embodiment and autobiography, has had a tremendous influence on visual art more broadly (Jones 1998; Mars and Householder 2004; Robertson 1991; Wark 2006).

6 Mieke Bal (2007) warns of "the traps of sentimentality ... when suffering is at stake" in visual artefacts (110). As "starees" – to use Rosemarie Garland-Thomson's (2009) language for the confrontational gaze produced by disability artists – the performers in *Worth* and *sum of the parts* create what Dominick LaCapra refers to as "'empathic unsettlement'" (quoted in Bal 2007, 110). This agitation of the viewer's relationship to the artwork is, we argue, a theoretical and spectatorial manoeuvre, an incommensurability of invitation and negation through which the artists underline the necessary uncertainty of how to read suffering (Bal 2007; Bennett 2005; Kozol, this volume; Simon 2005).

7 Margrit Shildrick (2009) recognizes the social anxiety that accompanies the anomalous body: "a body that inherently resists reduction to either sameness or difference, to the natural or unnatural, and in extreme cases to the human or non-human" (52). This anxiety manifests in a range of historical and contemporary transnational social practices, including eugenics, which we discussed in the introduction in relation to Fung's video works. Speaking specifically to disability, Shildrick notes that while "eugenics itself is widely discredited, contemporary 'biomedical' decisions are equally likely to be made on the basis of cultural values as to which disabilities are intolerable and should be eliminated at a genetic level or foetal stage, or which should be subjected to interventionary procedures" (53). As Shildrick notes, the anomalous or monstrous body, "embodied incompetency," and the "supposedly contaminatory potential of otherness" (53) may be marked by a range of differences, including, we suggest, gender, race, sexuality, class, and age.

References

Adbusters. 2009. "Obsession for Women." Accessed 30 Jan. 2009. http://www.adbusters.org/gallery/spoofads/fashion/obsession_women

Ahmed, Sara. 1999. "Home and Away: Narratives of Migration and Estrangement." *International Journal of Cultural Studies* 2 (3): 329–47.

Ahmed, Sara. 2000. *Strange Encounters: Embodied Others in Post-Coloniality*. London: Routledge.

Ahmed, Sara. 2004. *The Cultural Politics of Emotion*. New York: Routledge.

Ahmed, Sara. 2006. *Queer Phenomenology: Orientations, Objects, Others*. Durham, NC: Duke University Press.

Ahmed, Sara. 2008. "Open Forum Imaginary Prohibitions: Some Preliminary Remarks on the Founding Gestures of the 'New Materialism.'" *European Journal of Women's Studies* 15 (1): 23–39.

Ahmed, Sara. 2011. "Willful Parts: Problem Characters or the Problem of Character." *New Literary History* 42 (2): 231–53.

Ahmed, Sara, and Jackie Stacey. 2001. "Testimonial Cultures: An Introduction." *Cultural Values* 5 (1): 1–6.

Alaimo, Stacy. 2010. *Bodily Natures: Science, Environment, and the Material Self*. Bloomington: Indiana University Press.

Alaimo, Stacy, and Susan Hekman. 2008. "Emerging Models of Materiality in Feminist Theory." In *Material Feminisms*, ed. Stacy Alaimo and Susan Hekman, 1–22. Bloomington: Indiana University Press.

Alcoff, Linda Martín. 1995. "The Problem of Speaking for Others." In *Who Can Speak? Authority and Critical Identity*, ed. Judith Roof and Robyn Wiegman, 97–119. Urbana: University of Illinois Press.

Aliki. 1994. *The Gods and Goddesses of Olympus*. New York: HarperCollins.

Allison, Dorothy. 1996. *Two or Three Things I Know for Sure*. New York: Plume.

Allyson Mitchell: Ladies Sasquatch. 2009. Hamilton, ON: McMaster Museum of Art. Exhibition Catalogue.

Arndt, Lisa. 2003. "Pro Anorexia." Accessed 28 Apr. 2005. http://www.anorexicweb.com/InsidetheFridge/proanorexia.html

Am I Invisible Yet? 2004. "Am I Invisible Yet? Scow Rambles Again." Accessed 29 Feb. 2004. http://cannibalz.diaryland.com/021202_40.html

Ana's Underground Grotto. 2005a. Ana/mia Artwork. Accessed 24 May 2005. http://www.plagueangel.net/grotto/id14.html

Ana's Underground Grotto. 2005b. "Background/Philosophy – Background." Accessed 18 May 2005. http://www.plagueangel.net/grotto/id1.html

Ana's Underground Grotto. 2005c. "Reverse Triggers." Accessed 24 May 2005. http://www.plagueangel.net/grotto/id11/html

Ana's Underground Grotto. 2005d. "Thinspiration Photos." Accessed 9 May 2005. http://www.plagueangel.net/grotto/id2.html

Andrews, William L. 1990. "The Novelization of Voice in Early African American Narrative." *PMLA* 105 (1): 23–34.

Ang, Ien. 1997. "Comment on Felski's 'The Doxa of Difference': The Uses of Incommensurability." *Signs* 23 (1): 57–64.

Ankori, Gannit. 2006. *Palestinian Art*. London: Reaktion Books.

AnOreXic AdDiCt. 2002. "Letter from Ana." Accessed 28 Nov. 2002. http://myweb.ecomplanet.com/BOUC2329/mycustompage0005.htm

Antoni, Janine. 1998. "Mona Hatoum." *Bomb Magazine* 63 (Spring). Accessed 23 Aug. 2008. http://www.bombsite.com/issues/63/articles/2130

Anzaldúa, Gloria. 1987. *Borderlands/La Frontera: The New Mestiza*. San Francisco: Spinsters/Aunt Lute.

Appadurai, Arjun. 1990. "Disjuncture and Difference in the Global Cultural Economy." *Public Culture* 2 (2): 1–24.

Aquino, Rowena. 2007. "Negotiating the Spectre and Spectatorship of Trauma in Rithy Panh's *S-21: The Khmer Rouge Killing Machine* (2003)." *Asian Cinema* (Fall/Winter): 62–78.

Archer, Michael. 1997. Interview. In *Mona Hatoum*, ed. Michael Archer, Guy Brett, and Catherine de Zegher, 6–31. London: Phaidon.

Archer, Michael, Guy Brett, and Catherine de Zegher, eds. 1997. *Mona Hatoum*. London: Phaidon.

Arnold, Rebecca. 1999. "Heroin Chic." *Fashion Theory* 3 (3): 279–96.

Atkinson, Dorothy, and Jan Walmsley. 1999. "Using Autobiographical Approaches with People with Learning Difficulties." *Disability and Society* 14 (2): 203–16.

Augaitis, Daina, and Kathleen Ritter. 2008. "Rebecca Belmore: Rising to the Occasion." In *Rebecca Belmore: Rising to the Occasion*, 9–14. Vancouver: Vancouver Art Gallery.

Awkward, Michael. 2006. "A Black Man's Place in Black Feminist Criticism." In *The Womanist Reader: The First Quarter Century of Womanist Thought*, ed. Layli Phillips, 69–84. New York: Routledge.

Azoulay, Ariella. 2008. *The Civil Contract of Photography*. Trans. Rela Mazali and Ruvik Danieli. New York: Zone Books.

B., David. 2005. *Epileptic*. New York: Pantheon.

Baert, Renée. 1993. "Desiring daughters." *Screen* 34 (2): 109–23.

Baker, Joe. 2007. "Interventions: Making a New Space for Indigenous Art." In *Remix: New Modernities in a Post-Indian World*, ed. Joe Baker and Gerald McMaster, 15–35. Washington, DC: National Museum of the American Indian, Smithsonian Institution, and Phoenix, AZ: Heard Museum.

Bal, Mieke. 2004. "Light Writing: Portraiture in a Post-Traumatic Age." *Mosaic* 37 (4): 1–19.

Bal, Mieke. 2006. "Intention." In *A Mieke Bal Reader*, 236–63. Chicago: University of Chicago Press.

Bal, Mieke. 2007. "The Pain of Images." In *Beautiful Suffering: Photography and the Traffic in Pain*, ed. Mark Reinhardt, Holly Edwards, and Erina Duganne, 93–115. Chicago: University of Chicago Press.

Bal, Mieke. 2010. *Of What One Cannot Speak: Doris Salcedo's Political Art*. Chicago: University of Chicago Press.

Barad, Karen. 1996. "Meeting the Universe Halfway: Realism and Social Constructivism without Contradiction." In *Feminism, Science, and the Philosophy of Science*, ed. Lynn Hankinson Nelson and Jack Nelson, 161–94. Dordrecht: Kluwer Academic.

Barad, Karen. 2007. *Meeting the Universe Halfway: Quantum Physics and the Entanglement of Matter and Meaning*. Durham, NC: Duke University Press.

Barad, Karen. 2008. "Posthumanist Performativity: Toward an Understanding of How Matter Comes to Matter." In *Material Feminisms*, ed. Stacy Alaimo and Susan Hekman, 120–56. Bloomington: Indiana University Press.

Baron, Jaimie. 2007. "Contemporary Documentary Film and 'Archive Fever': History, the Fragment, the Joke." *Velvet Light Trap: A Critical Journal of Film and Television* 60 (Fall): 13–24.

Baron, Rebecca, dir. 1998. *okay bye-bye*. Film. United States. 39 min.

Barros, Carolyn A. 2001. *Autobiography: Narrative of Transformation*. Ann Arbor: University of Michigan Press.

Barthes, Roland. 1981. *Camera Lucida: Reflections on Photography*. 2nd ed. Trans. Richard Howard. New York: Hill and Wang.

Bartky, Sandra Lee. 1988. "Foucault, Femininity, and the Modernization of Power." In *Feminism and Foucault: Reflections on Resistance*, ed. Irene Diamond and Lee Quinby, 93–111. Boston: Northeastern University Press.

Bartky, Sandra Lee. 1990. *Femininity and Domination: Studies in the Phenomenology of Oppression*. New York: Routledge.

Batiuk, Tom. 2007. *Lisa's Story: The Other Shoe*. New York: Berkley Publishing Group.

Baucom, Ian. 2005. *Specters of the Atlantic: Finance Capital, Slavery, and the Philosophy of History*. Durham, NC: Duke University Press.

Baudrillard, Jean. 1981. *Simulacra and Simulations*. Trans. Paul Foss, Paul Patton, and Philip Beitchman. New York: Semiotexte.

Bauman, Zygmunt. 2009. *Does Ethics Have a Chance in a World of Consumers?* Cambridge, MA: Harvard University Press.

Baumgardner, Jennifer, and Amy Richard. 2000. *Manifesta: Young Women, Feminism and the Future*. New York: Farrar, Straus, and Giroux.

Beatie, Thomas. 2008. "Labor of Love: Is Society Ready for This Pregnant Husband?" *The Advocate* (8 Apr). http://www.advocate.com/news/2008/03/14/labor-love?page=full

Bechdel, Alison. 2005. *Invasion of the Dykes to Watch Out For*. Boston: Houghton Mifflin Harcourt.

Bell, Lynne. 2010–11. "From a Whisper to a Scream." *Canadian Art* 27 (4): 102–7.

Bell, Mebbie. 2009. "'@ the doctor's office': Pro-anorexia and the Medical Gaze." *Surveillance and Society* 6 (2): 151–62.

Belmore, Rebecca. 2001. *Wild*. Installation. Toronto: Art Gallery of Ontario.

Belmore, Rebecca. 2008. "Wild." In *Rebecca Belmore: Rising to the Occasion*, 49–51. Vancouver: Vancouver Art Gallery.

Belmore, Rebecca. 2010. *Worth*. Video. Canada. 14 min.

Benjamin, Harry. [1966] 1997. *The Transsexual Phenomenon*. Dusseldorf: Symposion. Accessed 22 May 2011. http://www.symposion.com/Benjamin

Benjamin, Walter. [1933] 2007. "On the Mimetic Faculty." In *Beyond the Body Proper: Reading the Anthropology of Material Life*, ed. Margaret Lock and Judith Farquhar, 130–2. Durham, NC: Duke University Press.

Bennett, Jill. 2005. *Empathic Vision: Affect, Trauma, and Contemporary Art*. Stanford, CA: Stanford University Press.

Berger, John. 1972. *Ways of Seeing*. London: BBC and Penguin.

Berger, Laurel. 1994. "Mona Hatoum: In Between, Outside and In the Margins." *ARTnews* 93 (7): 148–9.

Bergland, Betty Ann. 1994. "Representing Ethnicity in Autobiography: Narratives of Opposition." *Yearbook of English Studies* 24: 67–93.

Bernstein, Beth, and Matilda St John. 2009. "The Roseanne Benedict Arnolds: How Fat Women Are Betrayed by Their Celebrity Icons." In *The Fat Studies*

Reader, ed. Esther Rothblum and Sondra Solovay, 264–70. New York: New York University Press.

Biemann, Ursula, ed. 2003. *Stuff It: The Video Essay in the Digital Age*. New York: Springer.

Biressi, Anita, and Heather Nunn. 2005. *Reality TV: Realism and Revelation*. London: Wallflower Press.

Bloom, Mia. 2001. "Atrocities and Armed Conflict: State Consolidation in Israel, 1948–56." *Conflict, Security, and Development* 1 (3): 55–78.

Blum, Virginia. 2003. *Flesh Wounds: The Culture of Cosmetic Surgery*. Berkeley: University of California Press.

Boltanski, Luc. 1999. *Distant Suffering: Morality, Media, and Politics*. Trans. Graham Burchell. Cambridge: Cambridge University Press.

Bordo, Susan. 1993. *Unbearable Weight: Feminism, Western Culture, and the Body*. Berkeley: University of California Press.

Bordwell, Marilyn. 2002. "Jamming Culture: Adbusters' Hip Campaign against Consumerism." In *Confronting Consumption*, ed. Thomas Princen, Michael Maniates, and Ken Conca, 237–54. Cambridge, MA: MIT Press.

Bornstein, Kate. 1994. *Gender Outlaw: On Men, Women, and the Rest of Us*. New York: Routledge.

Bowen, Deanna. 2010. *sum of the parts: what can be named*. Video. Canada. 20 min.

Brabner, Joyce, and Harvey Pekar. 1994. *Our Cancer Year*. Philadelphia: Running Press.

Braidotti, Rosi. 1996. "Signs of Wonder and Traces of Doubt: On Teratology and Embodied Difference." In *Between Monsters, Goddesses, and Cyborgs: Feminist Confrontations with Science, Medicine, and Cyberspace*, ed. Nina Lykke and Rosi Braidotti, 135–52. London: Zed Books.

Braithwaite, Ann, Susan Heald, Susanne Luhmann, and Sharon Rosenberg. 2004. *Troubling Women's Studies: Pasts, Presents and Possibilities*. Toronto: Sumach Press.

Branagh, Kenneth, dir. 1994. *Mary Shelley's Frankenstein*. DVD. American Zoetrope Productions.

Bray, Abigail. 1996. "The Anorexic Body: Reading Disorders." *Cultural Studies* 10 (3): 413–29.

Brett, Guy. 1997. "Survey." In *Mona Hatoum*, ed. Michael Archer, Guy Brett, and Catherine de Zegher, 32–88. London: Phaidon.

Brock, Deborah. 2003. *Making Normal: Social Regulation in Canada*. Toronto: Nelson Thomson Learning.

Brodwin, Paul E. 2000. "Introduction." In *Biotechnology and Culture: Bodies, Anxieties, Ethics*. Ed. Paul E. Brodwin, 1–23. Bloomington: Indiana University Press.

Brophy, Sarah. 2004. *Witnessing AIDS: Writing, Testimony, and the Work of Mourning*. Toronto: University of Toronto Press.

Brophy, Sarah. 2008. "Troubled Heroism: Public Health Pedagogies in South African Films about HIV/AIDS." Special Issue: South African Cultural Texts and the Global Mediascape, ed. Patrick Flanery and Andrew van der Vlies. *scrutiny2: Issues in English Studies in Southern Africa* 13 (1): 33–46.

Brophy, Sarah, and Janice Hladki. Forthcoming. "Cripping the Museum: Pedagogy, Disability, and Video Art." Double Special Issue: Cripistemologies, ed. Merri Lisa Johnson and Robert McRuer. *Journal of Literary and Cultural Disability Studies* 8 (2–3).

Brown, Wendy. 2006. "American Nightmare: Neoliberalism, Neoconservatism, and De-democratization." *Political Theory* 34 (6): 690–714.

Bruzzi, Stella. 2005. *Bringing Up Daddy: Fatherhood and Masculinity in Post-war Hollywood*. London: British Film Institute.

Burke, Edmund. [1756] 1990. *A Philosophical Enquiry into the Origin of our Ideas of the Sublime and Beautiful*, ed. Adam Phillips. Oxford: Oxford University Press.

Butler, Judith. [1990] 1999. *Gender Trouble: Feminism and the Subversion of Identity*. 2nd ed. New York: Routledge.

Butler, Judith. 1993. *Bodies that Matter: On the Discursive Limits of "Sex."* New York: Routledge.

Butler, Judith. 2004a. *Precarious Life: The Powers of Mourning and Violence*. London: Verso.

Butler, Judith. 2004b. *Undoing Gender*. New York: Routledge.

Butler, Judith. 2005. *Giving an Account of Oneself*. New York: Fordham University Press.

Butler, Judith. 2009. *Frames of War: When Is Life Grievable?* London: Verso.

Butler, Judith, and Joan W. Scott, eds. 1992. *Feminists Theorize the Political*. New York: Routledge.

Byrd, Jodi A., and Michael Rothberg. 2011. "Between Subalternity and Indigeneity." *Interventions: International Journal of Postcolonial Studies* 13 (1): 1–12.

Cambodian Genocide Project. Genocide Studies Program, Yale Center for International and Area Studies. Online database. Accessed 18 Sept. 2008. http://www.yale.edu/cgp/

Cameron, Loren. 1996. *Body Alchemy: Transsexual Portraits*. San Francisco: Cleis Press.

Campbell, Colin. 1972. *True/False*. Video. Canada. 9 min.

Canadian Woman Studies/Les Cahiers de la Femme. 2001. Special Issue: Young Women: Feminist, Activists, Grrrls. 21 (4).

Carlson, Licia. 2001. "Cognitive Ableism and Disability Studies: Feminist Reflections on the History of Mental Retardation." *Hypatia* 16 (4): 124–46.

Cartwright, Lisa. 1995. *Screening the Body: Tracing Medicine's Visual Culture*. Minneapolis: University of Minnesota Press.

Cartwright, Lisa. 2008. *Moral Spectatorship: Technologies of Voice and Affect in Postwar Representations of the Child*. Durham, NC: Duke University Press.

Casper, Monica J., and Lisa Jean Moore. 2009. *Missing Bodies: The Politics of Visibility*. New York: New York University Press.

Cattaneo, Peter, dir. 1997. *The Full Monty*. DVD. Fox Searchlight.

Cauldwell, David O. 2001. "Psychopathia Transsexualis." *International Journal of Transgenderism* 5 (2). http://www.symposion.com/cauldwell/cauldwell_02.htm

Butterfly, Cerulean. 2005. "To those of you who come here looking to 'become anorexic,' or to yell at us…" Accessed 18 May 2005. http://www.cerulean-butterfly.com/disclaimer.html

Césaire, Aimé. [1955] 2000. *Discourse on Colonialism*. Trans. Joan Pinkham. New York: Monthly Review Press.

Chambers, Ross. 2004. *Untimely Interventions: AIDS Writing, Testimonial, and the Rhetoric of Haunting*. Ann Arbor: University of Michigan Press.

Chambers, Tod. 2004. "Virtual Disability: On the Internet, Nobody Knows You're Not a Sick Puppy." In *Cultural Sutures: Medicine and Media*, ed. Lester D. Friedman, 386–98. Durham, NC: Duke University Press.

Chandler, David P. 1999. *Voices from S-21: Terror and History in Pol Pot's Secret Prison*. Berkeley: University of California Press.

Chang, Elaine, ed. 2007. *Reel Asian: Asian Canada on Screen*. Toronto: Coach House.

Charles, Larry, dir. 2009. *Brüno*. DVD. Universal.

Chen, Anthony S. 1999. "Lives at the Center of the Periphery, Lives at the Periphery of the Center: Chinese American Masculinities and Bargaining with Hegemony." *Gender and Society* 13 (5): 584–607.

Cheng, Anne Anlin. 2001. *The Melancholy of Race: Psychoanalysis, Assimilation, and Hidden Grief*. New York: Oxford University Press.

Chivers, Sally. 2011. *The Silvering Screen: Old Age and Disability in Cinema*. Toronto: University of Toronto Press.

Chivers, Sally, and Nicole Markotić, eds. 2010. *The Problem Body: Projecting Disability on Film*. Columbus: University of Ohio Press.

Chow, Rey. 1996. "Where Have All the Natives Gone?" In *Contemporary Postcolonial Theory: A Reader*, ed. Padmini Mongia, 122–47. New York: St Martin's Press.

Chun, Wendy Hui Kyong. 2007. "Othering Space." In *The Visual Culture Reader*, 2nd ed., ed. Nicholas Mirzoeff, 243–54. New York: Routledge.

Chute, Hillary. 2008a. "Review of *Our Cancer Year*, by Joyce Brabner and Harvey Pekar; *Janet and Me: An Illustrated Story of Love and Loss*, by Stan Mack; *Cancer Vixen: A True Story*, by Marisa Acocella Marchetto; *Mom's Cancer*, by Brian Fies; *Blue Pills: A Positive Love Story*, by Frederik Peeters; *Epileptic*, by David B.; and *Black Hole*, by Charles Burns." *Literature and Medicine* 26 (2): 413–29.

Chute, Hillary. 2008b. "The Texture of Retracing in Marjane Satrapi's *Persepolis*." *Women's Studies Quarterly* 36 (1–2): 92–110.

Clare, Eli. 2001. "Stolen Bodies, Reclaimed Bodies: Disability and Queerness." *Public Culture* 13 (3): 359–66.

Claxton, Dana. 1994. *I Want to Know Why*. Video. Canada. 6:20 min.

Claxton, Dana, Melanie Townsend, and Steven Loft, eds. 2005. *Transference, Tradition, Technology: Native New Media Exploring Visual and Digital Culture*. Banff: Walter Phillips Gallery Editions.

Clewell, Tammy. 2004. "A Mourning Beyond Melancholia: Freud's Psychoanalysis of Loss." *Journal of the American Psychoanalytic Association* 52 (1): 43–67.

Cohen, Cathy J. 1999. "Punks, Bulldaggers, and Welfare Queens: The Radical Potential of Queer Politics?" *GLQ: A Journal of Lesbian and Gay Studies* 3 (4): 437–65.

Cohen, Jeffrey Jerome, and Gail Weiss, eds. 2003. *Thinking the Limits of the Body*. Albany: State University of New York Press.

Columbus, Chris, dir. 1993. *Mrs Doubtfire*. DVD. Twentieth Century Fox.

Cooper, Charlotte. 2009. "Fat Activism in Ten Astonishing, Beguiling, Inspiring and Beautiful Episodes." In *Fat Studies in the UK*, ed. Corinna Tomrley and Ann Kaloski Naylor, 5–11. York, UK: Raw Nerve Books.

Corliss, Richard. 2009. "Box-Office Weekend: *Brüno* a One-Day Wonder?" *Time* (13 July). Accessed 17 July 2012. http://www.time.com/time/arts/article/0,8599,1910059,00.html

Cotterill, Pamela, and Gail Letherby. 1993. "Weaving Stories: Personal Auto/biographies in Feminist Research." *Sociology* 27 (1): 67–79.

Couser, G. Thomas. 1997. *Recovering Bodies: Illness, Disability, and Life Writing*. Madison: University of Wisconsin Press.

Couser, G. Thomas. 2009. *Signifying Bodies: Disability in Contemporary Life Writing*. Ann Arbor: University of Michigan Press.

Crosbie, Lynn. 1997. *Click: Becoming Feminists*. Toronto: Macfarlane Walter and Ross.

Cvetkovich, Ann. 2003. *An Archive of Feelings: Trauma, Sexuality, and Lesbian Public Cultures*. Durham, NC: Duke University Press.

Cvetkovich, Ann. 2009. "Touching the Monster: Deep Lez in Fun Fur." In *Allyson Mitchell: Ladies Sasquatch*, 26–31. Hamilton, ON: McMaster Museum of Art.

Daldry, Stephen, dir. 2000. *Billy Elliot*. DVD. Focus Features.

Darke, Paul. 1998. "Understanding Cinematic Representations of Disability." In *The Disability Studies Reader: Social Science Perspectives*, ed. Tom Shakespeare, 181–97. London: Cassell.

DasGupta, Sayantani, and Marsha Hurst. 2008. "Death in Cyberspace: Challenging the Boundaries of Public/Private Dimensionality." Paper presented at "The Pulse of Death Now: The Austin H. Kutscher Memorial Conference," 29 Mar., at Columbia University, New York.

Davies, Bronwyn. 2000. *A Body of Writing 1990–1999*. Walnut Creek, CA: AltaMira Press, and Oxford: Rowman and Littlefield.

Davis, Kathy. 1995. *Reshaping the Female Body: The Dilemma of Cosmetic Surgery*. New York: Routledge.

Davis, Kathy. 2003. *Dubious Equalities and Embodied Differences: Cultural Studies on Cosmetic Surgery*. Lanham, MD: Rowman and Littlefield.

Davis, Lennard. 1995. *Enforcing Normalcy: Disability, Deafness, and the Body*. New York: Verso.

Davis, Noela. 2009. "New Materialism and Feminism's Anti-biologism: A Response to Sara Ahmed." *European Journal of Women's Studies* 16 (1): 67–80.

de Reynier, Jacques. 1969. *Mil neuf cent quarante huit à Jérusalem*. Neuchatel, CH: Éditions de la Baconnière.

Derrida, Jacques. 1998. *Right of Inspection*. Trans. Marie-Françoise Plissart. New York: Monacelli Press.

Derrida, Jacques. 2001. *Jacques Derrida: Deconstruction Engaged: The Sydney Seminars*, ed. Paul Patton and Terry Smith. Sydney, AU: Power Publications.

Derrida, Jacques. 2003. *The Work of Mourning*, ed. Pascale-Anne Brault and Michael Naas. Chicago: University of Chicago Press.

Deutsche, Rosalyn. 2010. *Hiroshima after Iraq: Three Studies in Art and War*. New York: Columbia University Press.

Donaldson, Roger, dir. 1995. *Species*. DVD. MGM.

Donger, Simon, with Simon Shepherd and ORLAN, eds. 2010. *ORLAN: A Hybrid Body of Artworks*. New York: Routledge.

Douglass, Frederick. [1855] 2003. *My Bondage and My Freedom*. New York: Penguin.

Doyle, Jennifer. 2013. *Hold It Against Me: Difficulty and Emotion in Contemporary Art*. Durham, NC: Duke University Press.

Driedger, Diane, and Michelle Owen, eds. 2008. *Dissonant Disabilities: Women with Chronic Illnesses Explore Their Lives*. Toronto: Canadian Scholars' Press / Women's Press.

Du Bois, W.E.B. [1903] 1994. *The Souls of Black Folk*. Mineola, NY: Dover.

Duggan, Lisa. 2005. *The Twilight of Equality? Neoliberalism, Cultural Politics, and the Attack on Democracy*. Boston: Beacon Press.

Duke, Bill, dir. 1992. *Deep Cover*. DVD. New Line Cinema.

Edut, Ophira, ed. 2000. *Body Outlaws: Young Women Write about Body Image and Identity*. New York: Seal Press.

Egan, Susanna. 1999. *Mirror Talk: Genres of Crisis in Contemporary Autobiography*. Chapel Hill: University of North Carolina Press.

Eisner, Will. 1985. *Comics and Sequential Art*. Tamarac, FL: Poorhouse Press.

Emberley, Julia. 2007. *Defamiliarizing the Aboriginal: Cultural Practices and Decolonization in Canada*. Toronto: University of Toronto Press.

Eng, David L. 1996. "In the Shadow of a Diva: Committing Homosexuality in David Henry Hwang's *M. Butterfly*." In *Asian American Sexualities: Dimensions of the Gay and Lesbian Experience*, ed. Russell Leong, 131–52. New York: Routledge.

Eng, David L., and David Kazanjian, eds. 2003. *Loss: The Politics of Mourning*. Berkeley: University of California Press.

Engelberg, Miriam. 2006. *Cancer Made Me a Shallower Person: A Memoir in Comics*. New York: HarperCollins.

Erevelles, Nirmala. 2011. *Disability and Difference in Global Contexts: Enabling a Transformative Body Politic*. New York: Palgrave Macmillan.

Evans, Jessica. 1999. "Feeble Monsters: Making Up Disabled People." In *Visual Culture: The Reader*, ed. Jessica Evans and Stuart Hall, 274–88. London: Sage.

Evans, Mary. 1993. "Reading Lives: How the Personal Might be Social." *Sociology* 27 (1): 5–13.

Evans, Michael Robert. 2008. *Isuma: Inuit Video Art*. Montreal and Kingston: McGill-Queen's University Press.

Faber, Alyda. 2002. "Saint Orlan: Ritual as Violent Spectacle and Cultural Criticism." *Drama Review* 46 (1): 85–92.

Faigley, Lester. 1999. "Material Literacy and Visual Design." In *Rhetorical Bodies: Toward a Material Rhetoric*, ed. Jack Selzer and Sharon Crowley, 171–200. Madison: University of Wisconsin Press.

Failler, Angela. 2006. "Appetizing Loss: Anorexia as an Experiment in Living." *Eating Disorders* 14 (2): 99–107.

Fanon, Frantz. [1952] 2008. *Black Skin, White Masks*. Trans. Richard Philcox. New York: Grove Press.

Farrelly, Bob, and Peter Farrelly, dirs. 2001. *Shallow Hal*. DVD. Twentieth Century Fox.

Fies, Brian. 2006. *Mom's Cancer*. New York: Abrams.

Findlen, Barbara, ed. 1995. *Listen Up: Voices from the Next Feminist Generation*. New York: Seal Press.

Finkelstein, Norman. 2005. *Beyond Chutzpah: On the Misuse of Anti-Semitism and the Abuse of History*. Berkeley: University of California Press.

Fiske, Robert. 2002. *Pity the Nation: The Abduction of Lebanon*. 4th ed. New York: Thunder Mouth Press.

Fiske, Robert. 2005. *The Great War for Civilization: The Conquest of the Middle East*. New York: Random House.

Foucault, Michel. [1975] 1995. *Discipline and Punish: The Birth of the Prison*. Trans. Alan Sheridan. New York: Vintage Books.

Foucault, Michel. 1976. *The History of Sexuality*, vol. 1. London: Penguin.

Foucault, Michel. 1980. "The Eye of Power." In *Power/Knowledge: Selected Interviews & Other Writings, 1972–1977*, ed. Colin Gordon, 146–65. New York: Pantheon.

Foucault, Michel. 1988. "Technologies of the Self." In *Technologies of the Self: A Seminar with Michel Foucault*, ed. Luther H. Martin, Huck Gutman, and Patrick H. Hutton, 16–49. Amherst: University of Massachusetts Press.

Foucault, Michel. 2008. *The Birth of Biopolitics: Lectures at the Collège de France, 1978–1979*, ed. Michael Senellart. Trans. Graham Burchell. New York: Palgrave Macmillan.

Fournier, Valérie. 2002. "Fleshing Out Gender: Crafting Gender Identity on Women's Bodies." *Body and Society* 8 (2): 55–77.

Francis, Margot. 2002. Review of *Sea in the Blood*. Accessed 20 Feb. 2011. http://www.richardfung.ca/index.php?/writings/margot-francis/

Francis, Margot. 2012. *Creative Subversions: Whiteness, Indigeneity, and the National Imaginary*. Vancouver: UBC Press.

Frank, Arthur W. 1995. *The Wounded Storyteller: Body, Illness, and Ethics*. Chicago: University of Chicago Press.

Frankenheimer, John, dir. 1996. *The Island of Dr Moreau*. DVD. New Line Cinema.

French, Lindsay. 2002. "Exhibiting Terror." In *Truth Claims: Representation and Human Rights*, ed. Mark Philip Bradley and Patrice Petro, 131–57. New Brunswick, NJ: Rutgers University Press.

Freud, Sigmund. [1917] 1976. "Mourning and Melancholia." In *The Standard Edition of the Complete Psychological Works of Sigmund Freud*, vol. XIV, ed. James Strachey, 237–58. New York: Norton.

Freud, Sigmund. [1923] 1998. *The Ego and the Id*, ed. James Strachey. Trans. Joan Riviere. New York: Norton.

Fudge Schormans, Ann. 2005. "Biographical Versus Biological Lives: Auto/biography and Non-speaking Persons Labelled Intellectually Disabled." In *Auto/biography in Canada: Critical Directions*, ed. Julie Rak, 109–28. Waterloo, ON: Wilfrid Laurier University Press.

Fung, Richard. 1988. *The Way to My Father's Village*. Video. Canada. 38 min.

Fung, Richard. 1990. *My Mother's Place*. Video. Canada. 49 min.

Fung, Richard. 2000. *Sea in the Blood*. Video. Canada. 26 min.

Gagnon, Monika Kin. 2000. "Worldviews in Collision: Dana Claxton's Video Installations." In *Other Conundrums: Race, Culture, and Canadian Art*, 33–47. Vancouver: Arsenal Pulp Press, Artspeak Gallery, and Kamloops: Kamloops Art Gallery.

Gale, Peggy, and Lisa Steele, eds. 1996. *Video Re/view: The (Best) Source for Critical Writings on Canadian Artists' Video*. Toronto: Art Metropole.

Garland-Thomson, Rosemarie. 2001. "Seeing the Disabled: Visual Rhetorics of Disability in Popular Photography." In *The New Disability History: American Perspectives*, ed. Paul K. Longmore and Laura Umansky, 335–74. New York: New York University Press.

Garland-Thomson, Rosemarie. 2007. "Shape Structures Story: Fresh and Feisty Stories About Disability." *Narrative* 15 (1): 113–23.

Garland-Thomson, Rosemarie. 2009. *Staring: How We Look*. New York: Oxford University Press.

George, Susan A. 2001. "Not Exactly 'Of Woman Born': Procreation and Creation in Recent Science Fiction Films." *Journal of Popular Film and Television* 28 (4): 176–83.

Gillman, Maureen, John Swain, and Bob Heyman. 1997. "Life History or 'Case' History: The Objectification of People with Learning Difficulties through the Tyranny of Professional Discourses." *Disability and Society* 12 (5): 675–94.

Gilman, Sander L. 1991. *The Jew's Body*. New York: Routledge.

Gilman, Sander L. 1995. "Damaged Men: Thoughts on Kafka's Body." In *Constructing Masculinity*, ed. Maurice Berger, Brian Wallis, and Simon Watson, 176–89. New York: Routledge.

Gilman, Sander L. 2005. *Franz Kafka*. London: Reaktion Books.

Gilmore, Leigh. 1994. *Autobiographics: A Feminist Theory of Women's Self-Representation*. Ithaca, NY: Cornell University Press.

Gilmore, Leigh. 1998. "Endless Autobiography? Jamaica Kincaid and Serial Autobiography." In *Postcolonialism and Autobiography*, ed. Alfred Hornung and Ernstpeter Ruhe, 211–32. Amsterdam: Rodopi.

Gilmore, Leigh. 2001. *The Limits of Autobiography: Trauma and Testimony*. Ithaca, NY: Cornell University Press.

Gilroy, Paul. 2005. *Postcolonial Melancholia*. New York: Columbia University Press.

Ginsburg, Faye D., Lila Abu-Lughod, and Brian Larkin, eds. 2002. *Media Worlds: Anthropology on a New Terrain*. Berkeley: University of California Press.

Go Pro: Ana Lives. 2010. "Thinspiration: Celebrities." Accessed 10 Jan. 2010. http://tilt214.tripod.com/id5.html

Goldberg, Elizabeth Swanson. 2007. *Beyond Terror: Gender, Narrative, Human Rights*. New Brunswick, NJ: Rutgers University Press.

González, Jennifer A. 2009. "The Face and the Public: Race, Secrecy, and Digital Art Practice." *Camera Obscura 70* 24 (1): 37–65.

González, Olga. 2009. "Culture and Politics in the Arts of the Occupied Palestinian Territories." *Macalester International* 23 (1): 202–20.

Goodley, Dan. 1996. "Tales of Hidden Lives: A Critical Examination of Life History Research with People Who Have Learning Difficulties." *Disability and Society* 11 (3): 333–48.

Goslinga-Roy, Gillian M. 2000. "Body Boundaries, Fiction of the Female Self: An Ethnographic Perspective on Power, Feminism, and the Reproductive Technologies." In *Biotechnology and Culture: Bodies, Anxieties, Ethics*, ed. Paul E. Brodwin, 113–46. Bloomington: Indiana University Press.

Grace, Sherrill. 2005. "Performing the Auto/biographical Pact: Towards a Theory of Identity in Performance." In *Tracing the Autobiographical*, ed. Marlene Kadar, Linda Warley, Jeanne Perreault, and Susanna Egan, 65–80. Waterloo, ON: Wilfrid Laurier University Press.

Gray, Brandon. 2009. "Weekend Report: 'Bruno' Not as Brawny as 'Borat.'" *Box Office Mojo* (13 July). Accessed 17 July 2012. http://boxofficemojo.com/news/ ?id=2603&p=.htm

Greensmith, Cameron. 2012. "Pathologizing Indigeneity in the Caledonia 'Crisis.'" *Canadian Journal of Disability Studies* 1 (2): 19–42.

Gremillion, Helen. 2003. *Feeding Anorexia: Gender and Power at a Treatment Center*. Durham, NC: Duke University Press.

Grewal, Inderpal. 2005. *Transnational America: Feminisms, Diasporas, Neoliberalisms*. Durham, NC: Duke University Press.

Greyson, John. 2008. "The Singing Dunes: Colin Campbell, 1942–2001." In *People Like Us: The Gossip of Colin Campbell*, ed. Jon Davies and John Greyson, 47–51. Oakville, ON: Oakville Galleries.

Griffith, D.W. dir. 1915. *Birth of a Nation*. Film. Epoch Film Co.

Grosz, Elizabeth. 1994. *Volatile Bodies: Toward a Corporeal Feminism*. Bloomington: Indiana University Press.

Grosz, Elizabeth. 2004. *The Nick of Time: Politics, Evolution, and the Untimely*. Durham, NC: Duke University Press.

Grosz, Elizabeth. 2008. *Chaos, Territory, Art: Deleuze and the Framing of the Earth*. New York: Columbia University Press.

Hafsteinsson, Sigurjón Baldur, and Marian Bredin, eds. 2010. *Indigenous Screen Cultures in Canada*. Winnipeg: University of Manitoba Press.

Halberstam, Judith. 1998. *Female Masculinity*. Durham, NC: Duke University Press.

Halberstam, Judith. 2005. *In a Queer Time and Place: Transgender Bodies, Subcultural Lives*. New York: New York University Press.

Haley, Alex, and Malcolm X. 1965. *The Autobiography of Malcolm X (as told to Alex Haley)*. New York: Ballantine Books.

Hall, Kim Q., ed. 2011. *Feminist Disability Studies*. Bloomington: Indiana University Press.

Hall, Rachel. 2009. "Of Ziploc Bags and Black Holes: The Aesthetics of Transparency in the War on Terror." In *The New Media of Surveillance*, ed. Shoshana Magnet and Kelly Gates, 41–68. New York: Routledge.

Hallas, Roger. 2010. *Reframing Bodies: AIDS, Bearing Witness, and the Queer Moving Image*. Durham, NC: Duke University Press.

Hammami, Rema. 2004. "Gender, Nakba and Nation: Palestinian Women's Presence and Absence in the Narration of 1948 Memories." *Review of Women's Studies* 2: 26–41.

Hansen, Mark B.N. 2004. "Digitizing the Racialized Body or the Politics of Universal Address." *SubStance* 33 (2): 107–33.

Haraway, Donna J. 1991. *Simians, Cyborgs, and Women: The Reinvention of Nature*. New York: Routledge.

Haraway, Donna J. 2003. *The Haraway Reader*. New York: Routledge.

Harper, Paula. 1998. "Visceral Geometry: Works of Mona Hatoum." *Art in America* (Sept.). Accessed 23 Aug. 2009. http://findarticles.com/p/articles/mi_m1248/is_n9_v86/ai_21268572/?tag=content;col1

Harris, Anita. 2007. *Next Wave Cultures: Feminism, Subcultures, Activism*. New York: Routledge.

Harris, Luke Charles. 1999. "My Two Mothers, America, and the Million Man March." In *Black Men on Race, Gender, and Sexuality*, ed. Devon W. Carbado, 54–67. New York: New York University Press.

Harvey, David. 2005. *A Brief History of Neoliberalism*. Oxford: Oxford University Press.

Hasso, Frances. 2000. "Modernity and Gender in Arab Accounts of the 1948 and 1967 Defeats." *International Journal of Middle East Studies* 32 (4): 491–510.

Hatoum, Mona. 1980. *Don't Smile, You're on Camera*. Performance. Beirut: Beirut Art Center.

Hatoum, Mona. 1981. *Look No Body!* Performance. Newcastle-upon-Tyne: Basement Gallery.

Hatoum, Mona. 1983. *The Negotiating Table*. Performance. Ottawa: SAW Gallery.

Hatoum, Mona. 1984. *Them and Us … and Other Divisions*. Performance. Bracknell, UK: South Hill Park.

Hatoum, Mona. 1986. *Unemployed*. Performance. Sheffield, UK: Streets Alive.

Hatoum, Mona. 1988. *Measures of Distance*. Installation. London: Tate Collection.

Hatoum, Mona. 1989. *The Light at the End*. Installation. London: The Showroom.

Hatoum, Mona. 1992–93. *Socle du Monde*. Sculpture. Paris: Galerie Chantal Crousel.

Hatoum, Mona. 1994. *Corps étranger*. Installation. Paris: Musée Nationale d'Art Moderne, Centre Georges Pompidou.

Hatoum, Mona. 1995. *Entrails Carpet*. Sculpture. London: Saatchi Gallery.

Havens, Richie. 1971. "Fire and Rain." *The Great Blind Degree*. CD. Stormy Forest Records. MGM.

Hawkins, Anne Hunsaker. 1993. *Reconstructing Illness: Studies in Pathography*. West Lafayette, IN: Purdue University Press.

Hayles, N. Katherine. 1999. *How We Became Posthuman: Virtual Bodies in Cybernetics, Literature, and Informatics*. Chicago: University of Chicago Press.

Hernández, Daisy, and Bushra Rehman, eds. 2002. *Colonize This!: Young Women of Color on Today's Feminism*. New York: Seal Press.

Herndl, Diane Price. 2002. "Reconstructing the Posthuman Feminist Body Twenty Years after Audre Lorde's Cancer Journals." In *Disability Studies: Enabling the Humanities*, ed. Sharon L. Snyder, Brenda Jo Brueggemann, and Rosemarie Garland-Thomson, 144–55. New York: MLA Press.

Hesford, Wendy S. 1999. *Framing Identities: Autobiography and the Politics of Pedagogy*. Minneapolis: University of Minnesota Press.

Hesford, Wendy S. 2000. "Visual Auto/biography, Hysteria, and the Pedagogical Performance of the 'Real.'" *JAC: A Journal of Rhetoric, Culture, and Politics* 20 (2): 349–89.

Hesford, Wendy S. 2004. "Documenting Violations: Rhetorical Witnessing and the Spectacle of Distant Suffering." *Biography* 27 (1): 104–44.

Hesford, Wendy S. 2011. *Spectacular Rhetorics: Human Rights Visions, Recognitions, Feminisms*. Durham, NC: Duke University Press.

Hesford, Wendy S., and Wendy Kozol, eds. 2000. *Haunting Violations: Feminist Criticism and the Crisis of the Real*. Bloomington: Indiana University Press.

Hevey, David. 1997. "The Enfreakment of Photography." In *The Disability Studies Reader*, 1st ed., ed. Lennard J. Davis, 332–47. New York: Routledge.

Hewitt, Nancy, ed. 2010. *No Permanent Waves: Recasting Histories of U.S. Feminism*. New Brunswick, NJ: Rutgers University Press.

Hickman, Timothy A. 2002. "Heroin Chic: The Visual Culture of Narcotic Addiction." *Third Text* 16 (2): 119–36.

Hillman, David A. 1997. "Visceral Knowledge." In *The Body in Parts: Fantasies of Corporeality in Early Modern Europe*, ed. David A. Hillman and Carla Mazzio, 81–106. London: Routledge.

Hird, Myra. 2004. "Feminist Matters: New Materialist Considerations of Sexual Difference." *Feminist Theory* 5 (2): 223–32.

Hirsch, Marianne. 1997. *Family Frames: Photography, Narrative, and Postmemory*. Cambridge, MA: Harvard University Press.

Hirsch, Marianne. 2002. "Nazi Photographs in Post-Holocaust Art: Gender as an Idiom of Memorialization." In *Crimes of War: Guilt and Denial in the Twentieth Century*, ed. Omer Bartov, Atina Grossmann, and Mary Nolan, 100–20. New York: New Press.

Hirschman, Jo. 2001. "TransAction: Organizing against Capitalism and State Violence in San Francisco." *Socialist Review* 4. Accessed 27 June 2011. http://findarticles.com/p/articles/mi_qa3952/is_200101/ai_n8932894/

Hladki, Janice. 2005. "Thresholds of the Flesh: Disability and Dis-ease and Producing 'Ability Trouble.'" *Review of Education, Pedagogy, and Cultural Studies* 27 (3): 265–85.

Hladki, Janice. 2009. "Mattering Media: Thinking Disability in Political Visual Practice." *Review of Education, Pedagogy, and Cultural Studies* 31 (2–3): 107–26.

Hladki, Janice, ed. 2010. *Fierce: Women's Hot-Blooded Film/Video*. Hamilton, ON: McMaster Museum of Art.

Hobbes, Thomas. [1651] 1996. *Leviathan*. Oxford: Oxford University Press.

Holahan, Catherine. 2001. "Yahoo Removes Pro-Eating-Disorder Internet Sites." *Boston Globe*. 4 Aug. Accessed 26 Sept. 2002. http://www.boston.com/

hooks, bell. 1992. *Black Looks: Race and Representation*. Boston: South End Press.

hooks, bell. 2004. *We Real Cool: Black Men and Masculinity*. New York: Routledge.

Horowitz, Irving Louis. 1997. *Foundations of Political Sociology*. New Brunswick, NJ: Transaction Publishers.

Houle, Robert. 2008. "Interiority as Allegory." In *Rebecca Belmore: Rising to the Occasion*, 19–23. Vancouver: Vancouver Art Gallery.

House of ED. 2005. "Welcome to the House of ED." Accessed 28 Apr. 2005. http://www.freewebs.com/ananeverdies/

Huffa, Joanne, Abi Slone, Mariko Tamaki, Tracy Tidgwell, Zoe Whittall, and Allyson Mitchell. 2004. *Big Judy*. Unpublished script.

Hughes, Rachel. 2003. "The Abject Artefacts of Memory: Photographs from Cambodia's Genocide." *Media, Culture, and Society* 25 (1): 23–44.

Huyssen, Andreas. 2003. *Present Pasts: Urban Palimpsests and the Politics of Memory*. Stanford, CA: Stanford University Press.

Hwang, David Henry. 1988. *M. Butterfly*. New York: Plume.

Irving, Dan. 2008. "Normalized Transgressions: Legitimizing the Transsexual Body as Productive." *Radical History Review* 100 (Winter): 38–59.

Irving, Dan. 2009. "The Self-Made Man as Risky Business: A Critical Examination of Gaining Recognition for Trans Rights through Economic Discourse." *Temple Political and Civil Rights Law Review* 18 (2): 101–21.

Jackson, Ronald L. 2006. *Scripting the Black Masculine: Identity, Discourse, and Racial Politics in Popular Media*. New York: State University of New York Press.

Jacobs, Harriet. [1861] 1988. *Incidents in the Life of a Slave Girl*. New York: Oxford University Press.

Jarrell, Donna, and Ira Sukrungruang, eds. 2005. *Scoot Over, Skinny: The Fat Nonfiction Anthology*. Orlando, FL: Harcourt.

Jay, Martin. 1988. "Scopic Regimes of Modernity." In *Vision and Visuality*, ed. Hal Foster, 3–28. Seattle, WA: Bay Press.

Jensen, Doreen, and Polly Sargent. [1986] 1993. *Robes of Power: Totem Poles on Cloth*. Vancouver: UBC Press, in association with the UBC Museum of Anthropology.

Joffee, Roland, dir. 1984. *The Killing Fields*. DVD. Warner Brothers.

Jones, Amelia. 1998. *Body Art / Performing the Subject*. Minneapolis: University of Minnesota Press.

Jones, Jordy. 2007. "Flex, Rex and Mister: Loren Cameron's Transhomosex Texts." In *The Art of Queering in Art*, ed. Henry Rogers, 7–20. Birmingham, UK: Article Press.

Juang, Richard M. 2006. "Transgendering the Politics of Recognition." In *Transgender Rights*, ed. Paisley Currah, Richard M. Juang, and Shannon Price Minter, 242–61. Minneapolis: University of Minnesota Press.

Juhasz, Alexandra. 1995. *AIDS TV: Identity, Community, and Alternative Video*. Durham, NC: Duke University Press.

Kacandes, Irene. 1999. "Narrative Witnessing as Memory Work: Reading Gertrude Kolmar's *A Jewish Mother*." In *Acts of Memory: Cultural Recall in the*

Present, ed. Mieke Bal, Jonathan Crewe, and Leo Spitzer, 55–71. Hanover, NH: University Press of New England.

Kaplan, Sara Clarke. 2007. "Souls at the Crossroads, Africans on the Water: The Politics of Diasporic Melancholia." *Callaloo* 30 (2): 511–26.

Karian, Lara, Lisa Rundle, and Allyson Mitchell, eds. 2001. *Turbo Chicks: Talking Young Feminisms*. Toronto: Sumach.

Kauffman, Linda S. 1996. "Bad Girls and Sick Boys: Inside the Body in Fiction, Film, and Performance Art." In *Getting a Life: Everyday Uses of Autobiography*, ed. Sidonie Smith and Julia Watson, 27–46. Minneapolis: University of Minnesota Press.

Kennedy, Helen. 2003. "Technobiography: Researching Lives Online and Off." *Biography* 26 (1): 120–39.

Kent, Le'a. 2001. "Fighting Abjection: Representing Fat Women." In *Bodies Out of Bounds: Fatness and Transgression*, ed. Jana Evans Braziel and Kathleen LeBesco, 130–50. Los Angeles: University of California Press.

Kenton, Erle C., dir. 1932. *Island of Lost Souls*. DVD. Paramount Pictures.

Kester, Grant H. 1997. "Aesthetics after the End of Art: An Interview with Susan Buck-Morss." *Art Journal* 56 (1): 38–45.

Kipnis, Laura. 1998. "Fat and Culture." In *In Near Ruins: Cultural Theory at the End of the Century*, ed. Nicholas B. Dirks, 199–220. Minneapolis: University of Minnesota Press.

Klein, Stephanie. 2008. *Moose: A Memoir*. New York: HarperCollins.

Koepnick, Lutz P. 2004. "Photographs and Memories." *South Central Review* 21 (1): 94–129.

Kozol, Wendy. 2004. "Domesticating NATO's War in Kosovo: (In)visible Bodies and the Dilemma of Photojournalism." *Meridians: Feminism, Transnationalism, Race* 4 (2): 1–38.

Kristeva, Julia. 1982. *Powers of Horror: An Essay on Abjection*. Trans. Leon S. Roudiez. New York: Columbia University Press.

Krotoski, Aleks. 2006. "Pregnancy and Virtual Prophylaxis." *The Guardian – Gamesblog*. Accessed 30 Nov. 2008. http://www.guardian.co.uk/technology/gamesblog/2006/jan/27/pregnancyandv

Kuppers, Petra. 2001. "Fatties on Stage: Feminist Performances." In *Bodies Out of Bounds: Fatness and Transgression*, ed. Jana Evans Braziel and Kathleen LeBesco, 277–91. Los Angeles: University of California Press.

Labaton, Vivien, and Dawn Lundy Martin, eds. 2004. *The Fire This Time: Young Activists and the New Feminism*. New York: Anchor Books.

LaCapra, Dominick. 2001. *Writing History, Writing Trauma*. Baltimore, MD: Johns Hopkins University Press.

Lancaster, Jen. 2008. *Such a Pretty Fat: One Narcissist's Quest to Discover if Her Life Makes Her Ass Look Big, or Why Pie Is Not the Answer*. London: Penguin.

Lane, Jim. 2002. *The Autobiographical Documentary in America*. Madison: University of Wisconsin Press.

Lather, Patti. 1993. "Fertile Obsession: Validity after Poststructuralism." *Sociological Quarterly* 34 (4): 673–93.

Latour, Bruno. 2005. *Reassembling the Social: An Introduction to Actor-Network Theory*. Oxford: Oxford University Press.

LeBesco, Kathleen. 2001. "Queering Fat Bodies/Politics." In *Bodies Out of Bounds: Fatness and Transgression*, ed. Jana Evans Braziel and Kathleen LeBesco, 74–87. Berkeley: University of California Press.

LeBesco, Kathleen. 2004. *Revolting Bodies? The Struggle to Redefine Fat Identity*. Amherst: University of Massachusetts Press.

Ledgerwood, Judy. 2002. "The Cambodian Tuol Sleng Museum of Genocidal Crimes: National Narrative." In *Genocide, Collective Violence, and Popular Memory: The Politics of Remembrance in the Twentieth Century*, ed. David E. Lorey and William H. Beezley, 103–22. Wilmington, DE: SR Books.

Lee, Helen, and Kerri Sakamoto, eds. 2002. *Like Mangoes in July: The Work of Richard Fung*. Toronto: Images Festival of Independent Film and Video.

Lee, Spike, dir. 1991. *Jungle Fever*. DVD. Universal.

Lendrum, Robert. 2006. *My Commonly Used Phrases*. Video. Canada. 8:56 min.

Lendrum, Robert. 2006. *My Favourite Jokes*. Video. Canada. 4:31 min.

Lendrum, Robert. 2006. *Chipmunks*. Video. Canada 5:58 min.

Lendrum, Robert. 2006–09. *Impostor: A Self Portrait*. Installation. Canada.

Lendrum, Robert. 2008. *Impostor: The Audition*. Video. Canada. 12:44 min.

Leong, Russell, ed. 1996. *Asian American Sexualities: Dimensions of the Gay and Lesbian Experience*. New York: Routledge.

Lepault, Sophie, and Capucine Lafait. 2006. *When men are pregnant*. Paris: Doc En Stock/Arte France. Accessed 30 Nov. 2008. http://www.youtube.com/watch?v=AiU-KZ_KADY

Lichtblau, Eric. 2008. "Arrests in Plan to Kill Obama and Black Schoolchildren." *New York Times* (28 Oct). Accessed 9 Dec. http://www.nytimes.com/2008/10/28plot.html

Lionnet, Françoise. 2001. "A Politics of the 'We'? Autobiography, Race, and Nation." *American Literary History* 13 (2): 376–92.

Liu, Phineas, and Virgil Wong. 2008. *Male Pregnancy, Designer Babies and Medical Nanotechnology*. Mary Ting (Curator). New York: John Jay College of Criminal Justice (CUNY), Department of Art, Music and Philosophy. 3 Apr. to 3 May.

Livingston, Jennie, dir. 1990. *Paris Is Burning*. DVD. Miramax.

Luhrmann, Baz, dir. 1992. *Strictly Ballroom*. DVD. Miramax.

Lupton, Deborah. 1995. "The Embodied Computer/User." In *Cyberspace/Cyberbodies/Cyberpunk: Cultures of Technological Embodiment*, ed. Mike Featherstone and Roger Burrows, 97–112. London: Sage.

Maasen, Sabine. 2005. "Schönheitschirurgie: Schnittflächen flexiblen Selbstmanagements." In *Artifizielle Körper – Lebendige Technik*, ed. Barbara Orland, 239–59. Zurich: Interferenzen.

Mack, Stan. 2004. *Janet and Me: An Illustrated Story of Love and Loss*. New York: Simon and Schuster.

Maclear, Kyo. 2003. "The Limits of Vision: *Hiroshima Mon Amour* and the Subversion of Representation." In *Witness and Memory: The Discourse of Trauma*, ed. Ana Douglass and Thomas A. Vogler, 233–48. New York: Routledge.

Madison, Soyini D. 2012. *Critical Ethnography: Methods, Ethics, and Performance*. 2nd ed. Los Angeles: Sage.

Magnet, Shoshana Amielle. 2011. *When Biometrics Fail: Gender, Race, and the Technology of Identity*. Durham, NC: Duke University Press.

Magnet, Shoshana, and Kelly Gates. 2009. "Communicating Surveillance: Examining the Intersections." In *The New Media of Surveillance*, ed. Shoshana Magnet and Kelly Gates, 1–17. New York: Routledge.

Malson, Helen. 1998. *The Thin Woman: Feminism, Post-structuralism and the Social Psychology of Anorexia Nervosa*. London: Routledge.

Manning, Erin. 2007. *Politics of Touch: Sense, Movement, Sovereignty*. Minneapolis: University of Minnesota Press.

Marchessault, Janine, ed. 1995. *Mirror Machine: Video and Identity*. Toronto: YYZ Books.

Marchetto, Marisa Acocella. 2006. *Cancer Vixen: A True Story*. New York: Random House.

Marcus, Eric R. 1999. "Empathy, Humanism, and the Professionalization Process of Medical Education." *Academic Medicine* 74 (11): 1211–15.

Marks, Laura U. 2000. *The Skin of the Film: Intercultural Cinema, Embodiment, and the Senses*. Durham, NC: Duke University Press.

Mars, Tanya, and Johanna Householder, eds. 2004. *Caught in the Act: An Anthology of Performance Art by Canadian Women*. Toronto: YYZ Books.

Martin, Emily. 1992. *The Woman in the Body*. Boston: Beacon Press.

Masayesya, Victor. 2000. "Indigenous Experimentalism." In *Magnetic North: Canadian Experimental Video*, ed. Jenny Lion, 229–39. Minneapolis: University of Minnesota Press.

Masco, Joseph. 2010. "Atomic Health: Or How the Bomb Altered American Notions of Death." In *Against Health: How Health Became the New Morality*, ed. Jonathan M. Metzl and Anna Kirkland, 133–56. New York: New York University Press.

Mauer, Barry M. 2005. "The Epistemology of Cindy Sherman: A Research Method for Media and Cultural Studies." *Mosaic* 38 (1): 93–113.

McCarthy, Anna. 2007. "Reality Television: A Neoliberal Theater of Suffering." *Social Text* 25 (4): 17–42.

McCarthy, Cormac. 1994. *The Crossing*. New York: Knopf.

McLaren, Margaret A. 2002. *Feminism, Foucault, and Embodied Subjectivity*. Albany: State University of New York Press.

McCloud, Scott. 1993. *Understanding Comics: The Invisible Art*. Northampton, MA: Kitchen Sink Press.

McRuer, Robert. 2006. *Crip Theory: Cultural Signs of Queerness and Disability*. New York: New York University Press.

McRuer, Robert, and Anna Mollow, eds. 2012. *Sex and Disability*. Durham, NC: Duke University Press.

McQueen, Steve. 2007–10. *Queen and Country: A Project by Steve McQueen*. Accessed 14 June 2010. http://www.artfund.org/queenandcountry/Queen_and_Country.html

Mellinkoff, Ruth. 1981. *The Mark of Cain*. Berkeley: University of California Press.

Memmi, Albert. 1965. *The Colonizer and the Colonized*. Boston: Beacon Press.

Merleau-Ponty, Maurice. 1962. *Phenomenology of Perception*. Trans. Colin Smith. London: Routledge.

Merleau-Ponty, Maurice. 1964. "Eye and mind." Trans. Carleton Dallery. In *The Primacy of Perception*, ed. James M. Edie, 159–90. Evanston, IL: Northwestern University Press.

Merleau-Ponty, Maurice. 1968. *The Visible and the Invisible*, ed. Claude Lefort. Trans. Alphonso Lingis. Evanston, IL: Northwestern University Press.

Merleau-Ponty, Maurice. 1973a. *The Prose of the World*, ed. Claude Lefort. Trans. John O'Neill. Evanston, IL: Northwestern University Press.

Merleau-Ponty, Maurice. 1973b. *Consciousness and the Acquisition of Language*. Trans. Hugh J. Silverman. Evanston, IL: Northwestern University Press.

Mersch, Dieter. 2003. "Körper/Spiegel/Bilder: Imagines des öffentlichen selbst." In *IABLIS – Jahrbuch für europäische Prozesse*, ed. Ulrich Schödlbauer, Geert Edel, and Renate Solbach, 58–71. Heidelberg: Manutius Verlag.

Metzl, Jonathan M., and Anna Kirkland, eds. 2010. *Against Health: How Health Became the New Morality*. New York: New York University Press.

Meyer, Manulani Aluli. 2008. *Indigenous and Authentic: Hawaiian Epistemology and the Triangulation of Meaning*. Thousand Oaks, CA: Sage.

Meyerowitz, Joanne. 2002. *How Sex Changed: A History of Transsexuality in the United States*. Cambridge, MA: Harvard University Press.

Michalko, Rod. 2002. *The Difference that Disability Makes*. Philadelphia: Temple University Press.

Miller, Nancy K. 2007a. "The Entangled Self: Genre Bondage in the Age of the Memoir." *PMLA* 122 (2): 537–48.

Miller, Nancy K. 2007b. "Out of the Family: Generations of Women in Marjane Satrapi's *Persepolis*." *Life Writing* 4 (1): 13–29.

Mingwei, Lee. [1995] 1998. *100 Days with Lily*. Accessed 30 Nov. 2008. http://www.leemingwei.com/mingwei-web/lily.htm

Mintz, Susannah B. 2007. *Unruly Bodies: Life Writing by Women with Disabilities*. Chapel Hill: University of North Carolina Press.

Mirzoeff, Nicholas. 2011. *The Right to Look: A Counterhistory of Visuality*. Durham, NC: Duke University Press.

Mitchell, Allyson. 2009a. "Deep Lez I statement." In *Allyson Mitchell: Ladies Sasquatch*, 12–13. Hamilton, ON: McMaster Museum of Art.

Mitchell, Allyson. 2009b. *Ladies Sasquatch*. Installation. Hamilton, ON: McMaster Museum of Art.

MMOrgy.com. 2005. *Bundle of Polys: MMO Pregnancy*. Accessed 30 Nov. 2008. http://www.mmorgy.com/2005/12/bundle_of_polys.php

Mohanty, Chandra Talpade. 1991. "Under Western Eyes." In *Third World Women and the Politics of Feminism*, ed. Chandra Talpade Mohanty, Ann Russo, and Lourdes Torres, 51–80. Bloomington: Indiana University Press.

Mohanty, Chandra Talpade. 1992. "Feminist Encounters: Locating the Politics of Experience." In *Destabilizing Theory: Contemporary Feminist Debates*, ed. Michèle Barrett and Anne Phillips, 74–92. Cambridge: Polity Press.

Moore, Judith. 2005. *Fat Girl: A True Story*. New York: Hudson Street Press.

Moraga, Cherríe. 1983. *Loving in the War Years: Lo que nunca pasó por sus labios*. Boston: South End Press.

Morris, Bernie. [1988] 2004. *The Birth of the Palestinian Refugee: 1947–1949*. Cambridge: Cambridge University Press.

Morris, Bernie. 1990. *1948 and After: Israel and the Palestinians*. New York: Oxford University Press.

Moynihan, Daniel Patrick. 1965. *The Negro Family: The Case for National Action*. Washington: Office of Policy Planning and Research, United States Department of Labor. http://www.dol.gov/oasam/programs/history/webid-meynihan.htm

Muller, Benjamin. 2004. "(Dis)qualified Bodies: Securitization, Citizenship and 'Identity Management.'" *Citizenship Studies* 8 (3): 279–94.

Mulvey, Laura. 1975. "Visual Pleasure and Narrative Cinema." *Screen* 16 (3): 6–18.

Muñoz, José Esteban. 1995. "The Autoethnographic Performance: Reading Richard Fung's Queer Hybridity." *Screen* 36 (2): 83–99.

Naficy, Hamid. 2001. *An Accented Cinema: Exilic and Diasporic Filmmaking*. Princeton, NJ: Princeton University Press.

Naghibi, Nima, and Andrew O'Malley. 2005. "Estranging the Familiar: 'East' and 'West' in Satrapi's *Persepolis*." *English Studies in Canada* 31 (2): 223–47.

Nakamura, Lisa. 2007. "'Where Do You Want to Go Today?' Cybernetic Tourism, the Internet, and Transnationality." In *The Visual Culture Reader*, 2nd ed., ed. Nicholas Mirzoeff, 255–63. New York: Routledge.

Nakamura, Lisa. 2008. *Digitizing Race: Visual Cultures of the Internet*. Minneapolis: University of Minnesota Press.

Namaste, Viviane. 2000. *Invisible Lives: The Erasure of Transsexual and Transgendered People*. Chicago: University of Chicago Press.

National Association of Anorexia Nervosa and Associated Disorders. 2009. "Eating Disorders and the Internet." Accessed 20 Jan. 2009. http://www.anad.org/621734/240600.html

Newbury, Darren. 1996. "Reconstructing the Self: Photography, Education and Disability." *Disability and Society* 11 (3): 349–60.

Niccol, Andrew, dir. 1997. *Gattaca*. DVD. Columbia Pictures.

Noble, Jean Bobby. 2006. *Sons of the Movement: FTMs Risking Incoherence in a Post-Queer Cultural Landscape*. Toronto: Women's Press.

Ocean, Billy. 1984. "Suddenly." *Suddenly*. CD. London and New York: Jive Records.

Orr, Jackie. 2006. *Panic Diaries: A Genealogy of Panic Disorder*. Durham, NC: Duke University Press.

Osborne, Peter, and Lynne Segal. 1993. Extracts from *Gender as Performance: An Interview with Judith Butler*. London. Full version originally published in *Radical Philosophy* 67 (Summer 1994). Accessed 30 Nov. 2008. http://www.theory.org.uk/ but-int1.htm

Palmer, Gareth. 2003. *Discipline and Liberty: Television and Governance*. Manchester: Manchester University Press.

Pappé, Ilan. 2006. *The Ethnic Cleansing of Palestine*. Arizona: Oneworld Press.

Pasquin, John, dir. 1994. *The Santa Clause*. DVD. Walt Disney Pictures.

Pattanaik, Devdutt. 2002. *The Man Who Was a Woman and Other Queer Tales from Hindu Lore*. Binghamton, NY: Haworth Press.

Patton, Tracey Owens. 2006. "Hey Girl, Am I More than My Hair?: African American Women and Their Struggles with Beauty, Body Image, and Hair." *NWSA Journal* 18 (2): 24–51.

Perfectly-Rotten. 2007. Accessed 26 Oct. 2007. http://www.perfectly-rotten.de.vu

Perpich, Diane. 2008. *The Ethics of Emmanuel Levinas*. Stanford, CA: Stanford University Press.

Perreault, Jeanne Martha. 1995. *Writing Selves: Contemporary Feminist Autography*. Minneapolis: University of Minnesota Press.

Perreault, Jeanne, and Marlene Kadar. 2005. "Tracing the Autobiographical: Unlikely Documents, Unexpected Places." In *Tracing the Autobiographical*, ed. Marlene Kadar, Linda Warley, Jeanne Perreault, and Susanna Egan, 1–8. Waterloo, ON: Wilfrid Laurier University Press.

Phelan, Shane. 2001. *Sexual Strangers: Gays, Lesbians, and Dilemmas of Citizenship*. Philadelphia: Temple University Press.

Phillips, Ruth B. 2011. "APEC at the Museum of Anthropology: The Politics of Site and the Poetics of Sight Bite." In *Imagining Resistance: Visual Culture and Activism in Canada*, ed. J. Keri Cronin and Kirsty Robertson, 171–91. Waterloo, ON: Wilfrid Laurier University Press.

The Pro Ana Lifestyle. 2007. "**Thinspiration – Kate Moss." Accessed 9 Jan. 2009. http://proanalifestyle.blogspot.com/2007/07/blog-post_12.html

Probyn, Elspeth. 2000. *Carnal Appetites: Foodsexidentities*. New York: Routledge.

Prothinspo. 2010. "About us." Accessed 10 Jan. 2010. http://pro-thinspo.com/aboutus.html

Puar, Jasbir K. 2007. *Terrorist Assemblages: Homonationalism in Queer Times*. Durham, NC: Duke University Press.

Puar, Jasbir K., and Amit Rai. 2002. "Monster, Terrorist, Fag: The War on Terrorism and the Production of Docile Patriots." *Social Text* 20 (3): 117–48.

Rak, Julie. 2004. "Are Memoirs Autobiography? A Consideration of Memoir and Public Identity." *Genre: Forms of Discourse and Culture* 37 (3–4): 483–504.

Rak, Julie. 2005. "Widening the Field: Auto/biography Theory and Criticism in Canada." In *Auto/biography in Canada: Critical Directions*, ed. Julie Rak, 1–30. Waterloo, ON: Wilfrid Laurier University Press.

Rancière, Jacques. 2010. *Dissensus: On Politics and Aesthetics*. London: Continuum Books.

Rascaroli, Laura. 2009. *The Personal Camera: Subjective Cinema and the Essay Film*. London: Wallflower Press.

Razack, Sherene. 2008. *Casting Out: The Eviction of Muslims from Western Law and Politics*. Toronto: University of Toronto Press.

Read, Jason. 2003. *The Micro-Politics of Capital: Marx and the Prehistory of the Present*. New York: State University of New York Press.

Reinhardt, Mark. 2007. "Picturing Violence: Aesthetics and the Anxiety of Critique." In *Beautiful Suffering: Photography and the Traffic in Pain*, ed. Mark

Reinhardt, Holly Edwards, and Erina Guganne, 13–36. Chicago: University of Chicago Press.

Reitman, Ivan, dir. 1994. *Junior*. DVD. Universal Pictures.

Renov, Michael. 2004. *The Subject of Documentary*. Minneapolis: University of Minnesota Press.

"Revolution, Grrrl Style." 1997. Special Issue of *Fireweed: A Feminist Quarterly*.

Richey, Warren. 1996. "Boycott Groups: Klein Ads Carry Scent of 'Heroin Chic.'" *Christian Science Monitor* 88: 232.

Rickard, Jolene. 2010. "Skin Seven Spans Thick." In *Hide: Skin as Material and Metaphor*, ed. Kathleen Ash-Milby, 81–96. New York: National Museum of the American Indian, and Washington, DC: Smithsonian Institution.

Robertson, Clive. 1991. "Performance Art in Canada 1970–1980: Tracing Some Origins of Need." In *Performance Art au/in Canada 1970–1990*, ed. Clive Robertson and Alain-Martin Richard, 8–19. Toronto: Coach House Press, and Quebec: Éditions Intervention.

Robins, Kevin. 2000. "Cyberspace and the World We Live In." In *The Cybercultures Reader*, ed. David Bell and Barbara M. Kennedy, 77–95. London: Routledge.

Robinson, Paulette. 2000. "The Body Matrix: A Phenomenological Exploration of Student Bodies On-line." *Journal of Educational Technology and Society* 3 (3): 249–60.

Rockhill, Kathleen. 1996. "And Still I Fight." *Canadian Woman Studies/ Les Cahiers de la femme* 16 (2): 93–8.

Rose, Nikolas. 2006. *The Politics of Life Itself: Biomedicine, Power, and Subjectivity in the Twenty-First Century*. Princeton, NJ: Princeton University Press.

Rosenberg, Sharon. 2000. "Standing in a Circle of Stone: Rupturing the Binds of Emblematic Memory." In *Between Hope and Despair: Pedagogy and the Remembrance of Historical Trauma*, ed. Roger I. Simon, Sharon Rosenberg, and Claudia Eppert, 75–89. Lanham, MD: Rowman and Littlefield.

Ross, Christine. 2008. "Introduction: The Precarious Visualities of Contemporary Art and Visual Culture." In *Precarious Visualities: New Perspectives on Identification in Contemporary Art and Culture*, ed. Olivier Asselin, Johanne Lamoureux, and Christine Ross, 3–16. Montreal and Kingston: McGill-Queen's University Press.

Rothberg, Michael. 2009. *Multidirectional Memory: Remembering the Holocaust in the Age of Decolonization*. Stanford, CA: Stanford University Press.

Russell, Catherine. 1999. *Experimental Ethnography: The Work of Film in the Age of Video*. Durham, NC: Duke University Press.

Ruttenberg, Danya, ed. 2002. *Yentl's Revenge: Young Jewish Women Write About Today's Feminism*. Seattle, WA: Seal Press.

Said, Edward. 1979. *Orientalism*. New York: Vintage.
Said, Edward. 1983. *The World, the Text, and the Critic*. Cambridge, MA: Harvard University Press.
Said, Edward. 2000. *Reflections on Exile and Other Essays*. Cambridge, MA: Harvard University Press.
Said, Edward, Sheena Wagstaff, and Mona Hatoum. 2000. *Mona Hatoum: The Entire World as a Foreign Land*. London: Tate Gallery.
Satrapi, Marjane. 2003. *Persepolis 1: The Story of a Childhood*. Trans. L'Association, Paris, France. New York: Pantheon.
Satrapi, Marjane. 2004. *Persepolis 2: The Story of a Return*. Trans. Anjali Singh. New York: Pantheon.
Satrapi, Marjane, and Vincent Paronnaud, dirs. 2007. *Persepolis*. DVD. Sony.
Sawchuk, Kim. 2000. "Biotourism, Fantastic Voyage, and Sublime Inner Space." In *Wild Science: Reading Feminism, Medicine and the Media*, ed. Janine Marchessault and Kim Sawchuk, 9–23. New York: Routledge.
Sawday, Jonathan. 1995. *The Body Emblazoned: Dissection and the Human Body in Renaissance Culture*. London: Routledge.
Sawicki, Jana. 1991. *Disciplining Foucault: Feminism, Power, and the Body*. New York: Routledge.
Sayigh, Rosemary. 1979. *Palestinians: From Peasants to Revolutionaries*. London: Zed Books.
Sayigh, Rosemary. 1994. *Too Many Enemies: The Palestinian Experience in Lebanon*. London: Zed Books.
Schaffer, Kay, and Sidonie Smith. 2004. *Human Rights and Narrated Lives: The Ethics of Recognition*. New York: Palgrave Macmillan.
Scott, Joan W. 1991. "The Evidence of Experience." *Critical Inquiry* 17 (4): 773–97.
Scott, Ridley, dir. 1979. *Alien*. DVD. Brandywine Productions.
Scott, Ridley, dir. 1982. *Blade Runner*. DVD. Ladd Company.
Sedgwick, Eve Kosofsky. 2003. *Touching Feeling: Affect, Pedagogy, Performativity*. Durham, NC: Duke University Press.
Seltzer, Mark. 1998. *Serial Killers: Death and Life in America's Wound Culture*. New York: Routledge.
Sharpe, Christina. 2010. *Monstrous Intimacies: Making Post-Slavery Subjects*. Durham, NC: Duke University Press.
Shelley, Mary. [1818] 2004. *Frankenstein*. New York: Simon and Schuster.
Shelton, Lynne, dir. 2009. *Humpday*. DVD. Magnolia Pictures.
Shildrick, Margrit. 1997. *Leaky Bodies and Boundaries: Feminism, Postmodernism and (Bio)ethics*. New York: Routledge.

Shildrick, Margrit. 2002. *Embodying the Monster: Encounters with the Vulnerable Self*. London: Sage.

Shildrick, Margrit. 2009. *Dangerous Discourses of Disability, Subjectivity, and Sexuality*. Basingstoke, UK: Palgrave Macmillan.

Shohat, Ella, and Robert Stam. 1994. *Unthinking Eurocentrism: Multiculturalism and the Media*. New York: Routledge.

Siebers, Tobin. 2010. *Disability Aesthetics*. Ann Arbor: University of Michigan Press.

Siegel, Deborah L. 1997. "The Legacy of the Personal: Generating Theory in Feminism's Third Wave." *Hypatia* 12 (3): 46–75.

Silverman, Kaja. 1996. *The Threshold of the Visible World*. New York: Routledge.

Simon, Roger I. 2000. "The Paradoxical Practice of Zakhor: Memories of 'What Has Never Been My Fault or Deed.'" In *Between Hope and Despair: Pedagogy and the Remembrance of Historical Trauma*, ed. Roger I. Simon, Sharon Rosenberg, and Claudia Eppert, 9–25. Latham, MD: Rowman and Littlefield.

Simon, Roger I. 2005. *The Touch of the Past: Remembrance, Learning, and Ethics*. New York: Palgrave Macmillan.

Singer, T. Benjamin. 2006. "From the Medical Gaze to *Sublime Mutations*: The Ethics of (Re)Viewing Non-normative Body Images." In *The Transgender Studies Reader*, ed. Susan Stryker and Stephen Whittle, 601–20. New York: Routledge.

Singleton, John, dir. 1991. *Boyz in the Hood*. DVD. Columbia Pictures.

Slaughter, Joseph. 2007. *Human Rights, Inc.: The World Novel, Narrative Form, and International Law*. New York: Fordham University Press.

Small, David. 2009. *Stitches: A Memoir*. New York: Norton.

Smith, Andrea. 2005. *Conquest: Sexual Violence and American Indian Genocide*. Cambridge, MA: South End Press.

Smith, Linda Tuhiwai. 1999. *Decolonizing Methodologies: Research and Indigenous Peoples*. New York: Zed Books.

Smith, Sidonie. 2002. "Bodies of Evidence: Jenny Saville, Faith Ringgold, and Janine Antoni Weigh In." In *Interfaces: Women/Autobiography/Image/Performance*, ed. Sidonie Smith and Julia Watson, 132–59. Ann Arbor: University of Michigan Press.

Smith, Sidonie, and Julia Watson, eds. 1996. *Getting a Life: Everyday Uses of Autobiography*. Minneapolis: University of Minnesota Press.

Smith, Sidonie, and Julia Watson. [2001] 2010. *Reading Autobiography: A Guide for Interpreting Life Narratives*. 2nd ed. Minneapolis: University of Minnesota Press.

Smith, Sidonie, and Julia Watson, eds. 2002a. *Interfaces: Women/Autobiography/Image/Performance*. Ann Arbor: University of Michigan Press.

Smith, Sidonie, and Julia Watson. 2002b. "Mapping Women's Self-Representation at Visual/Textual Interfaces." In *Interfaces: Women/Autobiography/Image/Performance*, ed. Sidonie Smith and Julia Watson, 1–46. Ann Arbor: University of Michigan Press.

Smythe, Hugh H. 1948. "The Concept 'Jim Crow.'" *Social Forces* 27 (1): 45–8.

Snyder, Sharon L., and David T. Mitchell. 2006. *Cultural Locations of Disability*. Chicago: University of Chicago Press.

Sobchack, Vivian. 2004. *Carnal Thoughts: Embodiment and Moving Image Culture*. Berkeley: University of California Press.

Sontag, Susan. [1978] 1990. *Illness as Metaphor/AIDS and Its Metaphors*. New York: Farrar, Strauss, and Giroux.

Sontag, Susan. 2003. *Regarding the Pain of Others*. New York: Farrar, Strauss, and Giroux.

Spence, Jo. 1995. *Cultural Sniping: The Art of Transgression*, ed. Jo Stanley and David Hevey. Foreword by Annette Kuhn. New York: Routledge.

Spielberg, Steven, dir. 2001. *AI – Artificial Intelligence*. DVD. Warner Brothers.

Spinelli, Claudia. 1997. "Interview (1996)." In *Mona Hatoum*, ed. Michael Archer, Guy Brett, and Catherine de Zegher, 134–41. London: Phaidon.

Spivak, Gayatri Chakravorty. 1999. *A Critique of Postcolonial Reason: Toward a History of the Vanishing Present*. Cambridge, MA: Harvard University Press.

Spry, Tamy. 2006. "Performing Autoethnography: An Embodied Methodological Practice." In *Emergent Methods in Social Research*, ed. Sharlene Nagy Hesse-Biber and Patricia Leavy, 183–212. Thousand Oaks, CA: Sage.

Squier, Susan M. 2007. "Beyond Nescience: The Intersectional Rights of Health Humanities." *Perspectives in Biology and Medicine* 50 (3): 334–47.

Squier, Susan M. 2008a. "Literature and Medicine, Future Tense: Making It Graphic." *Literature and Medicine* 27 (2): 124–52.

Squier, Susan M. 2008b. "So Long as They Grow Out of It: The Discourse of Developmental Normalcy, and Disability." *Journal of Medical Humanities* 29 (2): 71–88.

St. Pierre, Elizabeth, and Wanda S. Pillow, eds. 2000. *Working the Ruins: Feminist Poststructural Theory and Methods in Education*. New York: Routledge.

Stabile, Carol. 1998. "Shooting the Mother: Fetal Photography and the Politics of Disappearance." In *The Visible Woman: Imaging Technologies, Gender, and Science*, ed. Paula A. Treichler, Lisa Cartwright, and Constance Penley, 171–97. New York: New York University Press.

Stacey, Jackie. 1997. *Teratologies: A Cultural Study of Cancer*. London: Routledge.

Stainton, Tim. 2004. "Reason's Other: The Emergence of the Disabled Subject in the Northern Renaissance." *Disability and Society* 19 (4): 224–43.

Starks, Brian. 2003. "The New Economy and the American Dream: Examining the Effect of Work Conditions on Beliefs about Economic Opportunity." *Sociological Quarterly* 44 (2): 205–25.

Starr, Ann. 2005. "Looking in the Mirror: Images of Abnormally Developed Infants." *Journal of Medical Humanities* 26 (2–3): 97–106.

Steele, Lisa. 1974. *Birthday Suit – with scars and defects*. Video. Canada. 12 min.

Stone, Sandy. [1991] 2006. "The Empire Strikes Back: A Posttranssexual Manifesto." In *The Transgender Studies Reader*, ed. Susan Stryker and Stephen Whittle, 221–35. New York: Routledge.

Strick, Simon. 2008. "Vorher Nachher: Zur Erzählbarkeit des kosmetischen Selbst." In *Schön normal – Sozial und Kulturwissenschaftliche Perspektiven auf somatische Selbsttechnologien*, ed. Paula Villa, 199–218. Bielefeld: Transkript.

Stryker, Susan. 2006a. "(De)subjugated Knowledges: An Introduction to Transgender Studies." In *The Transgender Studies Reader*, ed. Susan Stryker and Stephen Whittle, 1–18. New York: Routledge.

Stryker, Susan. [1994] 2006b. "My Words to Victor Frankenstein above the Village of Chamounix: Performing Transgender Rage." In *The Transgender Studies Reader*, ed. Susan Stryker and Stephen Whittle, 244–56. New York: Routledge.

Sullivan, Martin. 2005. "Subjected Bodies: Paraplegia, Rehabilitation, and the Politics of Movement." In *Foucault and the Government of Disability*, ed. Shelley Tremain, 27–44. Ann Arbor: University of Michigan Press.

The Swan. 2004. Pro 7 Television GmbH. Pro 7 Germany.

Tagg, John. 1988. *The Burden of Representation: Essays on Photographies and Histories*. Amherst: University of Massachusetts Press.

Tanner, Laura. 2006. *Lost Bodies: Inhabiting the Borders of Life and Death*. Ithaca, NY: Cornell University Press.

Tapper, Evan. dir. 1996–99. *Unicorn Men*. Mixed Media Drawings. Canada.

Tapper, Evan. 2001. *Lot*. Video. Canada. 2:00 min.

Tapper, Evan. 2001. *Tumor*. Video. Canada. 3:00 min.

Tapper, Evan. 2001. *Untitled (Self-portrait in Blue)*. Video. Canada. 3:00 min.

Tapper, Evan. 2003. *Graphic Material*. Video. Canada. 2:00 min.

Tapper, Evan. 2003. *Self-portrait as a Teletubby*. Video. Canada. 3:00 min.

Tapper, Evan. 2006. *Artist Seeks …* Video. Canada. 1:30 min.

Tapper, Evan. 2008. *Sheh-asani Kirtzono*. Video. Canada 5:00 min.

Tapper, Evan. 2008. *I Teach Young Men How to Make Art*. Video. Canada. 1:30 min.

Taylor, Janelle S. 2000. "An All-Consuming Experience: Obstetrical Ultrasound and the Commodification of Pregnancy." In *Biotechnology and Culture: Bodies, Anxieties, Ethics*, ed. Paul E. Brodwin, 147–70. Bloomington: Indiana University Press.

Taylor, Janelle S. 2008. *The Public Life of the Fetal Sonogram*. Piscataway, NJ: Rutgers University Press.

Taylor, John, dir. 1977. *The Island of Dr Moreau*. DVD. American International Pictures.

Taylor, Louis. 2000. *Esther, Baby and Me*. Video. Canada. 20:49 min.

Thomas, Calvin. 2008. *Masculinity, Psychoanalysis, and Straight Queer Theory: Essays on Abjection in Literature, Mass Culture and Film*. New York: Palgrave Macmillan.

Thompson, Becky W. 1994. *A Hunger So Wide and So Deep: A Multiracial View of Women's Eating Problems*. Minneapolis: University of Minnesota Press.

Titchkosky, Tanya. 2007. *Reading and Writing Disability Differently: The Textured Life of Embodiment*. Toronto: University of Toronto Press.

Titchkosky, Tanya, and Rod Michalko, eds. 2009. *Rethinking Normalcy: A Disability Studies Reader*. Toronto: Canadian Scholars' Press.

Treichler, Paula A., Lisa Cartwright, and Constance Penley, eds. 1998. *The Visible Woman: Imaging Technologies, Gender, and Science*. New York: New York University Press.

Tremain, Shelley. 2002. "On the Subject of Impairment." In *Disability/Postmodernity: Embodying Disability Theory*, ed. Mairian Corker and Tom Shakespeare, 32–47. London: Continuum.

Tremain, Shelley, ed. 2005. *Foucault and the Government of Disability*. Ann Arbor: University of Michigan Press.

Tremain, Shelley. 2006. "On the Government of Disability: Foucault, Power, and the Subject of Impairment." In *The Disability Studies Reader*, 2nd ed., ed. Lennard J. Davis, 185–96. New York: Routledge.

Udovitch, Mim. 2002. "A Secret Society of the Starving." *New York Times Magazine* (8 Sept.). Accessed 26 Sept. 2002. http://www.nytimes.com/pages/magazine

US Department of State, Bureau of East Asian and Pacific Affairs. 2008, June. "Background Note: Cambodia." Accessed 15 Aug. 2008. http://www.state.gov/r/pa/ei/bgn/2732.htm

Van Alphen, Ernst. 2005. *Art in Mind: How Contemporary Images Shape Thought*. Chicago: Chicago University Press.

Van de Vall, Renée. 2009. "The Body Within: Art, Medicine and Visualization." In *The Body Within: Art, Medicine and Visualization*, ed. Renée Van de Vall and Robert Zwijnenberg, 1–14. Boston: Brill.
Victoria's Pro-Ana Journal. 2005. "Bone thinspiration." Accessed 10 May 2005. http://www.victoriasproana.com/5bone.html
Virgo, Clement, dir. 1995. *Rude*. DVD. Unapix.
Visweswaran, Kamala. 1994. *Fictions of Feminist Ethnography*. Minneapolis: University of Minnesota Press.
Wagner, Andrea T. 2000. "Re/Covered Bodies: The Sites and Stories of Illness in Popular Media." *Journal of Medical Humanities* 21 (1): 15–27.
Walcott, Rinaldo. 2003. *Black Like Who? Writing Black Canada*. Toronto: Insomniac Press.
Walker, Rebecca. 1995. *To Be Real: Telling the Truth and Changing the Face of Feminism*. New York: Knopf/Doubleday.
Walkerdine, Valerie. 1991. *Schoolgirl Fictions*. London: Verso.
A Walking Barbie. 2005. "The Journey to Perfectionism ..." Accessed 10 May 2005. http://www.freewebs.com/anaprincessheather/
Wark, Jayne. 2006. *Radical Gestures: Feminism and Performance Art in North America*. Montreal and Kingston: McGill-Queen's University Press.
Wasted Shadow. 2005. "The Pro-Ana Ribbon." Accessed 9 May 2005. http://www.wasted.fabpage/
Waugh, Thomas. 2006. *The Romance of Transgression in Canada: Queering Sexualities, Nations, Cinemas*. Montreal and Kingston: McGill-Queen's University Press.
Weber, Cynthia. 2003. "Oi. Dancing Boy! Masculinity, Sexuality, and Youth in *Billy Elliot*." *Genders* 37. http://www.genders.org/g37/g37_weber.html
Wendell, Susan. 1996. *The Rejected Body: Feminist Philosophical Reflections on Disability*. New York: Routledge.
Whitlock, Gillian. 2007. *Soft Weapons: Autobiography in Transit*. Chicago: University of Chicago Press.
Whittle, Stephen. 1995. "Gender Fucking or Fucking Gender." In *Blending Genders: Social Aspects of Cross-Dressing and Sex Changing*, ed. Richard Ekins, 196–214. London: Routledge.
Williams, Linda. 2003. "Film Bodies: Gender, Genre, and Excess." In *Feminist Film Theory: A Reader*, ed. Sue Thornham, 267–81. Edinburgh: Edinburgh University Press.
Wilson, Elizabeth. 2004. *Psychosomatic: Feminism and the Neurological Body*. Durham, NC: Duke University Press.

Wilson, Pamela, and Michelle Stewart, eds. 2008. *Global Indigenous Media: Cultures, Poetics, and Politics*. Durham, NC: Duke University Press.

Wilson, Shawn. 2008. *Research Is Ceremony: Indigenous Research Methods*. Winnipeg, MB: Fernwood.

Wolfe, Cary. 2009. *What Is Posthumanism?* Minneapolis: University of Minnesota Press.

Womack, Craig. 1999. *Red on Red: Native American Literary Separatism*. Minneapolis: University of Minnesota Press.

Wong, Virgil. 2008a. "Male Pregnancy." Presentation at the ISERP Faculty Seminar on Narrative Genetics, 23 Oct., at Columbia University, New York.

Wong, Virgil. 2008b. *Installations – Liu*. Accessed 30 Nov. 2008. http://www.virgilwong.com/installations/liu/index.shtml?name1=RYT+Hospital&type1=2Select&name2=Phineas+Liu,+MD,+PhD&type2=3Active

Wong, Virgil. 2008c. *RYT Hospital/Dwayne Medical Center: About Us*. Accessed 30 Nov. 2008. http://www.rythospital.com/about/

Wong, Virgil. 2008d. *RYT Hospital/Dwayne Medical Center: Clyven*. Accessed 30 Nov. 2008. http://www.rythospital.com/clyven/

Wong, Virgil. 2008e. *RYT Hospital/Dwayne Medical Center: Genochoice*. Accessed 30 Nov. 2008. http://www.genochoice.com/

Wong, Virgil. 2008f. *RYT Hospital/Dwayne Medical Center: Liu*. Accessed 30 Nov. 2008. http://www.rythospital.com/liu/

Wong, Virgil. 2008g. *RYT Hospital/Dwayne Medical Center: Nanodocs*. Accessed 30 Nov. 2008. http://www.rythospital.com/nanodocs/

Wong, Virgil. 2008h. *RYT Hospital/Dwayne Medical Center: POP! The First Male Pregnancy*. Accessed 30 Nov. 2008. http://www.malepregnancy.com

Wong, Virgil. 2008i. *RYT Hospital/Dwayne Medical Center: POP! The First Male Pregnancy – Science*. Accessed 30 Nov. 2008. http://www.malepregnancy.com/science/

Wong, Virgil. 2008j. *RYT Hospital/Dwayne Medical Center: POP! The First Male Pregnancy – Mr Lee Mingwei*. Accessed 30 Nov. 2008. http://www.malepregnancy.com/mingwei/

Whale, James, dir. 1931. *Frankenstein*. DVD. Universal Pictures.

Yosef, Raz. 2004. *Beyond Flesh: Queer Masculinities and Nationalism in Israeli Cinema*. New Brunswick, NJ: Rutgers.

Zack, Lizabeth. 2002. "Who Fought the Algerian War? Political Identity and Conflict in French-Ruled Algeria." *International Journal of Politics Culture and Society* 16 (1): 55–97.

Zimmermann, Patricia R. 2000. *States of Emergency: Documentaries, Wars, Democracies*. Minneapolis: University of Minnesota Press.

Notes on Contributors

Mebbie Bell Is an instructor in the Department of Women's and Gender Studies at the University of Alberta. Her work explores cultural intersections of post-structural feminist theory, health, and embodiment, focusing on disordered eating practices, discourses, and Foucauldian analyses. In the article "Re/forming the Anorexic Prisoner," published in *Cultural Studies/Critical Methodologies*, she examines the panoptic medical regimes of inpatient treatment protocols for anorexia through a Foucauldian feminist framework, and, in "@ the Doctor's Office," which appeared in the journal *Surveillance and Society*, she analyses the complex negotiations of medical surveillance and diagnostic authority by participants in the online pro-anorexia movement. Her recent post-doctoral fellowship in Community Service-Learning at the University of Alberta examined meanings of home, identity, learning, and recovery in second-stage women's shelters.

Sarah Brophy is an associate professor of English and Cultural Studies at McMaster University. Her research engages twentieth- and twenty-first-century life writing, fiction, and visual culture and participates in multiple fields including British literature and culture since 1945, autobiography studies, disability and the body, visual culture, gender and sexuality, critical race studies, and postcolonialism. She is the author of *Witnessing AIDS: Writing, Testimony, and the Work of Mourning* and of essays in the *Journal of Literary and Cultural Disability Studies* (with Janice Hladki, forthcoming), *End of Empire and the English Novel since 1945*, *Contemporary Women's Writing*, *Literature and Medicine*, *PMLA*, *scrutiny2*, and *Teaching Life-Writing Texts*. Collaborative work includes exhibitions on political video art and self-portraiture for the McMaster Museum of

Art as well as co-edited special issues of *Interventions: International Journal of Postcolonial Studies* (with Phanuel Antwi, Helene Strauss, and Y-Dang Troeung) and the *Review of Education, Pedagogy, and Cultural Studies* (with Janice Hladki). She is writing a book on queer and feminist cosmopolitanisms in postwar British literature and culture.

Adrienne Chambon is a professor at the University of Toronto's Factor-Inwentash Faculty of Social Work. She teaches courses on social exclusion, narrative knowledge, and the history and memory of social work and social welfare. She co-edited the volume *Reading Foucault for Social Work* with Allan Irving and Laura Epstein. Her more recent projects funded by the Social Sciences and Humanities Research Council of Canada (SSHRC) revisit the history of social work using local archives, focusing increasingly on notions of public space, the city, and its citizens. She participates in a SSHRC project led by Ann Fudge Schormans on public spaces for persons with cognitive disability. Chambon is the principal investigator on the project "Social Work and the 'Wished-For' City: Claiming Spaces for Women and Children in Early 20th Century Toronto."

Sayantani DasGupta, MD, MPH, originally trained in pediatrics and public health. She teaches in the Narrative Medicine Master's Program at Columbia University, as well as in the Health Advocacy Graduate Program at Sarah Lawrence College. She also co-chairs the faculty-level Columbia University Seminar on Narrative, Health and Social Justice. Widely anthologized and published, she is the co-author of *The Demon Slayers and Other Stories: Bengali Folktales*; author of a memoir about her time at Johns Hopkins Medical School, *Her Own Medicine: A Woman's Journey from Student to Doctor*; and co-editor (with Marsha Hurst) of *Stories of Illness and Healing: Women's Illness Narratives.*

Richard Fung is a video artist and writer whose work deals with the intersection of race and queer sexuality and with issues of postcolonialism, diaspora, and family. His award-winning tapes, which include *My Mother's Place, Sea in the Blood,* and *Dal Puri Diaspora,* are screened and collected internationally, and his essays, including the much anthologized "Looking for My Penis: The Eroticized Asian in Gay Video Porn," have been widely published. Fung is the co-author, with Monika Kin Gagnon, of *13: Conversations on Art and Cultural Race Politics*. A recipient of numerous grants and awards, including the Bell Canada Award for Video Art in 2000, Fung teaches at the Ontario College of Art and Design University in Toronto.

Janice Hladki is an associate professor of Theatre and Film Studies at McMaster University. Her research contributes to feminist, critical disability, and visual culture studies and explores the representational, discursive, and social implications of art and culture practices. She is interested in investigating the body in performance and moving image culture, social justice in the arts, autobiographical film, Indigenous art, and the politics of collaborative research. Recent publications include the exhibition book *Fierce: Women's Hot-Blooded Film/Video* for her curated exhibition; a co-edited special issue for the *Review of Education, Pedagogy, and Cultural Studies* (with Sarah Brophy); and essays in the *Journal of Literary and Cultural Disability Studies* (with Sarah Brophy), *Feminist Media Studies, ARIEL: A Review of International English Literature, Atlantis: Critical Studies in Gender, Culture, and Social Justice,* and the *International Journal of Qualitative Studies in Education*. Her artwork focuses on curatorial, theatre, and performance art projects, and she is known as one of the feminist performance collective, The Clichettes.

Dan Irving is an assistant professor in Sexuality Studies and in Human Rights in the Institute of Interdisciplinary Studies at Carleton University. Applying a critical political economy framework, his research focuses on the cultivation of transsexual subjectivities within a neoliberal context and on the ways that some transsexuals are incorporated into the workplace and broader society as "respectable" subjects. His article originally published in the "Queer Futures" issue of *Radical History Review* is reprinted in *The Transgender Studies Reader 2*. Other work has been published in *Transfeminist Perspectives in and beyond Transgender and Gender Studies*, as well as the *Temple Political and Civil Rights Law Review* and *Sexualities*.

Wendy Kozol is a professor of Comparative American Studies at Oberlin College with a concentration in visual culture studies. Her current research examines visual discourses about human rights, globalization, and US militarization through the perspectives of transnational feminist and cultural studies. Recent publications include (with Wendy Hesford) *Just Advocacy: Women's Human Rights, Transnational Feminism and the Politics of Representation*, and articles in *Feminist Studies, Peace Review, Reconstruction: Studies in Contemporary Culture, Photography and*

Culture, and *Theory and Event.* Her forthcoming book is entitled *Visible Wars and the Ambivalences of Witnessing.*

Laura McGavin is a Canada Graduate Scholar and Ph.D. candidate in the Department of English at Queen's University. Her current areas of research include feminist theories of embodiment, with a particular focus on illness and disability, and literary ecocriticism. Her dissertation investigates representations of cancer and environmental toxicity in contemporary literature by authors including Rachel Carson, Sandra Steingraber, Indra Sinha, and Nadine Gordimer. Her article "Terra Incognita," published in *ISLE: Interdisciplinary Studies in Literature and the Environment,* reads Werner Herzog's Antarctic documentary *Encounters at the End of the World* as compatible with recent theorizations of non-human agency. Other forthcoming projects include articles on literary close reading and medical humanism, and on artistic representations of the 1984 Bhopal disaster.

Allyson Mitchell is an assistant professor in Gender, Sexuality, and Women's Studies at York University, with a concentration in feminist and queer cultural theory and production. She is a visual artist working predominantly in sculpture, installation, and film. Mitchell's maximalist art articulates feminist theory in the round to play with contemporary ideas about activism, sexuality, autobiography, and the body, largely through the use of reclaimed textile and abandoned craft. Her work has been exhibited in numerous venues including the Tate Modern, the Warhol Museum, the Textile Museum of Canada, the Winnipeg Art Gallery, the Art Gallery of Ontario, Oakville Galleries, and the British Film Institute. Recent and forthcoming bodies of work include *Ladies Sasquatch, Killjoy's Kastle: A Lesbian Feminist Haunted House, Creep Lez,* and *A Girl's Journey to the Well of Forbidden Knowledge.* She is based in Toronto where she runs FAG, a feminist art gallery, with Deirdre Logue.

Peter Morin is a Tahltan Nation artist, curator, and writer currently based in Victoria, British Columbia. Morin's work investigates the places of impact between Indigenous culturally based practices and western settler colonialism. This work, defined by Tahltan Nation epistemological production, often takes on the form of performance interventions. Morin has participated in numerous exhibitions and performance events including *Team Diversity Bannock and the World's Largest Bannock,*

12 Making Objects AKA First Nations DADA, *Peter Morin's Museum*, and *This Is What Happens When You Perform the Memory of the Land*. Morin has curated exhibitions at the Museum of Anthropology, the Western Front, the Burnaby Art Gallery, and the Grunt Gallery, among others, and, in 2012, he co-curated *Carrying on Irregardless: Humour in Contemporary Native Art* for the Bill Reid Gallery of Northwest Coast Art.

Sheila Petty is dean of the Faculty of Fine Arts and a professor of Media Studies at the University of Regina. She has written extensively on issues of cultural representation, identity, and nation in African and African diasporic cinema and new media and has curated film, television, and new media exhibitions for galleries across Canada. Author of *Contact Zones: Memory, Origin, and Discourses in Black Diasporic Cinema*, she is co-editor (with Blandine Stefanson) of the forthcoming *World Directory of Cinema: Africa*. She is also the leader of an interdisciplinary research group and New Media Studio Laboratory spanning Computer Science, Engineering, and Fine Arts.

Kim Sawchuk is a professor in the Department of Communication Studies at Concordia University and Concordia University Research Chair in Mobile Media Studies. She is the current editor and co-founder of *Wi: Journal of Mobile Media*, the co-director of the Mobile Media Lab (Montreal-Toronto), and the past editor of the *Canadian Journal of Communication*. Her most recent publications include *Sampling the Wireless Spectrum*, co-edited with Barbara Crow and Michael Longford; *USED/Goods*, a collection of essays with Gisele Amantea and Lorraine Oades; *Embodiment/Verkörperungen* a German-English co-production with Christina Lammer and Catherine Pilcher; *Wild Science: Reading Feminism, Medicine and the Media*, co-edited with Janine Marchessault; and *When Pain Strikes*, a collaboration with Cathy Busby and Bill Burns. In 1996, she co-founded Studio XX, a Montreal-based feminist media production centre.

Ann Fudge Schormans is an assistant professor in the School of Social Work at McMaster University. Her many years of social work practice and ongoing activist work have focused on supporting people with intellectual and developmental disabilities. Her scholarship and research pursuits are similarly concerned with issues important to people with disabilities. Increasingly, questions of self-advocacy and self-representation by people labelled intellectually disabled, through auto/biography and inclusive and collaborative research methodologies, have dominated her work. Her related publications include essays in *Auto/biography in Canada: Critical Directions; Australian Social Work; The Review of Education, Pedagogy and Cultural Studies; Disability and Society*; and a chapter co-authored with people labelled intellectually disabled in *Developmental Disabilities in Ontario*, 3rd ed.

Simon Strick is a researcher at the Center for Literary and Cultural Research (ZfL) Berlin, where he works on contemporary somatechnologies. He received his Ph.D. in American Studies at Humboldt University, Berlin, with a dissertation on discourses of pain in the nineteenth century. His forthcoming book is entitled *American Dolorologies: Pain, Sentimentalism, Biopolitics*. He has published several essays on gender, embodiment, and affect in *Feministische Studien/Feminist Studies, Amerikastudien/American Studies*, and *Plurale*. He is a member of the theatrical collective panzerkreuzer.rotkäppchen and has worked in several performances and plays dealing with issues of animality, gender, and German postsocialist identity.

Cultural Spaces

Cultural Spaces explores the rapidly changing temporal, spatial, and theoretical boundaries of contemporary cultural studies. Culture has long been understood as the force that defines and delimits societies in fixed spaces. The recent intensification of globalizing processes, however, has meant that it is no longer possible – if it ever was – to imagine the world as a collection of autonomous, monadic spaces, whether these are imagined as localities, nations, regions within nations, or cultures demarcated by region or nation. One of the major challenges of studying contemporary culture is to understand the new relationships of culture to space that are produced today. The aim of this series is to publish bold new analyses and theories of the spaces of culture, as well as investigations of the historical construction of those cultural spaces that have influenced the shape of the contemporary world.

Books in the Series:

Peter Ives, *Gramsci's Politics of Language: Engaging the Bakhtin Circle and the Frankfurt School*

Sarah Brophy, *Witnessing AIDS: Writing, Testimony, and the Work of Mourning*

Shane Gunster, *Capitalizing on Culture: Critical Theory for Cultural Studies*

Jasmin Habib, *Israel, Diaspora, and the Routes of National Belonging*

Serra Tinic, *On Location: Canada's Television Industry in a Global Market*

Evelyn Ruppert, *The Moral Economy of Cities: Shaping Good Citizens*

Mark Coté, Richard J.F. Day, and Greg de Peuter, eds., *Utopian Pedagogy: Radical Experiments against Neoliberal Globalization*

Michael McKinnie, *City Stages: Theatre and the Urban Space in a Global City*

David Jefferess, *Postcolonial Resistance: Culture, Liberation, and Transformation*

Mary Gallagher, ed., *World Writing: Poetics, Ethics, Globalization*

Maureen Moynagh, *Political Tourism and Its Texts*

Erin Hurley, *National Performance: Representing Quebec from Expo 67 to Céline Dion*

Lily Cho, *Eating Chinese: Culture on the Menu in Small Town Canada*

Rhona Richman Kenneally and Johanne Sloan, eds., *Expo 67: Not Just a Souvenir*

Gillian Roberts, *Prizing Literature: The Celebration and Circulation of National Culture*

Lianne McTavish, *Defining the Modern Museum: A Case Study of the Challenges of Exchange*

Misao Dean, *Inheriting a Canoe Paddle: The Canoe in Discourses of English-Canadian Nationalism*

Sarah Brophy and Janice Hladki, eds., *Embodied Politics in Visual Autobiography*

www.ingramcontent.com/pod-product-compliance
Lightning Source LLC
LaVergne TN
LVHW090805070826
844660LV00022B/1085

9781442616097